T0351801

Wrong Turnings

Wrong Turnings

HOW THE LEFT GOT LOST

Geoffrey M. Hodgson

The University of Chicago Press   CHICAGO & LONDON

The University of Chicago Press, Chicago 60637
The University of Chicago Press, Ltd., London
© 2018 by The University of Chicago
All rights reserved. No part of this book may be used or reproduced in any manner
whatsoever without written permission, except in the case of brief quotations in critical
articles and reviews. For more information, contact the University of Chicago Press, 1427 E.
60th St., Chicago, IL 60637.
Published 2018
Printed in the United States of America

27 26 25 24 23 22 21 20 19 18   1 2 3 4 5

ISBN-13: 978-0-226-50574-9 (cloth)
ISBN-13: 978-0-226-50588-6 (paper)
ISBN-13: 978-0-226-50591-6 (e-book)
DOI: 10.7208/chicago/9780226505916.001.0001

Library of Congress Cataloging-in-Publication Data
Names: Hodgson, Geoffrey Martin, 1946– author.
Title: Wrong turnings : how the left got lost / Geoffrey M. Hodgson.
Description: Chicago ; London : The University of Chicago Press, 2018. | Includes
    bibliographical references and index.
Identifiers: LCCN 2017029424 | ISBN 9780226505749 (cloth : alk. paper) |
    ISBN 9780226505886 (pbk : alk. paper) | ISBN 9780226505916 (e-book)
Subjects: LCSH: Right and left (Political science)—History. | Liberalism. | Democracy. |
    Socialism.
Classification: LCC JA83.H625 2018 | DDC 320.53—dc23
LC record available at https://lccn.loc.gov/2017029424

♾ This paper meets the requirements of ANSI/NISO Z39.48-1992 (Permanence of Paper).

To my grandchildren, with the hope of a better future for all humanity

CONTENTS

Everywhere, the Left is in crisis. Despite global economic turbulence, the Left often concentrates on slogans rather than practical solutions. Elsewhere the Left has acquiesced with austerity and welfare cuts, and lost much of its distinctive identity. Others on the Left have embraced Left populism, offering seemingly simple solutions—such as public ownership and 'democratic control'—to complex politico-economic problems.

This book explores some of the historical roots of the Left's malaise. In major part it is a matter of lost and mistaken identity. It is shown that the very meaning of 'Left' has shifted radically from its origins in the French Revolution. Today, the term 'Left' is associated with state intervention and public ownership, which is remote from its meaning in 1789.

We are not obliged to follow the doctrines of the original Left, but it is important to understand how strains of Left thinking have twisted and turned from their original source. This book argues that the Left must rediscover its roots in the Enlightenment, and re-adopt vital Enlightenment values that it has abandoned.

Much of this book is historical and analytic. So when, for example, I explain the original meaning of the term 'Left', the reader should not automatically assume that I adopt that position. I reveal my own normative views in later chapters.

There is another health warning. My evidence and arguments may be disconcerting for those with unbendable notions of Left or Right. I am proposing a different way of positioning varied political views. The result may be troubling. It may interfere with your political satnav. Do not read further if you are unprepared to reconsider your political road map.

Readers looking here for a plan for a future utopia will be disappointed. This book argues that progressive thinkers should retrieve many ideas that have been previously and recklessly jettisoned. I am not a socialist (in the original sense of that term): I argue for a reformed capitalism. Within a democracy I am not a revolutionary: all reform should be careful and experimental. Nordic countries offer some of the best exemplars, with relatively lower inequality, effective social welfare and strong economic performances.

Do not look here for alternative radical blueprints, or skip to the end in search of utopian visions or detailed policy prescriptions: they are not there. Some of the biggest lessons spring from an understanding of the wrong turnings of the past, and from an appreciation of what must be preserved. I am an evotopian, not a utopian.

In particular, on the big debate concerning public versus private ownership of enterprises, it is very much a question of what works, in regard to economic performance and the preservation of human rights (including liberty, sociality, autonomy and development). While such a pragmatic evaluation is unavoidably framed by ideology, it is not ideologically axiomatic in the sense of starting from the presupposition that private or public ownership (or some specified mix of the two) is superior. Instead, it is a matter of learning from experience and experiment, with respect to human rights as well as economic performance. Given this, I have no optimal mixture of private and public to offer.

Several chapters depend on their predecessors. For example, the significance of chapter 9 on religion cannot be fully appreciated unless the critique of religion as a source of authority by Enlightenment thinkers is understood. This Enlightenment question of legitimate authority is addressed in chapters 1 and 2.

This is not intended to be an academic text. I raise many complex issues, but I omit many important thinkers and numerous vital references to the academic literature. This book is more of a *crie de cœur* in the current crisis. In part I write for my contemporaries of the heady 1960s, who have become politically lost as the world has changed, and for others who have sadly descended into impracticality, obscurantism, apathy or indifference. I write too for those who are newer on the journey, including those who are concerned about economic austerity, widening inequality and neoliberalism, and are looking for a progressive way forward.

I am not the first progressive thinker to become seriously alarmed about today's Left. Christopher Hitchens, Nick Cohen and others led the way, although I differ from some of their views, and I find much earlier origins of the Left's malaise. Maajid Nawaz coined the term 'Regressive Left', which marks its tragic retreat from former ideals. This book charts this regression, and offers a new route for its revival.

I warmly thank Jess Agnew, Paul Dale Bush, Robbie Butler, Ha-Joon Chang, Nicolai Foss, Ian Gough, Peter Hain, Jim Hodgson, David Knibb, Peter Leeson, Vinny Logan, John Maguire, David Morgan, Guinevere Nell, Ugo Pagano, Pedra Pereira Hors, Barkley Rosser, Colin Talbot, Alex Tylecote, Andrew Tylecote, Mehrdad Vahabi, anonymous referees and others for very helpful discussions, comments and criticisms.

INTRODUCTION

One . . . ought to recognise that the present political chaos is connected with the decay of language, and that one can probably bring about some improvement by starting at the verbal end.

GEORGE ORWELL, 'Politics and the English Language' (1946)

This book addresses enduring modern themes concerning human rights, human liberty and human fulfilment. But while these topics have been discussed for millennia, some crucial terms that we use to describe key positions in the struggle for emancipation have changed beyond recognition in the last two hundred years.

The term *Left* originated in the French Revolution, to describe doctrines of liberty, rights, solidarity and equality under the law. At that time, the *Right* supported monarchy, state privileges and the established church. The *Left* denied that legitimate authority derived from religion or from noble birth. *Left* meant opposition to monarchy, aristocracy, theocracy, state monopolies and institutionalized privileges. It meant liberty (including freedom to own and trade property), equality of rights (under the law) and fraternity (in the community). These rights and principles were held to be universal.

But the meanings of Left and Right have changed. Much of political discourse has been turned upside down, in multiple, spectacular, linguistic revolutions.

Henceforth in this book I adopt a convention where *Left* and *Right* (in italics) are used to refer to the original meanings of those terms, as they were established during the French Revolution, from 1789 to the high watermark of reform in 1792. Left and Right (without italics) are used to refer to other varied actual uses of those terms.

THE BROKEN LANGUAGE OF TODAY'S POLITICS

The language of politics is broken: it needs to be mended. For instance, I might now describe myself as 'a social democrat', 'of the centre-left' or 'a left-leaning liberal'. But such descriptions immediately raise problems and major ambiguities. For example, the term *social democrat* has changed radically in meaning since its inception (when it was used by Marxists) in the nineteenth century. And the word *liberal* means different things in the United States, in Britain and in Continental Europe.

In the nineteenth century the Left became *socialist*. But to reconstruct its identity today, the Left must re-evaluate this historic turning. The word *socialism* has also mutated in meaning. When it became established in the 1830s it referred to the abolition of private property. It retained that prominent definition until the Cold War, when more moderate usages appeared.

When Labour and Social Democratic Parties in Europe accepted a market-oriented, mixed economy after 1950, many chose to bowdlerize the history of the term, rather than to abandon it explicitly. It became vaguely associated with 'values', rather with a different politico-economic system with the common ownership of property. *Socialism* became a dead albatross, hanging around the neck of the stranded Left.

Despite the global economic crash of 2008, which for some signalled the beginning of the end of the economic system, the Left as a whole has not outlined a persuasive, feasible and democratic alternative to capitalism. Its 'democratic socialist' alternative to capitalism has lacked viable expression in both theory and practice.

The Left also must counter woolly concepts and bad habits of thinking that prevent creative engagement. For example, far too often the Left uses the term 'right-wing' as if it were sufficient to dismiss a doctrine, rather than to construct an argument against it.

Obversely, in the United States, 'left wing' has become for some a term of abuse, to hurl at anyone who is not a Tea Party Republican or who defends any economic role for the state.

The terms 'Left' and 'Right' have become ambiguous and self-contradictory. Today the term 'right-wing' is applied to diverse and opposed views such as the following:

Those who favour private ownership and markets are sometimes placed on the political Right, irrespective of their attitude to democracy, equality or human rights.

Those who venerate the nation state are sometimes placed on the political Right, irrespective of their attitude to democracy, equality or human rights.

Hence the debased term Right now covers democrats and authoritarians, peacemongers and warmongers, nationalists and individualists, egalitarians and inegalitarians, and defenders and opponents of human rights. There is nothing about private ownership and markets that necessarily implies racism or belligerent nationalism. Yet these different things are conflated under the same label.

The word Left has also slipped into different usages:

Those who advocate substantial state intervention in the economy, typically involving planning and nationalized enterprises, are typically placed on the Left, often irrespective of their degree of support for democracy and human rights.

Champions of extended democracy, decentralization, popular sovereignty, individual liberty and freedom of expression are often described as Left.

Accordingly, the term 'Left' is now applied to both decentralizers and statist centralizers, to both democrats and totalitarians, and to both defenders and sacrificers of liberty.

Consider regimes that use nationalist rhetoric and nationalize some large firms. Are such regimes Left (because of nationalization) or Right (because of nationalism)? Consider a market economy of small private enterprises, taxed and governed in a manner to reduce inequality. Are such systems Right (because of markets) or Left (because of relative equality)? The answers are unclear, showing that the key terms have become loose and ambivalent.

CHANGING PLACES

When the term *socialism* emerged in the 1820s, it underlined equality and solidarity, but sometimes to the detriment of liberty, autonomy or democracy. Prominent early socialists, such as Robert Owen, envisioned rational, harmonious communities, and saw division, voting and organized political parties as counter-productive.[1] I see this as a big wrong turning for the Left.

Then, in the 1840s, Karl Marx and Frederick Engels joined their version of socialism to the predicted victory of the proletariat in the class struggle, and to its expropriation of the capitalist ruling class. Marx and Engels described the principles and rights of the French Revolution as nothing more than 'bourgeois' ideals—the ideology of the rising capitalist class. Marx and Engels thus sacrificed these universal principles and rights at the altar of class struggle. This was another wrong turning.

The first Marxist government was established in Russia in 1917, and it quickly evolved into a one-party state. Purges and terror ensued. But many on the left supported the Soviet regime. The Left label became associated with totalitarianism, with minimal human rights, sham trials, mass executions, limited freedom and arbitrary confiscations of property. Tragically, the unchallengeable ideological rule of a Marxist party resembles the equally incontestable rule of the aristocracy and the church, against which the earliest *Left* protested. The original meaning of *Left* was turned upside down.

The term *Right* has long been linked with authoritarianism, racism or other discrimination, the rejection of popular sovereignty and the denial of equality under the law. In this vein, it was coupled with the rising fascism of the 1920s and 1930s, in Italy, Germany, Spain and elsewhere.

But the fascist and Nazi regimes of the *Right* were rivalled in terms of mass repression by the Soviet Union. Their similarity was obscured by the military alliances and ideological obfuscations of the Second World War. Both Left and Right acquired repressive and authoritarian connotations. Repression from the Left was often excused, because of its adopted façade of egalitarian and collectivist ideology.[2]

The Marxist dissident Leon Trotsky wrote that that there was little difference between Stalinism and fascism, apart from the nationalization of the means of production.[3] Public ownership was his key demarcation criterion. But for those millions in both types of regime, suffering famine, torture, death or deprivation of their rights, the dominant form of ownership made little difference to their misery.

The original *Left* criticized state ownership: state-sponsored monopolies were strongly opposed by the French revolutionaries in 1789. Since then, in several countries, nationalizations of firms have been carried out by conservative or nationalist governments. Trotsky was right in noting the similarity of Stalinism and fascism, but nationalization was less significant as a remaining difference than he implied.

There is a strong case for regarding Stalinism and Maoism as reactionary or *Right*, and close to fascism. Many of the twentieth-century experiments in large-scale national planning, including in capitalist countries, were provoked by the needs of war or defence, rather than Left ideology.[4]

While Marxists wrenched the term 'Left' from its original roots, the militant nationalisms and fascisms of the first half of the twentieth century delayed any major shift in the meaning of the word Right. As late as the 1960s it still had strong associations with traditionalism, nationalism, theocracy and fascism. Conservatives in Europe and the United States supported dictatorships in Latin America, or were apologists for South African Apartheid: these conservatives were appropriately described as *Right*.

But eventually the term 'Right' also shifted massively, from nationalist and traditionalist apologies for the privileges of aristocracy, to greater advocacy of free markets and private ownership, which ironically had been the territory of the original *Left* in the French Revolution.

With the collapse of the Keynesian welfare consensus in the 1970s, a now-confident free-market neoliberalism took ground. By 1980, some thinkers on the Right had captured a swathe of liberal territory that had been long vacated by the original Left. Consequently, both free marketeers, as well as condoners of dictatorships, were seen as Right.

But many on the Right—including US President Ronald Reagan and UK Prime Minister Margaret Thatcher—were inconsistent in their promotion of individualism and liberty. They championed powerful large corporations no less than tiny firms. They supported dictatorships and opposed sanctions against South African Apartheid. Their claimed ultra-free-market and libertarian views were compromised by their negative attitudes to drugs and prostitution and by their devotion to conservative and non-individualistic 'family values'.[5] By contrast, many other libertarian advocates of free markets support democracy and oppose all dictatorships.

The collapse of major 'socialist' experiments in China and the Soviet Bloc in the 1980s led to a further seismic shift. Within the Eastern Bloc countries, the rising radicals promoted free enterprise and democracy: they were against the status quo. By contrast, promoters of nationalization and comprehensive planning on the contemporary Western Left were seen as reactionary defenders of a doomed social order. This bewildered some radicals from the West, who discovered in the 1990s that the Eastern European revolutionaries were libertarian advocates of free enterprise and private property.[6]

At least since 1990, the term 'Right' has meant support for market solutions, alongside its enduring associations with nationalism and authoritarianism. But the original *Left* advocated free markets. Since then, for well over a century, the Left has been associated with state intervention and ownership. Ironically, in key respects, these terms have now swapped places.

ABANDONING UNIVERSAL RIGHTS

The original *Left* defended universal human rights. But many on the Left took a major wrong turning when they promoted class struggle: they supported the working class, but denied the rights of others. This retraction of universal rights was most obvious in Marxism, with disastrous consequences in Communist regimes.

Many 1960s radicals were critical of Soviet-style totalitarianism, as well as of capitalism. There was a huge movement of opposition to the war in Vietnam. There were also demonstrations against the 1968 Soviet invasion of Czechoslovakia.

But, with important exceptions, the 1960s Left failed to give sufficient prominence to universal human rights. Many on the Left were suspicious of such language and Marxists argued explicitly against it.

The 1960s sensitized many on the Left against militaristic attempts by major powers to impose their will on others. Some on the Left went further; they opposed any exportation of Western ideas, and rejected any notion that poorer countries deserved to enjoy the same human rights that are promoted and (partly) realized in Western Europe and North America. Even peaceful proposals to extend these rights or values were seen as apologies for 'Western imperialism' or for the 'US Empire'.[7]

Hence universal principles and rights, held up by the French revolutionary *Left* of the 1790s, were seen by some of the 1970s Left as excuses for Western militarism or oppression. Many leftists saw such principles and rights as a sham: they abandoned central defining ideas of the original *Left*.

This reaction against attempts to impose Western values and institutions on other nations gave rise to a version of normative *cultural relativism*, where one culture was regarded as no better or worse than another. In flawed attempts to undermine the rhetoric of the Western warmongers, it was claimed that universal values were problematic, peculiarly Western, or even illusory. A major section of the anti-war Left mocked universal rights and principles, thus mimicking the 1789–1792 *Right*.

In Britain, France and elsewhere, under the ambiguous terminology of 'multi-culturalism', state-funded religious schools were increased in number, with more religions included. Cultural relativism had other adverse effects. When dealing with ethnic or religious minorities, police forces and prosecuting authorities were sometimes slow in dealing with cases of violence against women, forced marriages, female genital mutilation, brutality in the name of family honour, witchcraft rituals involving mutilation or murder, and the grooming and rape of girls. Cultural relativism made it more difficult to criticize harmful practices in other cultures.

Even worse, some on the Far Left now defend the violence and terrorism of religious extremists. In the name of 'the struggle against Western imperialism' or the battle 'to defeat the US Empire' several members of the Far Left have supported al-Qaeda and other jihadists in Iraq, given 'critical' support for the theocratic regime in Iran, or even supported the so-called Islamic State in Iraq and Syria. One tiny UK Left group proposed that the Left 'has to acknowledge and accept the widespread call for a Caliphate (an Islamic government led by a caliph) among Muslims as valid and an authentic expression of their emancipatory, anti-imperialist aspirations'.[8]

The bombing of thousands of innocent civilians and the use of torture by Western powers do not justify *any* form of resistance, or *any* alternative to Western domination. While there have been noble struggles for national liberation from Western powers—Ireland and India come to mind—we should not ignore the behaviour and declared aims of the nationalists. Struggles for human rights, pluralist democracy and national independence are very different from those for a sectarian and reactionary caliphate.

CURTAILING FREEDOM OF SPEECH

Step by step, the Left abandoned core principles of the Enlightenment. In 1989 a *fatwa* was proclaimed against Salman Rushdie, for his allegedly blasphemous depiction of the Prophet Mohammed in his novel *The Satanic Verses*. The *fatwa* was issued by Ayatollah Khomeini, the Supreme Leader of Iran. He called upon other Muslims to kill Rushdie, along with his editors and publishers, 'without delay'. Across the world, many Muslims demonstrated and agitated for Rushdie's murder. Many on the Left were critical of Rushdie, for stirring up this violent antagonism and causing deep offence to a cultural minority.

Voltaire was one of the great inspirations of the French *Left* of 1789–1792. He argued eloquently for freedom of non-violent expression, and against laws that made blasphemy an offence. In a spectacular bicentennial inversion of the 1789 *Left*, part of the 1989 Left criticized blasphemy.

The pattern was repeated in 2005 when there were death threats against the drafters and publishers of the Danish cartoons depicting Mohammed. Confusing mockery with persecution, some on the Left blamed the artists and journalists for satirizing the Prophet, and failed to defend the freedom of non-violent expression. The horrific murders in Paris in 2015 of the *Charlie Hebdo* journalists may hopefully prompt a rethink, because they were followed by huge demonstrations in favour of such freedom.

Many radical and progressive thinkers have failed to distinguish racism from criticism of religion, or from criticism of laws, norms and practices within a religion. For example, in a television interview in October 2014 the famous American actor Ben Affleck described Sam Harris's criticism of some explicit doctrines in Islam as 'racist'. Harris was not advocating discrimination against a race, or against Muslims.[9]

Intelligent leftists have described protest in the UK against Sharia law as 'right-wing'. Yet much opposition to Sharia law is on the grounds of its discriminatory rules, particularly against women. How could such opposition be always intrinsically 'right-wing'?[10]

To be sure, many of these demonstrators have acted for racist rather than anti-theocratic reasons, and some of them have shouted racist or anti-Muslim slogans. But unfortunately all political parties from Left to Right contain racists. If having racist members makes a party Right, then no sizeable political party would escape this description. Peaceful, reasoned opposition to Sharia law is much more in the spirit of Voltaire than of the obnoxious thugs who want to destroy mosques or beat up Muslims.[11]

Many on the Left have done excellent work since the 1930s in campaigning against racism and fascism. But since the 1990s the frequent confusion of criticism of religion with racism has diluted their anti-racist efforts. Their resources have been misdirected into campaigns against legitimate, democratic, political parties that are not necessarily racist in terms of their official policies (although, like all large political groupings, they contain some racists).

For example, in March 2014 the anti-racist 'Hope not Hate' campaign group circulated an email appeal for funds to campaign against the United Kingdom Independence Party (UKIP), on the grounds that it had held a closed session discussing Sharia law. Many members of UKIP have exhibited racism or advocated violence against Muslims, and such actions should be condemned.[12] But Hope not Hate also targeted peaceful *discussion* of Sharia law.

Sharia law is an Islamic doctrine. But Islam is a religion, not an ethnicity. Critical discussion of Sharia law—even in a closed session—should not be opposed in principle by tolerant and civilized people, even if some of the participants in that discussion are neither tolerant nor civilized.[13]

Hope not Hate has called for limits to freedom of expression, to prohibit 'hate speech' against a religion. In June 2013 Matthew Collins, a spokesman for Hope not Hate, was quoted: 'There is a line in the sand between freedom of speech and the right to use hate speech. . . . People will now quote Voltaire but he never had the benefit of going to the gates of Auschwitz and seeing where unfettered free speech ends up'.[14]

It is ridiculous to suggest that the Holocaust was a result of too much free speech. When the Nazis came to power in 1933 they did not unfetter free speech: they ended it, through violent repression. They brutally silenced their critics. Their fanatical racism was promoted by violence and intimidation: those who supported or protected Jews had their free speech quickly curtailed.

Hatred of a religious doctrine does not mean hatred of individuals. Voltaire campaigned against religion but defended the right of anyone to peaceful religious worship. His notion of free speech included the right to offend others. He mocked, but he did not incite others to violence. Hope not Hate should vigorously defend free speech (short of incitement to violence), rather than imposing limits upon it. It is deeply tragic that an organization proclaiming hope over hate promotes considerable limits on free speech.

Of course, there is a danger that criticism of a religion can help to prepare the conditions for racist or other violence. But criticism of *any* doctrine can help to create conditions that may help to engender anger or violence against those that hold it. The possibility of such reactions is no excuse for censorship.

Terrorists and mass murderers have apparently drawn inspiration from a number of diverse thinkers. Twisted minds can easily turn doctrines to serve hateful and violent ends. Hence we cannot ban an idea or criticism simply because it may be misused.

For example, Anders Breivik, the notorious anti-Muslim terrorist and murderer of seventy-seven innocent young people, quoted Edmund Burke, Winston Churchill, Mahatma Gandhi, Thomas Jefferson, John Locke, George Orwell, Melanie Phillips, Roger Scruton and others, in his attempts to justify his atrocious killings in Norway in 2011. Surely this does not mean that the works of these writers should be banned? Misplaced concerns about 'unfettered free speech' might suggest that they should.

Instead of banning anything that might inspire a psychotically deranged murderer, it is important to maintain open discussion and criticism of all ideas. Some criticism may offend others. But if we allowed free speech only when it did not cause anyone any offence, then we would allow very little. Free speech should be allowed, short of incitement to violence.

In particular, we enter a very dangerous zone when criticism of religion is restricted. While the human rights of religious devotees, including their freedom to worship, must emphatically be protected, tolerance of religion does not mean that we should remain silent about acts of discrimination or oppression that have been carried out by religious followers. Like any doctrine, religion should remain under intellectual scrutiny. People have the right to criticize or protest peacefully against any religious tenet or practice. It is absurd and dangerous to dismiss automatically such criticism as 'right-wing'.

THE CONTRIBUTION OF THIS BOOK IN BRIEF

The first six chapters of this book are a selective history of some radical ideas, from the 1381 Peasants' Revolt in England to the theory and practice of Marxism. These chapters are not simply historical: the relevance of key ideas is demonstrated for today.

Chapter 1 concentrates on European ideas in the period from 1381 to 1789, noting that many early revolts appealed to religion for justification. Some called for communal ownership, but typically on a small scale. Contrary to a widespread misinterpretation, the English Levellers of the 1640s defended private property. They saw the legitimacy of government as grounded on the will of the people. Previously, the Reformation in Europe had led to rival claims of possible religious legitimation of authority. There were Catholics and multiple Protestant groups, each with its own religious legitimation of political power. Facing and rebutting these rival claims, radicals were impelled to call for religious toleration and a secular state. This secular trajectory, combined with the growth of science, formed the background for the Enlightenment, which argued for the supremacy of reason over superstition.

Chapter 2 explains how the original terms *Left* and *Right* emerged in the French Revolution in 1789–1792. The *Left* and *Right* were divided primarily on the question of the legitimate source of authority for government, and secondly on the question of universal and equal human rights. The *Right* defended religion and aristocratic birth as sources of authority. The *Left* rejected these, and sought somehow to root authority in the will of the people. The *Left* leaders of the French Revolution advocated an individualistic, property-owning, market economy, just as the English Levellers had done in the 1640s and the American revolutionaries in the 1770s. This chapter also contests the Marxist notion that 1789 was a 'bourgeois revolution'. It was not primarily a victory of capitalists over feudal aristocrats.

Chapter 3 is devoted to the contribution of Thomas Paine, who developed an alternative way forward for the *Left*. He has been wrongly described as a socialist. His innovative arguments for a guaranteed income and for a redistribution of wealth are shown to be highly relevant for today's capitalist economies. Paine charted a different route for the *Left*, which was quickly but regrettably eclipsed by socialism and collectivism.

Chapter 4 examines three early 'utopian socialists', namely Claude-Henri de Saint-Simon, François Marie Charles Fourier and Robert Owen. Each attempted to justify his planned society on the basis of some version of science. But their schemes were inflexible and they all abandoned some Enlightenment principles concerning democracy and universal human rights.

Chapter 5 is the first of two chapters on Marxism. It critically examines the Marxist notion of class struggle, with its elevation of the proletariat as the 'universal class'. It argues that the Marxist depiction of class as the most basic social unit is incoherent, because the definition of class itself depends on prior legal relations. The chapter also examines the incipient utopia in Marxism of a future planned economy. It summarizes diverse criticisms of collective planning from Albert Schäffle to Friedrich Hayek. Marx ruled out an economy consisting of autonomous worker cooperatives, but such a scheme is more viable than nationwide collectivization and the abolition of markets.

Chapter 6 continues the discussion of Marxism. It argues that the rule of one class over another, even if the ruling class is a majority, nullifies the principle of universal human rights, and paves the way for a totalitarian system. The realities of organization in any large-scale society (numbering in the thousands or millions) mean that effective direct rule by the whole population is impossible and some kind of leadership or elite is necessary. Marxists are also negligent concerning the rule of law. For example, in the Soviet Union, rights were deemed to be granted by the state, to be withdrawn if it desired. Acting against the state, or 'against the revolution' became a vague, catch-all crime. For reasons outlined in the chapter, Marxism generally carries the seeds of totalitarianism.

Chapter 7 is a defence of democracy and human rights. It opens with some examples of Left apologetics for repressive Communism in Russia, China and Cambodia. There is a comparison of death tolls, first between capitalism and Communism and second between democratic capitalism and despotisms of all kinds. It is argued that democratic systems, where there is some protection of human rights, can evidently reduce the risks of famine and war. Democracy may also help economic development, at least for countries above relatively low levels of output per capita. The penultimate section discusses rights and their possible justifications. If rights are difficult to justify *a priori* by reason alone, the evidence of the twentieth century shows decisively that the protection of rights helps to reduce human suffering. The chapter ends with some diagrammatic depictions of different views in relation to the originally defined notions of *Left* and *Right*.

Chapter 8 is an attack on normative cultural relativism, described as 'cultural relativism' for short. Cultural relativists argue that we (especially those of us from the West) should not criticize the moral values of other cultures. Its proponents allege that such criticism furthers Western globalization or imperialism by imposing Western values on the rest of the world. Cultural relativism was fuelled by reactions against Western military intervention in Vietnam, Iraq and elsewhere. But being critical of Western brutality and hypocrisy does not mean that one should be indifferent to female genital mutilation, wife-burning or dowry murder, as some prominent 'feminists' seem to propose. Such arguments are internally contradictory and immoral.

Chapter 9 addresses religion, with a primary focus on Islam. Criticism of a religion is not racist. But the ill-defined charge of 'Islamophobia' has prevented critical discussion of the nature of Islam. The immense contribution of Islam to world art and culture is acknowledged. But Islam today differs from other major religions—including Christianity and Judaism—in important respects. It has not yet accomplished an adequate separation of religion from law. In Islam as still practised in many communities, basic laws derive directly from religious texts and are regarded as the word of God. By contrast, legislation in the modern West is legitimated via the authority of representative democracy. Islam still devolves the implementation of several legal-religious rules onto the believers themselves, who under God's instruction from the Qur'an, may take the law into their own hands, and mete out prescribed punishment to rule-breakers. These factors make the reconciliation of existing Islamic cultures with post-Enlightenment societies difficult. Some Muslims are trying to modernize Islam, but the blanket charge of Islamophobia dissuades critical discussion that may help reform.

Criticizing Islam as a doctrine is not the same as criticizing Muslims as people. I do not criticize Muslims as persons. I have no time for populists like US President Donald Trump who made discriminatory statements against Muslims in his election campaign. It is important to uphold the right of people to believe in anything. What matters most is practice. A key problem is the practical unification within Islam of law and religion, which is incompatible with the post-Enlightenment separation of religion from the state. This chapter, like the others, is above all a defence of Enlightenment principles and institutions.

Chapter 10 contains two letters to imaginary friends. This epistolary device is intended to help clarify my own position to the reader, in relation to two prominent currents of opinion. The first letter is to a free-market libertarian. I recognize the strengths in her position but argue that the basic libertarian stance needs to be updated in the light of massive developments in the financial and corporate world, of ongoing threats of financial instability, of growing inequalities in the distribution of wealth in developed economies, of the growing economic importance of information and knowledge, and of the need for state intervention in some spheres, including to deal with the problem of climate change. The second letter is to an enduring socialist, who still wishes to maximize public ownership and minimize markets. I argue that this position has received fatal blows in the twentieth century, from theoretical critiques and from practical catastrophes. Socialism—at least in the classic sense—is dead. The welfare state, perhaps also with a significant public sector, is not. Dealing with inequality within capitalism is also vital. The real debate concerns what direction we would wish to take capitalism.

Chapter 11 concludes the book by outlining a policy agenda for a New Old *Left*. There are foremost emphases on the problem of inequality and on the survival of democracy in a complex world. Possible measures to deal with inequality include the enhancement of educational provision, a guaranteed basic income and a politically viable mechanism for a substantial redistribution of wealth. I emphasize a gradual and experimental approach, which I describe as evotopian. I modernize the classic French revolutionary slogan, to 'liberty, equality, democracy and solidarity'.

CHAPTER 1

Progressive Radicalism before the *Left*

When Adam delved and Eve span, who was then the gentleman?

JOHN BALL, 1381 Sermon to the People

For millions of years, our ancestors have lived in tribal units of hunter-gatherers, rarely numbering more than two hundred individuals. For group survival, we evolved propensities to cooperate with each other. Relying on emotions and facial expressions, we developed sophisticated social mechanisms to engender trust and cooperation, and to enforce social rules. Everyone knew everyone else within the tribe, and rule-breaking was punished by shaming, mocking, shunning or sometimes more severe sanctions. Tribal groups were relatively egalitarian, but still structured by gender and status, and governed by custom.[1]

Conflict between tribal groups was sometimes lethal. Groups that sustained internal cooperation, reciprocity and other solidaristic behaviour would act more cohesively and could be more successful against other groups. This provided an evolutionary selection mechanism for advancing cooperation in human cultures.[2]

Much of this changed with the rise of civilizations and large-scale urban settlements. About fourteen thousand years ago in the Levant in the Middle East, there emerged the first large permanent settlements in human history (even before the development of agriculture).[3] Civilizations in Egypt, Sumer, the Indus, China and elsewhere spawned even larger communities with powerful elites, stratified social orders and highly sophisticated divisions of labour.

While it continued to play a major role in these civilizations (and it is still vital even in modern societies), custom alone cannot regulate any complex, large-scale system. It is impossible to know everyone else in the community; hence, individual reputation is a less useful device for the enforcement of rules. Instead of custom, humans had to develop fuller notions of law and property to deal with the allocation and exchange of resources. Political and legal authority ceased to be entirely customary, and became codified and more institution-alized.[4]

The emergence of human civilization with permanent, large-scale settle-ments (numbering in the thousands or more) and complex institutions meant that humans faced new problems concerning governance and the legitimation of political and legal authority. How could powerful, unelected rulers justify their authority over many thousands of others? What gave them the right to make those decrees and rules?

Complex societies have often been stabilized through force and despotic rule. But to endure and work on human minds, hierarchy and authority have also to be ideologically legitimated in some way. Hierarchy and authority had to be sanctioned by ideology as well as defended by force.

Formerly, for millions of years of human history, questions of authority and legitimacy were largely resolved by custom and religious ritual. Then, from fourteen thousand years ago—a small fraction of the lifetime of the hu-man species—the problems of governance, authority and legitimacy were compounded by the rise of large-scale communities, located in cities. This was a major change, requiring new institutions to organize production and distribution, and prompting new questions concerning the righteousness of government or law. To sustain the government of large-scale communities, the innocence of custom had to be subjugated to institutionalized authority. But how could such authority be justified?

In ancient civilizations, religion was used to legitimate authority. Accord-ingly, there was a priesthood of some kind, as well as a bureaucracy and an army. Religious ceremonies and rituals legitimized the ruling elite. Since then, in many societies, religion has continued to play this important role.

Once open discussion became possible, justice and authority became cen-tral topics of political analysis and debate. Ancient Greek philosophers such as Plato considered the nature of justice and the rationale of the ideal state. But in practice, religious and mythological beliefs were still used to buttress authority.

Then, in the eighteenth century, the precursors of the original *Left* chal-lenged the religious legitimation of authority. Instead they proposed that valid political authority derives ultimately from the people. The role of religion was not, and still is not, a marginal issue. It is central to an appreciation of the rise and meanings of *Left* and *Right*.

Varieties of radicalism and progressive thinking are recorded in the earliest of literatures, from Plato to the Bible. We focus here on dissident and reform-ing ideas in the four centuries that preceded the French Revolution of 1789.

Hence this chapter is a selective rather than a comprehensive account of pre-1789 radical thought.[5]

FROM THE PEASANTS' REVOLT TO *UTOPIA*

The English Peasants' Revolt of 1381 targeted the great feudal inequalities of status and wealth. An attempt to collect poll taxes in Brentwood in Essex led to a violent confrontation, which rapidly spread across the south-east of England and into East Anglia. Many rose up in protest, burning court records and opening the local gaols. The rebels sought a reduction in taxation, an end to serfdom and the removal of the King's senior officials.

In addition, the radical priest John Ball called for the levelling of wealth and status and argued that things would not go well 'till everything be made in common . . . we shall all be united together, and the lords shall be no greater masters than ourselves'. Note the themes of equality and unity, as well as of common ownership.

After the rebels entered London, King Richard II temporarily acceded to most of their demands. Violence broke out at an open meeting with the rebels, and the rebel leader Wat Tyler was killed. Richard gathered his forces and expelled the rebels from London. After several days, most of the rebels were tracked down and executed.

Ball was hanged, drawn and quartered in his birthplace of St Albans in Hertfordshire. While his ideas were revolutionary at the time, he drew from tradition as well as from the Bible. A form of common possession was already familiar to the peasants: rural communities had rights to share and use common lands.[6]

Before the Enlightenment, European radicals often made reference to Christian scriptures as grounding for their claims. Ball skilfully used the creation story in Genesis to argue against permanent inequality of status. The Peasants' Revolt called for the abolition of serfdom, but deployed rather than challenged the authority of religion. Religion was the ideological centre of feudal life. Even after the decline of classical feudalism in England, the role of religion remained pivotal for centuries.

Ball was aligned to the dissident Lollard sect, which called for religious and political reform. The Lollards upheld that the Catholic Church had been corrupted by greed and power; expensive church ornament had diverted funds from the needy. In 1394 a group of Lollards marched on London and presented a petition to the English Parliament. Eleven of its twelve demands called for the reform of religious institutions. The twelfth preached against 'unnecessary trades' as 'the occasion of pride and luxury'.[7]

The Lollards were precursors of Protestant reformers. The sixteenth century in England saw the Protestant Reformation of Henry VIII and the dissolution of the monasteries in the 1530s. There were increasing enclosures of common lands. These seismic changes provoked a number of ill-fated popular rebellions.

The division of a population between Protestants and Catholics meant that there were rival sources of allegiance and rival religious justifications of authority. Europe was plunged into successions of religious revolts and wars, where the legitimation of royal authority depended on the imposition of the monarch's religion. Hence the rivalry between Protestants and Catholics meant political as well as ecclesiastical turmoil.

In the Peasants' War of 1524–1525 in Germany, the radical Protestant Thomas Müntzer was one of the peasant leaders. He proposed a biblically inspired communism. In France the Wars of Religion lasted from 1562 to 1598, and were followed in the seventeenth century by several Protestant rebellions. There were eighty years of religiously motivated war in the Low Countries, from 1568 to 1648. In England, major Catholic revolts erupted in 1536 and 1569.

Sir Thomas More was a devout Catholic. He tortured and burned Protestant dissidents, and was executed for failing to endorse Henry VIII's divorce from his first wife. But his famous 1516 book *Utopia* has been an inspiration for radical thinkers. In this work he criticized the dividing and enclosure of common lands and attacked the greed of the rich. Set in the context of a mostly rural economy, *Utopia* proposed taking everything into common ownership and abolishing internal trade. People would receive goods on the basis of their needs. The working day would be limited to six hours. There would be institutions for the care of the sick and the elderly. A hierarchy of elected officials would determine needs and allocate labour and goods. Contrary to More's own practices, there would be toleration in matters of religion: people would be free to worship as they wished. But women would be subordinate to men. Slavery would be a form of punishment for disobeying some laws or the elected authorities. *Utopia* is a sermon against greed and waste, grounded on a Christian faith that humankind can abandon these sins. Its religious tolerance meant that there would be no one theological justification for authority and power. It hinted at the idea that the legitimacy of government could be founded on a limited form of democracy.

By suggesting the democratic legitimation of power, *Utopia* signalled a new radical discourse for the modern era. This underdeveloped feature was just as important as its advocacy of common ownership. After all, the English peasantry was long familiar with allocated common land, and its shared use and management. The democratic legitimation of authority was much more radical, and even more pertinent for future, larger-scale, urban-based societies.

Other revolts in England from 1500 to 1640 were less about religion and more in protest against enclosures and other encroachments upon common land. Often they would appeal for justice to the King or other authorities, rather than challenge their legitimacy or right to rule. This was the case in the Kett Rebellion in Norfolk in 1549 and the Midland Revolt of 1607. Notwithstanding their communal sentiments, these uprisings appealed for the preservation of existing arrangements in rural communities, rather than envisioning a new world.

THE ENGLISH CIVIL WAR

The English Civil War erupted in 1642, as a conflict of authority between the King and Parliament. King Charles I claimed to rule by divine right, deriving his sovereignty from religion. By contrast, Parliament professed to represent the will of the people. But only a small minority of males had the right to vote in parliamentary elections. Women had no vote.

Parliamentarians and Royalists warred throughout Britain until the defeat and execution of Charles I in 1649 and the installation of a republic under Oliver Cromwell. The Civil War stimulated seminal debates concerning power and authority. There was a growth of dissident Protestant groups, who saw the established Protestant Church of England as too hierarchical and conservative. In religious terms, Britain became deeply divided between followers of the established church, various types of Nonconformist and Catholics. These ongoing schisms forced the question of the legitimation of government authority onto the immediate agenda.

Prompted by debates over what to do with the monarchy and the King after his defeat, a major political movement developed within the Parliamentarian army. Participants in the anti-enclosure uprising in the Midlands in 1607 had been called 'levellers' because they levelled hedges and fences. The Levellers of the 1640s were given this nickname by their enemies, and they repeatedly repudiated the description. They often protested that they were not promoting the 'levelling' of landed estates or any general redistribution of property. Their leader John Lilburne explained in 1647 that the term *Leveller* applied to him and his party only in the sense of equality under the law, namely their 'desire that all alike may be levelled to, and bound by the Law'. But much later their socialist admirers assumed that they wished to 'level' all property as well. There is no basis for this supposition in their writings.[8]

The Levellers emphasized popular sovereignty, an extended male franchise, equality before the law and religious tolerance. They believed in natural and inalienable rights, bestowed by God. The inalienability of these rights put limits on the powers of any majority in Parliament, because democracy cannot stifle inalienable rights. But otherwise they were strong supporters of democracy. While they defended private property, they railed against undemocratic tyranny. Hence their position was different from some modern libertarians such as Ludwig von Mises or Friedrich Hayek, who, while generally supporting liberty, argued on occasions that if private property rights were threatened, then democracy might justifiably be replaced by temporary dictatorship.[9]

From 1647 to 1649 the Levellers published a series of manifestos entitled the *Agreement of the People*. William Walwyn—a Christian freethinker and one of their leaders—echoed Thomas More in his pleas for religious tolerance. John Milton in his *Areopagitica* of 1644 had already made an eloquent appeal for freedom of expression. The Levellers were the first political movement in Europe to call for the separation of church and state and for a secular republic.

The Levellers were influential in Cromwell's army. At a rendezvous near Ware in Hertfordshire on 15 November 1647, two regiments carried copies of the *Agreement of the People* and stuck pieces of paper in their hatbands with the Leveller slogan 'England's Freedom, Soldiers' Rights'. With swords drawn, Cromwell and some of his officers rode into their ranks and ordered them to take the papers from their hats. One of the soldiers was swiftly executed for mutiny.

The Levellers argued for a constitution based on an extended manhood suffrage and biennial Parliaments.[10] Authority would be vested in the House of Commons rather than in the King or the House of Lords. Specified 'native rights' were declared sacrosanct for all Englishmen: freedom of conscience, freedom of worship, freedom from impressment into the armed forces and equality before the law.

Lilburne, the Leveller leader, came from County Durham. He was originally a Puritan and he later converted to Quakerism. Arrested in 1637 for circulating unlicensed pamphlets, he was fined £500, whipped, pilloried and imprisoned. During the Civil War he served as an officer in the Parliamentarian army. For his agitation against the Cromwellian authorities he spent several more years in prison. Lilburne coined the term *freeborn rights*, defining them as rights with which every human being is born, as opposed to rights bestowed by government or by its laws. He advocated an extended male suffrage, equality under the law and religious tolerance.

The Levellers declared that rights to liberty and property were innate to every person. Individuals had rights over their thoughts and bodies, without molestation or coercion, and everyone had the natural right to own private property. The Levellers did not promote common ownership, except when it resulted from the voluntary pooling of the property of everyone involved.[11]

By the 1640s, much of the formerly common lands in England were already enclosed, and the Levellers did not wish to return this land to its previous state. They did not write much about land reform. In one 1647 pamphlet, the Leveller Richard Overton briefly suggested that 'ancient' enclosures should be made accessible for the common use of the poor. But generally the Leveller leaders did not campaign against the enclosure of common lands. Instead they upheld legally acquired rights of property. The Marxist historian Christopher Hill pointed out that the Levellers 'sharply differentiated themselves from the Diggers who advocated a communist programme'.[12]

A defence of private property and a rebuttal of 'levelling' appears in the final, May 1649 version of the Leveller *Agreement of the People*, in a passage addressed to Members of Parliament: 'We therefore agree and declare, That it shall not be in the power of any Representative . . . [to] level men's Estates, destroy Propriety, or make all things Common'.[13] Even if representatives in the legislature were democratically elected, they did not have the right to overturn individual rights to property.

Likewise, Lilburne was repeatedly obliged to rebut the charge that the Levellers desired to 'level' all property. He wrote in 1652:

In my opinion and judgment, this Conceit of Levelling of property . . . is so ridiculous and foolish an opinion, as no man of brains, reason, or ingenuity, can be imagined such a sot as to maintain such a principle, because it would, if practised destroy not only any industry in the world, but raze the very foundation of generation, and of subsistence or being of one man by another. For as industry and valour by which the societies of mankind are maintained and preserved, who will take the pains for that which when he hath gotten is not his own, but must be equally shared in, by every lazy, simple, dronish sot? Or who will fight for that, wherein he hath no interest, but such as must be subject to the will and pleasure of another, yea of every coward and base low-spirited fellow, that in his sitting still must share in common with a valiant man in all his brave noble achievement? The ancient encouragement to men that were to defend their Country was this: that they were to hazard their persons for that which was their own, to wit, their own wives, their own children, their own Estates. And this give me leave to say, and that in truth, that those men in England, that are most branded with the name of Levellers, are of all in that Nation, most free from any design of Levelling, in the sense we have spoken of.[14]

As well as rebutting the charge of 'levelling', Lilburne here defended the institution of private property in terms of its incentives for 'industry' and maintaining 'subsistence'. If everything were 'equally shared', then the 'lazy' would benefit as much as those 'who will take the pains', thus diminishing incentives for individual effort. Incentives to work hard would be lessened.

With these words, Lilburne pointed to the crucial problem of scale in all communistic ventures. It relates to what economists call 'the free-rider problem'. As the size of the community increases, the free-rider problem can be exacerbated. If the number of people in a working community that shares its income is n, then individual incentives to contribute to community output are very roughly in proportion to $1/n$. As n increases, the extra effort of any single individual is rewarded less, because the output from extra effort is shared between n people. I call this the $1/n$ problem. As far as I am aware, Lilburne was the first person to identify it.[15]

Crucially, at low values of n, such as in a family or in a small cooperative, incentives to work hard can be enhanced by face-to-face mechanisms involving reciprocity, trust, commendation, satisfaction, shame, scorn or punishment. These social mechanisms are effective because they have evolved in human tribes over millions of years. At higher levels of n, these interpersonal mechanisms become relatively less effective.

The Levellers advocated free trade. For them, the basic division in society was not between workers and owners of property: it was between the rich and influential—who profited from monopolies and government favours—and the rest of the people. A clause in the May 1649 version of the *Agreement of the People* tells Parliament: 'That it shall not be in their power to continue or make any Laws to abridge or hinder any person or persons, from trading or merchandizing into any place beyond the Seas, where any of this Nation are free to trade'.[16]

Lilburne, Overton and Walwyn attributed the existence of low wages to monopolies, restrictions on trade and excise taxes. In 1652 Walwyn presented to the Parliamentary Committee for Trade and Foreign Affairs a defence of free trade against the Levant Company, urging the abolition of monopolies and trade restrictions. In *Walwyn's Conceptions; For a Free Trade*, the author saw free trade as a common right, conducive to common good.

Siding with the Levellers in the Putney Debates of 1647, Colonel Thomas Rainsborough argued that both the rich and poor had a right to a decent life, and that 'every man that is to live under a government ought first by his own consent to put himself under that government'. But in 1649, Rainsborough was killed, Leveller-led army mutinies in Bishopsgate in London and Banbury in Oxfordshire were crushed, and Cromwell effectively destroyed the Levellers as a political force.[17]

Yet the myth that the Levellers promoted common ownership persists. Tony Benn often mentioned the Levellers favourably, but he ignored their strong commitment to private ownership, and instead suggested that their arguments pointed to 'common ownership and a classless society'. The prominent British Labour politician Fenner Brockway published a book in 1980 called *Britain's First Socialists: The Levellers, Agitators and Diggers of the English Revolution*. But of these, only the Diggers were socialists. An entertaining four-part television series set during the English Civil War entitled *The Devil's Whore* (released in North America as *The Devil's Mistress*) has Rainsborough speaking in favour of common ownership, without any objection from Lilburne. There is no historical evidence to sustain such depictions. They are fantasies promoted by Benn, Brockway and others.[18]

By contrast, the Diggers opposed private property. From 1649 to 1650 groups of Diggers squatted on several stretches of common land in southern England. They set up communes whose members worked together on the soil and shared its produce. The Digger leader Gerrard Winstanley published a series of pamphlets advocating common ownership of land.

In his *New Law of Righteousness* (1649), Winstanley equated Christ with 'the universal liberty' and regarded all political authority as corrupting. He declared 'an equal privilege to share in the blessing of liberty' and regarded the institution of property as a limitation of the freedom of others. Land was bestowed to all by God. Winstanley criticized trade, because it led to cheating and discontent. He envisioned an agrarian society, in which all goods would be communally owned, and all commerce and wage labour would be outlawed.[19]

Hence the Levellers and Diggers had very different ideological positions. The Levellers advocated individual autonomy, private ownership and free trade. Although they appealed to religion, they saw democratic legitimation as the source of government authority. By contrast, the Diggers proposed a rigid, small-scale, religiously inspired, agrarian communism.

THE ENLIGHTENMENT

The Enlightenment refers to the great flowering of scientific and political ideas in Europe (most notably in Britain, France, Germany and the Netherlands) in the seventeenth and eighteenth centuries. Enlightenment thinkers questioned traditional authority and argued that the human condition could be improved through the use of reason and the development and application of science. A succession of great thinkers emphasized reason, enquiry, analysis, religious toleration and individual rights. In politics, they challenged attempts to legitimate power via appeals to religion, to family lineage or to traditional authority. Their ideas were a major influence on the struggle for American independence from 1765 to 1783 and on the French Revolution of 1789.

Inspirational philosophers of the Enlightenment include Francis Bacon (1561–1626), Thomas Hobbes (1588–1679), René Descartes (1596–1650), Baruch Spinoza (1632–1677), John Locke (1632–1704), Isaac Newton (1642–1727), Charles-Louis Montesquieu (1689–1755), Voltaire (1694–1778), David Hume (1711–1776), Jean-Jacques Rousseau (1712–1778), Adam Smith (1723–1790), Immanuel Kant (1724–1804), Thomas Paine (1737–1809), Mary Wollstonecraft (1759–1797) and many others.

The Enlightenment began with the scientific revolution of the late sixteenth and seventeenth centuries. Just as the new science made the natural world subject to rational enquiry, the Enlightenment also aimed to show that systems of justice and authority could be based on reason rather than custom or religion. These revolutions in thinking swept away the medieval world view and ushered in the modern Western world.

Notwithstanding the diversity of Enlightenment thought, reason remained its supreme principle. Reason was commended as a source of systematic knowledge of nature and as an authoritative guide to practical and political life, although crucially some recognized the limits of its power. Confidence in reason was generally paired with hostility toward other claims of authority, particularly those emanating from tradition or religion. Enlightenment thinkers proclaimed a set of universal human rights, and sought to inspire governments that would honour these rights and be subject to reason.

Enlightenment political thought was highly varied, with a number of internal controversies, including on the extent of democratic suffrage. But there were prominent common themes, such as these:

all people are born with the same legal and moral rights, including those to life, liberty and property;

people should have freedom of worship, of assembly and to express their opinions (at least short of incitement to violence);

that ultimately government must be founded upon the consent of the governed, rather than upon religion or dynastic inheritance;

and that government should include checks and balances to limit despotism and to safeguard the rights of dissenters and other minorities.

One of the most remarkable and persistent omissions from the penetrating gaze of Enlightenment rationalism was the recognition of equivalent rights for women. Most Enlightenment thinkers took it for granted that rights to vote and even own property were male, and that unmarried women were subject to the authority of their fathers, just as married women were to be ruled by their husbands.

Even Robert Burns's poem 'The Rights of Woman' (1792), which suggested that 'the rights of woman merit some attention', saw females as 'tender flowers' in need of 'protection' and wanting 'admiration' for their 'charms'. Despite the poem's title, there was nothing about women sharing equal political and economic rights with men. Burns voiced the prominent view, which prevailed even among enlightened progressives, that women were emotional creatures, with diminished powers of reason.

There were some important exceptions. In 1649 Katherine Chidley led a group of Leveller women to argue that their sex had rights and liberties equal to men. But she did not write of female suffrage. Mary Wollstonecraft in her *Vindication of the Rights of Women* (1792) put forward a forceful case for gender equality. But while this tract highlighted the rights of women to an education, it too failed to call for female suffrage. The gendered political business of the eighteenth-century Enlightenment remained unfinished until well into the twentieth century. Income inequality between men and women persists today.

The era of the Enlightenment was a great period of nationalism and nation building in Europe. England completed a unification with Scotland in 1707. Italian and German unifications were completed in 1871. But the consolidation of nations and their borders had twin effects. While it typically asserted a national identity in terms of values, history and language, it had to cope with internal minorities with different ethnicities, religions, languages or cultures. Neither persecution, propaganda, interbreeding, nor education could completely eradicate these differences.

This internal diversity within a nation state, combined with migrations across borders, led to questions concerning national identity and the assignment of rights to minorities. Enlightenment reason dictated that a national government rested on the consent of its people. But who were its people? Who were to be included or excluded?

Even in the United States, whose Declaration of Independence in 1776 announced the most important practical experiment in Enlightenment political thought, this problem was acute from the beginning. The American Constitution, first drafted in 1787, opened with the famous words: 'We, the people of the United States'. But, at least in practice, this excluded Native Americans and black slaves from full political and other rights. Tribal groups of Native Americans were treated as separate 'nations'. This reflected the persistent usage of the term *nation* to refer to an identifiable group of people, typically defined by ethnic, cultural or linguistic criteria. Even after the abolition of slavery in 1865, the granting of full citizenship rights to Native Americans in 1924 and the *de facto* enfranchisement of African Americans in 1965, there remains the problem of dealing with illegal immigrants and long-term resident aliens.

Nations and states are different things, and their political reconciliation shall remain a difficult problem, unless and until there is world government, and rights are then no longer partitioned by states. The Enlightenment left unresolved these otherwise enduring problems of national identity and political geography, which have remained major causes of persecutions, revolts and wars ever since. In our era of globalization, we face challenges of openness and assimilation to a much greater degree than ever before.

THE LIMITS TO REASON

While making reason their guiding principle, Enlightenment thinkers had to get to grips with the limits to reason and rational argument. These limits were explored by Kant, in great works such as his *Critique of Pure Reason* (1781), *Critique of Practical Reason* (1788) and *Critique of Judgment* (1790). Kant wrote: 'Human reason has this peculiar fate that . . . it is burdened by questions which, as prescribed by the very nature of reason itself, it is not able to ignore, but which, as transcending all its powers, it is also unable to answer'.[20]

Edmund Burke was a Whig Party Member of the British Parliament and a highly original political thinker. He had been sympathetic to the complaints of the American colonists before they declared independence. But at the outbreak of the French Revolution, and before the horrors of Maximilien Robespierre's Reign of Terror (1793–1794), Burke in 1790 explored limits to the use of reason as a guide for politicians and governments. Against the tide of his time, he cautioned against declarations of abstract and universal human rights. He warned that they could be retracted as quickly as they were affirmed. Because of the complexities of human affairs, and the limits to our understanding of institutional mechanisms, society could not be redesigned simply by the application of reason. Given the huge complexities of both human nature and social institutions, there were clear limits to the rational organization of human affairs. Burke wrote:

> [T]he constitution of a state, and the distribution of its powers, [is] a matter of the most delicate and complicated skill. It requires a deep knowledge of human nature and human necessities, and of the things which facilitate or obstruct the various ends which are to be pursued by the mechanism of civil institutions. . . . The science of constructing a commonwealth, or renovating it, or reforming it, is, like every other experimental science, not to be taught *à priori*. . . . The science of government being therefore so practical in itself . . . [is] a matter which requires experience, and even more experience than any person can gain in his whole life, however sagacious and observing he may be.[21]

For Burke, the careful science of government was a grand historic experiment, spanning multiple generations, where each generation might learn incrementally from the practical experience of its predecessors. The founts of wisdom and justice were tried-and-tested tradition. Traditional institutions should be respected, because they had been built up and tested over time. Individual powers of reason were smaller than the inherited, tacit wisdom embedded in tried-and-tested institutions.

Burke's argument should be taken seriously, especially in the context of highly complex societies and economies. It did not mean abandoning all notions of justice or rights, and Burke did not abandon them himself. The trouble with his argument was that it then provided little practical advice, other than a generally cautious conservativism plus a small dose of restrained experimentation. In the face of the revolutionary convulsions of the 1790s, his doctrine seemed a general apology for the *status quo*. For this reason he was lambasted by Thomas Paine and others.[22]

Burke's strictures concerning complexity and experimentation are especially important in the modern context. They warn against blueprint designs for politico-economic systems that involve all-embracing rational plans.

But the experience of numerous, diverse, socioeconomic experiments in the nineteenth and twentieth centuries gives us a much richer guide to what should be avoided, and to what successes might be achieved. With all this accumulated experience, we may heed Burke's warnings concerning social and human complexity, and nevertheless experiment a little more boldly than he was inclined, as long as we experiment in directions that have been productive in the past, and avoid paths that have led to disaster.

Burke qualified the predominant Enlightenment view of liberty: 'But what is liberty without wisdom, and without virtue? It is the greatest of all possible evils; for it is folly, vice and madness, without tuition or restraint'.[23] For him, the pursuit of unqualified and unrestrained liberty ignored the problem that the individual might act foolishly, immorally or unjustly. The individual was not always the best judge of his or her interests.

Even if the individual was restricted to actions that did not harm others, then, as John Stuart Mill worried later, he or she may prefer playing push-pin to reading poetry. Freedom of choice does not necessarily lead to human development or flourishing. For Mill, education was necessary to improve our understanding of our choices and of their consequences—and to reduce folly. Education can bring greater appreciation of poetry and the arts. Accordingly, the uneducated individual is an imperfect judge of his or her welfare. The problem remained of ascertaining what was and was not, on balance, a harmful act to others.

All this made the maximization of individual liberty problematic. Any constraint on liberty brings the dangers of authoritarianism; but liberty unleashed allows the perils of folly and injustice. Mill's solution, later elaborated and refined by John Dewey, among others, was for the constrained authority of education, guided by the evolving principles of empirically grounded science.[24]

CONCLUSION: THE ENDURING RELEVANCE OF THE ENLIGHTENMENT

The Enlightenment underlined the roles of both reason and experimentation in human affairs. Against the claims of aristocracy and religion, Enlightenment thinkers proclaimed universal and inalienable human rights. Unlike previous radical doctrines, these rights were not founded on Christian or other religious scriptures. As European nations became internally less homogenous in terms of religion, this move was necessary as well as admirable. It helped to avoid the descent of politics into an irresolvable conflict of religious dogmas, with everyone claiming that they were following the word of God.

The ultimate later expression of Enlightenment ideas on human emancipation was the Universal Declaration of Human Rights, adopted by the General Assembly of the United Nations in 1948. It was drafted shortly after a devastating world war, waged against fascist regimes that had trampled over human rights in Europe and Asia. This Universal Declaration was later buttressed by the European Convention for the Protection of Human Rights and Fundamental Freedoms (drafted 1950) and the International Covenant on Economic, Social and Cultural Rights (adopted by the United Nations in 1966).

Enlightenment principles, including universal rights, are opposed by fascists, despots and extreme conservatives. They are also criticized by Marxists: while they welcome the Enlightenment's attacks on privilege and religion, they see these as part of a passing phase in the class struggle. According to Marxists, Enlightenment ideas are neither natural nor universal. Instead they represent the aims and interests of the rising bourgeoisie. Hence, depicting the French Revolution as a triumph of Enlightenment thought, Frederick Engels wrote:

> Now, for the first time, appeared the light of day, the kingdom of reason; henceforth superstition, injustice, privilege, oppression, were to be superseded by eternal truth, eternal Right, equality based on Nature and the inalienable rights of man. We know today that this kingdom of reason was nothing more than the idealized kingdom of the bourgeoisie; that this eternal Right found its realization in bourgeois justice; that this equality reduced itself to bourgeois equality before the law; that bourgeois property was proclaimed as one of the essential rights of man; and that the government of reason, the *Contrat Social* of Rousseau, came into being, and only could come into being, as a democratic bourgeois republic.[25]

According to Marxism, the champions and beneficiaries of Enlightenment values were the economically rising bourgeois class, including merchants, entrepreneurs, financiers and manufacturers. Hence, for example, the Marxist writer Guy Robinson described the Enlightenment as the ideology of the bourgeoisie: 'The . . . Enlightenment view expressed little more than the sense of emancipation of one particular class from the constraining bonds of feudalism and a sense of the infinite possibility of the new order of society for that class, which was the motor and representative of that new order'.[26] While acknowledging Enlightenment ideas, in their limited historical context, as progressive, Marxism depicts them as bourgeois rather than universal, and hence partly or wholly dispensable in the socialist future.

In particular, Marxists reject the 'bourgeois' Enlightenment defence of private property. They look instead to past radicals who have promoted common ownership. Indeed, the idea of holding property in common goes back to Plato and the Bible. Many feudal peasants jointly used and managed their village common lands. In parts of Europe, common management of land was once relatively commonplace on a small scale, and similar arrangements persist today in many developing countries. Marx and Engels also pointed to the so-called 'primitive communism' of the tribal era.[27]

But as noted earlier in this chapter, the predominant vision of common property, when it appeared, was rural or agricultural, and often shrouded in backward-looking, religious doctrine. After the Diggers of the seventeenth century, schemes for common ownership had little recurrence in England until the 1830s. In their major study of Western utopian thought, Frank E. Manuel and Fritzie P. Manuel noted that, during the Enlightenment, 'egalitarian doctrines were concentrated in France, without significant echo in eighteenth-century England or elsewhere on the Continent, where outright attacks on the private ownership of property were virtually non-existent before 1789'.[28]

As noted in later chapters, it was principally within Marxism that a new view of common ownership, freed of religious justification and of rural confinement, and extended to the national scale, became prominent. Marxism linked the struggle for nationwide common ownership with the rising proletariat, and saw this goal as destined not by religion, but by the 'scientific' analysis of history.

We shall return to these central and vital themes later. Beforehand, in the next chapter, we survey the huge social convulsion of the French Revolution, which was inspired by Enlightenment ideals and gave birth to the terms *Left* and *Right*.

CHAPTER 2

The French Revolution and the Original *Left*

Bliss was it in that dawn to be alive,
But to be young was very heaven! . . .
When Reason seemed the most to assert her rights . . .
Not favoured spots alone, but the whole earth . . .
Not in Utopia, subterranean fields,
Or some secreted island, Heaven knows where!
But in the very world, which is the world
Of all of us,—the place where in the end
We find our happiness, or not at all!

William Wordsworth, 'As It Appeared to Enthusiasts at Its Commencement' (1805)

The French Revolution of 1789–1799 was one of the most important events in human history. Inspired by Enlightenment ideals, it altered the course of modern society, by triggering the decline of absolutist regimes and by announcing a long and still-unfinished global struggle for democracy and universal human rights.

The revolution led to the execution of Louis XVI, who had become King of France in 1774. In the first part of his reign he tried to accomplish some reforms. He attempted to abolish serfdom and to grant more rights to non-Catholics. But the nobility successfully resisted their implementation. The failures of his reforms stoked up resentment at home.

Privileges enjoyed by the clergy and the aristocracy fuelled growing popular resentment. There were years of bad harvests. King Louis removed some regulations on the grain market, but this led to higher prices. The monarchy was deeply in debt, and it attempted to raise revenue through unpopular taxation.

In January 1789, Louis summoned the French Parliament—known as the Estates General—to address these financial problems. There were three sets of deputies, or 'Estates', each with its quota of seats. The First Estate was made up of representatives of the Catholic clergy. The Second Estate comprised representatives of the aristocracy. The Third Estate consisted of commoners; it held fewer than half of the seats in the Estates General, but represented 95 per cent of the French population. According to the rules at that time, each Estate would vote separately on an issue, but the collective vote of each Estate would be weighed equally. Consequently, the representatives of 95 per cent of the people would together have only a third of the voting power.

After the election of their representatives, the Estates assembled in Paris in May. The Third Estate demanded that all three Estates should meet together as one unified body, with every individual delegate having one vote. This was resisted by the King and the other two Estates, and the legislature reached an impasse. Eventually the Third Estate decided to begin its deliberations on its own. It invited the other two Estates to take part, but resolved not to wait for them. On 17 June the Third Estate declared itself as the representative body of the entire people.

But the King annulled its decrees and attempted to deprive it of a meeting place. Representatives of the clergy and nobility then joined with those of the Third Estate, and together they declared themselves as the National Constituent Assembly. The people feared that the King was planning to attack Paris and disband the Assembly. Riots erupted as people broke into buildings in search of arms to defend the city. The Bastille was stormed on 14 July 1789.

On the night of 4 August 1789 the Assembly proclaimed the abolition of feudalism and of the laws and privileges of the *Ancien Régime*. On 26 August 1789 the Assembly published its *Declaration of the Rights of Man and of the Citizen*. This upheld freedom of thought, of worship, of assembly and from arbitrary arrest; it enshrined equality under the law and hailed private property as a basic right. Article Six read: 'The law is the expression of the general will. All citizens have the right to contribute personally, or through their representatives, to its formation. It must be the same for all, whether it protects or punishes'. The concept of the 'general will' derived primarily from Jean-Jacques Rousseau, who was a major inspiration for the revolutionaries.[1]

Their constitutional deliberations were also influenced by Charles-Louis Montesquieu, who had studied the English system of government and pointed to the need for checks and balances within the state: 'In order that power is not abused, things should be so disposed, that power checks power'. Montesquieu argued for the separation of the legislature, the executive and the judiciary. Leading French revolutionaries understood the dangers in the concentration of power in few hands.[2]

On 6 October 1789 the King and the royal family were obliged to move from Versailles to Paris under the 'protection' of the National Guard. The French

Republic was proclaimed in September 1792 and the King was executed in January 1793.

Through its 1792 elections, France became the first modern democracy, based on near-universal male suffrage. But unfortunately it did not last long. It was followed by dictatorships, or partial democracies with more limited suffrage, until well into the nineteenth century. The year 1792 was a global high watermark for democracy, only to be reached again in the twentieth century.

By comparison, after declaring independence from Britain in 1776, the United States proclaimed individual liberty and the rights of man. But initially the franchise was limited to a subset of white men, and slaves (mostly of African descent) were deprived of rights. White men without a significant amount of property could not vote in all US states until 1856. White women did not get the vote in all US states until 1920. Native Americans did not get US citizenship or the right to vote until 1924. Although nominally emancipated in 1865, African Americans were prevented from voting in some states until 1965.

The United Kingdom did not have universal male suffrage until 1918 and universal female suffrage until 1928.

The origins of the terms *Left* and *Right* are found in the deliberations of the French legislative assemblies from 1789 to 1792. Before we turn in more detail to that crucial period, we may briefly note what followed.

For much of the 1790s France was at war with Britain, Austria, Prussia, Spain or the Dutch Republic. Because of war, the new constitution of June 1793 was not put into force. Consequently, those accused of acting 'against the people' or of 'crimes against liberty' had little effective legal protection. Under Maximilien Robespierre, the Reign of Terror lasted from 1793 to 1794, involving political purges and mass executions.[3] In a *coup d'état* in July 1794, Robespierre was overthrown and then executed. After five years of further political instability, Napoléon Bonaparte took power in November 1799.

THE ORIGINAL *LEFT*

In the National Constituent Assembly of 1789, those deputies most critical of the monarchy began to congregate on the seats to the left of the President's chair. Conservative supporters of the aristocracy and the monarchy would congregate on the right side of the Assembly. The Baron de Gauville explained: 'We began to recognize each other: those who were loyal to religion and the king took up positions to the right of the chair so as to avoid the shouts, oaths, and indecencies that enjoyed free rein in the opposing camp'.[4]

Those seated to the *Left* of the National Constituent Assembly wished to limit the powers of the monarchy, and eventually to create a democratic republic. From 1789 to 1792 the Assembly divided over the issues of whether the King should have a veto over legislation, over whether there should be a second chamber, and over the nature and extent of the franchise for the election of deputies. Those on the *Right* wished to maintain the authority of the crown by means of a royal veto, to preserve some rights of the aristocracy, to have an unelected upper house, and to maintain major property and tax qualifications for voting. By contrast, the *Left* demanded an end to aristocratic privileges, limitations to the power and privileges of the church, a single-chamber legislature in which all power rested with democratically elected representatives, and a broad popular—but wholly male—franchise.[5]

In 1789, Jacobin Clubs sprung up all over France. They took their name after the first club, formed in a Jacobin monastery near the Assembly in Paris. The Jacobins were the agitators and activists of the revolution. Like most political groupings, they amalgamated different opinions. Originally the Jacobin Clubs were an inclusive forum for all revolutionaries; people later described as Girondins and Montagnards were among their number. The Girondins acquired that name because a number of them came from the *département* of the Gironde. The Montagnards were a radical faction within the Jacobins; they took their name from their occupation of the higher seats behind the President of the Assembly. By 1791 the Jacobin Clubs were dominated by Girondin intellectuals and orators. Hence Girondins, such as Jacques-Pierre Brissot and Thomas Paine, were also Jacobins.

At least from 1789 to 1792, when the label was most inclusive, the Jacobins as a whole were the *Left*. Like other Enlightenment thinkers, they believed that ideal governments were founded on natural rights and by the will of the people, rather than on religion or tradition. Hence, as well as defending the nation and promoting a republic, they opposed an attempt in 1790 to reinstate Catholicism as the national religion. The re-introduction of an established church would have made religion a superior authority over the people.[6]

Accordingly, the *Left* and *Right* were divided on the question of the legitimate source of authority for government, and on the question of universal and equal human rights. To be *Left* was to reject aristocracy or religion as sources of authority, and instead claim authority in the will of the people. The *Left* differed internally on the question of how a suitably enlightened general will could be detected and interpreted.

How can *Left* politicians determine what is the enlightened popular will? What institutions and mechanisms should be constructed to best represent that will, especially in a large and diverse nation? Answers to these questions are far from obvious. Hence defining the original *Right* is easier than defining the *Left*.

The Girondins and other Jacobins supported the use of force to defend the gains of the revolution and took an aggressive stance against hostile foreign powers. The Girondins campaigned with other Jacobins for the end of the monarchy, but then they resisted the spiralling, violent momentum of the revolution.

Like the English Levellers of the 1640s, most Girondins were committed democrats. But some militant Jacobins argued for suspensions of democratic powers to facilitate a more rapid purging of feudal or aristocratic powers. Some supported the execution of the King, despite a prominent earlier Jacobin sentiment in favour of the total abolition of the death penalty.

Elected on the basis of near-universal male suffrage, the National Convention was inaugurated in September 1792.[7] The Girondins did not match the fanaticism or the ruthlessness of the Montagnards. Vengeful mobs invaded the prisons of Paris and killed hundreds of prisoners. While the Girondins favoured a democratic republic, some of them proposed that Louis XVI should remain in power until it be shown by his actions that he was blocking the will of the people. Instead of the rule of the mob, the Girondins desired democracy, justice and order.

The Girondins had a majority in the National Convention; they controlled the executive council and filled the ministries. But the Montagnards held vital Parisian institutions including its mayoralty, its municipal council (Commune), its Jacobin Club, its mass assemblies and its regiment of the National Guard. Girondin dominance of the government was undermined by the Parisian uprisings of 27 and 31 May 1793. On 2 June the Parisian National Guard was deployed to purge the National Convention of the Girondins. Most leading Girondins were imprisoned and executed, and thus began the Reign of Terror.

After the purge against the Girondins, the term *Jacobin* acquired a narrower meaning, connoting vigorous, uncompromising and violent revolutionary action, in line with the Montagnards.

WHAT THE *LEFT* WAS NOT

If energy and determination are Left, then the Montagnards were to the Left of the Girondins. But degrees of fanaticism, activism and violence are poor criteria to differentiate political doctrines. We should be concerned more with the nature of an ideology than the manner in which it is pursued or expressed.

Consider the death penalty. In 1792 there was an important division of opinion over whether the King should be executed. Paine was among the opponents, arguing that 'an avidity to punish is always dangerous to liberty' because it can establish a precedent for others. Many of the original Jacobins opposed the death penalty and the growing bloodlust of some of their number was inconsistent with the original principles of the *Left*.

In his popular volume *The Left in Europe since 1789*, David Caute referred to the French Revolution and proposed definitions of Left and Right. Caute argued that the defining and enduring feature of the Left is its advocacy of 'popular sovereignty', against the supremacy of the monarchy and the church, as upheld by the Right.[8]

Caute did not analyse the concept of popular sovereignty in depth, or consider its practical limits in complex, large-scale societies. But he stressed that 'popular sovereignty' was not necessarily the same as democracy and that it would 'be wrong to conclude automatically that the agents of dictatorship had ceased to be of the Left'. But it is difficult to see how 'popular sovereignty' could remain secure within a dictatorship.

Caute depicted Robespierre as the main campaigner for universal suffrage. For Caute, 'the Left in 1793 constituted those to the left of the Girondins'. He also wrote of the 'moderate liberal' Girondins and the 'radical democratic' Jacobins. His depictions do not square up with the facts and are easily refuted.[9]

Consider two influential revolutionaries. Jacques-Pierre Brissot played such a central role among the Girondins that for a while their whole group was called Brissotins. Before 1789, in advance of Robespierre, Brissot advocated a democratic republic in France. He argued against electoral qualifications based on income or property and instead proposed a representative government based on universal male suffrage. Brissot also took the abolitionist lead in campaigning against slavery.[10]

Nicolas de Condorcet was another leading abolitionist and also aligned with the Girondins. A renowned mathematician, philosopher and political scientist, Condorcet was one of the first few advocates of female suffrage. He was not followed by Robespierre in that respect.

Contrary to Caute's depiction, the prominent examples of Brissot and Condorcet show that leading Girondins were earlier and more inclusive in their proposals for a democratic franchise than Robespierre. The Girondins as a whole were no less democratic in their aims than Robespierre and other Jacobins.

Caute was wildly inaccurate when he wrote that the Girondins 'were deeply opposed to absolute democracy'.[11] Girondin deputies came from several regions of France and represented the country as a whole. But the National Convention was at the mercy of the Paris mobs. The Girondins argued that the neither the Paris Commune nor its people had the right to decide policy for the nation as a whole. The Girondins denounced the domination of the National Convention by Parisian interests, and summoned provincial levies to their aid.

Generally the Girondins argued against the suspension of democratic powers. By contrast, Robespierre and other Montagnards were more willing to suspend democracy in times of alleged emergency.

Caute's notion of popular sovereignty was designed to link the 1789 *Left* to 1960s New Left sentiments for vaguely specified 'democratic socialism'. To do this, he had to bring some notion of common ownership into the picture. Caute wrote: 'One man, one vote . . . achieves only a fake popular sovereignty so long as the means of production remain under private control'. Like many others Caute failed to detail how such popular control would work. Furthermore, the attempt to link 'democratic socialism' to the French revolutionary *Left* fails dismally when confronted with the facts.[12]

THE ORIGINAL *LEFT* AND PRIVATE ENTERPRISE

Caute's opposition to 'private control' and private ownership contradicted the entire French revolutionary *Left* of 1789–1792. The French revolutionaries furthered the rights of private property and were opposed to public ownership or control of the means of production.

In pre-revolutionary France under King Louis XVI there were numerous corporations closely tied up with royal power and bureaucracy. They linked the worlds of business and politics. The sale of corporate offices provided an important source of royal revenues. In return, numerous corporations and guilds received privileges from the King. This era of 'Colbertism' involved bureaucratic meddling, regulation, nepotism and corruption.

In search of an individualistic utopia, and against the despised institutions of the *Ancien Régime*, the French revolutionary authorities enacted laws from June 1791 that prohibited organizations of workers, professionals and entrepreneurs, and ended much state regulation of business. Business coalitions, guilds and even business corporations were abolished. The Preamble to the French Constitution of September 1791 noted that the National Assembly 'abolishes irrevocably the institutions that were injurious to liberty and equality of rights'. In addition it declared: 'Neither *jurandes* [associations] nor corporations of professions, arts, and crafts any longer exist'. Individuals were free to pursue their business interests but forbidden to combine together for business purposes.[13]

The key point is that, from the Girondins to the Montagnards, the *Left* leaders of the French Revolution advocated an individualistic, property-owning, market economy, just as the English Levellers had done in the 1640s and the American revolutionaries in the 1770s. Under the monarchy, the French revolutionaries had experienced the ill effects of state monopolies and other large agglomerations of economic power. They wanted none of them. They defended private property and private enterprise in an extremely individualistic form. As the Fabian socialist R. H. Tawney put it: 'the dogma of the sanctity of private property was maintained as tenaciously by French Jacobins as by English Tories'. Frank E. Manuel and Fritzie P. Manuel concurred:

> The Jacobin utopia of the little people makes no dogmatic demand for a communal system. The Jacobin sansculottes of Paris, who had few 'proletarians' among them—their ranks being filled with shopkeepers, artisans, and members of the poorer professions— . . . were not opposed to individual property because most of them had a bit of it.[14]

Instead, Caute proposed that the 'French revolution provided three main models' for the future Left. Alongside the 'moderate liberal' and 'radical democratic' tendencies in the 1790s, he noted the 'socialist' movement, led by Gracchus Babeuf. Caute thus outlined a family lineage of multiple Left descendants from the original French *Left*, including varieties of liberalism, anarchism, communism, socialism and social democracy.

But having sketched this family tree, Caute devoted very few pages to liberalism. John Stuart Mill, for example, was mentioned dismissively on one page only. Caute devoted much more attention to the nineteenth- and twentieth-century 'Left', which wished to abolish private property and had dramatically limited liberty and democracy. This was entirely contrary to the Jacobins of 1789–1792.[15]

Who was Babeuf? Born François-Noël Babeuf in 1760, he later adopted the first name Gracchus, after the plebeian politician of Republican Rome who wished to redistribute wealth from the rich to the poor. Babeuf agitated against feudal privileges and became embroiled in the revolution. He supported the Reign of Terror and was imprisoned in 1794 for his criticism of the group that seized power, ended the Terror and executed Robespierre.

After his release from prison in 1795, during a time of famine, Babeuf advocated common ownership and the abolition of private property, to be achieved if necessary by the methods of terror. He was the first revolutionary communist of modern times. He wanted an equal distribution of income and wealth, irrespective of the work done. He opposed rights to inheritance and proposed the breakup of large cities into smaller communities. All would be compelled to do physical work and live in the same manner. Babeuf and his followers planned to seize national power, and then rule on behalf of the masses, until the people were educated and deemed able to rule through locally elected bodies. Babeuf's conspiracy was uncovered in 1796 and he was then executed.[16]

Babeuf had a point. How could equality of rights, equality under the law and the abolition of inherited privileges be squared with the concentrated inheritance of wealth, much of it being a hangover of the feudal era? How could the abolition of feudalism be reconciled with the persistence of luxury alongside squalor?

But by focusing on this problem alone, Babeuf and his followers pushed the revolutionary slogan of equality far beyond the matter of equivalent treatment under the law. Despite their claim that they wanted to preserve and extend existing rights, they negated several other important rights that the revolution had enshrined, including the rights to individual property and of freedom of expression and assembly.

Although linked with the thinking of the time, the short-lived conspiracy of Babeuf was hardly representative of the revolution as a whole. While his slogan was absolute equality, the abolition of private property went against prevalent Jacobin opinion. He was a product of the revolution, but he was not typical of it. Using Babeuf to establish that socialism and communism have a *Left* lineage is no less absurd than suggesting that mass executions, terror, dictatorship and Bonapartism are all *Left*. It is much more sensible, first and foremost, to apply the term *Left* to the doctrines that prevailed in 1789–1792, rather than to the upheavals and transgressions that followed.

POPULAR SOVEREIGNTY VERSUS THE POPULAR LEGITIMATION OF AUTHORITY

For Caute, Left meant advocacy of popular sovereignty. With this definition, he tried to link the French revolutionary radicals with both Soviet-style totalitarian Communism and the vague 1960s ideals of 'democratic socialism'. This definition is flawed and the linkage does not work. We have noted already the defence of private property by the French revolutionaries. In later chapters it will be argued that 'democratic socialism' (if it means wholesale public ownership plus extensive democratic management) is not feasible in large, complex societies. It will also be shown that Marxist ideology carries the seeds of totalitarianism, and that Soviet-style systems are marked departures from the ideals of the original *Left*.

But the task here is to understand the original *Left*. It pursued representative democracy, but that was not its only *raison d'être*. Instead, rather than the monarchy or religion, it saw the people as a whole as the ultimate source of political legitimacy. A key claim was that political authority derives somehow from the people, and not from God, religion or inherited position.

In addition, the *Left* stressed a number of basic individual rights, including freedoms of expression, assembly and worship; rights to ownership of property; and equal treatment under the law. The original *Right* denied or limited such rights. Crucially, these allegedly natural or inalienable rights put severe limits on the use of *any* authority, whether it is an expression of the popular will or not. These rights were not simply a protection against despots; they also placed limits on democratic or popular sovereignty over any individual or minority group.

Hence the grounding of political authority in a mandate from the people does not give the government or people any authority to override these human rights. Individual rights are exercised in civil society: their existence puts major constraints on the government and the legislature. *This puts severe limits on any exercise of popular sovereignty.* Caute's flawed definition of the Left overlooks the vital constraints imposed by inalienable human rights.

Logically, rights must precede any expression of majority rule: the latter implies the right to vote, at least by those who are enfranchised. Any system of majority rule or popular sovereignty implies prior rules to determine those sovereign voting powers.

While popular sovereignty suggests ongoing popular control, the popular legitimation of political authority is a very different matter. Popular legitimation is consistent with a plebiscite on the national constitution, followed by periodic elections of political representatives. Ongoing popular influence is expressed through individual interactions and contracts with others, within civil society and a market economy. Whatever its limitations, this was the general view of the revolutionary *Left* of 1789–1792.

One of several major problems is to determine how legitimate political authority is to be expressed or validated. Here, since its inception, the *Left* has divided into different positions. Understanding this problem, conservatives on the *Right* argue that many inherited laws and institutions—typically including the monarchy—should be respected and preserved, because they have been tested by time. But a task in this chapter is to identify the nature of the original *Left*, and neither to resolve nor deny its problems.

A BOURGEOIS REVOLUTION?

The achievements of the Enlightenment, and of the French revolutionaries of 1789–1792, have enduring modern relevance. One way of diminishing these achievements is to describe them as the passing historical product of a rising, sectional, minority and ultimately doomed social class. In this interpretation, the French Revolution is a 'bourgeois revolution': it is seen as an important prelude to the big class act to come, when the proletarian revolution will overthrow the bourgeoisie and proclaim a new era of equality.

Marxists are famous for this interpretation, but it has precursors. Before 1830, early historians of the French Revolution, such as François Mignet and Adolphe Thiers, depicted it as a triumph of the bourgeoisie over other social classes.

The next step was to characterize the epoch after 1789 in terms of the struggle of the suppressed working class against the triumphant bourgeoisie. Hence the political activist Louis Auguste Blanqui sided with the 'proletariat' in the revolutionary struggle against the capitalist order. Inspired by Babeuf, Blanqui linked the struggle for communism to growing industrialization and the aspirations of the industrial working class.[17]

Aware of such precedents, Karl Marx wrote to Joseph Weydemeyer in 1852: 'no credit is due to me for discovering the existence of classes in modern society, nor yet the struggle between them. . . . What I did that was new was to prove . . . that the class struggle necessarily leads to the *dictatorship of the proletariat*'. Marx and Engels declared in the *Communist Manifesto*: 'The history of all hitherto existing society is the history of class struggles'. And they went further to claim that the 'fall' of the bourgeoisie and 'the victory of the proletariat are equally inevitable'.[18]

Marxists picture history as a succession of rising classes, each struggling against others, leading to bourgeois revolutions in past centuries and proletarian revolutions in the future. Marx saw the bourgeois victory over the aristocratic class as a necessary precursor of the eventual triumph of the proletariat.

Unfortunately for Marxists, the depiction of the French Revolution as a triumph of the bourgeoisie has been under severe factual and analytic attack from several historians since the 1960s. Alfred Cobban revealed that the French revolutionaries were typically lawyers or state officials rather than capitalists. Capitalists played an insignificant role in the revolution itself. George V. Taylor and other historians have shown that the genuine capitalists in France collaborated with the royalist state before 1789 and that their share of economic activity was then small. Industrial capitalist production in France did not grow to major significance until well into the nineteenth century. Hence the capitalist (or bourgeois) class did not mount a challenge to the old order in the eighteenth century, and this was not the nature of the 1789 revolution. Given this evidence, the interpretation of the revolution as a class conflict between the aristocracy and the rising bourgeoisie had to be abandoned.[19]

This was a severe challenge to Marxist historians. Their orthodox interpretation became untenable. By the bicentenary of the revolution in 1989, the classic Marxist interpretation of the revolution had been completely undermined.

Sensible attempts to rescue Marxism from the fray had to concede the revisionist case. In his 1987 book *Rethinking the French Revolution: Marxism and the Revisionist Challenge*, the Marxist George C. Comninel admitted the following: 'The French Revolution was essentially an *intra-class* conflict . . . It was a civil war within the ruling class . . . The Revolution was not fought by capitalists, and did not produce capitalist society . . . it may be better simply to drop the idea of bourgeois revolution once and for all'.[20]

Conceding so much makes it difficult for Marxists, because the eagerly anticipated proletarian revolution becomes a historically lonely event. When the foremost historical claim of a victory of one class over another proves to be nothing of the sort, then the grand historical picture of one social class replacing another becomes questionable. Hopes for the future class victory of the proletariat may begin to fade.

Marxists might respond that by class struggle they mean a struggle between *representatives* rather than *members* of a social class. These proxies may come from any social stratum, as long as they represent the 'interests' of the class they are deemed to represent. But this is a politically dangerous interpretation. How are we to know what these interests are and how are we to decide who is the true represented of the social class in question? If the class struggle is not between social classes but their representatives, then the grand claim that the 'history of all hitherto existing society is the history of class struggles' could become little more than a standard history of individuals, factions or parties, retold with each bearing a class badge, donated by historians after the event.

Analytically, social classes are not the elemental building blocks of any social system. Classes are not separable or independently constituted entities; they are themselves defined in terms of institutional relations of property and power. These relations involve the state and civil society, and they constitute and precede classes as such. It is analytically essential to regard institutions as more fundamental than social classes.[21]

The history of all hitherto existing society is the history of institutional change; it involves confrontations and innovations concerning rules and rights.

The French Revolution was a massive institutional convulsion, leading to major changes in the institutional order. It is in these terms that it must be examined or understood rather than primarily in terms of the supposed class interests of the actors who were involved in the drama. Instead of one class building block displacing another, it was a revolution concerning human rights and the legitimation of authority. It smashed feudal institutions and paved the way for a modern state.

Marxists will resist this argument because otherwise their cherished notion of a proletarian revolution would have to go. Instead they would have to look at the petty details of institutional change—past, present and future. Their grand, revolutionary depiction of history as class struggle would be challenged. They would become unglamorous piecemeal reformers instead.

In sum, the French Revolution was neither the victory of one class nor a victory in the interests of a minority alone. In proclaiming universal rights and liberties, as well as a secular basis for government, it was potentially a victory for all humankind, notwithstanding its limitations and problems. The great tragedy was that the progressive vision of the French revolutionaries in 1789–1792 was then crushed by terror and dictatorship. While these rights and liberties took many decades to be revived, the French Revolution is a milestone in the global history of human emancipation.

CONCLUSION: WHO IS *RIGHT?* WHAT IS *LEFT?*

We now summarize the most important points. The political term *Right* originally referred to the use of religion or tradition as the grounding or political legitimation of authority and law, and as justifications of unequal legal rights or aristocratic privileges. By contrast, the *Left* rejected religion and tradition as sources of legitimation of law or political power. Instead, the *Left* argued that all legitimate political authority rested on a mandate from the masses, expressed by universal suffrage or other means. But the French *Left* of the 1790s overlooked women: that major omission was rectified much later.

Under the monarchy, the *Right* had been the champion of state intervention, state regulation and state monopolies. By contrast, the *Left* argued for a minimal state: its desired role was largely confined to national defence and the administration of justice, within the confines of a national constitution.[22] This constitution would express and safeguard several vital individual rights, including equality under the law; freedom of expression, assembly and worship; and rights to own and trade property. This kind of political standpoint had been prefigured by the English Levellers in the 1640s and the American revolutionaries in the 1770s.

The trump card of the *Right*, as played most eloquently by Burke, was to point out that governing a country was a highly complex business, that relying on the popular will or on democracy was an inadequate and highly fallible solution, and that to a large degree it would be better to rely on tried-and-tested institutions. Cautious attitudes toward democracy explain why neither the English Levellers nor the early American revolutionaries supported complete male suffrage. (But to explain is not to excuse.) Even the French Constitution of 1792 withheld the right to vote from waged employees and the unemployed, as well as from women.

For the French *Left* the concept of the 'general will of the people' was inspired by Rousseau, but it is a notoriously obscure, problematic and even dangerous concept. Its problems have given rise to a large literature, many pointing to the possible slide toward forms of totalitarianism. The key point is that the French revolutionary *Left* claimed to ground political and legal institutions on some expression of the 'general will', but was divided on the question of how that will would be ascertained or represented.

The *Left*'s notion of natural or inalienable rights also has many problems. The 1776 American Declaration of Independence proclaimed: 'We hold these truths to be self-evident, that all men are created equal, that they are endowed by their Creator with certain unalienable Rights, that among these are Life, Liberty and the pursuit of Happiness'.[23] But to assert a truth as self-evident is hardly an answer to a request for its justification. Furthermore, the sentence suggested that these rights had been bestowed by God; but aristocrats and Kings made the same argument in defence of their special rights and privileges. Better arguments in defence of natural or inalienable rights were made by Thomas Hobbes, John Locke and Immanuel Kant. Notwithstanding the doctrinal difficulties, it is clear that the original *Left* upheld a set of natural or inalienable rights.

A major problem for the *Left* remained largely untouched by the French revolutionaries, save for the efforts of Babeuf and his conspirators. Babeuf decried the severe and enduring anomaly of inequality of wealth and income in France. He pointed out that the revolution had left feudal-scale inequalities of wealth largely intact. How could a revolution, which had proclaimed equality and overthrown tradition, sustain the inheritance of huge inequalities of wealth? The problem of dealing with inequalities of power and wealth in capitalist economies remains a foremost agenda item for all radical thinkers.[24]

A further unresolved problem for the original *Left* was that pursuit of liberty—to express opinions, make contracts, trade property, pursue happiness and so on—depended on the satisfaction of some basic human needs. Without health, food, shelter and other necessities, all such liberty would be impaired. This put on the agenda the requirements of healthcare, and provisions to meet other basic needs for human survival and social engagement.

All these problems needed to be addressed by the intellectual descendants of the original *Left*. Their responses defined different currents of opinion within the subsequent Left. As in the case of Babeuf, some streams of opinion went so far as to jettison some of the *Left*'s most important principles and achievements, but with relatively little positive gain. Others on the *Left* reacted with plans for the redistribution of some wealth and for the development of a welfare state. But they would be resisted by others on the *Left* who saw these measures as overturning the sanctity of property and the limited role of government. The *Left* also divided into multiple currents on the relative importance of democracy, compared to (say) the protection of private property, or the struggle against inequality.

We may summarize the nature of the original *Left* in a nutshell. First, the original *Left* maintained a set of universal and inalienable individual rights—including to life, to property, to equality under the law, to freedom of expression, of assembly and of worship. By contrast, the original *Right* limited these rights and freedoms and sustained institutionalized inequality under the law. Second, the original *Left* rejected any legitimation of authority or government in terms of religion, aristocratic status or tradition. Instead, the legitimation of authority was said to derive from a mandate from the people. Government should operate within the constraints of a constitution that protected individual freedoms and rights.

In these terms, who would not be *Left* in this original sense? Rulers and regimes that deny such individual rights, including fascists and other dictators, are not *Left*. Regimes that deny full and equal rights to their whole adult population, on gender, ethnic or other grounds, are not *Left*. Regimes that draw their legitimacy from religion are not *Left*. Monarchies and regimes where sovereign power or privilege are inherited within dynasties are not *Left*.

The reader may be reminded of an old argument that puts classical liberalism on the Left, and all authoritarian doctrines—including fascism and Soviet-style socialism—on the Right. Well yes, liberalism is a fruit of the Enlightenment, and the French Revolution was its culmination. And liberalism too is faced with the dilemmas raised above. In later chapters we shall consider these dilemmas and appraise how both liberals and socialists dealt with them.

The first requirement is to understand what the original *Left* meant in 1789–1792 and how it split and evolved to deal with its unfinished agenda.

It is not intended here to hold up the canons of the original *Left* of 1789–1792 as the standard by which every succeeding doctrine is to be judged. The world has evolved, and new political doctrines are required to deal with it. Some tenets of the original *Left* require major revision. At the same time, we should not ignore their enduring principles. The emphasis on human liberty and secular government has lost none of its relevance today.

In the following chapters we look at some of the problems and challenges faced by the *Left* of 1789–1792 and how they were tackled by socialists and other radicals.

CHAPTER 3

Thomas Paine and the Rights of Man

Two roads diverged in a wood, and I—
I took the one less travelled by,

ROBERT FROST, 'The Road Not Taken' (1920)

Thomas Paine was born in 1737, in Thetford, Norfolk, England. His father was a Quaker and his mother an Anglican. Thomas attended the local grammar school. Leaving at the age of thirteen, he was then apprenticed to make stays for ships. After completing his apprenticeship, his own stay-making business collapsed and his first wife died in childbirth. He became an excise officer, living at various towns in England. In 1768 he moved to Lewes in Sussex, where he became involved in local politics and married for a second time. Six years later, in a rootless and aimless state, he separated from his second wife and moved to London. There he met Benjamin Franklin, who suggested emigration to British colonial America, and gave him a letter of recommendation.

After a sickness-ridden voyage, Paine arrived in Philadelphia in 1774. Becoming embroiled in American politics, he supported the 1776 Declaration of Independence and served in the American revolutionary army. His *Common Sense* (1776) was the first pamphlet to advocate US independence and it was an inspirational banner for those fighting British rule. He returned to England in 1787 and visited revolutionary France in 1790–1791. The two parts of his book on the *Rights of Man* were published in England in 1791 and 1792. Pursued by the British authorities, he fled England for France in 1792. In his absence, he was tried and convicted for seditious libel. He never returned to England.

Paine was awarded French citizenship and elected to the National Convention, where he sided with the majority Girondins. He voted for the transformation of France into a republic but supported banishment rather than execution of the King. He was an opponent of the death penalty, and he foresaw the danger of the revolution descending into orgies of bloody retribution.

After the anti-Girondin *coup* of June 1793, Paine was imprisoned in Paris during the Terror, where by a fluke of fate he narrowly escaped execution. The gaoler marked the doors of the cells of condemned prisoners with chalk, signalling their execution the following day. At that time, Paine was receiving official visitors; his door was open, with its inside facing the corridor. The dim-witted gaoler marked his door. The next morning the door was closed, with the mark out of sight. Paine was released in November 1794, after the fall and execution of Robespierre. He returned to the United States in 1802 and died in New Rochelle in the state of New York in 1809.

Paine was largely self-educated. But there is clear evidence of the influence of Thomas Hobbes, John Locke and others in his writing. He wrote in a popular style for a mass readership. He was also influenced by Deism—a belief in a God who is known to us not through scripture, but through reason and our reflections upon nature. Deism was popular among other Enlightenment thinkers. Paine's work is sometimes dismissed as derivative or unoriginal. But beneath the popularly written prose, there is much original thinking, the relevance of which endures into the twenty-first century.

Like many others, Paine promoted the concept of universal human rights. He called for the abolition of slavery, and he was one of the first to advocate universal male suffrage. He sat on the left of the French National Convention: politically he was wholly of the *Left*. In Britain today he is widely acknowledged as Left, along with Robert Owen and other socialists. But Paine was not a socialist: he did not advocate common ownership and he strongly supported the right to hold private property.

As one of the 'founding fathers' of the United States—who knew Benjamin Franklin, Thomas Jefferson and George Washington—Paine is also a shining star in the American historical firmament. Yet in the United States he finds less support on the Left and more among Tea Party Republicans. Interpretations of his legacy vary widely from Europe to America.

This chapter shows how Paine has been misinterpreted and misplaced politically. Key aspects of his thought are summarized. The chapter concludes with an assessment of the strengths and weaknesses of Paine's political thought, and points to its relevance for today.

MISPLACING PAINE

In the United States, Paine is often seen as an advocate of rugged individualism, unfettered markets and limited government. In 2009, Glenn Beck—the conservative political commentator, bestselling author, television personality and radio host—published *Glenn Beck's Common Sense: The Case against an Out-of-Control Government, Inspired by Thomas Paine*. He also used dramatized 'messages' from Paine in his Fox News show. Other Tea Party sympathizers jumped on the bandwagon. Among these was Sarah Palin, the 2008 Republican candidate for the US Vice Presidency. In her two-million-copy, bestselling autobiography *Going Rogue*, Palin quoted Paine with approval.[1]

In severe contrast, many leftists claim that Paine was a socialist. But by the original meaning of the word *socialism*—the common ownership of the means of production—these claims are also violations of the truth. Paine was a firm and enduring advocate of private ownership, of a market economy and of limited government. But for reasons outlined later below, Paine would also feel out of place in the US Republican Party of today.

Leftists have ritually paraded Paine, alongside Robert Owen and Karl Marx, as a milestone along the long road of radical history, leading from the Diggers and other early communistic utopians to modern socialism and communism. During the Second World War, when Britain, France, the United States and Russia were allies against fascism, it was convenient for British and American Marxists to co-opt Paine. The story of Paine's life connects the first three of the four Allies. In celebration of this alliance, Marxists wished to connect Paine with Russian Communism as well. Consider two prominent examples.

Philip S. Foner was a prominent American Marxist and labour historian. In 1945 he edited two collections of Paine's writings. In one of these he added the editorial claim that in his *Agrarian Justice* 'Paine supported the communist aspect of Babeuf's theories'. But there is no evidence for this statement. Paine briefly mentioned Babeuf, but to rebuke his unconstitutional insurrectionism, not to support his communism. Paine was consistently in favour of private property and free enterprise.[2]

The famous American writer Howard Fast—author of the famous novel *Spartacus*—joined the Communist Party in 1943 and later suffered a short prison sentence under McCarthyism. The Soviet Union awarded him the International Stalin Peace Prize in 1953. In 1948 he introduced and edited a popular selection of Paine's writings, which was published in London. Fast was fulsome in his praise of Paine as a revolutionary, glossing over his advocacy of private ownership, of a market economy and of limited government.

But on the critical side, Fast wrote that Paine 'fell in with the party of Condorcet, and he mistook their reactionary stand for an enlightened programme: his lack of knowledge of the French knowledge abetted his misunderstanding'. This is inaccurate. Paine was a friend of Nicolas de Condorcet and they both inclined to the Girondins. They agreed on the abolition of slavery and of the death penalty. Although Paine had imperfect French, he regularly used the services of translators and was capable of making speeches in the National Convention. There is no evidence that he misunderstood Condorcet or the Girondins at the time. Fast did not explain why 'the party of Condorcet' was 'reactionary'.

On the last page of the same book, Fast depicted an ageing and disillusioned Paine as falling back on mystical discussions of God, knowing that 'his much-dreamed-of utopia and brotherhood of man would not be realized for perhaps many, many generations'. Presumably Fast referred here to Paine's Deist theological excursions in his *Age of Reason*, which was published in three parts in 1794, 1795 and 1807. Paine was a strong believer in God throughout his life. But he was not a utopian dreamer. He continued to be concerned by practical politics, as in his important 1797 essay *Agrarian Justice*. His proposals for the abolition of slavery and for redistributive taxes were far from utopian. Fast misplaced Paine on the long road toward the glowing future of Soviet-style socialism.[3]

To the modern reader, Paine's long theological essay in *The Age of Reason* might seem a diversionary and non-urgent preoccupation for his pen, especially in the turbulent and revolutionary 1790s. But, in those pre-democratic times, its principal aim was to undermine the idea that religion could validate the authority of government. By mocking claims in the Bible, Paine undermined Christian monarchy and theocracy. He argued instead that the authority of government should be grounded on the ultimate consent of the governed.

Marxists like Foner and Fast attempted to move Paine from his place on the *Left* in 1789–1792 to a very different version of the Left. This redefined Left had emerged with Owen and Marx, was consolidated in the first half of the twentieth century, and was bolstered by the alliance between the UK, the United States, France and the USSR against fascism in the Second World War.

Distorted views of Paine persisted on the Left. Up to his death in 2014, the former Labour Party Cabinet Minister Tony Benn was President of the Thomas Paine Society of the UK. Sure enough, both Benn and Paine wanted to abolish the British monarchy. But beyond that, they diverged on several fundamental issues. In particular, Benn was an enduring defender of the original version of Clause Four of the Labour Party Constitution, which advocated the 'common ownership of the means of production, distribution and exchange'. This provided for no exception: all production would be in common ownership and there would be no private sector. Benn favourably quoted Clement Attlee: 'If you look around the world, what are the problems? They're all caused by the private ownership of the means of production, distribution, and exchange'.[4]

In 1959 the Labour leader Hugh Gaitskell attempted to end his party's formal commitment to wholesale common ownership in favour of a mixed economy. So Benn switched his allegiance to Harold Wilson. Thirty-six years later, the Labour Party leader Tony Blair successfully changed the wording of this clause and thus ended the Labour Party's long-standing constitutional commitment to far-reaching common ownership. But Benn still wished to retain the original wording and protested: 'Labour's heart is being cut out'.[5] By contrast, common ownership was ever far from Paine's heart or soul. Benn's Presidency of the Thomas Paine Society obscured Paine's political legacy.

Contrary to Benn, Paine believed that private property was a human right. For him it was a pillar of liberty and an indispensable basis for fruitful interaction in society. But Paine was also well aware that markets could be dysfunctional: they could exacerbate distributional injustices, creating a duty for government to intervene with regulation.

Paine's much subtler position has been long overshadowed by the simplistic but enduring binary rhetoric of capitalism versus socialism, where the latter meant widespread nationalization and the marginalization or abolition of markets. Benn took that same binary view of the political options. For him the choice was between *either* wholesale common ownership *or* 'market forces as the sole determinant of economic activity'. The possibility of a mixed economy was sidelined. But there are always coexisting modes of allocation, even under capitalism. Rich historical experience shows that the most dynamic systems in world history have been capitalist economies that synergized healthy public and private sectors.[6]

Given these mistaken appraisals of Paine, and the failures of conventional socialism, he is ripe for re-interpretation. After 1792 the *Left* had some difficult choices. One of these was the way of American-style, free-market individualism and libertarianism. Others sought greater equalities of income and wealth, but acquiesced with totalitarianism. Paine illuminated a different road: it advocated democracy within a constitution that endorsed natural and inalienable rights; it retained most private property but stressed individual duties as well as rights; it upheld the rights of the individual but saw individuals as dependent upon one another; it would limit the powers of government but also upheld that government had a duty to address the problems of poverty, infirmity and excessive economic inequality. This is a road less travelled.[7]

Paine's road became overgrown with weeds through limited use. By the 1840s much radical thought had instead switched to socialism. From the 1870s the rise of Marxism further exacerbated the neglect. Leading historians influenced by Marxism have wrongly pigeon-holed Paine as an 'ideological spokesman for the bourgeoisie'.[8]

Below I outline some salient points in Paine's thought. I also consider some of the limitations of his position. Later, in the final chapter of this book, I attempt to show how the line of direction in Paine's thinking can be amended and developed with relevance for today.

PAINE ON RIGHTS, GOVERNMENT AND DEMOCRACY

Paine's political theory is outlined principally in his *Common Sense* and *Rights of Man*. The first part of the latter was a response to Edmund Burke's *Reflections on the Revolution in France*, which is the classic conservative critique of the revolution.

Burke denied that people had natural, fixed and inalienable rights. By contrast, Paine claimed that every individual since the creation of humankind has been endowed with rights, including to liberty and property. He made a distinction between rights that were relatively easy to secure (such as freedom of conscience) and rights (such as to property) that required society or government actively to protect them.[9]

To an extent, Paine followed Hobbes, Locke and Rousseau by using 'state of nature' reasoning as a heuristic to establish some basic principles. But unlike these three, he did not start from the mythically isolated individual and then try to show how society was established. Instead, his primary focus was on the transition from small-scale tribal units to larger national conglomerates requiring new systems of government.

Paine understood that cooperation and reciprocity could work well on a small scale and would then 'render the obligations of law and government unnecessary' when 'bound together in a common cause'. But small, self-governing communities cannot serve modern needs, involving far-reaching trade and adequate military defence. Cooperation and reciprocity depend on trust, familiar interpersonal relations and small numbers.

But if a larger society relied on trust and commitment alone, then people 'would begin to relax in their duty and attachment to one another'. Focusing on the shift from a small-scale, tribal society to the large-scale societies of modern times, Paine considered how incentives to share and cooperate might be sustained. Common ownership was not the solution for bigger social units, because incentives to contribute would dwindle. Paine thus hinted at what I described previously as 'the $1/n$ problem'.[10]

In his *Common Sense*, Paine argued that there was a distinction between government and society. Civil society—as we might call it today—is the sphere of human interaction governed by the pursuit of our wants. Despite self-interest, these aims can sometimes unite us. They may involve cooperation and lead to social order, independent of government. But Paine warned that we also have vices, and we sometimes trample selfishly on the interests of others. Paine's political biographer John Keane has argued that '*Common Sense* was the first political essay in modern times to make and defend the distinction—now enjoying renewed popularity two centuries after Paine—between civil society and the state'.[11]

Paine understood that trade could encourage greed, corrupt public virtue and undermine solidaristic needs, such as for national defence. But trade was also a manifestation of human interdependence. Despite being driven by self-interest, it also brought people together. He defended the market system but understood some of its limitations. Hence there was a legitimate but limited role for government in economic affairs. For Paine, government had a limited right to interfere in 'society', but this had to be firmly constrained: 'government even in its best state is but a necessary evil; in its worst state an intolerable one'.[12]

Paine did not portray individuals as isolated atoms. On the contrary, he believed that a society that protected the rights of property and contract would enhance human communality: 'The mutual dependence and reciprocal interests which man has upon man, and in all parts of a civilized community upon each other, create that great chain of connection which holds it together'. Every business occupation 'prospers by the aid which each receives from the other. Common interest regulates their concerns, and forms their law; and the laws which common usage ordains, have a greater influence than the laws of Government'. Paine criticized the view that commerce simply meant disharmony, inequality and strife. His position was thus very different from that of socialists such as Robert Owen and Karl Marx.[13]

Paine argued in the second part of the *Rights of Man* that many rights had to be mediated, if possible by society, and if not by government: 'Government is no farther necessary than to supply the few cases to which society and civilisation are not conveniently competent'. He admitted a role for government that was substantial for his time. Nevertheless, when civil society is 'competent', by due standards of need and justice, the state should not step in.[14]

But Paine did not believe in *laissez faire*. Keane has summarized how Paine saw a market system as dependent on other institutions, including the state:

> He was adamant that market exchanges must be controlled and nurtured politically. A self-regulating market is undesirable. It motivates individuals not on the basis of commitment to serve and be served by their fellow citizens, but through a mixture of greed and fear. . . . Paine therefore concluded that . . .

market transactions within a republic must always be crafted by political and legal relations. A republic requires nonmarket support mechanisms such as public discussion, voluntary associations, taxation schemes, judgments by elected, public-spirited civil magistrates, and government controls. . . . The best system of government, in short, is one that nurtures its citizens' civil and political liberties and mutual aid by means of a civil society structured by restricted and regulated market exchanges.[15]

Paine also understood that in larger societies, direct and complete participatory democracy is impossible. Problems of complexity, scale and location place severe limits on democratic involvement. Given the impracticalities of large-scale direct democracy, nations should adopt systems of *representative* democracy, relying on professional and trained experts in government offices. He also opposed the anarchistic views of his friend William Godwin, who wished to get rid of government altogether. Paine would have also rejected the ultra-democratic utopian dreaming of some socialists, such as those of Tony Benn or of Lenin in *The State and Revolution*.[16]

Initially Paine was sceptical of Montesquieu's proposal for checks and balances in government, and he argued for unicameral parliaments. But he became increasingly aware of the problem of the potential despotism of the majority over the minority, and by 1792 he had become more sympathetic to a bicameral system. Paine also insisted that the judiciary should be separated from the legislature and the executive. For example, against the proposals of Georges Danton in 1792, Paine argued in the Assembly that law had to be administered by trained judges and not by 'the people' or by their political representatives.[17]

Like other radicals, Paine argued that legitimate political sovereignty derived from a mandate from the people. But this was not simply a contract between the individual and the state: it also involved agreement between the people of a nation. As Paine argued in 1786: 'When a people agree to form themselves into a republic . . . it is understood that they mutually resolve and pledge themselves to each other, rich and poor alike, to support this rule of equal justice among them'.

Furthermore, as Locke had argued earlier, the people had a right and a duty to resist despotism. 'A republic, properly understood, is a sovereignty of justice, in contradistinction to a sovereignty of will'. Paine limited legitimate collective power to the securing of civil and natural rights, within a framework of just laws. His augmented notion of rights included rights to a liveable income, to provide for basic needs, as well as to liberty and property.[18]

PAINE ON PRIVATE PROPERTY AND REDISTRIBUTION

As noted above, Paine used the heuristic device of an original 'natural state', with a small human population of hunter-gatherers. All land was then uncultivated and possessed in common. But, for Paine, the return to this communal 'natural state' was both undesirable and impossible. Civilization had increased the human population, and through trade and large-scale production it had achieved a substantial increase in productivity. If the large contemporary population were to return to the 'natural state' then economic output would fall massively: their right to sustenance and other basic needs would be threatened. Paine was no sentimentalist for the original state of nature.[19]

Paine saw the right to private property in land as emanating from the efforts of cultivation, which had led to increased yields. But he had to square the circle: if land was the legitimate common property of all in the 'natural state', then why shouldn't its common ownership persist? In response, Paine was in no doubt about the sanctity of private ownership: 'though every man, as an inhabitant of the earth, is a joint proprietor of it in its natural state, it does not follow that he is a joint proprietor of cultivated earth'. But how could this private ownership be justified?[20]

Paine's answer was quite original, and differed from other justifications, such as Locke's argument in the second of his *Two Treatises on Government*. Locke argued that ownership becomes legitimate when it is 'mixed with' and improved by the labour of its owner: property rights derive from the exertion of labour upon natural resources. Ownership of the entire resource was thus justified by the beneficial improvements or creations of labour. Up to this point, without citing the English philosopher, Paine argued similarly. In the 'natural state' there was no cultivated land. Subsequently, those who cultivated the land and raised its use value had the right to own it. Consequently, 'nothing could be more unjust' than common ownership of cultivated land.

But thereafter Paine departed from Locke. While private ownership was justified, for Paine the owner does not have *full* rights to *all* the revenues from that ownership. In contrast to Locke, for Paine an individual's entitlement to the benefits of an object does not extend beyond the added value that their labour has created. For Paine, the mixing of labour with land or objects does not give rights to *all* the revenues from those resources. Rightful revenues derive from what labour has created anew and in addition to the original gifts of nature. These previous gifts place obligations on the owners of such property: society should be compensated because these gifts were once the property of all. For Paine, uncultivated land was a gift to all from God; everyone had the right to some remuneration for this bequest. Justifiable private ownership was substantial but not absolute: there were obligations to pay taxes on inherited wealth.[21]

Paine wanted to 'advocate the right . . . of all those who have been thrown out of their natural inheritance by the system of landed property' and, at the same time, to 'defend the right of the possessor [of landed property] to the part which is his'. Because of the original gift of land to everyone, every proprietor owes the community a ground rent for the land he holds, which should be used as a right of inheritance for all.[22]

Paine then extended this argument concerning the taxation of wealth beyond wealth in land alone. Much social wealth was the work of past generations. It was achieved not by individuals alone, but in society via mutual co-operation and exchange. Hence everyone has some entitlement to this wealth, because of the conferred symbiotic benefits of living in a society:

> All accumulation, therefore, of personal property, beyond what a man's own hands produce, is derived to him by living in society; and he owes on every principle of justice, of gratitude, and of civilization, a part of that accumulation from whence the whole came.[23]

This argument was entirely consistent with Paine's enduring view that every part of society was interdependent with the others and 'no one man is capable, without the aid of society, of supplying his own wants, and those wants, acting upon every individual, impel the whole of them into society, as naturally as gravitation acts to a centre'. This claim carries greater strength today, because we are dependent on many others in highly complex social institutions for our health, education and livelihood. Any business enterprise relies on a labour force that was educated and kept healthy by many other vital institutions in society; all business depends on a massive social infrastructure, all of which typically involves the state as well as other enterprises.[24]

But it is impossible to separate an object of property into those parts that the original private owner acquired (such as raw materials or uncultivated land), on the one hand, and those bits that were added and created by the owner, on the other. So for obvious practical reasons, as well as the preservation of individual incentives and autonomy, private ownership must remain. But because the owner benefits from a bequest of the original 'natural state', taxation of this wealth is morally just. Consequently, a major redistribution of wealth through taxation is warranted.

Paine proposed a one-off, state-funded distribution 'to every person, when arrived at the age of twenty-one years, the sum of fifteen pounds sterling, as compensation in part, for the loss of his or her natural inheritance, by the introduction of the system of landed property'. The effect of this benefit would be to provide every adult with an amount of wealth that could be used to invest in property or personal development, irrespective of the income or status of his or her parents.[25]

Paine's analysis of property rights is an underestimated contribution to political theory. Paine combined a libertarian defence of private ownership with a redistributive egalitarianism, founded on the individual right to both property and personal development. He understood that an essential source of prosperity in modern society was devolved ownership; its abolition would reduce incentives and the size of the cake to be shared. Private ownership of many assets, protected by the law, is necessary to guarantee individual autonomy and the vibrancy of civil society. Other policies that might address inequality—like wholesale collectivization—were counter-productive because they would reduce incentives to work and innovate, and result in a fall in overall output.[26]

The English proto-socialist Thomas Spence had proposed in 1775 that land should be taken from private hands and owned in common at the parish level (rather than being nationalized). Spence is said to have been the first writer in English to use the term *rights of man*. But despite their shared phraseology, Spence attacked Paine's 1797 proposal on the grounds that it retained individual ownership of land. Spence claimed that without dealing with the concentrated private ownership of land by a rich minority, power could never pass to the majority of the people.[27]

Paine did not respond to Spence, but it is clear that he took a different view. Paine's defence of private ownership simultaneously retained economic incentives for the improvement and effective use of the land in large-scale societies. Paine also addressed the problem of economic inequality. As Keane wrote in his biography of Paine:

> Paine favoured the preservation of a private-property, market-driven economy, but he argued that its self-destructive dynamism—its tendency to generate wealth by widening the income gap between classes—could be tamed by institutionalizing the basic principle of each person's entitlement to full citizens' rights.[28]

PAINE AND THE WELFARE STATE

For the French revolutionaries, universal rights allowed a free people to improve their well-being, notwithstanding differences in talent, circumstances or wealth. As Napoléon Bonaparte later put it, when in exile on St Helena: 'My maxim was, *la carrière est ouverte aux talents* [the career is open to talents], without distinction of birth or fortune, and this system of equality is the reason why your [British] oligarchy hate me so much'.[29]

But Paine went further. The second part of the *Rights of Man* promoted schemes of welfare and redistributive taxation that would be an anathema to many modern individualists and libertarians. He stressed that we are all dependent on one another and we all have duties to others. He argued that while individual careers should be open to talents, our debts to past and current generations put moral limits on the concentration of wealth in a few hands. Consequently, he devised measures to alleviate poverty and to redistribute a portion of social wealth.

Paine proposed that poor relief be replaced by provision from central government funds; that state pensions be offered for those above fifty years old, rising in amount until sixty years, then to continue until death; that state provision be made for the free education of the poor; that state maternity benefits be granted to all women after the birth of a child; and that state support be provided for the young to move and find work. He also argued that there should be a progressive taxation on landed property, coupled with the abolition of primogeniture, and a progressive tax on income from investments.

His 1787 pamphlet *Agrarian Justice* provided a principled defence of welfare provision, rooted in a conception of the original equality of man and the equal right to some subsistence from the earth. Paine identified 'the greatest evil' as the 'landed monopoly' that has 'dispossessed more than half the inhabitants of every nation of their natural inheritance' and 'created a species of poverty and wretchedness that did not exist before'. He pointed to the offensive injustice of extreme inequality: 'The contrast of affluence and wretchedness continually meeting and offending the eye, is like dead and living bodies chained together'.[30]

Gregory Claeys has emphasized Paine's contribution to the theory of the welfare state. Paine argued 'that it was the government's duty, as the expression of the common good, to promote sociability and a higher level of civilization by maintaining and enhancing the rights of the poor'. This required a significant amount of state intervention:

> Paine's scheme for state-enforced pensions, progressive taxation, universal education and assistance to the poor involved a massive redistribution of wealth and restatement of rights wholly alien to the Smithian as well as any jurisprudential vision. . . . Government now had a positive function which 'society'

could not perform, which was to alleviate the chief vice of society, the failure of the system of exchange to support the population at all times. . . . This was a fundamental turning-point in modern radicalism.[31]

All this is a very long way from the scribblings on Paine by leading members of the modern Republican Party of the United States and equally remote from attempts by Marxists and their fellow travellers to associate Paine with the common ownership of all means of production.

The real Paine was very different from both: he was a definite man of the *Left*. He pioneered a genuine *Left* alternative to the ultra-individualism of some of the American and French revolutionaries. His vision is entirely consistent with Article 29(1) of the United Nations Universal Declaration of Human Rights: 'Everyone has duties to the community in which alone the free and full development of his personality is possible'.[32]

PAINE'S LIMITATIONS

Paine advocated a theory of natural rights, where rights are deemed inalienable and independent of actual social or political conditions. A major pioneer of this approach was Locke, who argued that natural rights flowed from natural law, which came from God. Paine offered a Deist version of this argument. Deists circumvented controversy over scriptural interpretation. They argued that the existence of a God could be established by reason, and by reflection on the wonders of nature.

But both Theist and Deist approaches require belief in the existence of a God. There is no way of knowing His wishes (or even Her gender). Why not instead appeal directly to reason and nature?

This alternative approach was taken by Kant. His justification of rights started from the ideal of equality and moral autonomy of rational human beings. He thus provided a means for justifying human rights as the basis for self-determination, grounded within the authority of human reason. In this respect Paine's approach was inferior to that of the German philosopher, and Kant has had a much greater impact on the subsequent development of the theory of rights.[33]

Nevertheless, Paine was clear about the importance of rights, and he turned the natural rights approach to considerable advantage. For instance, he argued that because these rights were natural, they were not granted by governments. If they were, then they could just as readily and justifiably be taken away. Rights were not necessarily the same as enacted laws. Paine's natural theory of rights meant that they were universal. Hence he urged the abolition of slavery and became convinced of the need for universal male suffrage.

But he did not propose that women should have the vote. Paine was a man of his time, and advocacy of female suffrage was very rare before 1850. But Spence had advocated female suffrage as early as 1775, as had Paine's friend Condorcet during the French Revolution. It is no small matter that Paine failed to take this up.[34]

Paine's rationalist and ahistorical approach to the theory of rights is also open to criticism. Later chapters of this book refer briefly to alternative approaches. These include accounts of rights that refer to human needs or interests. We have needs for basic human sustenance and for institutions necessary to provide for individual welfare, social interaction and human flourishing.[35]

Paine's theory of the right to property also needs improvement and updating. Both Locke's and Paine's justifications for private property are special and conditional. By contrast, G. W. F. Hegel saw property as universally necessary for the ethical development of the individual. Property may thus be seen as a general right that derives from the universal need for significant autonomy and for control over some means of livelihood. Accordingly, Jeremy Waldron has provided a justification of private property rights based on general needs and entitlements, rather than special or contingent rights, as in the cases of Locke or Paine.[36]

Also Paine exaggerated the remedies and powers of reason in government. France showed how quickly that government could shift from reasoned argument to bloody terror and dictatorship. Burke had a point: to act justly, governments could not rely on reason alone. They also had to draw from the tried-and-tested experiences of earlier generations. Although his criticisms of monarchy, theocracy and despotism hit their targets, Paine was too reckless in pitting reason against existing institutions, and too optimistic about the possibility that reason alone may design our affairs. His notion that revolution could wipe the slate clean for the edicts of a new rational order was naïve and dangerous, as events in France from 1793 demonstrated. Burke may have been mistaken in his support for the French monarchy and the *Ancien Régime*, but he was right in advising experimental, adaptive and incremental changes to most political institutions.[37]

Paine adopted another limitation that was typical at the time. Experience in Britain, France and elsewhere showed that organized interests could conspire with sovereigns in the exercise of tyranny. Consequently, a deep suspicion of 'factions' (including organized parties) in the political sphere, and of corporations in the economic sphere, was commonplace among Enlightenment thinkers. The Scottish philosopher David Hume expressed such concerns in an essay published in 1777. In his *Federalist Papers* of 1788 the future US President James Madison saw 'factions' as adverse to the interests of the community. In 1791 the French revolutionaries went so far as to prohibit all organizations of workers, professionals and entrepreneurs. Paine took a similar stance, declaring in his *Rights of Man* against corporations and political parties. This too reflects his over-optimistic notion that individuals, enlightened and guided by reason, could be the principal guardians of liberty against despotism.[38]

But the abolition of corporations and political parties could also have grave, adverse effects. Without adequate, organized, countervailing power in civil society, the individual was vulnerable to the power of the state. Paine and his contemporaries believed in a minimal state, but Paine had eventually allowed the state a potentially much larger role by arguing for schemes of redistribution and welfare. These problems are much more evident to us today. Experience tells us that effective countervailing power is essential to keep the modern state in check and to provide a secure foundation for democracy.[39]

Rare among political theorists of that time, Burke argued in favour of political parties. His main argument was not one of countervailing power, but it was informed by his understanding of the limits of individual reason in political affairs. He made the persuasive argument that political parties would bring together people with shared goals; their combined, interactive experience was a valuable means of nuancing policy and legislation to take into account complex and fluid circumstances. Political parties can be justified, not only in terms of countervailing power, but also because they create epistemic communities that can enhance understanding and improve policy. Paine's excessive faith in the powers of individual reason prevented him from appreciating these points.[40]

Paine's work points to the possibility of a modern, redistributive welfare state but it remains rooted in the late eighteenth century. He wrote in an era when financial institutions were already important, but he had little prevision of the huge growth of capitalist financial power. He understood that markets were indispensable for a modern economy but insufficient as an expression of social interests. He deeply appreciated the inherited and ongoing problem of inequality, but with little knowledge of political economy he could not gauge whether burgeoning capitalism would exacerbate or ameliorate this severe defect.

These limitations and deficiencies opened the door for his socialist opponents. Marx in particular offered a much richer understanding of the capitalist era. Socialists and Marxists sidelined Paine, only much later to resurrect him as a convenient symbol, to celebrate the alliance between liberal capitalism and Soviet Communism in the Second World War. Subsequently he was again adopted and distorted by American Tea Party Republicans. But all this was to bury his message. After the end of the Cold War and what has been described as 'the death of socialism' we are in a much better position to appreciate Paine's relevance today.

CHAPTER 4

Socialism's Wrong Responses to the Right Problems

If our brains were simple enough for us to understand them, we'd be so simple that we couldn't.

Jack Cohen and Ian Stewart, *The Collapse of Chaos* (1994)

Alongside liberty, the French revolutionaries called for equality and fraternity. In 1796 the communist Gracchus Babeuf pointed out that while the revolution may have established equality of political and legal rights, these were defied by massive inequalities of wealth, power and income. Dealing with this economic inequality was unfinished revolutionary business. The problem was further dramatized in the nineteenth century, by growing industrialization and the creation of a massive urban workforce, living in appallingly squalid conditions. Men, women and children were obliged to labour for dreadfully long hours on minimal wages, while capitalists were enriched from the profits.

While the rich could protect their interests through access to law and the courts, the poor could not afford to hire legal support. Equality under the law was a sham unless the rights of the poor could be protected as well. Although declared equal under the law, the owners of capital and labour did not engage each other on equal terms. While the rich, with their social connections, could influence judges or politicians, the poor had negligible legal or political power. Throughout Europe, until the latter part of the nineteenth century, trade unions were illegal. Until 1875, even in relatively liberal Britain, breaking an employment contract, such as by quitting before it expired, was a criminal offence, which could be punished by whipping, imprisonment or transportation to the colonies.

As outlined in the preceding chapter, Thomas Paine recognized the severe problem of inequality under capitalism, and developed proposals to alleviate it within the framework of a market economy. Others followed Paine in some respects, but eventually struck out in a very different direction. These were the 'utopian socialists', as Karl Marx and Frederick Engels described them. The three most important were Claude-Henri de Saint-Simon (1760–1825), François Marie Charles Fourier (1772–1837) and Robert Owen (1771–1858). But neither Saint-Simon nor Fourier described their doctrines as *socialist*: that term was adopted by Owen.

As children of the Enlightenment, these thinkers followed science and reason. But they looked back to an imagined past, as well as forward to the future. Amid growing industrialization, they wanted to reverse the process of urbanization. Like most previous socialist or communist proposals, theirs outlined their wish to return to small-scale communities, set out on rigid lines.[1]

Today's large-scale, dynamic, complex and innovative economies depend on institutional variety and economies of scale that these utopian proposals did not provide. In addition, these utopians paid insufficient attention to the functional preservation of rights and autonomy. Everyone had to conform to their ideal state.

SCIENCE AND PSYCHOLOGY: SAINT-SIMON AND FOURIER

Claude-Henri de Saint-Simon was born in Paris as a French aristocrat. When he was a young man he went to America and enlisted in the revolutionary army in the War of Independence. Serving under General Washington, he took part in the siege of Yorktown in 1781. He then returned to France and supported the ideals of its 1789 revolution. During the Terror he was imprisoned on suspicion of engaging in counter-revolutionary activities. He was released in 1794. Up to this point, his life followed tracks remarkably close to those of Paine. But their political views were different. Saint-Simon became rich through currency speculation, but his fortune was then stolen by his business partner. He subsequently devoted himself to study and writing.

In a number of works published from 1802 to 1821, Saint-Simon called for an industrial society organized in accord with scientific knowledge. Society should be studied scientifically and empirically. A healthy society would be well-organized according to scientific principles. His highly influential follower Auguste Comte developed this line of thinking and coined enduring terms such as 'positivism' and 'sociology'.

Saint-Simon proposed the abolition of inheritance, but not of private property. Instead there would be public intervention in the private sector. He suggested that 'general directors', appointed by public authorities, could ensure that rules based on scientific principles were applied effectively in production and in management. Their interventions would reduce shirking and waste in the private sector.

For Saint-Simon, the principal economic roles of government were to reduce idleness and to ensure that production was guided by the best available scientific knowledge. Beyond this, he criticized any expansion of government intervention into the economy. He argued that if the government were to go further, then it would become a 'tyrannical enemy of industry' and would precipitate industrial decline. Influenced by Adam Smith and other economic liberals, Saint-Simon proposed low taxes and a low level of government involvement in an economy. But he wished to minimize the destructive effects of competition, and to ensure that private businesses, guided by science, would all serve the needs of society as a whole. This was more like 'utopian capitalism' than 'utopian socialism'.

Saint-Simon disliked aristocratic and other inherited privileges. He proposed a meritocratic society where individuals could rise in station by achievement. There would be hierarchical, merit-based organizations of managers and scientists, who would be the key decision makers in government. He was not an advocate of popular democracy.[2]

Saint-Simon was less concerned with the *Left* project of establishing institutions for the protection of liberty. For him, notions of popular sovereignty or liberty had little practical meaning. Instead, science would be the guide within his grand system of industry. While he opposed feudalism and aristocracy, he did not see legitimate government as grounded on some kind of popular mandate. Instead, government would be legitimated by its guardianship and judicious application of science, as well as by its minimization of waste. Saint-Simon was not a democrat: science was advanced by enlightened reason and experiment, not by votes. The furtherance of humanity was the task of the scientifically educated intelligentsia.

Although he did not advocate the abolition of private property, Saint-Simon had a crucial influence on future socialism in at least two respects. First, as Don Lavoie put it: 'the very notion of organizing industry according to a common plan traces directly to Saint-Simon and had as its original models military and feudal organizations'. Second, the elevation of science, rather than democracy or rights, as the source of guiding political principles is also traceable to Saint-Simon and had a major influence on subsequent socialism.[3]

In his later years, Saint-Simon turned to Christianity. Perhaps sensing the moral void in his earlier 'scientific' schemes for society, he wished to promote love and cooperation. Some of his followers began to argue for the abolition of private ownership.

François Marie Charles Fourier had relatively little formal education but was able to devote time to his schemes because of an inheritance. Fourier, as Leszek Kolakowski wrote, 'enjoys the deserved reputation of a visionary and a crank of the first order' who 'described the future socialist paradise in more grandiose detail than any of the utopians who preceded him throughout history'.[4]

For Fourier, the goal of social organization was pleasure. He laid down rules for procreative relations between the sexes, including the possibility of multiple partners and of casual sex. The family as a unit would disappear. Some of his speculations are bizarre, such as his vision of future oceans of lemonade. But other ideas have proved influential, and he is credited with the coining of the word *feminism*.[5]

Fourier looked to psychology, developing his own idiosyncratic taxonomy of basic human passions. He argued that people differed in terms of their capacities and propensities. Production would be organized so that everyone would take the role most suited to his or her character. Work would cease to be drudgery; greater individual fulfilment would make it more pleasurable. Factory and machine production would be reduced to the minimum.

Fourier believed that there were 12 common passions which resulted in 810 types of character, so the ideal community would have exactly 1,620 people. Conflicts of interest or preference could not be eradicated, but had to be understood and ameliorated through the creation of social arrangements that were conducive to harmony. Beyond that, the search for complete economic equality was chimerical.

According to Fourier, political rights were universal. Most importantly, women would enjoy full equality with men. Fourier did not call for the abolition of private property or of its inheritance. But instead of capitalist firms with employees, most production would be carried out by cooperatives.

Everyone would receive a minimal but guaranteed basic income for their subsistence. Limited political decisions would be made on a democratic basis, but in this harmonious society there would be little role for government, other than for overseeing the bureaucratic administration, which in turn would be steered by science.

Like Saint-Simon, Fourier drew upon the Enlightenment idea of science as a major guide to progress. Saint-Simon constructed a primitive sociology; Fourier derived his psychology of passions. But they both overlooked much of the Enlightenment's contribution to political philosophy. In particular, apart from Fourier's endorsement of political rights for women, they wrote little on human rights more generally, and they bypassed the need for secular legitimation of political authority via a popular mandate. Everything was based on science alone.

They both lacked an understanding of the provisional and fallible nature of all science, which requires more than experiment to make progress. Instead, they held an optimistic view of scientific advancement, conceived as establishing one certainty after another. This naïve vision of science prevailed well into the twentieth century. In the social sciences it has been an important buttress for socialism and Marxism. Today we understand scientific processes as being socially embedded, complex, provisional and fallible.

Science is also limited in the sense that it cannot itself provide a complete guide to ethical behaviour. While morality must be informed by science, it cannot be reduced to science. Perhaps Saint-Simon understood this scientific deficit in the end, and that is why he moved toward Christianity.[6]

If politico-economic decisions must be guided by science, as interpreted by an enlightened elite of experts, then democracy must be constrained, because perceived scientific truth would trump any vote. This outlook can nurture an incipient totalitarianism, partly against those who would question the findings of science. The language of universal rights may also be diminished, as the scientists and their administrators might be said to know best and what is in the interests of each individual.

Saint-Simon and Fourier paid insufficient heed to the complexities and uncertainties of the modern socioeconomic order. They overlooked the severe limits to prescriptive planning and system design, neglecting the need for experimental testing of socioeconomic principles or methods. While Saint-Simon admired Smith, he did not seem to take on board his enduring argument that much socioeconomic order was a result of spontaneous self-organization, and that there are limits to what can be achieved by overall design.

Accordingly, the schemes of Saint-Simon and Fourier drew from the scientific achievements of the Enlightenment but not so much from its advances in economics or political philosophy. They veered away from main-line Enlightenment tracks. They started a sideways journey that was later followed by others, most importantly by Owen, Marx and Engels. It proved to be so powerful that they were able to capture the term 'Left' for themselves.

But other branches of thought sprung out as well. Philippe Buchez was a follower of Saint-Simon. He proposed the formation of worker cooperatives as early as 1831, and his ideas became prominent during the French Revolution of 1848. Eventually, Buchez and his followers argued for autonomous worker cooperatives, linked by contracts and trade. Despite the ostensible viability and attractiveness of this radical proposal, it was explicitly rejected by Marx and Engels because it retained a role for competition and markets.[7]

Communities inspired by Fourier's ideas were founded in the United States and Europe. His followers also promoted worker cooperatives. One disciple was Jean-Baptiste Godin, who founded in 1859 a Fourierist experimental co-operative, or *familistere*, in Guise in northern France. It survived until 1968.[8] Another enduring proposal by Fourier was his notion of a guaranteed basic income. Last but not least, Fourier stands out as one of the earliest proponents of equal rights for women.

But if socialism means the abolition of private property—as others would soon define it—then neither Saint-Simon nor Fourier were socialists. Advocates of worker cooperatives in the nineteenth century typically described themselves as anarchists or anarcho-syndicalists, rather than socialists.

THE PATERNALISTIC SOCIALISM OF ROBERT OWEN

Robert Owen was a tireless and charismatic enthusiast for his socioeconomic schemes, and he gathered a huge following. But his legacy is surrounded by mythology that needs to be debunked. Owen was neither a libertarian nor a democrat. Often he opposed agitation for political reform on the grounds that it would endanger progress toward social harmony.[9]

Born in Newtown in Wales as the son of a poor craftsman, Owen left school at the age of ten. After working in a draper's shop for a few years, he moved to London in 1787. The following year he travelled to Manchester, where he was employed at another drapery. By 1792 he was managing and partly financing a cotton-spinning mill. In 1793 he was elected as a member of the Manchester Literary and Philosophical Society, where Enlightenment ideas prevailed. He also became a committee member of the Manchester Board of Health, which, among other things, strove to improve the working conditions of factory workers.

Owen acquired a cotton factory in New Lanark near Glasgow, and moved there in 1800. He employed two thousand workers including about five hundred pauper children. Convinced that poor working conditions caused low productivity and bad behaviour, he set out on a major experiment in industrial relations. Fines were abolished; good work was praised. Through a combination of kindness and working improvements, Owen won the confidence and trust of his workforce. He provided them with basic education and healthcare. New Lanark became famous for its humane working conditions and for the quality of its cotton thread. Owen reaped considerable profits.

Following the utilitarian philosopher Jeremy Bentham, Owen argued that the guiding principle of all policy was the maximization of happiness. He wrote of the social conditions necessary for the cultivation of happiness, creating guidelines for paternalistic intervention. The Benthamite social engineer would put these principles into practice. The individual had the duty to live for the happiness of the greatest number. Owen was concerned less with matters of liberty, autonomy or rights.

Owen argued that individuals were products of their social environment: we are all creatures of our circumstances. In this premonition of the behaviourist psychology of the twentieth century, he saw 'the science of the influence of circumstances' as 'the most important of all the sciences'. According to Owen, the application of this science would remove the need for rewards and punishments. Once people were treated with sympathy and kindness, they would respond with diligence and loyalty.[10]

The post-Enlightenment veneration of science was central to Owenism. 'For a period of twenty years after 1825 the "science of society" carried Owenite implications and when the Owenites acquired buildings in which to meet they were called Halls of Science'.[11]

Owen came to the view that reform was needed, not in industrial relations alone, but in the entire politico-economic system. Evil lay in competition and the pursuit of profit, which encouraged people to place their own greed above the social good. People should be educated and united in associations of combined interests, which would provide sufficient incentives for productive work and good behaviour. In these communities 'the natural wants of human nature may be abundantly supplied; and the principle of selfishness . . . will cease to exist'.[12]

Advocates of self-interested 'economic man' will reject Owen's claim that selfishness can or should disappear. They argue that self-interest is the wellspring of prosperity. But human nature is more complex than both Owen and the economists presumed. There is now much evidence to show that human cooperation and altruism are evolved propensities among humans because of the survival advantages they provide for groups. But the complete *elimination* of self-interest would be dysfunctional in evolutionary terms; it would remove all impulses to survive and leave the individual vulnerable. That is why most people are both cooperative and selfish, to some degree. Both Owen and the orthodox economists were mistaken.[13]

A problem for utopians is that humans vary hugely in their moral and altruistic dispositions. Incentives are required to ensure that moral and altruistic norms prevail. Owen heralded an enduring problem for socialist thought—a failure to consider specific incentives for cooperation, while wrongly assuming that durable social concord would prevail readily when the right conditions were present.

Another problem is that Owen's extreme environmental determinism diminished the role of individual initiative and inventiveness. If people are simply a product or reflection of their environment, then how could they change that environment? But somehow the environment had to be changed. The driver of change had to be an exception to the principle of environmental determination.

Perhaps what was needed was an enlightened paternalist who had escaped the clutches of the grim world of the present and could show people the way into the future. There had to be a visionary—a person somehow immune to the law of environmental determination. Needless to say, that benevolent autocrat was Owen, who felt that he 'should be given full control of any community until its members had reached his level of rationality'. Many of Owen's collaborators, including the famous Ricardian socialist William Thompson, became critical of Owen's authoritarian and anti-democratic tendencies.[14]

Owen began to develop utopian plans for a 'social system' consisting of 'villages of union' of up to about 1,500 people, situated in the countryside. Among his inspirations were the Shaker religious communities in the United States. With the help of modern machinery, his villages could become largely self-sufficient. Owen saw private property as a major source of social disharmony and discord. Eventually all property would be owned in common. The family was seen as a pillar of private property, so it too had to be abolished for the community to exist as an undivided whole with common interests.

Owen had an additional objection to private ownership. He complained of 'the complicated arrangements necessary to procure and obtain all the rights . . . of private property'. The institutions of private property meant 'forming society into a machine too complex to be understood by almost any mind, in consequence of the innumerable laws, customs, and regulations'.[15]

But why does social complexity need to be understood by a single mind? Unlike systems of central planning, which require decisions to be made at the centre by a single authority (as if by a single mind), private property allows decentralization and much more autonomy. Owen's complaint was that private property and decentralized authority would increase complexity and prevent the whole system from being run by a single person or committee.

Following Adam Smith, the economist David Ricardo developed a labour theory of value. Ricardian socialists such as Thompson took this a step further: if labour was the source of value then it should receive the whole product. By 1820 Owen was promoting labour time as the ideal standard of value and remuneration, thus eliminating all money except for notes denominating hours of labour.

An obvious problem with this scheme was that a vigorous and efficient hour of work would reap the same reward as sixty minutes of grudging or token effort, thus removing individual incentives for exertion, care and efficiency. But Owen was confident that under the right social conditions this problem would become marginal: all workers would become devoted to the common good. Selfishness and greed would completely disappear.

While Owen defended freedoms of expression and worship, he was very wary of democracy, which meant disagreement of opinion and competition for votes. Instead, the solution to social ills lay in the reconstruction of the social environment by an enlightened minority. Once established, the harmonious community would supersede democracy.

Owen opposed elections as competitive, disharmonious and divisive. He showed no enthusiasm for the great Reform Bill of 1832, which extended the right to vote beyond a narrow elite and quickly led to major advances. For example, following this reform, the year 1833 saw the abolition of slavery in the British Empire and major restrictions on child labour. But under Owen's 'social system' there would be concord and harmony, making electoral contests redundant.[16]

Owen prescribed an age-related allocation of responsibilities. As they reached defined age thresholds, people would move from education, to production, to distribution and then to administer 'foreign affairs', before taking retirement. But they would not be given a chance to change the system itself or its defining rules.

Owen was fiercely critical of all professions and wished to abolish them all, including in medicine. At the top of his hit list were lawyers. He regarded law as an instrument of the wealthy and powerful, and he proposed the complete abolition of courts and lawyers. But while it is true that the law can often be manipulated by the rich and influential, it did not occur to Owen that the abolition of courts would undermine the protection of individual rights. Courts are essential to safeguard rights. People must be able to litigate in their own defence. By contrast, Owen proposed to deal with the problem of unequal access to the law by abolishing law itself.[17]

OWENISM IN PRACTICE

Upon these shaky intellectual foundations, Owen built his first communities. In 1825 Owen purchased a large tract of land in Indiana in the United States and founded the community of New Harmony. It attracted a motley group of adventurers, radicals and freethinkers. Although Owen was an inspirational leader, many 'were unwilling to submit unquestioningly to his teachings, and preferred governing themselves'. Some of the Owenites in New Harmony called for the immediate establishment of common ownership, but Owen was reluctant to comply.[18]

Additional Owenite communities appeared. New Harmony was quickly divided into two, and then further subdivided several times over. But by 1828 all the Owenite communities in the New World had failed. Internal dissentions had arisen over failures to install the common ownership of property; however, in another case, it was attempted and the community then collapsed. There were also disputes over religion and sexual behaviour. Some became disenchanted with rigid community life.[19]

By the same year, other Owenite communities had been formed in the UK, including one in Orbiston near Glasgow and another in London. Others followed in the 1830s, including in Ralahine in Ireland, Manea Fen in Cambridgeshire, and Pan Glas in Merionethshire in Wales. Again, fundamental differences arose on matters such as the organization of activity and the community of property. These experiments did not endure. Few Owenite communities lasted more than three years.[20]

Typically the members of these communities were from dispersed backgrounds, and they lacked any previous experience of interaction and cooperation. Owenite doctrine contested any family ties that might bind some of them together. In such circumstances, more enduring communal experiments—such as those of the Shakers in the United States—relied on religious zeal to prevent fragmentation and promote cohesion. But Owen relied on reason instead of religion and severe problems of community cohesion remained. The Irish landowner John O'Driscol was an early critic of Owenism. Only 'despotic power' or 'religious zeal', he argued, would be sufficient to hold a community together: Owenism proclaimed neither.[21]

In this riven context, the term *socialist* emerged in English for the first time. It appeared in 1827 in the *Co-operative Magazine*, published in London by Owen's followers. It was used in the *Poor Man's Guardian* in 1833, and moved into wider usage thereafter. For Owen and his followers, socialism meant the abolition of private property. It also acquired the broader ideological connotation of cooperation, in opposition to selfish individualism. The instigation of communal property was seen as its institutional foundation.

As Owen argued in 1840, 'virtue and happiness could never be attained' in 'any system in which private property was admitted'. He aimed to secure 'an equality of wealth and rank, by merging all private into public property'. From the 1830s until the 1950s, socialism was almost universally defined in terms of the abolition or minimization of private property and some form of widespread common ownership.[22]

More successful than Owenite communities were the retail cooperatives set up by some of Owen's followers. They aimed to make profits to fund new Owenite communities. By 1830 there were about three hundred retail cooperatives throughout Britain. Acquiring a viable logic and momentum of their own, many cut loose from Owen's unsuccessful utopian schemes.

The consumer cooperative movement was given a lasting impetus by the Rochdale Society of Equitable Pioneers, founded by a group of Owenite weavers in 1844 and based on agreed written rules and principles. Within ten years there were over one thousand similar cooperative societies in Britain. These were the beginnings of the substantial and enduring retail cooperative movement in Britain. It is both telling and deeply ironic that Owen's most lasting institutional legacy is in a retail sphere where contracts, competition and profit prevail.

After the complete failure of the early Owenite communities, in the 1830s Owen turned to another institutional innovation. This was his notion of 'labour exchanges', where artisans bought and sold their products using labour notes, reflecting the number of hours involved in their production. Against profit and competition, the aim was to reward workers with the fruits of their labour.

Such exchanges were in operation in 1832–1833 and involved hundreds of artisans. Owen himself supervised a large labour exchange in London. Another opened in Birmingham. But by mid-1834 all these exchanges had collapsed. Alongside the difficulty that labour notes were not widely transferable, there had been predictable and widespread complaints concerning the claimed labour hours involved in pricing the products. Why should all hours of labour time be rewarded and measured the same when they varied hugely in terms of skill and diligence?

But Owen did not give up. In 1835, when he was aged sixty-four, he formed a new communitarian organization, which came to be known as the Rational Society. Eventually it had over sixty branches, involving tens of thousands in its meetings. The Rational Society leased land in Hampshire, and there set up the new Owenite community of Queenwood in 1839. Owen spent much of the available funds on a large and lavish building. By 1845 the funds were exhausted. The folly of Queenwood bankrupted the Rational Society.

But in the nine years of its existence, the Rational Society published millions of pamphlets and drew many thousands to its meetings. Attending one such gathering in Manchester in 1843 was the young Frederick Engels. From lectures by John Watts and other Owenites, Engels learned of their brand of socialism.

Frederick Engels was born in Prussia in 1820. In 1837 his father co-founded a cotton-spinning factory in Manchester. Hoping that the practical experience of managing the Ermen and Engels Company might move his son away from his radical-liberal views, in late 1842 he sent Frederick to manage the enterprise. What a fateful miscalculation!

Inspired by Owenite meetings in Manchester in 1843, and against his father's wishes, the young Engels became a resolute socialist. The socialist gatherings in Manchester were at the heart of Britain's industrial economy, with its stark contradictions between burgeoning wealth and dire poverty. Following the Owenites, Engels resolved that the abolition of private property was the way forward. He surmised that extensive popular support for socialism among the rising industrial working classes was possible. Marx was independently converted to socialism in the same year.[23]

In the following year, Engels met Marx in a café in Paris. They became lifelong friends and collaborators. Hence those 1843 Owenite meetings in Manchester played a role in world history. But ironically, by 1844, the Manchester Owenite leader Watts 'had come to the conclusion that Owen's ideal community was impracticable and many of its adherents self-seeking'.[24]

In 1854, despite his antipathy to religion and his championship of science, and two years before his death at the age of eighty-three, Owen was converted to spiritualism, at a time when it had become a craze among the population at large and in the Owenite movement. He claimed to have contacted the spirits of Benjamin Franklin and Thomas Jefferson, who had called for the improvement of the human condition and for a world of universal peace.[25]

CONCLUSION: THE RIGIDITY AND AUTHORITARIANISM OF UTOPIAN SOCIALISM

As we have seen, Saint-Simon, Fourier and Owen all appealed to science in different ways to justify their utopian schemes. Marx and Engels described their own position as 'scientific socialism'. In this respect they were all children of the Enlightenment, which upheld science in place of superstition.

Yet Saint-Simon, Fourier and Owen went further: science and reason would become the source of all authority. Marx and Engels took a different turn, as discussed in the next chapter. But they all—'utopian' and 'scientific' socialists alike—rejected some key principles of the Enlightenment.

Unlike the French revolutionary *Left* of 1789–1792, legitimate political power was to be grounded on science rather than the popular will. Rights ceased to be inalienable and were subject to political and scientific authority. The newborn socialism challenged both democracy and preceding notions of universal and inalienable rights.

In their view and application of science, Saint-Simon, Fourier and Owen were mistaken. Their use of the supposed findings of science was highly selective and idiosyncratic. They did not understand how science evolves; they did not appreciate that its findings are always provisional. Instead they saw science as cumulatively placing one piece of eternal truth upon another. They neglected the social context of scientific discovery.

Science is always a social process. Advances attributed to a few individuals are often the cumulative results of many small incremental advances, sometimes in diverse areas and over a long period of time. The social institutions of the scientific community are vital. Through networks and various social and pecuniary incentives, they help to generate a consensus on some core issues so that science does not bury itself under endless scepticism and criticism. But they also need to accommodate a sufficient diversity of views so that scientific innovation can take place.[26]

The provisional nature of all science means that claims concerning truth cannot be fixed for all time. Yet the 'utopian socialists' set out a permanent plan for society that took little heed of the possibility that science might change its view. If they had recognized the provisional nature of science, then their politico-economic plans would have included institutional provisions to allow for revision and further politico-economic experimentation. Powers of experimentation should not be vested in leaders alone, because they, like science, are also fallible.

Such considerations suggest in any utopian system a role for democracy, where amendments could be proposed and debated. But for the utopians of the early nineteenth century, democracy was a threat to social harmony rather than a mechanism that might allow institutional revision and development. They stuck to a fixed plan.

But democracy is an inadequate solution to the problem of the fallibility of scientific and political judgments. Anyone with any experience of committees knows that they are often conservative and can block innovative progress. Especially as society and technology get more complex, democratic committees would be hugely overburdened if they took on every decision concerning investment or changes in routine. Additional institutional provisions are required.

Every politico-economic proposal should envisage its own fallibility. There must be some provision for claims concerning rights or grievances against the authorities. In cases where matters cannot be resolved, the possibility of exit needs to be left open. To avoid despotism, individuals must have the option, and the practical means, of leaving any utopian community. Short of such provisions, utopian schemes are bound to slide into authoritarianism.

By contrast, these radical thinkers proposed rigid schemes of social ordering, with limited individual autonomy and little possibility of exit. This autonomy was most limited with the proposals of Babeuf and Owen, who, by banning private property, denied people the means to escape the communal scheme so that they could work on their own account.

It is best to allow those with new ideas, about what should be done and how, to experiment in their own way, as long as their projects place no obvious threat to the community. To allow for voluntary exit or experiment, it is desirable to retain the rights of private property and private enterprise, to allow people to produce things on their own.

Of course, setting up a business is costly, risky and difficult. Some modern technologies require huge amounts of investment to get off the ground. Exit is not always feasible in the same line of work. But the 'utopian socialists' wrote of a time when small-scale trades made up most of the economy. It is significant that Owen and others, by backing the abolition of private property, ruled out this option. It is also relevant today, when many businesses are still small in scale.

Crucially, rights to private property are also matters of justice and human rights. This was understood by the French revolutionaries and it is upheld today. Article 17 of the Universal Declaration of Human Rights, adopted by the General Assembly of the United Nations in 1948, declares: 'Everyone has the right to own property alone as well as in association with others. No one shall be arbitrarily deprived of his property'.[27]

Why is private property a human right? The philosopher John Finnis established a principle of subsidiarity, meaning that 'the proper function of association is to help the participants . . . to help themselves' or 'constitute themselves', where individuals or families or groups 'can help themselves by their own private efforts and initiatives without thereby injuring . . . the common good, they are entitled in justice to do so'. Autonomy and self-management suggest 'that the opportunity of exercising some form of private ownership, including of means of production, is in most times and places a requirement of justice'.

Accordingly, following similar proposals by G. W. F. Hegel, the philosopher Jeremy Waldron argued that private property is vital for individual autonomy and ethical development, including the enhancement of a sense of care and personal responsibility.[28]

The general right to private property implies that property should be widely distributed, rather than concentrated in a few hands. The right to private property derives from the universal rights to a degree of autonomy and self-development. Notwithstanding our general dependence on others, we have the right to as much self-determination as possible that is consistent with the common good. This does not rule out substantial public ownership in some sectors, but it means that viable options for private enterprise are also crucial.

Private property never confers absolute rights or powers of control: it is a way of organizing society that confers obligations to others as well as individual or corporate rights. It entails a complex mesh of reciprocal entitlements and duties. Within a regulated system of law, the system of property can provide incentives and autonomy. Contrary to the original socialists, a much better maxim than the abolition of private property would be its fairer distribution.

Among the bundle of rights that ownership may confer is the possible right of alienation, meaning the right to sell property to a buyer. This general right to trade has an accordant justification: it opens up possibilities of improvement through voluntary engagement with others, meaning, it is a means of sociability for mutual benefit. Contrary to the original socialists, a much better maxim than the abolition of markets would be their careful regulation.

It is notable that the utopian proposals of Babeuf, Saint-Simon, Fourier and Owen all proposed an end to large cities, and a population shift to small, rural towns or villages. In a small community, some form of communism may be possible because social discipline can be enforced by reputation and by face-to-face recognition and interaction. Shirking and other transgressions can be dealt with by disapproval, by ostracization or by other punishments.

But theory and experience tell us that these mechanisms of social order are undermined when the size of the population extends into the thousands, and when social complexity greatly increases. In 1822 the former US President Thomas Jefferson addressed 'the principle of a communion of property', noting that 'small societies may exist in habits of virtue, order, industry, and peace' and claiming that he had 'seen its proofs in various small societies which have been constituted on that principle'. But could this 'principle of a communion of property' be applied to larger societies? Jefferson did 'not feel authorized to conclude . . . that an extended society, like that of the United States . . . could be governed happily on the same principle'.[29]

Nobel Laureate Elinor Ostrom's inspiring studies of the management of common-pool resources are relevant here. She showed that resources—such as medieval common land, fisheries or agricultural irrigation schemes—can be effectively managed by relatively small communities with long historical ties of association.

Their small size means that they can overcome the $1/n$ problem, where n is the number of people in a community that shares its output, and $1/n$ is the likely reward to an individual for every extra bit of his or her effort. With smaller values of n, participants are able to monitor each other to ensure that necessary tasks are carried out and that the interests of the community are served. Enforcement mechanisms range from praise to punishment.

Within relatively small and cohesive groups, Ostrom emphasized individual reputation, trust and targeted sanctions as mechanisms for encouraging cooperation, reciprocity and compliance with customary rules. Ostrom's case studies show that effective management rules and routines evolve less by design and more by evolution and experiment over long periods of time. Accordingly, cooperative utopias may be possible on a small scale, but even within such confines, they are too complex to be effectively and completely designed from above.[30]

While embracing science, the so-called 'utopian socialists' had failed to learn many of the important *political* lessons of the Enlightenment—particularly concerning democracy and individual rights. They also failed to envisage societies involving much larger populations, more complex divisions of labour, restless technological innovation and institutional dynamism. To a degree they harked back to a restful, bygone rural era.

But while Marx and Engels learned from Owen and others, they abandoned their utopian visions of small-scale communities. Likewise embracing an Enlightenment view of science, they rode the tiger of capitalist expansion and innovation toward a different dawn.

CHAPTER 5

Marxism's Wrong Turnings: Class War and Wholesale Collectivization

What Marx accomplished was to produce such a comprehensive, dramatic, and fascinating vision that it could withstand innumerable empirical contradictions, logical refutations, and moral revulsions at its effects. The Marxian vision took the overwhelming complexity of the real world and made the parts fall into place, in a way that was intellectually exhilarating and conferred such a sense of moral superiority that opponents could be simply labelled and dismissed as moral lepers or blind reactionaries. Marxism was—and remains—a mighty instrument for the acquisition and maintenance of political power.

Thomas Sowell, *Marxism: Philosophy and Economics* (1985)

Karl Marx was born in Prussia in 1818. His involvement in the failed German Revolution of 1848 led to exile from his homeland. In 1849 he moved with his wife and children to London, where he spent the rest of his life, supported financially by his friend Engels, from the proceeds of his cotton-spinning enterprise in Manchester. They witnessed the first country to develop large-scale industrial capitalism. Marx studied the dynamics of this system, in the belief that it would falter into crisis and prepare the conditions for socialism.

Like the 'utopian socialists' before them, Karl Marx and Frederick Engels claimed that their approach was scientific. But their grounds for this assertion were very different. Engels argued in 1892 that the 'utopian socialists' saw ideas and reason as the remedies for social ills: 'The solution of the social problems, which as yet lay hidden in underdeveloped economic conditions, the Utopians attempted to evolve out of the human brain. Society presented nothing but wrongs; to remove them was the task of reason'.[1]

Rather than ideas, Marx and Engels saw economic developments and social classes as the underlying forces of change. The proletariat was the agent of progressive change: its victory over the bourgeoisie would lead to the creation of socialism. Through the study of history, politics and economics, science would reveal the forces leading to socialism.

The 'scientific' approach developed by Marx and Engels rested on claims that

(a) social classes are constituted by 'economic' conditions;
(b) class struggle is always the motor of history;
(c) the development of capitalism enlarges and coalesces the proletariat; and
(d) the proletariat is the 'universal class'.

By (d) it is meant that the proletariat alone, by overthrowing the bourgeoisie and the capitalist system, could act in the interest of humanity as a whole and build a new society based on rational planning.

Proposition (a) springs from their conception of social class. The detailed examination of the next two propositions—(b) and (c)—occupied the writing and research of Marx and Engels for much of their adult lives. Along the way they made major contributions to historiography and social science. Above all, Marx's analysis of capitalism in *Capital* is a titanic achievement. Notwithstanding its theoretical flaws, it ranks as one of the most important contributions to our understanding of capitalism in the last two hundred years.[2]

The utopians had attempted to use the results of science to design their perfect societies. By contrast, Marxism postponed any detailed explanation of how the socialist future would work. Instead it concentrated on the examination of the social and economic forces that supposedly would bring about the new social order. The design of the socialist future was not the task of Marxist intellectuals, but of the proletariat when it had seized power.

While utopian socialism involved 'the play of the imagination on the future structure of society', Marx argued that socialism had to be grounded on real, material, 'economic' forces. Marx and Engels argued that their principles were not 'invented, or discovered, by this or that would-be reformer'. Instead: 'They merely express, in general terms, actual relations springing from an existing class struggle, from a historical movement going on under our very eyes'.[3]

In two ways 'economic forces' were said to point to the society of the future. First, capitalism brought the workers together in large production units, creating the possibility of their united struggle against the system. Second, Marx predicted growing capitalist crises, as with his theory of the tendency of the rate of profit to fall, found in the third volume of *Capital*.[4]

Marx saw capitalism as its own gravedigger. Fortified by Marx's theory, Marxists are ever in anticipation of capitalism ripening the prerequisites for proletarian revolution. Even when the system is booming, they use this theory to fortify their patience for the great crisis to come.

This 'scientific' intellectual strategy made Marxism a system of great power and attractiveness. For any critic of poverty, inequality, commercialization, greed, exploitation and social disharmony, Marxism offered the slogan of socialism, but without the need to worry about how this alternative society would work. In its place, Marxism provided an inspiring analysis of history and of capitalism that seemed to make all developments understandable in terms of the interests of the social classes involved.

Instead of offering a detailed blueprint of the socialist future, Marxism pointed to the working class as the agent of social change and the ruling class of the future. It was necessary to support the proletariat in its struggle so that it could become the new ruling class. Only then the detailed nature of the future society would be revealed. So Marxists remained vague about the detailed nature of socialism.

Marxism inspired several twentieth-century revolutions. Vladimir Ilyich Lenin led the Bolshevik Marxists to seize power in Russia in 1917. Mao Zedong's Communist Party gained supremacy in China in 1949. Subsequently, both countries suffered terror and famine. Marxists developed tactics to resist the criticism that these regimes were totalitarian and repressive. Their massive defects could be blamed on their relative backwardness and isolation, on the attacks and subversions of their capitalist enemies, or on the alleged impossibility of fully developed 'socialism in one country'. Alternatively some Marxists argued that these regimes were not socialist, but 'degenerated workers' states' or even 'state capitalist' in character.

Precisely because Marxism offered no detailed picture of the nature of socialism, there was no clear set of socialist benchmarks against which postrevolutionary reality could be evaluated. Multiple excuses became possible. Marxism developed a powerful and adaptable autoimmune system to deal with any criticism or empirical challenge.

Marxism relied on the Enlightenment's successful elevation of the status and role of science. Marxism was also influenced by those Enlightenment thinkers who rashly believed that all human affairs could be subject to rational design, neglecting the importance of experiment and the limits to reason itself.

But Marxism ditched much of the other baggage of the Enlightenment, including its claims concerning human rights and the political ideals of the insurgent French *Left* of 1789–1792. Enlightenment aims and principles were described by Marxists as 'nothing more than the idealized kingdom of the bourgeoisie'.[5]

Hence Marx and Engels jettisoned many *Left* principles. Some of their most dubious arguments for doing so were based on claims that these principles were already largely defunct. In their *Communist Manifesto*, Marx and Engels addressed an imaginary critic: 'You are horrified at our intending to do away with private property'. Their response was that 'private property is already done away with for nine tenths of the population'. Marx and Engels were not inclined to defend or re-instate even 'the property of the petty and of the small peasant' on the spurious ethical grounds that 'to a great extent' it was 'already destroyed'. They answered 'bourgeois' complaints concerning the 'abolition of individuality and freedom' with a candid response: 'The abolition of bourgeois individuality, bourgeois independence, and bourgeois freedom is undoubtedly aimed at'. Their linking of individuality and freedom with an allegedly doomed social class was sufficient to overrule any complaint about limitations on freedom in general.[6]

In the remainder of this chapter, problems are exposed with the Marxian account of social classes and its notion of 'economic' conditions. It is pointed out that their notion of the proletariat as the 'universal class', which is destined to run society in the interests of all, has no scientific basis whatsoever. It is also shown that Marx and Engels, while rejecting utopianism, did indeed adopt and scale-up some 'utopian' design features in their preferred socialism.

The viability as well as the desirability of these features is questioned here. It is shown how their statist vision of socialism was perpetuated by Fabians, among others. Vital questions concerning the feasibility of this socialism are reviewed. Finally, the entire strategy of basing normative political principles upon the supposed destiny of a social class is shown to be both logically flawed and politically dangerous.[7]

SOCIAL CLASSES AND THE 'ECONOMIC BASE'

Marx and Engels depicted social classes as fundamental components of modern society. The 'economic base' of society consisted of the 'economic' relations between those component classes. Law, ideology, politics and religion were part of the 'superstructure' built upon the 'economic base'.[8]

But Marx and Engels failed to define terms such as 'economic structure', 'relations of production', 'economic conditions of production', or 'economic relations'. The meanings of these concepts are not self-evident from their writings. Yet they have to be sufficiently clear to make sense of their attempted strict dichotomy between 'economic' and 'legal' relations. Their failure to define the 'economic' deprives their argument of analytic force and clarity.[9]

They conceived classes in terms of their relationship to the means of production. In an attempt to define the two main classes of modern capitalism, the bourgeoisie and the proletariat, Engels added a note to an 1888 edition of the *Communist Manifesto*:

> By bourgeoisie is meant the class of modern capitalists, owners of the means of social production and employers of wage labour. By proletariat, the class of modern wage labourers who, having no means of production of their own, are reduced to selling their labour power in order to live.[10]

Clearly, in these definitions, Engels was obliged to refer to *ownership*, the *employment* of waged labourers and the *selling* of labour power. None of these terms can be adequately understood without reference to law. Ownership implies legal rights, enforced by the legal powers of the state. The employment contract is a specific legal form, differing from a contract for sales or services.

Marx frequently used terms such as 'owner' and 'property' to describe social classes. In the third volume of *Capital*, in its unfinished chapter entitled 'Classes', Marx wrote: 'The *owners* of mere labour-power, the *owners* of capital and the land*owners* . . . in other words wage-labourers, capitalists and landowners . . . form the three great classes of modern society based on the capitalist mode of production'. Once again, social class was defined by means of what are ostensibly legal terms.[11]

Attempts to prioritize social class in explanations of political, economic and historical phenomena always face the problem of identifying the nature of class itself. Consequently, social formations such as capitalism and socialism cannot be categorized simply by noting which class is in power, because social classes themselves are constituted in terms of legal and other social rules or relations. The configuration of class power is in part an expression of such legal rules or relations.

The argument here is over the constitutive role of law, not whether its outcomes are just. The allocation of legal rights may be unfair, but this allocation is a real social force. Law is not all on the surface. In modern societies it is a central mechanism of social power; legal rules matter. Marx and Engels saw law as secondary to class struggle. On the contrary, law is primary and necessary for the definition of modern social classes. Marx and Engels were unconvincing in their rejection of law from the economic base.

Marx once asked rhetorically: 'Are economic relations regulated by legal conceptions of right or is the opposite not the case, that legal relations spring from economic ones?' His implied positive answer in the final six words was incorrect. His question was also incoherent because it is impossible to separate 'legal' from 'economic' relations. 'Legal relations' cannot 'spring from economic ones' alone, because the 'economic' relations to which Marx referred were themselves defined partly in legal terms.[12]

The Marxist demotion of law is both theoretically unsatisfactory and (as argued later below) politically dangerous.

IS THE PROLETARIAT THE 'UNIVERSAL CLASS'?

At an early stage of their collaboration, Marx and Engels developed the idea of the proletariat as the 'universal class'. They meant that it was the class whose particular interests are identical to the general interests of society, such that the pursuit of the interests of this class would amount to the furtherance of the interests of humanity as a whole. The emancipation of this universal class would produce a 'universal emancipation' from oppression and exploitation.

Marx and Engels argued in 1845 that 'the proletariat can and must emancipate itself' but it cannot do this 'without abolishing *all* the inhuman conditions of life of society today'. The proletariat was the sole agent of the destruction of capitalism and of the building of socialism.

But the working class may not be aware of the historic destiny that Marx and Engels ascribed to them: 'It is not a question of what . . . the . . . proletariat . . . *regards* as its aim. It is a question of *what the proletariat is*, and what, in accordance with this *being*, it will historically be compelled to do'. The proletariat by its nature was unified and energized through capitalism.[13]

While hitherto all history was seen as the history of class struggle, and every previously ascendant social class had *claimed* to represent the interests of humanity as a whole, in reality each was acting in its particular class interest, including its promotion of the form of property by which it exploited others and accumulated its wealth. By contrast, the proletariat, having nothing but its capacity to work and to produce children, could seize power and truly act in the interests of all humanity.

Behind the technical analysis in *Capital* was the vision of the proletariat, built up and brought together by the system, and with a historical destiny to overthrow it. As Engels explained:

> Then it was seen that *all* past history, with the exception of its primitive stages, was the history of class struggles; that these warring classes are always the products . . . of the *economic* conditions of their time; that the economic structure of society furnishes the real basis, starting from which we can alone work

out the ultimate explanation of the whole superstructure of juridical and political institutions . . . From that time forward socialism was no longer an accidental discovery of this or that ingenious brain, but the necessary outcome of
the struggle between two historically developed classes—the proletariat and
the bourgeoisie.[14]

The destiny of the proletariat became the great, teleological, organizing principle of Marxism. It forged its nuggets of philosophy, politics, economics and
history into a grand and enticing schema that has few (if any) rivals in scope
in modern secular thought.

But crucially, it belittled many achievements of the Enlightenment as 'bourgeois', including its great proclamations of liberty, equality, toleration and human rights. The turn to class by Marx and Engels was a turn away from the
Left political principles proclaimed in the French Revolution of 1789–1792.

Even if socialism was superior to capitalism, it would not mean that the
overthrow of capitalism and the building of socialism were the mission and
destiny of the working class. As Leszek Kolakowski rightly pointed out: 'Marx
was convinced that the proletariat was destined by history to establish a new
classless order; but this conviction was not based on any argument'.[15]

We cannot refute any argument by Marx or Engels on this point, quite simply because there is no argument to be found. The vision of the proletariat as
the liberator of humanity played a crucial synthetic part in their grand system
of social thought. But it was basically an article of faith.

It was also a device to avoid detailed discussion of the socialist future. By
seeing socialism as the victory of a class, Marx and Engels could avoid engagement with the complex practicalities in the comprehensive planning of
a large-scale, modern economy, without private property or markets. To this
we now turn.

MARXISM'S INCIPIENT UTOPIA

Marx and Engels often used the term *communism* instead of *socialism*. But this
was primarily to distance themselves from the analytic, strategic and tactical
ideas of contemporary socialists rather than to postulate a radically different
objective. For them, 'communism' was a label for their movement, rather than
their goal. Thus in about 1845 they wrote: 'Communism is not for us a *state of
affairs* which is to be established, an *ideal* to which reality [will] have to adjust
itself. We call communism the *real* movement which abolishes the present state
of things'.[16]

In the *Communist Manifesto* of 1848, Marx and Engels echoed Robert Owen and others and called for the 'abolition of private property'. In 1850 Marx declared: 'Our concern cannot simply be to modify private property, but to abolish it'. Marx and Engels proclaimed an economic order in which 'capital is converted into common property, into the property of all members of society'. They wanted the complete abolition of the 'free selling and buying' of commodities. They advocated common ownership of all means of production and the abolition of commodity exchange and markets. But by emphasizing national ownership, they went much further than Owen. They welcomed efforts 'to centralize all instruments of production in the hands of the state' and looked forward to a time when 'all production has been concentrated in the hands of a vast association of the whole nation'.[17]

This state-socialist utopia persisted in their writings. It appeared, for example, in the second volume of *Capital*, where Marx wrote of the planned system of 'social production' in which 'society distributes labour-power and means of production between the various branches of industry'. Likewise, in one of his last manuscripts, completed in 1880, Marx remarked that in the society of the future, 'the "social-state" will draw up production from the very beginning . . . The scope of production . . . is subject in such a state to rational regulation'.[18]

Throughout their lives, Marx and Engels refrained from giving any more than the barest hints of the form of organization of the future socialist society. It is thus all the more significant and remarkable that the singular notion of 'a vast association of the whole nation' involving collective production 'fostered by national means' re-appeared several times in their writings over the decades, without any amendment or qualification. There is no evidence in any of their works that they saw any value in institutional and structural diversity, under capitalism or socialism. They wanted the entire economy to be under state control.

While offering no detailed picture of a socialist future, Marx and Engels rejected socialist blueprints as 'idealist' and 'utopian'. Nevertheless, they adopted a utopian scheme in outline, and they wrongly took its feasibility for granted. Like the utopian socialists before them, they upheld that an entire economic system could be governed by reason. But it was to be on a much larger scale than proposed by the utopian socialists. Their nationwide socialist utopia was seen as the obvious, self-evident outcome of the application of science and rationality to human affairs. It would replace the chaos and irrationality of the market. Its workability on a national scale was taken for granted, and no attention was paid to organizational details.

Socialism of a kind might work on a small scale, albeit lacking the economies of large-scale production and the technological dynamism of competitive capitalism. If socialist societies were any larger, then individual incentives for effort and innovation would be diminished, and compensatory, face-to-face, trust-based mechanisms to sustain cooperation would be relatively less effective.

Most communists and 'utopian socialists' preceding Marx and Engels proposed near-independent communities of a relatively small size. By contrast, Marx and Engels advocated common ownership on a national scale—typically involving millions of people—and thus ruled out the possibility of a small-scale socialism using community-based, intimate, interpersonal mechanisms of reciprocity, trust, cooperation and reputation.

Marx and Engels ignored the broader question of individual incentives and, in particular, what I have called the $1/n$ problem, which refers to the particular problem of incentivization in large-scale communities. Instead they proposed collectivization on a nationwide scale, involving millions of people. Communism on this scale would be unprecedented, and the problems of incentivization all the more severe.

Instead of addressing such issues, their primary goal was the victory of the proletariat in the struggle against the capitalist class and the overthrow of the existing and allegedly irrational system. But they retained a utopian faith in a rational socialist system, once the working masses were elevated to political power. After the revolution, the guidance of a future and complex society could be entrusted to the emancipated powers of proletarian reason, freed from vested interests deriving from property and greed.

Here Marx and his followers made three crucial errors. First, they downgraded the task of detailed exposition of the structure and workings of a future socialist society. The failure of Marx and his followers to produce an adequate outline of a planned economy was little short of disastrous when the Bolsheviks came to power in 1917. The subsequent socialist Left has compounded the omission for another century, lacking any adequately detailed explanation of how a feasible socialism would work, how production would be organized and how people would be incentivized to work productively and skilfully.

Second, in their few words on the economic organization of socialism, they betrayed an overwhelming adherence to the national ownership and organization of the means of production, without any concession to economic pluralism or to a mixed economy. They had excessive faith in the power and scope of human reason. They inherited this weakness from the Enlightenment, while rejecting many of its strengths.

Third, in particular, they jettisoned a foremost achievement of the Enlightenment—the assertion of universal human rights. Rights to property and autonomy were emphatically rejected. While supporting the proletariat, they granted no political or legal rights to other social classes. This move was disastrous, especially for those who were to suffer the oppressions of Marxist regimes.

The idea that private property and markets should be abolished was thematic to socialism and unconfined to Marxism. It pervaded the writings of socialists as diverse as the Continental revolutionary communists, German 'state social-ists' and British Fabians. It is important to stress that, at least until the 1950s, hostility toward markets and private property were thematic for socialism as a whole. The founding influences of Owen and Marx were long-lasting.

Some non-Marxist socialists tried to lay out more detail on how social-ism would work. For example, Fabian socialists Sidney and Beatrice Webb had an ultimate vision of a fully planned and consciously controlled socialist economy where all markets and private ownership of the means of production were gradually marginalized to insignificance. They wanted private ownership of the means of production to be ended: it was a 'perversion'. They envis-aged a massive, complex structure of national, regional and local committees, all involved in decision-making over details of production and distribution. How would these cope with the huge amounts of information and specialized knowledge in modern complex economies? It was simply assumed that this was relatively easy to sort out in some rational manner.[19]

The British Fabian G. D. H. Cole is sometimes described as a 'libertarian socialist' and as an advocate of 'decentralized' 'guild' socialism. But he sup-ported the wholesale nationalization of industry and the abolition of private enterprise. To his great credit, and unlike most Marxists, Cole did actually try to explain how a future socialist society would work. But his explanation is a failure. He did not show how devolved democracy could function and en-dure in a society where private property was abolished. His hyper-democratic account of socialism, where individuals make decisions throughout indus-try as well as the polity, failed to consider the problems of necessary skill in judgment, of obtaining relevant knowledge and the overwhelming number of meetings and decisions involved.[20]

Cole's vision of socialism was of an integrated, national system where 'a single authority is responsible both for the planning of the social production as a whole and for the distribution of the incomes which will be used in buying it'. Within this 'single authority' he also sought devolved worker control. He wanted local autonomy of manufacturing, modelled on the medieval guild. But he was tragically unclear about how the two were to be reconciled. How would the autonomous powers of the latter be protected from the control and centralizing ambitions of the 'single authority'? There was no adequate answer. As Don Lavoie put it in his critique of national planning:

> national economic planning involves *by its very nature* the concentration of immense political and economic power in a single agency. This agency would have to be capable of mobilizing the vast resources of a nation. Such concentration will naturally lend itself to abuse by those hungry for such power and eminently competent in its exercise.[21]

Routinely adding the word 'democratic' to 'planning', and trying to make a planning hierarchy more democratic, does not overcome this problem. As long as we are dealing with a single planning hierarchy, with inadequate countervailing power by some separate authority to hold it in check, then that supreme hierarchy will always be a prized object of seizure by power-hungry politicians, or by those simply determined 'to get important things done' in the face of perceived urgency. Even if extensive democracy were feasible within large and complex hierarchies—which Robert Michels and others gave us reason to doubt—genuinely democratic sentiment and practice cannot endure within such a prized monopoly of massive political and economic power.[22]

Cole did not understand that genuine and enduring decentralization can only be achieved by devolving legal property rights to local enterprises. These rights must include the right to trade with other organizations; otherwise the central authority has ultimate control. In other words, viable and enduring decentralization requires devolved rights over private property, and these imply the possibility of trade or markets. Cole shunned this view. Instead he advocated the abolition of capitalism and of most private property.[23]

Cole downplayed the fact that the medieval guilds were corporate entities, with independent rights to own and trade property. By contrast, his socialist guilds would have much less effective powers in reality. Cole upheld that they would have the right to *propose* prices for their output. But if there were no willing buyers, then the matter would be referred to a higher authority—first local, then national—to make a 'final decision' on what the price should be. Hence Cole's guilds would lack devolved autonomy on decisions over sales or prices.

He also insisted that they would not decide on their own what investments in equipment they would make. Instead, all investment would be decided by a higher authority or 'commune'. Guilds would not be autonomous entities with the right to conclude contracts on their own account. The presence of higher authorities with the right to impose prices, and make other crucial decisions, would greatly limit their autonomy. In practice the guilds would be under the heel of local and national bureaucracies, with all the attendant problems of deliberation, delay and disincentivization.[24]

Karl Polanyi was a major figure in twentieth-century social science. In the 1920s he proposed a form of socialism, building on the ideas from his friend Cole. Another major inspiration for Polanyi was Owen. Polanyi wished to avoid the impersonality of the market and build a socialism infused by the empathy and cooperation of the community. To Cole's impractical notions of local devolution and democracy, he added a 'pseudo-market mechanism' with non-tradable 'token money', while retaining overall state ownership and ultimate control. Polanyi did not fully grasp that interpersonal empathy and intimate cooperation can serve as the sufficient basis of social integration and economic production in small-scale communities only. Like Cole, he did not understand that the autonomy of groups or individuals is deeply compromised if they are deprived of rights to own and trade property.[25]

Classical socialists condemned the market for fostering competition, encouraging greed, generating inequality and promoting exploitation. They believed that markets can and should be abolished and replaced by collective planning. They often insisted on democratic control as well. While they sometimes differed on matters such as democracy and decentralization, they agreed on the abolition of private property and markets.

Eight years before he became Prime Minister in the UK, Clement Attlee wrote of the 'evils' of capitalism: their 'cause is the private ownership of the means of life; the remedy is public ownership'. Attlee then approvingly quoted the words of Bertrand Russell: 'Socialism means the common ownership of land and capital together with a democratic form of government. . . . It involves the abolition of all unearned wealth and of all private control over the means of livelihood of the workers'. The word *socialism* endured from the 1830s to the 1950s with these collectivist connotations, in opposition to private firms and markets.[26]

It still preserves this meaning in some quarters. For example, similar collectivist plans have been proposed by the American Marxist Robin Hahnel and (more vaguely) by the famous British politician Tony Benn. Their unfeasible rhetoric of hyper-democracy masked their antagonism to private property and their preference for wholesale nationalization.[27]

The severe problems with collectivist planning are massively confounded if all decisions are subject to widespread democratic discussion. Fabian socialists, like Cole and the Webbs, proposed a collectivized economy run by a maze of democratic councils and committees. None of these authors considered the unfeasibility of the enormous number of meetings required in a large-scale, complex economy to bring everything under democratic control.

Greater industrial democracy, with worker participation in some workplace decisions, can improve productivity and make work more enjoyable. But it is impractical to have votes on more than a tiny fraction of the important decisions that have to take place every day in any large, complex economy. Everyone's participation in every major decision that concerned them would be a crushing burden of endless decision-making on every citizen. It would guarantee economic paralysis. Oscar Wilde was right: socialism is impossible because it would take too many meetings.[28]

Whatever the limitations of a market system, it has the advantage that it does not require majority agreement before a decision can be made to produce or distribute a good or service. Private property and contracts permit zones of partial autonomy within an interrelated system; agents may reach decisions through negotiated contracts with others. The costs and benefits are devolved to individuals or firms.

Through private enterprise it is possible for many technological or institutional innovations to be pioneered without the prior agreement of (democratic) committees or (undemocratic) bureaucrats. This analysis is borne out by experience. The former Soviet-type economies in Russia and China lacked devolved autonomy, secured by private ownership. They had limited capacity to innovate.

AN EARLY CRITIQUE OF THE FEASIBILITY OF THE SOCIALIST UTOPIA

Many critics have argued that public ownership and planning on a national scale is *undesirable*. Others claim that this vision is *unfeasible*. Some of these critics have argued that socialism is impossible in general terms. Others have argued that it is impossible while retaining economic growth or democracy. Despite their vital importance, accounts of debates on the feasibility of socialism appear rarely in the textbooks of economics or other social sciences. They are seldom taught to students.

In particular, the pioneering critical contribution of the German 'historical school' economist Albert Schäffle has been almost entirely ignored. Schäffle was born in Germany in 1831. After becoming a professor at the University of Vienna, and a brief spell as the Austrian minister of finance, he obtained a pension that allowed him to devote his time to writing.[29]

In a series of works from 1870, Schäffle appraised socialism. He did not argue that socialism was impossible. Instead, he focused on the difficulties of organizing and planning a collectivist system, especially while retaining democracy. He identified problems concerning individual incentives for work and innovation in large-scale, collectivized systems.

When any extra output is automatically divided and shared with thousands of others, what is the individual incentive to work harder? With a large number of workers sharing in the output, some of the more selfish may slacken or shirk, knowing that they will always benefit from their share of the output of many others. Making this simple but important point, Schäffle depicted a society with one million workers:

> My income from my social labour is conditional upon my 999,999 co-operating comrades being as industrious as I. . . . Socialism would have to give the individual at least as strong an interest in the collective work as he has under the liberal system of production . . .[30]

This problem of incentives with large numbers thwarts any socialist scheme of large-scale cooperation. This is the $1/n$ problem. If everything is shared, then incentives for extra individual effort can be much less than the likely individual rewards. When thousands of people are brought together, and rewards are shared, then there is less incentive to make the extra effort because the rewards from that additional work would be hugely diluted. As noted in chapter 1 above, the English Leveller John Lilburne made a similar argument over two hundred years earlier.

Much later, this point was illustrated dramatically in post-Mao China. After the Communist Revolution of 1949, agriculture in China was organized into large collective farms. Mao died in 1976, opening up the possibility of reform. In 1978 some peasant farmers decided to withdraw from collective farms and take responsibility for production at the household level, where the household (instead of the collective) received the revenue from its sold output. Individual households had much greater incentives to work harder and to innovate. They overcame the $1/n$ problem. After decades of slow growth under Mao, China's explosive economic growth began with those changes. As a result, millions were lifted out of poverty.[31]

Schäffle also argued that a system trying to use labour time as its unit of account would face intractable problems, including the heterogeneity of labour and the inaccessibility of relevant data. Measuring labour inputs in this way would also undermine individual incentives to increase productivity. This was an effective response to Owen and other socialists who proposed using labour as a unit of account.

What would happen if large-scale collectivization was attempted? Schäffle argued that a state collectivist system of production would have to counter the incentive and monitoring problems by the installation of a strong central authority. Mechanisms of social interaction, that effectively pressure people to cooperate and pull together in groups, would not work in large-scale societies. People would have to be bullied or forced to work.[32]

This would undermine any egalitarian or democratic distribution of power. As Schäffle wrote: 'collective production without firm hands to govern it, and without immediate individual responsibility, or material interests on the part of the participators' is 'impossible for all time'. Schäffle elaborated:

> Without a sufficiently strong and attractive reward for individual or corporate pre-eminence, without strongly deterrent drawbacks and compensatory obligations for bad and unproductive work, a collective system of production is inconceivable, or at least any system that would even distantly approach in efficiency the capitalistic system of today. But democratic equality cannot tolerate such strong rewards and punishments.[33]

Hence socialism administered by democratic means was unfeasible. Schäffle thus presented a choice between socialism and democracy. We cannot have both.

Market competition is absent or much diminished in a centrally planned economy. Instead, the pressure to perform comes from the state. Consequently, strong state discipline would be necessary to sustain production, and larger-scale socialism would engender authoritarianism and bureaucracy.

Twentieth-century evidence strongly supports Schäffle's argument. After the attempts to establish socialism in Russia, China, Eastern Europe and elsewhere, Schäffle's stance on the relationship between large-scale collectivist planning and democracy is highly prescient. In no case has an adequate democracy prevailed within a centrally planned economy. In this and other vital respects, his analysis has stood the test of time. Amazingly, Schäffle also predicted the likely survival of a regulated capitalism with democratic political institutions beyond the year 2000.[34]

To a degree, Schäffle's $1/n$ argument concerning incentives applies to any large-scale organization, including big private corporations. Large corporations try to incentivize people by splitting up their organizations into divisions and work teams, and giving performance targets to each division or team.

An obvious socialist response would be to argue that similar measures could be applied to nationalized industries. But what is lacking under classical socialism is market discipline. By contrast, corporations are subject to some degree of national or global competition and are under constant pressure to innovate and seek new products. Planning within firms proceeds against the necessary backdrop of markets. These markets provide the firms with benchmark prices against which planning decisions can be made. Competition for sales and finance put pressure on the corporate planners to seek efficient solutions.

Because of diminished competitive pressures, nationalized industries in centrally planned economies have been less impressive in terms of innovation and flexibility. Peter Murrell showed empirically that the former Communist countries were apparently no less efficient in allocating resources than capitalist economies. Where they lagged was in terms of dynamic efficiency: the ability to innovate.[35]

THE AUSTRIAN CRITIQUES OF THE FEASIBILITY OF THE SOCIALIST UTOPIA

A major controversy concerning the feasibility of socialism erupted in 1920 after the publication in German of an important article by Ludwig von Mises. This became known as the socialist calculation debate. Von Mises and his student Friedrich Hayek were born in Austria. They were important figures in the so-called Austrian school of economics. This school underlined the nature and role of knowledge, especially in regard to incentives, innovation and entrepreneurship. Their socialist opponents—including Oskar Lange and Henry Dickenson—used mainstream economic theory and overlooked these problems of obtaining and using information and knowledge.[36]

Revaluations of the debate by careful scholars have overturned the preceding consensus that von Mises and Hayek were on the losing side. Lange and his followers did not adequately answer the criticisms of von Mises and Hayek in the debate, and they failed to provide a satisfactory outline of a workable and dynamic socialist system.[37]

Many socialists ignore the arguments of the Austrian school against socialism because they regard von Mises and Hayek as ideological neoliberals. But we must look beneath the ideology and dissect the analysis. Although there are some important analytical defects in the Austrian school position (in chapter 10, below I challenge some aspects of their politics), their arguments concerning the feasibility of classical socialism are very strong.

Consider the problem of managerial incentives. How are managers to be encouraged to take some risks, but not to be too reckless? Dickenson proposed a system of managerial bonuses to reward competent entrepreneurs. But these would provide limited encouragement for risky entrepreneurship. Hayek rightly pointed out that 'managers will be afraid of taking risks if, when the venture does not come off, it will be somebody else who will afterward decide whether they have been justified in embarking on it'. Unless the system gives them incentives to take risks, managers would eschew risk-taking, minimize personal exposure to responsibility and stick to established routine. Hayek pointed out that Lange and Dickenson were 'deplorably vague' about key issues, including how competent managers were to be selected.[38]

Hayek also pointed out that these socialist theorists had a naïve view of the availability of knowledge in socio-economic systems. They assumed that all relevant technical and economic information would be readily available to the decision makers. As Dickenson wrote naïvely: 'All organs of the socialist economy will work, so to speak, within glass walls'. As a result, the central planning authority would be the 'omnipresent, omniscient organ of the collective economy'. Similarly, Lange argued that under socialism all relevant information concerning production would be widely available, with the result that 'everything done in one productive establishment would and should also be done by the managers of each productive establishment'.[39]

Lange and Dickenson acquired this flawed view of knowledge from the mainstream economic theory that they embraced. Criticizing this, Hayek concluded that by depicting 'economic man' as 'a quasi-omniscient individual', economics has hitherto neglected the problem that should be its major concern, namely the analysis of 'how knowledge is acquired and communicated'. The mainstream models adopted by Lange and others did not deal adequately with this central problem. Tacit knowledge was overlooked. The assimilation of new technical knowledge was wrongly assumed to be unproblematic.[40]

Innovation depends on hunches about the future. Successful innovation takes into account local, tacit and other knowledge concerning circumstances and possibilities. Much of this knowledge involves context-dependent interpretation of complex details, and cannot all be brought together and utilized by a central committee or planning authority.

For Hayek, the 'economic problem of society is thus not merely a problem of how to allocate "given" resources . . . it is a problem of the utilization of knowledge which is not given to anyone in its totality'. He emphasized the 'particular information possessed by every one of the participants in the market process'. These facts in their totality 'cannot be known to the scientific observer, or to any other single brain'. All systems of comprehensive planning face this problem of accessing dispersed information. By contrast, market systems allow particular local information to be expressed and processed through the price mechanism. Overall, markets allow much more knowledge to be utilized—knowledge that 'exists only dispersed among uncounted persons' and is more 'than any one person can possess'.[41]

Generally, Hayek saw government interference in the economy as a distortion of the free-market, information-processing system. Even if we acknowledge significant economic and regulatory roles for the state, then the market is still vital to coordinate vast amounts of complex, dispersed and tacit information. There is no viable alternative to the significant use of markets in large-scale, complex, economic systems. Proposals for planning that overly limit, or even remove, the role of the market overlook this fact.

In their schemes to bring all knowledge together into the hands of planners, advocates of comprehensive planning overlook the time and other difficulties involved in gathering and dealing with available information. Also they give inadequate consideration to how innovations are to be incentivized, tested and promoted.

The arguments of von Mises and Hayek point decisively in favour of substantial private ownership and market competition. Von Mises underlined the importance of meaningful prices to make effective allocative decisions. Hayek's powerful epistemic critique highlighted the impossibility of bringing all knowledge together to make a comprehensive overall plan.

But they took an extreme view: they did not favour a mixed economy of public and private enterprises. Yet in practice all actual and successful capitalist economies are mixed economies. Experience suggests that it is possible to reconcile some public ownership with a vibrant entrepreneurial economy. It is not a matter of dogma, but of what works, as tested by experience.[42]

MARKETS, PLANNING AND PROBLEMS OF SCALE

In their criticisms of the market economy, Marxists point out that commercial relations reduce sociability and make human interactions calculative and impersonal. They yearn for a non-market system, where people can interact on the basis of trust and personal consideration, rather than for the pursuit of profit.

Small communities can run on this basis. Is this a possible way forward? Should we advocate a small-scale socialism, based on autonomous communities of fewer than two thousand people?

It would come at a massive human cost. Small-scale, independent, socialist units would lose the huge benefits since 1800 from the national and global divisions of labour. Without the innovation and growth brought by this dynamic global system, which is integrated by markets, we would be much poorer, not only in terms of wealth, but also in terms of health, life expectancy and cultural riches.

Impersonal relations occur in bureaucracies as well as in markets. Large-scale systems of national planning also make much interaction impersonal. People become numbers to be processed by bureaucrats and computers.

The experience of centrally planned economies in Russia, China and Eastern Europe shows that systems of state planning can be cesspits of human alienation and corruption, governed impersonally by disillusioned bureaucrats and corrupt state officials. Corruption is endemic to such systems, partly because to get anything done, people are obliged to break inflexible bureaucratic rules.

Given that impersonal relations appear in bureaucracies as well as markets, it is evident that they are more to do with large-scale operations. These reduce the relative importance of interpersonal intimacy and familiarity, which survive mainly in the small-scale excesses of community and family.

Marxists either overlook these problems of alienation and impersonality in large-scale planned economies, or they immunize themselves from the lessons, by proclaiming that these planned economies were not really socialist.

Marxists make a much better case when they warn of the dangers of reducing all social interactions and economic decisions to matters of contract, money or profit. This is a valuable argument against the contractualization and commercialization of all social life. But Marxists also overlook the fact that, at the micro level, even a market or contract-based system depends essentially to a degree on trust and other non-pecuniary considerations.[43]

A way out here is to nurture the elements of trust and cooperation that survive within capitalism—in the workplace, community and family—but accept a major role for private property and markets in the economy as a whole, alongside viable and effective economic intervention by the state.

ANOTHER ROAD NOT TAKEN

During Marx's lifetime, there were alternative radical movements and different visions. Philippe Buchez's proposals for worker cooperatives were mentioned in the preceding chapter. In the 1830s he argued that these cooperatives should gradually merge into a single 'universal association'. But eventually, and contrary to most contemporary socialists and communists, Buchez and his followers recognized the need for multiple, autonomous worker cooperatives, linked by contracts and markets. Hence Marx in 1875 described Buchez's ideas as 'reactionary', 'sectarian', opposed to the workers' 'class movement', and contrary to the true revolutionary aim of 'cooperative production . . . on a national scale'.[44]

A similar system with markets and worker cooperatives was suggested by Pierre-Joseph Proudhon. His position came to be described as anarchism, because of its opposition to statist socialism. He proposed a system of 'mutualist associations' involving groups of workers who would pool their labour and their property, holding these resources in common. He realized that without a decentralization of contractual powers, meaningful economic decentralization could not flourish. He thus proposed that each cooperative association would be able to enter into contractual relations with others. But these contracts were assumed to be mutually defining and self-policing, without recourse to a legal system, a government or a state. Proudhon's anarchist society was to be sustained by contracts between politically and economically autonomous associations.[45]

But Marx and Engels emphatically rejected the proposition that contracts and competition should survive after the proletarian revolution. In accord with most socialists and communists of their time, they proposed that all the means of production should be owned by society as a whole, not by autonomous communes or associations.

Within capitalism, worker cooperatives can demonstrate that workers are capable of managing production without capitalists. Marx supported them for that reason. In his draft 'Inaugural Address of the International Working Men's Association' of 1864, he praised the established producer cooperatives, but did not see them as having an autonomous future under socialism. Instead, he saw their salvation in their development 'to national dimensions . . . fostered by national means'. Marx proposed that all worker cooperatives would amalgamate into nationalized industries, which would be owned and controlled at the national level.[46]

By rejecting all markets, Marx and Engels ruled out a system that could embrace small-scale common ownership through worker-owned cooperatives, and could encourage innovative dynamism by promoting competition between enterprises. They thought that market competition between cooperatives, while giving groups of workers control at an enterprise level, was incompatible with their notion of working-class power at national and higher levels. But this was a dogmatic illusion: social classes as singular bodies can never control a large-scale economy, making decisions together on everything. In any large-scale, complex system, power always has to be delegated and compartmentalized.

The idea of a permanent 'socialist' alternative to central planning became more prominent after Josip Tito's 1948 break with Joseph Stalin and the beginnings of the Yugoslav experiment in the self-management of enterprises in the 1950s. Tito's government promoted semiautonomous worker cooperatives selling their outputs on markets.

The Yugoslav system was closer to the associationism of anarchists such as Pierre-Joseph Proudhon than it was to the anti-market, centralist socialism of Marx. An economic model of worker cooperatives in a market context was first formulated in 1958 by the American economist Benjamin Ward. At first he described his model as 'market syndicalism' but later he described it as 'socialism'. Accordingly, over a century after it was coined, the word 'socialism' began belatedly to broaden its meaning, beyond the confines of a system in which contractual exchange and markets would be entirely absent.

A minority of socialists, desiring a genuine decentralization of economic and political power, began to realize that the only way to safeguard against overcentralization was to devolve property rights and employ the market mechanism and hence allow a substantial number of production units to make their own decisions concerning output and prices. Buchez and Proudhon had come to similar conclusions more than a century earlier.

Because workers are free (as long as there is work elsewhere) to quit a capitalist firm, employers have insufficient incentive to invest fully in the skills of employees. A capitalist employer must bear the risk that investment in training will be lost, because the trained worker can readily leave the firm after a contracted period. Worker cooperatives offer a remedy for this problem. The workers become shareholders, with a common interest in training all workers with relevant skills. Several prominent 'proofs' of the alleged suboptimality of cooperatives are typically based on static efficiency models that do not consider ongoing processes of learning and hence overlook this advantage.[47]

The New Zealand–born Communist and writer Rewi Alley lived in China from 1927 until his death in 1987. In 1937, during the Japanese invasion, he initiated and organized the *Gong He* (Gung Ho) movement for industrial cooperative factories in both Nationalist and Communist areas of unoccupied China. By 1942 his movement had set up about two thousand worker cooperatives. They helped to provide the Nationalist and Communist zones with the manufactured goods needed to sustain their territory economically and to fight the Japanese army. Alley was later honoured by Mao for his efforts in support of the Chinese people. But when Mao gained power in 1949, and in accord with Marxist dogma, all the cooperatives that he had helped to build and inspire were nationalized or closed down.[48]

MARXISM'S WRONG TURNINGS: SUMMARY AND CONCLUSION

While the 'utopian socialists' had called upon science to help design their future society, Marxism adopted science for the alternative aim of explaining how the development of capitalism would lead 'inevitably' to socialism. Science was alleged to reveal the progressive driving forces of history, to which all enlightened humanity should submit. Hence science was used to bypass any discussion of desirability or morality. Marxists described people who placed ethical considerations above the science of history as 'reactionary'.

Apart from a few meagre sketches, Marxists abandoned attempts to explain how the future socialist society would work. This was an irresponsible and disastrous omission. Marx and Engels simply assumed that comprehensive common ownership and planning were possible on a national scale, without any consideration of how such a system would work and how problems of large-scale planning and individual incentivization would be resolved.

Previously, very few utopian thinkers had proposed nationwide common ownership. Instead they built on small-scale, rural experiences of common ownership or community management. Such schemes can work because they rely on close familiarity and frequent face-to-face contact. Hence they can overcome the $1/n$ problem. Ignoring this crucial question of individual incentives, Marx and Engels simply assumed that there was no major problem in scaling up wholesale common ownership to national dimensions.

Marxism described how capitalism enlarged and brought together the working class, which was then expected to overthrow capitalism. Unfortunately, the constitution of social classes depends on legal and other institutions. Social formations such as capitalism and socialism cannot be categorized simply by determining which class is in power, because social classes themselves are constituted in terms of prior legal and other rules.

Marxists claim that the proletariat is the 'universal class'; this means that it is the class whose particular interests are identical to the general interests of society. While stressing that the working class must emancipate itself, they also argued that the working class may not always be aware of its true interests and historic role. In these circumstances it was the job of Marxists to tell the workers about these things.

Marxism's supreme focus on class struggle treats other important advances as secondary to this dominant narrative. Take slavery. Its abolition in the British Empire in 1833 and in the United States in 1865 conceded a major part of the population their legal rights. Of course, Marx welcomed the abolition of slavery. But generally he saw abolition as part of the general struggle of the working class rather than the installation of important universal rights.[49]

Marx commendably observed that women's position in society was a measure of development of society as a whole. But he wrote relatively little on the emancipation of women. Marx and Engels claimed that women could not be emancipated without the abolition of private property, and they focused principally on the class struggle. Hence the UK Married Women's Property Acts of 1870 and 1882, which made married women legal persons with the right to own property as individuals, were underestimated by Marxists.

While Marxists were involved in the struggle for female suffrage, it was depicted as a matter of 'bourgeois' right, secondary to the class struggle between employees of both genders and their bosses. As the German Marxist Rosa Luxemburg wrote, the 'struggle for the political equality of women is only one expression and one part of the general liberation struggle of the proletariat'.[50]

Of course, for Marxists, the emancipation of slaves and the enfranchisement of women were positive events. But they matter 'only' insofar as they can be fitted into the dominant narrative of workers against capitalists. Everything worth considering is forced into the schema of class struggle. Battles over political or legal rights are thus subservient.

The dominant Marxist historical picture of rising and falling social classes meant that socialists did not have to think about how their proposed future would work. This was part of its appeal. It pointed to the growth of the proletariat and proclaimed it as the agent of socialist revolution. The tricky problem of explaining in messy detail how socialism could work in complex, large-scale societies could be postponed and addressed later when the working class had 'emancipated itself'. It was part of its historic destiny, and who could argue with destiny?

This left a gaping hole in the Marxist argument. Theoretical debates over the feasibility of socialism have shown convincingly that such a system—where most private property and trade are abolished—would face huge problems and it would slide toward totalitarianism. Twentieth-century experiences have amply confirmed these arguments.

With its wholesale abolition of non-state property and markets, Marxism blocked the road toward an alternative collectivist system involving worker cooperatives trading on markets. Marxism not only failed; it also ruled out more viable alternatives to capitalism.

CHAPTER 6

Down the Slippery Slope
to Totalitarianism

My suspicion is that this was both Marx's anticipation of perfect unity of mankind
and his mythology of the historically privileged proletarian consciousness which were
responsible for his theory being eventually turned into an ideology of the totalitarian
movement: not because he conceived of it in such terms, but because its basic values
could hardly be materialized otherwise.

Leszek Kolakowski, 'Marxist Roots of Stalinism' (1977)

This chapter continues the discussion of Marxism. Marxists advocate the rule
of a majority class over another, where the minority class is deprived of its
property and other liberties. Marxism's notion of proletarian rule entailed the
suppression of rights for other social classes. This abandons the principle of
universal human rights, as established by the French revolutionary *Left*. It
paves the way for totalitarian rule, where accusations such as being 'bourgeois'
or a 'counter-revolutionary' serve as a pretext for punishment. In practice this
means that human rights are lost for the proletariat as well.

In any large-scale society, direct popular rule is impossible and some kind of
leadership or elite is necessary. Consequently, institutional checks and balances
are essential to avoid abuse of power. Because Marxists focus on the myth of
class rule, where a social class can somehow exercise power as a whole, they
have neglected the importance of checks, balances and separations of power.

Consequently, for the above reasons, Marxist regimes have dismal records
in terms of human rights and the rule of law. Contrary to Marxist apologists,
this shortfall does not result from particular circumstances. Instead it flows
from the nature of Marxism itself.

CLASS RULE AND INDIVIDUAL RIGHTS

Marxists regard legal and individual rights under capitalism as expressing
'nothing more than the idealized kingdom of the bourgeoisie'. Their normative

arguments in favour of socialism are not based on any alleged rights. Instead, socialism is seen as historic destiny. Marx tried to show that crises within capitalism are recurrent and inevitable, and that capitalism digs its own grave by enlarging and empowering the working class. This, as Marx and Engels put it, was the trajectory of history 'going on under our very eyes'.[1]

Marx saw socialism as the class destiny of the proletariat, who by overthrowing capitalism would emancipate humankind from inequality and exploitation. Socialism was not validated by an appeal to justice or rights. Instead it was grounded on 'material' and 'economic' developments within capitalism that were leading to growing internal crises and the rise of the proletariat.

His 1843 essay 'On the Jewish Question' was one of the first tracts where Marx criticized the general notion of rights and began to call for the abolition of private property. For Marx, liberal rights are premised on the notion that each of us needs protection from others. Hence liberal rights are rights of separation concerning freedom from interference. Marx rightly retorted that our full freedom and development must depend on cooperation with others. He correctly pointed out that human flourishing and freedom depend on our ongoing relations with other people.[2]

But Marx's attempted counter-argument does not nullify individual rights and freedoms. While Marx was right in arguing that human development always depends on others, he overlooked the possibility that human relationships can be despotic as well as fulfilling. As well as being helpful and cooperative, other people can bully, repress, inhibit and make mistakes. We depend on others, but not on all their possible behaviours. For this reason individuals need, and have rights to, autonomy and protection, even if they will always depend on others for their personal fulfilment. No one can be free if these rights are removed.

Free cooperation can be virtuous and fulfilling; forced cooperation is a despotic nightmare. Marxists shunned the conditions for freedom and opened the door for totalitarianism.

Marx rejected appeals to rights or justice. In his 1875 'Critique of the Gotha Programme' he attacked socialists who argued for a 'fair' distribution of wages, and more generally he condemned talk about rights and justice as 'ideological, legal and other humbug so common among the democrats and the French socialists'. In a letter of 1877, Marx complained: 'In Germany a corrupt spirit is asserting itself in our party'. This alleged 'corruption' had nothing to do with money or greed. Instead it was manifest among 'immature undergraduates and over-wise graduates who want to give socialism a "higher idealistic" orientation'. Instead of the 'scientific' and 'materialistic basis' of socialism revealed by

Marx, these German socialists wanted to substitute 'a modern mythology with its goddesses of Justice, Freedom, Equality and *Fraternité*'.[3]

For Marx and Engels, matters of law, rights, justice, morality and religion were an ideological—and often illusory—component of the social superstructure. The grounding of all political action was neither justice nor morality, but the 'material forces of production' within the vaguely defined 'economic' base. In their economics, Marx and Engels treated individuals as robots maximizing their material consumption, unmotivated by matters of justice or morality.[4]

Marx and Engels bypassed the issues of morality and justice by focusing on the real social forces allegedly leading to socialism. But neither the driving forces of history nor the supposed destiny of a social class make this socialist future just, or morally right. Even if Marx's economic analysis of capitalism was broadly valid and the working class was getting more agglomerated and powerful, this would not itself show that socialism was morally superior to capitalism by any standards of ethics or justice. Analysis of reality is insufficient for ethical judgments.

Destiny does not imply justice. If a horse is destined to win a race it does not mean that this is a just or moral outcome. When he pulled the sword out of the stone, the young Arthur may have shown that he was destined to become King, but this does not mean that he had the moral right to rule Britain. Equally, saying that the proletariat is destined to overthrow the bourgeoisie does not mean that its future empowerment will be morally superior to rule by the bourgeoisie.

The difference between ethics and analysis is illustrated by the views of the great economist Joseph Schumpeter. He was strongly influenced by Marxism. He thought that socialism was likely to replace capitalism. He (wrongly) believed that mainstream economists such as Oskar Lange (who had used mainstream general equilibrium theory to try to show that socialism was feasible) had won their debate with Ludwig von Mises and Friedrich Hayek. But politically and morally, Schumpeter preferred capitalism: he was a conservative and an anti-socialist. His analytical belief in the feasibility and likelihood of socialism did not logically require him to be a socialist.[5]

For Marxists, all moral sentimentality must surrender to the momentum of history and to the findings of Marxist political economy. Marx and Engels argued that appeals to morality would not be required in their future utopia: 'communism abolishes all religion and all morality, instead of constituting them on a new basis'. They saw all means as justified to serve that end. By describing important human rights as 'bourgeois', and by regarding any moral discussion of rights or justice as corrupting and diversionary, Marxism paved the way for totalitarianism.[6]

It is a complex and uncertain world; all individuals are fallible. Even under communism, people would make mistakes. They can make decisions that are ethically or practically flawed. This applies to parties that are struggling to further the perceived interests of the working class. All individuals, leaders, organizations and political parties are fallible. For this reason, a variety of views must be sustained: such diversity serves as a vital source of varied perspectives and different diagnoses. There is also a need for open discussion, so that new information can be acted upon, and mistakes can be identified and rectified.

To make these measures real, people need rights, including the right to appeal against decisions and generally to express their own views. If they have no acknowledged rights, which are protected institutionally by law, then they are vulnerable. By shunning all discourse on rights in favour of the rhetoric of proletarian destiny, Marxism is always on the slippery slope toward totalitarianism.

THE MYTH OF CLASS RULE AND THE REALITY OF PARTY DICTATORSHIP

Marxists define the working class (or proletariat) as those people who live primarily through wages or salaries, obtained from contracts of employment with an employer. Such employees have become the majority, at least in developed capitalist countries. So does Marxism herald an era of democratic rule by the majority? Unfortunately not.

For Marxists, rule by a social class meant rule in the supposed interests of that class, and not by its democratic vote, unless that class was deemed to be sufficiently aware of its interests. As noted previously, Marx and Engels dismissed what the proletariat '*regards* as its aim'. Marxists see themselves as entitled to decide what is in the interests of the proletariat, even if the proletariat itself expresses a different aim.[7]

A Marxist party must struggle against elements of 'false consciousness' among the proletariat, as well as against other social classes. Opponents are seen as duped by bourgeois ideology, even if they are not bourgeois themselves. By this logic, a Marxist party could override democratic expressions of opinion with the claim that it was acting in the interests of the majority, even when that majority thought differently.[8]

A more cautious strategy would be for a Marxist party to attempt first to bring around the majority of the proletariat to their point of view. It would root itself in working-class communities and engage in struggles for better wages and working conditions, while trying to educate the workers about socialism and their alleged true interests. This type of strategy was attempted in several countries in Europe, most notably in several large cities in Germany and Austria, from 1880 to 1933. But it still requires a Marxist party to persuade the workers of their interests and historic destiny, and it takes little account of the possibility that any Marxist view could be mistaken.

All political action requires organization. Marxist organizations have to decide on policies that allegedly align with proletarian interests. Another key problem is to determine how policy decisions are to be executed, administered and monitored. All substantial organizations have to process vast amounts of information, to make decisions and to implement them. For Marxists, these difficulties were obvious by the 1890s, when mass Marxist parties had become well-established in Germany and had sprung up in other countries in Europe.

Given these problems, Max Weber argued that bureaucracy was an unavoidable outcome in large-scale organizations and politico-economic systems. The general need for bureaucratic structures and processes is not obviated by higher levels of education or improved means of communication. Improved education or communications are likely to increase information inputs and to enlarge rather than diminish bureaucratization.[9]

Robert Michels was a student of Weber and a follower of Werner Sombart, another German historical school economist. Michels argued persuasively that full democratic control was impossible in large-scale, complex organizations. For individuals to coordinate and act together, sizeable organizations need leaders, who then delegate administrative tasks to complex bureaucracies. Leaders and bureaucrats manage information flows between members of the organization. They develop skills, and acquire expertise and knowledge, that are peculiar to their roles. Knowledge is specialized and the management of information has unavoidably to be selective. It is impossible for everyone to become a specialist in more than a few areas, or to take account of every piece of information in the organization. Inevitably, this leads to oligarchy, with some power shifting away from individuals at the base.[10]

Michels underlined the oligarchic distribution of knowledge and power in large, complex organizations. Because of localized knowledge, specialisms, complexities and massive amounts of information, a direct democracy, where everyone votes on everything, is not viable. It is impossible to involve everyone in every significant decision. Michels argued in detail that 'the principle cause of oligarchy in the democratic parties is to be found in the technical indispensability of leadership'.[11]

Some form of representative democracy is possible in times of stability, with elected leaders who are held to account by regular meetings. But there still would be leaders with greater power than their followers.

But revolutions are times of urgency, with little time to gather information or debate details. They do not permit the niceties of election or representative democracy. The victory of the proletariat is likely to mean the victory of its self-declared and unelected leadership. This has been the way of all Marxist insurrections, in Russia, China, Cuba and elsewhere.

This importance of party leadership was acknowledged by Marx and Engels in the *Communist Manifesto*, when they wrote of the Communist Party being 'the most advanced and resolute section of the working-class parties of every country, that section which pushes forward all others; on the other hand, theoretically, they have over the great mass of the proletariat the advantage of clearly understanding the lines of march, the conditions, and the ultimate general results of the proletarian movement'.[12]

In his 1902 pamphlet *What Is to Be Done?* Lenin proposed that a revolutionary vanguard party should lead the political struggle because it was the only way that the proletariat could successfully achieve a revolution.

In his 1917 booklet *The State and Revolution*, Lenin saw 'the dictatorship of the proletariat' as 'the organisation of the vanguard of the oppressed as the ruling class for the purpose of crushing the oppressors'. But instead as seeing rule by the 'vanguard' as a perhaps temporary limitation of democracy, he argued the opposite. It meant 'an immense expansion of democracy, which for the first time becomes democracy for the poor, democracy for the people, and not democracy for the money-bags'. Note the qualification: this 'democracy' was not for all. It meant the 'suppression by force, i.e. exclusion from democracy, of the exploiters and oppressors of the people'.[13]

Lenin's 1917 account suffers from a number of major problems. He overlooked the practical problems of an 'immense expansion of democracy' in a large-scale, complex, modern, politico-economic system. Then he upheld that the victory of the working class would bring more democracy for the majority, but none for the rich. By making democracy a non-universal, class privilege and by suppressing a minority 'by force', universal suffrage and universal human rights were abandoned.

Lenin thus compromised democracy and rights for everyone. Any expressed point of view could be deemed 'bourgeois' and suppressed. Consequently, as Anthony Polan put it: 'What the Bolsheviks could not do was to accept the characterization of any political difference as genuine, i.e. an opinion which a person or group had a right to hold and negotiate over as an equal partner in the process of will-formation'. This rendered any democracy highly fragile. Once democratic rights cease to be universal, then they can more readily be made insignificant. This was rapidly demonstrated in practice after 1917.[14]

A further problem was the planned democratic institutions themselves. A Bolshevik revolutionary slogan was: 'All power to the soviets!' Lenin proposed the dissolution of parliament and the transfer of power to the soviets—or workers' councils—which had first arisen in Russia in the 1905 Revolution. As well as from the capitalists, this measure would clearly remove the right to vote from those in workplaces without soviets, including women working solely in the home and self-employed workers. (By Marx's definition, the self-employed are not capitalists because they do not employ labour. They are workers, but not wage labourers.) Even if these groups were given some representation in factory-based workers' councils, they would not be as closely involved as other workers. Marx proposed severe discrimination against the bourgeoisie. Lenin went further, not only to disenfranchise that class, but to deny power to a large numbers of workers, including housewives.[15]

Within Marxism, are there democratic alternatives to Leninism? In her 1918 booklet on *The Russian Revolution*, the German Marxist Rosa Luxemburg warned that the 'dictatorship of the proletariat' should not undermine democracy:

> But this dictatorship [of the proletariat] consists in the *manner of applying democracy*, not in its *elimination*, but in energetic, resolute attacks upon the well-entrenched rights and economic relationships of bourgeois society, without which a socialist transformation cannot be accomplished. But this dictatorship must be the work of the *class* and not of a little leading minority in the name of the class—that is, it must proceed step by step out of the active participation of the masses; it must be under their direct influence, subjected to the control of complete public activity; it must arise out of the growing political training of the mass of the people.[16]

Superficially this looks like a defence of democracy. But what Luxemburg proposed is both undesirable and unfeasible. Like Lenin, she endorsed unrestricted and 'resolute attacks upon the well-entrenched rights . . . of bourgeois society'. The clear danger would be that everyone's rights would be lost, including the right to own and trade property. Luxemburg made no attempt to qualify this phrase or to underline those important rights—such as freedom of assembly and the right to vote—that need to be resolutely protected.

Luxemburg argued for the 'active participation of the masses' that would place the leadership 'under their direct influence, subjected to the control of complete public activity'. But it is implausible to place the leadership under continuous and complete democratic control. She overlooked the complexities of modern, large-scale society and the sheer impossibility of having mass meetings or referendums on every important decision. Even with modern computer technology, it would be impossible to have everyone voting meaningfully on anything more than a fraction of the significant issues. Crucial, detailed, expert knowledge is always going to be concentrated in the hands of some minority.

Luxemburg is sometimes depicted as providing a more democratic Marxist alternative to Leninism. But in truth her proposals are just as unprotective of human rights and just as unfeasible in practical terms. Her unworkable plans for ultra-democracy would both raise and disappoint expectations, leading to the impatience of all and a likely authoritarian reaction.

In sum, the Marxist dogma of the dictatorship of the proletariat faces unavoidable problems that impel it toward totalitarianism rather than democracy. The Marxist notion of class domination removes rights from major segments of the population. Gone is the original *Left* defence of universal rights. Removing rights from a segment of the population—whether it is to suppress a social class, an ethnic group or followers of a particular religion—undermines universal rights and liberties that apply to everyone.

The idea of the proletariat having class interests and a historic destiny, of which it is not necessarily aware, provides a rationale for a party to substitute for that class, claiming to act in its interests. It would act to suppress its opponents. But without countervailing power and open debate, any organizational monopoly slides toward totalitarianism. Dissent from the party line can be suppressed by claims that the dissenters are undermining the revolution. Without political checks and balances, such dissenters have no effective legal protection. The removal of rights from the bourgeoisie or their agents provides the precedent and excuse for their widespread suppression.

RIGHTS AND THE RULE OF LAW

Laws get in the way of revolutionary struggle. Hence, along with their dilution of the notion of rights, Lenin and others proposed that all laws should be abolished. Writing in 1918, Lenin described the 'dictatorship of the proletariat' as 'rule based directly upon force and unrestricted by any laws. The revolutionary dictatorship of the proletariat is rule won and maintained by the use of violence by the proletariat against the bourgeoisie, rule that is unrestricted by any laws'.[17]

Despite these words, the young Soviet Union *did* establish a legal system and a constitution, in which some rights were codified. But these rights were depicted explicitly as granted by the state, rather than being inalienable. If rights draw their legitimacy solely from the state, then the state may legitimately withdraw those rights.

Furthermore, the declared rights were not universal. The 1918 Soviet constitution distinguished between the rights of the workers and the rights of others. The state also announced that it 'deprives all individuals and groups of rights which could be utilized by them to the detriment of the socialist revolution'. A major problem here was that the criteria used to decide what was detrimental were unspecified, opening the door to arbitrary repression by the authorities. This is exactly what happened.[18]

Under such a system, it is inevitable that law becomes an instrument of politics and government, instead of helping to keep government in check. Simple acts, such as the buying and selling of small items of property, can be deemed 'detrimental to socialism' or 'counter-revolutionary'. In the Soviet Union such offences were punishable by death. Instead of a means of defending rights, the law became an instrument of oppression by the Communist Party. Stalin's collectivization of agriculture in 1928–1931, involving the forced deportations or deaths of millions of peasants, was carried out formally according to the letter of Soviet law.

Of course, law has been abused as an instrument of politics in capitalist countries as well. But a wider distribution of power and ownership—which is feasible under capitalism but not under Soviet-style socialism—makes possible the development of countervailing power, which is essential to keep such abuses in check and to help defend the legal system from political manipulation. These countervailing mechanisms are much less effective when most property and economic power is concentrated in the hands of the state.

Concerning law, Mao's China was even worse than the Soviet Union. When Mao was in power, little effort was made to develop a legal system. Mao preferred that the Communist Party should rule without any legal restriction. Mao died in 1976 and economic reform began in 1978. China then began to develop a new system of law, which was necessary as part of the foundation of its emerging market economy. But despite many important achievements in this direction, the enforcement of declared rights and other elements of the constitution are often in practice subject to the discretion of the Communist Party.

Article 33 of the Constitution of the People's Republic of China (adopted in 1982 and revised in 2004) declares that all 'citizens of the People's Republic of China are equal before the law'. But, in clear violation of this principle, China still operates the *hukou* system in which roughly half of the population is endowed with lesser rights. Redolent of residence permits in ancient China, the modern version of this *hukou* system was established in 1958 during the development of the command economy, primarily to control the movement of labour between rural and urban areas and secure food supplies in a planned economy. It divides the Chinese population into two classes according to registration at birth. According to the *hukou* system, every Chinese citizen has a registered principal residence and a registered status as a rural or urban citizen. Urban and rural citizens have different rights and entitlements. In China today, urban registrants are entitled to the better-paid jobs, education, housing and healthcare, some of which are unavailable to those with rural registration.[19]

Several relaxations of the *hukou* system have been introduced since 1980. Nevertheless, the division of the population into two groups, with an unequal allocation of basic rights, still remains. In a country that is rapidly modernizing and enjoying much greater freedom than it did before 1978, the *hukou* system is an inegalitarian relic of both imperial and Maoist China.

The development of rights and freedoms in China will require a more consistent and egalitarian system of law, which crucially must operate with some autonomy from the Communist Party.

The 'socialist' experiments in Russia and China did not simply abolish private property rights. By regarding law as a cynical political instrument of a ruling class, rather than a potential safeguard of human rights, they undermined the very notion of the rule of law, and overturned personal rights and civil liberties. The human cost was massive.[20]

There were some achievements in Russia and China under Communist rule. Russia was lifted out of backwardness and became a more developed country, capable of defending itself against Nazism. Mao unified China and brought education to its masses for the first time. But fuller assessments should consider what a progressive, non-Bolshevik government might have achieved in Russia after 1917 and what comparative progress a reforming Nationalist government might have made in China from 1949 to 1978.[21]

After 1978, the Chinese Communist Party abandoned Soviet-style collectivism and introduced private enterprise. Consequently, hundreds of millions were lifted out of poverty. But these gains were made after dropping wholesale collectivization, and when private enterprise and markets were promoted.

Marxists rightly point out that rights such as freedom of expression or assembly have less relative significance when people are starving or lacking in other basic necessities. The most fundamental rights include the right to a livelihood: destitution denies such rights. Legal rights may be unenforceable when access to a lawyer is unaffordable. But these facts do not imply that other legal and human rights are unimportant or can be ignored. The deaths of millions under Communism testify to their importance.

CONCLUSION: THE SEEDS OF TOTALITARIANISM AND THE CLIMATE OF LIBERTY

The origins of totalitarianism in Marxism are not simply a result of Marx's promotion of the 'dictatorship of the proletariat'. They lie in the view that one class has the destiny to triumph over others, and the belief that this justifies the removal of basic rights—including freedom of expression and the right to vote—from other social classes.

Some hierarchical mechanism of representation and decision-making is unavoidable in any complex, large-scale society. Specialization and hierarchy are necessary to deal with complexity. But all hierarchies contain the seed of oligarchy. Unless such an oligarchy is checked by enforceable rights and countervailing powers, dictatorship is the likely outcome.

Marxists presume to know the interests of the proletariat. But explicit proletarian opinion is suspect: the people have been duped by consumerism and have acquired capitalist habits. Marxism decrees that the proletariat has the warrant and historical destiny to rule over other classes, but it cannot be trusted to do so.

Class war means the suppression of universal human rights and opens the door for totalitarianism. Non-Marxists on the Left cannot simply brush this conclusion aside. Marxism has diverted the entire social democratic Left.[22] This was visible after the end of the Cold War in 1991. Not only did Soviet-style regimes collapse: social democratic parties everywhere lost their way. Many had been fellow travellers with Marxism and sentimentalists for large-scale, bureaucratic collectivization.

In 1956 C. Anthony Crosland published *The Future of Socialism*: this began a slow reconciliation with markets, private enterprise and a mixed economy. In 1959 the (West) German Social Democratic Party abandoned the goal of widespread common ownership. In the same year, Hugh Gaitskell tried to get the British Labour Party to follow this lead, but met stiff resistance. The party did not ditch its Clause Four commitment to the complete 'common ownership of the means of production, distribution and exchange' until 1995.

Some social democrats see their primary role as to advance the interests of the working class, rather than to provide a vision of a viable and humane society for everyone. Hence the name 'Labour Party' remains as a burden on any social democratic party that wishes to broaden its appeal beyond its traditional working-class base, including to those millions that regard themselves as 'middle class'.

Some social democratic parties that have moved away from the old rhetoric of nationalization and class struggle have sought some mythical 'middle ground' in politics by embracing some of the values of their conservative and pro-austerity opponents. In the process they have sometimes downplayed the issue of inequality and the need for redistributive remedies. Some social democratic governments—such as the New Labour government of Tony Blair in the UK—have a blemished record on civil liberties, curtailing some freedoms of speech and assembly at home, as well as exhibiting some complicity in the use of torture abroad.

Social democracy must understand that a mixed economy with countervailing power is the necessary foundation of democracy and freedom. It must turn toward, rather that dismiss, radical liberalism. Marxists describe liberal ideas as 'petit-bourgeois'. But it is precisely those 'petit-bourgeois' liberties and aspirations that should be at the centre of a revived social democracy.

After the Left has ditched its class-war rhetoric and its prejudices against private property, trade and markets, it should be the foremost champion of Enlightenment values, including the protection of the individual from oppression, whether it is from abuses of state or corporate power. This radical liberalism has to be fused with a foremost concern to reduce extreme inequalities of income and wealth, as well as establish universal care for the sick and needy.

This is not to argue for a free-market policy where the state retreats from the economy and purportedly leaves everything to the market. Because the state plays an indispensable role in constituting institutions such as property, markets, corporations and money, it is impossible for the state to retreat from its constitutive functions. Successful modern economies retain a vital strategic role for the state.[23]

But we have also to be aware of the omnipresent dangers of excessive bureaucracy and state corruption. Many politicians and bureaucrats genuinely want to serve the public. But the temptations of power are always great. Also, as shown in the next chapter, intelligent and caring people can become blind to injustice or evil through their adoption of a deluding ideology. It is precisely because the state is indispensable, and the state has to be monitored and kept in check, that Enlightenment rights and liberties are of renewed importance.

APPENDIX: BLAIRISM AS MARXISM TURNED UPSIDE DOWN

In 1994 Tony Blair was elected as leader of the Labour Party in the UK. He went on to win three general elections in 1997, 2001 and 2005. His decision to join the United States in the 2003 invasion of Iraq was highly controversial, but he was a highly effective and charismatic leader and brought about several important reforms, including devolution and the national minimum wage. Spending on health and education increased. For a while, Blair's 'New Labour' or 'third way' politics was trumpeted as a modern way forward for the Left in other countries.

Blair admitted that his knowledge of Marxism was limited to reading Isaac Deutscher's monumental three-volume biography of Leon Trotsky. He also claimed to adhere to the Christian socialism of John Macmurray. The evidence suggests that these influences were relatively superficial. Macmurray was a classical socialist who argued that the state should 'assume control of the economic and financial activities of society', which was very far from Blair's own view.[24]

Abandoning the Labour Party's traditional Clause Four commitment to the common ownership of the means of production, Blair promoted 'social-ism', which now meant recognizing individuals as socially interdependent. It also signalled social justice, cohesion and the equal worth of each citizen, with equal opportunities.

In a short 1994 pamphlet, Blair laid out his credo. He emphasized a distinction between ethical socialism and Marxism, aligning himself with the former rather than the latter. But his account of the former was vague and flawed, leaving the latter unexplored. He claimed that the non-Marxist, ethical socialists of the past saw 'socialism' as 'defined by certain key values and beliefs' and not by common ownership. This claim is false.[25]

For so-called ethical socialists such as John Macmurray, R. H. Tawney, Beatrice Webb, Sidney Webb and G. D. H. Cole, it is clear from their rhetoric that their 'key values and beliefs' included a moral distaste for profit-making from private ownership of the means of production.

Blair wrongly suggested that 'ethical socialism' had been opposed to common ownership. On the contrary, its original devotion to this goal was no less than that of Marxism. Macmurray's Christian socialism involved common ownership. Cole proposed a 'guild socialism' under which much of the economy would be under common ownership. Cole's explicit aims were to overthrow capitalism and to replace it by collective ownership and democratic organization. Originally, at the time when Tawney was developing his ethical stance, he supported guild socialism. He wrote that the notions of 'absolute rights to property and to economic freedom' had 'been discredited'. But Tawney later became an advocate of a mixed economy.[26]

Tawney followed Owen and Marx to qualify the importance of individual rights. He wrote: 'The individual has no absolute rights; they are relative to the function which he performs in the community of which he is a member'. For Tawney, the rights were conditional on service performed in the interests of the community. We are all for serving the community, but who is to judge whether adequate service is performed, and thereby establish our entitlements? In this way, Tawney's abandonment of absolute, inalienable, individual rights opened the door for totalitarianism. Tawney's ethical socialism was itself deeply flawed and is symptomatic of common failure, from Owen to Blair, to give sufficient weight to individual rights.[27]

The relationship between means and ends is important. Marxism famously separates ends from means, claiming that 'the ends justify the means'. For Marxism, the moral evaluation of any means is simply in terms of the imagined ends. In ethics, *consequentialism* is the doctrine that means should be evaluated solely in terms of the ends they serve. Steven Lukes has forcefully criticized this 'extreme consequentialism' in Marxism. Part of the problem with consequentialism is that in a complex world we cannot be sure that specific means will lead to their assumed ends. Hence means must be placed under moral constraints as well.[28]

Blair argued that any emphasis on common ownership or nationalization confused means with ends. He argued that the ends of social harmony and social justice, for example, might be achieved by means other than common ownership.[29] Ironically, by separating means and ends so completely, Blair mirrored Marxism. Blair used a Marx-like separation of ends from means to abandon classical socialist ends.

But means and ends are rarely separable. In particular, if there is only one way to achieve a goal, then that means assumes the status of an end as well. The classical socialists believed that common ownership was the only way to reduce greed, inequality and social deprivation. Hence, for them, common ownership was an end as well as a means.

John Dewey pointed out that the pursuit of a goal is a learning process that can modify our ends. Furthermore, the use of particular means might modify our ends, as we discover unforeseen problems or benefits. Crucially, the end we uphold is a spur to action, hence also a means of energizing change. Dewey wrote: 'there is no end which is not in turn a means'.[30]

In a free society, and within important limits, people must be given the means to reach their own ends. Accordingly, the legal and constitutional means of pursuing individual satisfaction might also become ends. This is particularly the case for classical liberalism, which professes a set of institutions that may best serve the pursuit of individual ends, whatever they may be. Within constraints, the individual is left to choose. An important debate within liberalism concerns what those limits should be.

Even the revised Clause Four of the Labour Party Constitution, which was adopted under Blair in 1995, fails in its attempt to disentangle ends from means. It calls for 'the means to realise our true potential' in the same sentence as the end of 'a community in which power, wealth and opportunity are in the hands of the many not the few'. Then this clause goes on to refer to both of these terms as 'ends'. In practice, all political parties propose means as well as ends.

Blair adopted another dichotomy from Marxism. This is the separation of the sphere of 'values and beliefs' from economic structures and patterns of ownership. This is redolent of Marx's distinction between 'superstructure' and 'economic base'. But Blair reversed their importance: for him 'values and beliefs' assumed primacy. Adopting the same dichotomy, Marxism was turned upside down.

The dichotomy is false. All economic activity involves beliefs, evaluations, expectations and value-laden motivations. Values and beliefs are intrinsic to the economy. The economy is not a machine that can be considered separately from the knowledge, beliefs and expectations of the human agents within it.

This emphasis on 'values and beliefs' over institutional structures allowed Blair to privatize some public services, including parts of the National Health Service. His claim was that the same esteemed values could endure within any system of ownership. This argument aligned Blair's Labour Party with other social democratic parties who were also pursing privatization.

But changes to institutional structures affect the habits and beliefs of those involved. Extending the scope for contracts and markets means—rightly or wrongly—that pecuniary and profit-orientated values can become more pervasive, unless checks are put in place.

Generally, Blair's 'third way' lacks robust theoretical underpinnings. It is not a well-articulated or coherent alternative. Relying on 'values and beliefs', without much notion of the desired politico-economic institutions, makes a political party vulnerable to focus groups, ideological fashions and lobbyist incursions.

Blair was absolutely right to stress that individuals are socially interdependent, and to advocate social justice, cohesion and equal opportunity. But such arguments pointed to versions of social liberalism, including the radical thought of Thomas Paine, Thomas H. Green, John A. Hobson and John Dewey. In Britain it was Liberals such as David Lloyd George that laid the foundations of its welfare state. President Franklin D. Roosevelt consolidated the American liberal tradition.

But Labour's nostalgic devotion to the word *socialism* was too strong. Blair wrote of *social-ism*, but with or without the hyphen it had already become a zombie term—a mere badge of identity. Enduring a slow death from the 1950s, the word was re-animated and hyphenated by Blair, using a false history of its meaning.

Blair was an outstanding politician, but when he stepped down from office in 2007 he left an ideological as well as a charismatic vacuum. Labour retained the term *socialism*, but added further distortions to its meaning. This theoretical, ideological and personal void explains why the Labour Party could choose the retro-Marxist Jeremy Corbyn as its leader in 2015. He seized the enduring s-word and tried to give it new life. A version of semi-Marxist, Bennite socialism, combined with a quasi-Leninist foreign policy, was back on the agenda.

CHAPTER 7

Keeping *Left*:
In Defence of Democracy
and Individual Rights

It seems to me that the questions we urgently need to ask ourselves are these: is totalitarianism the only means of eliminating capitalism? If so, and if . . . we abhor totalitarianism,
can we continue to call ourselves anti-capitalists? If there is no humane and democratic
answer to the question of what a world without capitalism would look like, then should
we not abandon the pursuit of unicorns, and concentrate on capturing and taming the
beast whose den we already inhabit?

George Monbiot, 'Rattling the Bars' (2003)

After the rise of Marxism in the twentieth century, other socialists abandoned
the idea of universal human rights. This was one of the greatest tragedies in
the history of the Left. Through its association with Marxist regimes, the Left
became linked with the deaths of millions, dwarfing the tragedy of the French
revolutionary Terror of 1793-1794. For some, democracy became a luxury
rather than an ideal. When the Left was in power, elections could stand in the
way of 'getting things done'. Leftists were persuaded that noble ends justified
ruthless means.

Events pushed them into the arms of expediency. In the dangerously polar-
izing world of the 1930s, many saw Soviet Communism as a bulwark against
rising fascism in Europe. In the midst of the Great Depression, capitalism
seemed to be in its death throes. The liberal middle ground looked insecure.
It seemed that everyone had to take to extremes: it was either fascism or Communism.

Prominent intellectuals saw Joseph Stalin's Soviet Union as a beacon of
progress. American fans of Stalin included the journalist Walter Duranty and
the singer Paul Robeson. In Britain they included the political thinkers Sidney
and Beatrice Webb; the famous writers H. G. Wells, George Bernard Shaw and
Aldous Huxley; and the scientists John D. Bernal and Julian Huxley.

It is alleged (but unconfirmed by evidence) that Lenin described such sympathizers from the West as 'useful idiots'. They were not a homogeneous group. Some later recanted, claiming that they were not fully aware of what was going on. Others were more enduring in their enthusiasm.

The socialist novelist H. G. Wells wrote in 1932 that despite being 'ruled by a permanent Terror, Russia nevertheless upholds the tattered banner of World-collectivity and remains something splendid and hopeful in the spectacle of mankind'. But thereafter Wells became more critical of Stalin's regime.[1]

A more notorious Soviet sympathizer was the Irish writer and Fabian socialist George Bernard Shaw. After visiting the Soviet Union in 1931 and meeting Stalin, Shaw became a strong supporter of the regime. He declared that Russia was becoming 'a Fabian society'. This was at a time of mass famine and forced collectivization. In the preface to his 1933 play *On the Rocks*, he defended the Russian secret police's 'liquidation' of detainees who could not give satisfactory answers to queries about 'pulling your weight in the social boat' or 'giving more trouble than you are worth' or had not 'earned the privilege of living in a civilized community'. In a letter published in the *Manchester Guardian* in 1933, Shaw and others dismissed reports of famine in the Soviet Union as 'slander' resulting from a 'lie campaign' against the 'Workers Republic of Russia'. In fact, from 1932 to 1933, about six to eight million people died there from hunger. Shaw subsequently attempted to justify the extermination of the Russian peasantry: 'For a Communist Utopia we need a population of Utopians. Peasants will not do'. In 1936 Shaw defended Stalin's purges and mass executions. In 1948 he declared that Stalin was 'a first rate Fabian'.[2]

Leading Fabians Sidney and Beatrice Webb were highly influential in the British Labour Party and they founded the London School of Economics in 1895. In 1932 they made a three-week visit to the Soviet Union. Their generally favourable impressions were reported in 1935 in their massive two-volume study, *Soviet Communism: A New Civilisation?* In the 1937 edition the question mark was removed from the title. Their assessments of the Soviet Union were more cautious than those of Shaw, but they also denied the existence of a famine in the Ukraine in 1932–1933 and they opined that the liquidation of rich peasants (*kulaks*) may have been necessary to collectivize agriculture and increase its productivity. Their book received favourable reviews from Left writers and it played a role in nurturing sympathy in the Labour Party for the Soviet Union, at least until the onset of the Cold War in 1948.[3]

During the emergency of the Second World War, even more extreme views emerged. G. D. H. Cole is often depicted as a 'democratic', 'decentralist' or even 'libertarian' socialist. But in 1941 Cole wrote:

I would much sooner see the Soviet Union, even with its policy unchanged, dominant over all Europe, including Great Britain, than see an attempt to restore the pre-war States to their futile and uncreative independence and their petty economic nationalism under capitalist domination. Better be ruled by Stalin than by the destructive and monopolistic cliques which dominate Western capitalism. Nay more: much better to be ruled by Stalin than by a pack of half-hearted and half-witted Social Democrats who do not believe in Socialism.[4]

Communism achieved another victory when Mao Zedong came to power in 1949. Professor Joan Robinson was a leading Cambridge economist, influenced by both Marx and John Maynard Keynes. An enthusiastic supporter of Mao, she visited China several times. Despite this first-hand experience, she failed to acknowledge that Mao's Great Leap Forward in 1958–1961 had been an economic disaster: it led to catastrophic famine and about forty million deaths. In defiance she wrote: 'the Great Leap [Forward] was not a failure after all, but the Rightists were reluctant to admit it'.[5]

In the 1960s she lauded the Cultural Revolution, approving of attempts by Mao and the Red Guards to root out 'capitalist roaders' within Chinese society. She praised Mao's 'moderate and humane' intentions. In fact, the Cultural Revolution led to at least half a million and perhaps as many as two million deaths. Violent struggles ensued across the country and paralyzed the economy for years. Many more millions of people were persecuted at whim by the Red Guards: they suffered public humiliation, arbitrary imprisonment, torture or execution. Countless more died when the army tried to re-establish order. In China's totalitarian system they had no refuge or legal protection.[6]

As late as 1973 Robinson opposed 'market socialism' and advocated a centrally planned economy. She wrote of the 'success of the Chinese economy in reducing the appeal of the money motive'. After extolling the virtues of Mao's system, she reported that 'Chinese patriotism and socialist ideology are pulling together'. But a few years later, shortly after Mao's death in 1976, the country overturned many of the policies that Robinson had celebrated in her writings.[7]

In 1964 Robinson visited Communist North Korea and extolled the 'Korean miracle' in its economy. Its claimed success was attributed to public ownership and central planning. But, within fifteen years, capitalist South Korea was surging ahead of its Northern neighbour. By the 1990s North Korea was experiencing mass famines. By 2010, GDP per capita in the South was about seventeen times greater than in the North.[8]

The historian Edward P. Thompson left the British Communist Party after the 1956 Hungarian Uprising and subsequently played a major part in the formation of the *New Left Review*. But as late as 1973 he had sufficient residual sentimentalism for the Soviet Union to write of the 'times when [Soviet] communism has shown *a most human face*, between 1917 and the early 1920s, and again from the battle of Stalingrad to 1946'.

Leszek Kolakowski's response to these rose-tinted words was devastating. He asked what Thompson might have meant by the 'human face' of the Soviet Union during these years. Did it mean the 'attempt to rule the entire economy by police and army, resulting in mass hunger with uncountable victims, in several hundred peasants' revolts, all drowned in blood'?

> Or do you mean the armed invasion of seven non-Russian countries which had formed their independent governments . . . ? Or do you mean the dispersion by soldiers of the only democratically elected Parliament in Russian history . . . ? The suppression by violence of all political parties, including socialist ones, the abolition of the non-Bolshevik press and, above all, the replacement of law with the absolute power of the party and its police in killing, torturing and imprisoning anybody they wanted? . . . And what is the most human face in 1942–46? Do you mean the deportation of eight entire nationalities of the Soviet Union with hundreds of thousands of victims . . . ? Do you mean sending to concentration camps hundreds of thousands of Soviet prisoners of war handed over by the Allies?

Kolakowski searched for an explanation of Thompson's incredible description of these events as 'a most human face' of Communism. Perhaps this phrase is being used 'in a very Thompsonian sense which I do not grasp'? A commentator on Kolakowski's response wrote: 'no one who reads it will ever take E. P. Thompson seriously again'.[9]

Robinson and Thompson were not the only top-rank academics to be deluded by ideology. Consider the most important linguist of the twentieth century. Noam Chomsky loathed the American war in Vietnam. For him, to hide its own acts of oppression and mass murder, the West had duped the masses with its slick corporate propaganda. The West was fascism, with a fake mask of democracy.[10]

But when reports emerged that the Communists were also capable of mass atrocities, he suspected an American conspiracy to exaggerate and to draw attention away from their own crimes. Then the evidence emerged of the killing fields of the Khmer Rouge in 1975–1979. Chomsky accused the publishers of the evidence of 'extreme anti-Khmer Rouge distortions'. We now know that the Khmer Rouge obliterated about two million people—a quarter of the Cambodian population—in the pursuit of their Communist utopia. Chomsky's reputation as a political thinker has never recovered.

By an overwhelming majority, Jeremy Corbyn was elected as British Labour Party leader in 2015 and re-elected in 2016. He too is hostile to American foreign policy. In his foreword to a re-issue of John A. Hobson's classic work *Imperialism*, Corbyn compared the Soviet empire with the imperial practices of the West, coming to the conclusion that the latter were worse. Arguing that Soviet influence over its client states 'was always different' from Western colonialism, he pointed to Cuba to illustrate its 'quite independent foreign policy'.

Was this 'independent foreign policy' manifest when Cuba agreed to site Soviet missiles in its territory in 1962 and supported the Soviet invasion of Czechoslovakia in 1968? And was the suppression of the Hungarian Uprising in 1956 the expression of the 'independence' of another country within the Soviet sphere of influence?

Corbyn's opposition to 'Western imperialism' led him to conclude that Russian-sponsored military action in the Ukraine from 2014, including the illegal annexation of the Crimea, was largely the fault of NATO provocation. He opposed sanctions against Russia for its illegal invasion, and saw Russia and China as leading the world of the future: 'As the US moves into relative economic decline, China's expansion and Russia's huge energy reserves and location are moving the politics of the world to a different place'.

Corbyn has also given speeches supporting Colonel Muammar Gaddafi's regime in Libya and Slobodan Milosevic, the butcher of Bosnian Muslims. In a display of Marxist revolutionary romanticism, Corbyn wrote in 2011: 'What the Cubans and . . . Che Guevara were preaching in the 1960s has an even greater resonance today'.[11]

Was Corbyn asking for more Marxist insurrections in Latin America and elsewhere, even in countries that now have democratic governments? Or did he wish to emulate the Cuban economy? Cuba has suffered severely from US sanctions, but that is not the whole story. The idea that the Fidelistas can tell us how to run a polity or an economy is, at best, naïve. Cuba has impressive public education and health systems, but its state-controlled agriculture is so inefficient that, despite abundant cultivable land, Cuba has to import about 60 per cent of its food. Cuba's economy has been stagnant for decades, except for its tourist sector, which is now dominated by private enterprises.[12]

Corbyn also supported the socialist governments of Hugo Chávez and Nicolás Maduro in Venezuela, which since 1998 have led to many state takeovers of private enterprises, extensive corruption, widespread starvation, lethal riots, growing dictatorship and the erosion of human rights.[13]

Apart from Cuba and Venezuela, where was this Left to turn after the allure of Stalin's Russia and Mao's China receded, after the beginnings of pro-market reforms in China in 1978 and after the fall of the Berlin Wall in 1989? In pursuit of an agenda 'against Western imperialism', they turned to non-Communist despotic regimes. They were not hailed because they were on the road to a socialist future. They were supported, whatever their defects, as allies in 'the struggle against Western imperialism'.

Consider some examples. The Workers Revolutionary Party is one of many Trotskyist sects that sprouted in Britain since the Second World War. It would not be worth a second look if it did not once count leading actors Vanessa Redgrave and Corin Redgrave among its members, and if its sympathizers did not once include the former Labour Mayor of London Ken Livingstone and Labour MP John McDonnell, who became Jeremy Corbyn's Shadow Chancellor of the Exchequer.

In its 'struggle against Western imperialism' the Workers Revolutionary Party made some unsavoury allies. It received money from the Iraqi dictator Saddam Hussein. In return, its members were asked to spy on Iraqi dissidents in London and pass on the information to the Iraqi embassy. But by 1985 it had switched allegiance to the dictatorial Libyan regime of Colonel Gaddafi, allegedly receiving about half a million pounds from that source.[14]

Another example is the former British Member of Parliament George Galloway. He visited Iraq in 1994 and delivered a speech to Saddam Hussein. He ended with the statement: 'Sir, I salute your courage, your strength, your indefatigability'. Galloway continued: 'just as Stalin industrialized the Soviet Union, so on a different scale Saddam plotted Iraq's own Great Leap Forward'. He did not mention the millions that died at the hands of Stalin and Mao.[15]

As noted above, others on the Far Left have given 'critical' support for the theocratic regime in Iran, including support for this regime in its catastrophic war with Saddam Hussein's Iraq in 1980–1988. Supporters of Iran in this vicious war included the Socialist Workers Party (UK), which ironically later formed the 'Stop the War' movement against Western attacks on Iraq!16

COMMUNISM AND CAPITALISM: THE DEATH TOLLS

While researching this book I came across a grisly battle of words on the Internet concerning the relative death tolls under Communism and capitalism. It revealed appalling death tolls under both types of system.

Published in 1999, the *Black Book of Communism* calculated the premature death toll under Communist regimes to be about ninety-four million.[17] These estimated deaths include: sixty-five million in China under Mao, twenty million in the Soviet Union and about two million in Cambodia under Pol Pot and his Khmer Rouge. Famines explain large numbers of these deaths, including an estimated toll of up to forty-five million in the Great Leap Forward in China in 1958–1961 and up to eight million in the Ukraine in 1932–1933. Some critics say that this figure of ninety-four million is too much, others that it is too conservative an estimate. Either way, the toll of death and misery under Communist regimes is enormous.[18]

In response, there have been attempts to estimate excess mortality under capitalism. It depends how 'capitalism' is defined, but by some assessments the toll is massive. We should not overlook the fact that capitalism has been in existence for much longer than any Communist regime. But also we should not make excuses or diminish the scale of brutality under any system. Capitalism too can be lethal.

For example, the African slave trade caused many millions of early deaths. European conquests of the Americas caused about one hundred million Native American deaths, through combinations of disease and genocide. The British rule of India led to about sixty million deaths, much of them through massacres and famines. The Irish potato famine cost over a million lives. Before 1945, Japanese imperialism in Asia cost tens of millions of lives. Indonesian purges against communists in the 1960s led to about a million dead. And there have been numerous lethal capitalist wars and invasions, reaching an overall total that is certainly well above the estimated ninety-four million premature deaths under Communist regimes.[19]

Game over? Communism is less bad that capitalism? End of story?

No. The point here is not to compare capitalist with Communist regimes. We need to compare democratic regimes, enjoying substantial human rights, with regimes where democracy and human rights are absent or limited. Meaningful democracy—where it is legal and possible for an opposition to organize and vote to remove the incumbent party or elite—has not existed under any Communist regime. Human rights have also been highly limited under Communism.

But there have been both democratic and despotic capitalisms. There have been many brutal capitalist dictatorships, including fascist regimes, where democracy and rights have been denied. In much of the capitalist world today, human rights are routinely violated and many countries are undemocratic.

We need to compare democratic with despotic regimes. Death tolls from despotic capitalist regimes must be added to those deaths under Communism, on the despotic side of the balance sheet.

After despotic capitalist countries are subtracted, the remaining brutalities in capitalist countries are confined mostly to cases when a partially democratic regime attacked a population who lacked the vote and other rights, or caused a famine among a population that lacked democratic and other rights of expression.

Consider the one hundred million Native Americans who died as a result of European colonizations of North and South America. Most of these deaths occurred in South and Central America, after they were invaded by Spain and Portugal, which were then absolutist monarchies rather than democratic regimes.

The highest available reputable estimate for North America is eighteen million premature Native American deaths, most of which were the result of disease. Most of the deliberate killings in the United States occurred in the Indian Wars of the nineteenth century, when the right to vote was also denied to many African Americans and there was incomplete adult male suffrage for whites. The North American genocide was a dreadful crime, but it occurred when democracy in the United States was confined to white males.

Similar remarks apply to the brutal role of the British in India. While most of the deaths were due to famines, the savage repression and killing of several millions after the Indian Mutiny of 1857 should not be excused or forgotten. But all those under British colonial rule were denied the vote, and very limited male suffrage then existed in the United Kingdom. These were hardly democratic circumstances.

These two cases of genocide in the United States and in British India are more complex because the regimes fit readily into neither the democratic nor despotic category. They both involved the killing, by partly democratic colonial regimes, of subject native peoples with limited legal rights. But even if we place these deaths on the democratic side of the balance sheet, the despotic death toll is still much greater.

FAMINE, WAR, DEMOCRACY AND RIGHTS

By democracy we mean a type of political system in which governments are selected through free and contested elections. There are different types of democracy and they vary on the extent of the franchise. Notwithstanding these differences, democracy contrasts with other systems where there are no elections, or where elections cannot be effectively contested.

Nobel Laureate Amartya Sen has famously argued that famines are much less likely in countries with democratic political institutions. He wrote: 'The diverse political freedoms that are available in a democratic state, including regular elections, free newspapers and freedom of speech, must be seen as the real force behind the elimination of famines'. Sen argued that when people have difficulty obtaining food, free speech and democratic institutions can help signal information that help facilitate both private and public responses. While democracy cannot itself guarantee that everyone gets enough to eat, it is of enormous positive assistance in avoiding famine.[20]

Consider the famine that resulted from the Great Leap Forward in Mao's China. In 1958 the Communist government ordered massive increases in steel production. Throughout the country, peasants were obliged to produce backyard steel furnaces. In addition, many thousands of workers were deployed on large irrigation projects. Fearing retribution by the Communist leadership, local party members hugely inflated their production figures, which led to even higher production targets being handed down from the centre. Because of the huge dislocation of labour off the land, the production of food fell and famine set in. Deemed responsible for such failures, many peasants and local officials were tortured or killed. Party officials who reported food shortages were decried as 'bourgeois' or 'counter revolutionaries' and suffered similar fates. By 1962 about forty million people had died. They were victims of a reckless and misconceived economic policy imposed from the centre, plus a totalitarian political system that distorted flows of information and allowed no effective criticism or correction of that policy.[21]

War is a major cause of famine. It has long been argued that democracy is also an antidote to war. This is known as the *democratic peace theory*. Among its originators were Immanuel Kant, Thomas Paine and Alexis de Tocqueville. The basic claim is that wars between two or more democracies are less likely than wars where not all combatants are democratic.

Wars between democracies are relatively rare. Of course, it depends on the definitions of democracy and war. The exceptions depend crucially on these definitions. For example, was Germany democratic in 1914–1918? Arguably not: the franchise was limited. In Prussia those with a vote were represented in the parliament in a highly unequal allocation of seats according to social classes, and the Reichstag had limited power beneath the Kaiser. If the definition of democracy is stringent enough to exclude Germany in 1914–1918, then the exceptions to the democratic peace theory are relatively minor.

But correlation is not causation. We need to search for causal explanations as well. It has been argued that democratically elected leaders may be held to account for war losses by their electors and are hence less likely to go to war, that democracies are more inclined to establish diplomatic institutions for resolving international tensions and that democracies are less inclined to view countries with similar political institutions as hostile.[22]

It must be emphasized that the democratic peace theory concerns wars *between* democracies. Democracies themselves have conducted many devastating and brutal wars of offence or defence *against non-democracies*. And of course, the democratic status of a belligerent does not itself justify any war.

In his important book *The Better Angels of Our Nature*, Steven Pinker attempted to explain a long-term decline in deaths by violence from wars and homicides, from tribal societies to the present. He marshalled extensive evidence and argued that the decline in violence is enormous in magnitude. It is visible in many domains, including downward trends in military conflict, homicide, genocide and torture. But he also stressed that the decline is neither historically smooth nor its continuance inevitable.

In trying to explain the reduction in violence, Pinker pointed to the Enlightenment of the sixteenth and seventeenth centuries, which instigated movements to protect human rights, to abolish slavery and to ban torture. He emphasized the settlement after the Second World War, which led to the United Nations Universal Declaration of Human Rights and a number of movements and institutions to limit military conflict.[23]

Despite the massive carnage since 1960 in Vietnam, Laos, Cambodia, Iraq and elsewhere, the data show a clear overall decline in deaths from warfare in the last sixty years. In the 1950s, for every million people, there were almost 250 annual deaths caused by war. By 2013 there were fewer than ten per million deaths.[24]

On the other hand, we have to take into account the possibility of future nuclear conflict. Nuclear weapons have proliferated in several countries and there is the risk of fanatical terrorists laying their hands on them. They can also be detonated accidentally. One nuclear explosion might kill many millions of people and provoke further deadly retaliation. The downward trend in deaths from war needs to be safeguarded by international action to reduce the nuclear threat.

Even short of nuclear Armageddon, modern democracies are heavily involved in the production and sale of arms, providing powerful vested interests in favour of the prolongation of conflict. Alongside democracy is the military-industrial complex with its capacity to lobby governments and make money out of war.

But democracy is still beneficial. Detailed data are available with indices on different aspects of democratization, including the extent of the franchise and civil liberties. By these measures, global democratization has increased significantly since 1950. According to the democratic peace theory, the concurrent declining trend in deaths from war may be partly explained by this democratic progress.[25]

Consequently, the reduction of death and misery from famine and war is best pursued by opposition to all forms of despotism, whether capitalist or Communist. The Biblical Four Horsemen of the Apocalypse are conflict, war, famine and death. The antidote is clear: the chances of war, famine and premature death can be diminished through a society with democratic institutions and universal human rights.

Preceding chapters showed that socialism—as traditionally defined in terms of the abolition of private property—cannot offer a secure foundation for democratic institutions and human rights. The options that remain are forms of capitalism that have been able to sustain such institutions and rights, an economy consisting of worker cooperatives and markets, or a mixture of economic arrangements including capitalist, state and cooperative firms.

CAN DEMOCRACY HELP ECONOMIC DEVELOPMENT?

There is a predictable reaction to the argument in the preceding section. By arguing for global democracy and universal human rights, I will be accused of imposing Western values and institutions on other nations and cultures. This reaction often stems from a version of normative cultural relativism. This syndrome will be discussed in the next chapter. But sceptics have additional arguments, which I address right away.

The British economist John Williamson coined the term *Washington Consensus* in 1990. He referred to a specific set of policies, involving macroeconomic stabilization, free trade, privatization and deregulation. The Left has used this term as a swear word, to criticize the promotion of property rights, markets and democracy in developing countries. Yet property rights, markets and democracy were precisely the prescriptions of the original *Left*, from the English Levellers to the French Revolution.[26]

Leaving the normative case for democracy aside, it is a legitimate scientific question to ask whether democracy can help economic development or not. To answer this question we need to look at the evidence.

At first sight, the argument that democracy helps development looks thin. As noted previously, all currently developed economies were at best limited democracies until well into the twentieth century. Britain had a very limited male franchise until 1868, by which time it had experienced almost a century of impressive industrial development and had achieved substantial increases in living standards. While pioneering its Industrial Revolution, Britain was no more than a minimal democracy, with the vote confined to male property owners. As the development economist Ha-Joon Chang has noted: 'Whatever one's position is on the relationship between democracy and economic growth in today's world, it is indisputable that today's developed countries did not develop under democracy. Until the 1920s, universal male suffrage was a rarity, not to mention the even lower extent of female suffrage. It was not until the late twentieth century that most developed countries became truly democratic'.[27]

There are spectacular cases of economic growth that did not depend on democracy. Japan developed enormously from 1868 to 1945 without being a democracy. China's achievements as a one-party Communist state have been remarkable. From 1979 until 2010, China's average annual GDP growth rate was about 10 per cent. Hundreds of millions of people were lifted out of poverty. It is a hugely impressive case of development without democracy, affecting about one-fifth of the world's population.[28]

It has been argued that autocracies are better able to marshal the resources necessary to promote economic development. Underdeveloped countries lack the financial or other institutions to start the process of building infrastructure or large-scale industry by private means. The histories of Japan, China, Singapore, Taiwan and South Korea show how the state stepped in to start this process long before any democratic government appeared.

Democratic institutions are extremely difficult to build up, especially in countries with corrupt or dysfunctional states. They took centuries to emerge in the West. They cannot easily be imposed on other countries by invasion, as recent experiences in Iraq and Afghanistan testify. Are those that argue for democracy in developing countries expecting too much?

But look a little closer, taking China as a first example. After more than three decades of spectacular growth, Chinese GDP per capita in 2014 was 24 per cent of that in the USA in the same year. China is still a long way behind the leading capitalist countries.[29]

In any given year since 1900, the level of GDP per capita in the United States is a useful benchmark for other countries. The United States has had the highest levels of GDP per capita in this entire period, with the exceptions of some smaller or oil-rich countries. Moving in a few decades, from less than 10 per cent of US GDP to 24 per cent US GDP, is spectacular. But how many countries have progressed much further and passed through what has been described as the 'middle-income trap'?[30]

More specifically, how many countries since 1900 have managed to move from 20 per cent or less of US GDP per capita, to urban, industrial countries of (say) 60 per cent or more of US GDP per capita? The answer seems to be only five: Japan, Taiwan, South Korea, Singapore and Hong Kong.

Of these, Singapore and Hong Kong are relatively small, city-based territories, each of fewer than eight million people. They are now among the richest countries in the world. Hong Kong belatedly acquired limited democratic institutions under the British before 1997. Singapore is a limited democracy. Given these caveats, and especially taking their small size into account, they offer less decisive evidence for or against the thesis that democracy helps economic development.

It is better to focus on the cases of Japan, South Korea and Taiwan. These cases are very important in developmental terms, particularly when we consider the prospects for other countries that have experienced rapid growth from low levels of GDP per capita.

Japan's GDP per capita grew at an average annual rate of 1.5 per cent from 1870 to 1913 and 0.9 per cent from 1913 to 1950. Then it took off. While sheltering under US military hegemony; adopting a Western-style, democratic political system; imitating Western know-how; and developing new organizational and manufacturing techniques, it saw its per capita GDP explode from 1950 to 1973 at an average annual rate of about 8 per cent. It moved into the ranks of developed economies. In 1950 its GDP per capita was 20 per cent of that in the United States. In 1990 it reached 81 per cent of the US level.[31]

Crucially, Japan's explosive growth began after 1945, after Japan became a substantial democracy.

South Korea and Taiwan—both former colonies of Japan—also grew rapidly after 1950. But unlike Japan they did not falter in the 1990s. From 1950 to 2001 their average growth rates of GDP per capita were both about 6 per cent. In 1950 the absolute GDPs per capita of South Korea and Taiwan were 8 and 10 per cent, respectively, of that of the United States. In 2014 they reached 65 and 84 per cent, respectively, of the US level.[32]

From 1960 to 1987, South Korea was, at best, a very limited democracy, suffering periods of authoritarian military rule. But after the establishment of the Sixth Republic in 1987, South Korea has developed into a modern democracy with free elections and robust civil liberties.

Democratic reforms accelerated in Taiwan after 1988, when Lee Teng-hui was elected President. Lee Teng-hui was re-elected in 1996 in the first direct presidential election in the country's history. In 2000 the ruling Kuomintang Party was defeated in a free presidential election. Further major democratic reforms followed in 2005.

By 1990, albeit to different degrees, both these countries had established democratic political institutions. In that year the GDPs per capita of South Korea and Taiwan were 37 and 43 per cent, respectively, of that of the United States. This was still way below their 2014 levels of 65 and 84 per cent.[33]

This exercise shows that no major country (of more than eight million people) has developed from less than 20 per cent of US GDP per capita to more than 60 per cent of US GDP per capita without it being a democracy when it reached the level of 45 per cent of US GDP per capita. *In all the countries that have moved from underdeveloped to developed industrial economies since 1900, democracy has been adopted before they reached the 45 per cent mark.* Democracy may help countries pass over the middle-income trap.

More extensive and robust studies have examined the relationship between democracy and economic development in larger samples of countries. The literature on this topic is huge, and it is impossible to review it here. Attempts to study the relationship are beset by several problems, including specification or measurement errors in the democracy indices and the likelihood of a two-way causal relationship: development might help stimulate democracy as much as the other way round.

Another analytical problem is that few countries have developed successfully. About half of all countries (for which we have data) are currently below 20 per cent of US GDP per capita. These include populous countries such as India, Indonesia, Nigeria, the Philippines and the Ukraine. About 30 per cent of all countries (for which we have data) are below 10 per cent of US GDP per capita. These include large countries such as the Democratic Republic of the Congo, Bangladesh and Pakistan. Many of these low-income countries are weak, corrupt or failed states, where democracy at best is fragile. The wealth of some countries derives from natural assets such as oil, and several of these resource-rich states are undemocratic.[34]

Given these analytical problems it is not surprising that controversy continues over whether democracy aids development or not. A 2005 survey of the academic literature on this topic by John Gerring and his colleagues noted the apparent consensus that the net effect of democracy on growth performance cross-nationally since 1950 has been 'negative or null'. But their own analysis began to turn the tide of debate. They challenged this consensus by considering lagged and cumulative effects of democracy, which indicated positive effects. Their analysis suggested that states with extensive democratic histories tended to adopt sounder policies, allowing them to outperform authoritarian regimes in the long run.[35]

In the same year, Dani Rodrik and Romain Wacziarg provided more empirical evidence of the growth-promoting nature of democracy. Their systematic analysis uncovered another picture that is considerably more favourable to democratization, showing its positive effects on development.[36]

A subsequent study by Daron Acemoglu and his colleagues also suggested a robust and sizeable positive effect of democracy on economic growth. Their central estimates suggested that a country that switches from non-democracy to democracy achieves about 20 per cent higher GDP per capita in the following thirty years. However, their results indicated no clear differential effect of democracy on economic growth at low levels of economic development.[37]

Using evidence from an extensive global data set, Carl Henrik Knutsen argued that democracy can help promote technological innovation, which is an important determinant of long-term economic growth. He cited evidence to show that autocracies have slower technological change than democracies.[38]

The reasons why democracy may aid development are complex. As well as reducing the likelihood of famine and war, democratic governments have to take greater account of the people. This can help to promote greater investment in primary schooling and better health. Democratic legitimacy may also help sustain higher levels of taxation to help build up welfare states. Finally, effective democracy requires a separation of powers and a degree of countervailing power, within and against the state. These conditions can help protect business interests and reduce fears of arbitrary confiscation of property.[39]

It is fashionable for leftist development economists to challenge the idea that democracy helps to promote economic growth. They suspect that the pro-democracy arguments are a ploy by the Washington Consensus to install capitalist institutions. Of course, we may criticize the devastating American-led wars in Vietnam, Iraq and elsewhere that ostensibly had the aim of installing democracy, but ended up with carnage. But objections to Western aggression are not themselves an argument against democracy in the developing world. We should not reject a thesis simply because we suspect the motives of some people promoting it. The question concerning the relationship between democracy and development must be considered empirically, and through rigorous scientific investigation.

Overall, studies of the relationship between democracy and development are complex and do not give a decisive verdict, but it seems that the evidence in favour of a positive relationship is increasing. While the evidence in favour is not yet overwhelming, the case against it has been undermined.

We also need to be reminded of the intrinsic virtues of democracy. It would be a noble aim even if it did nothing to promote economic growth. Enlightenment thinkers upheld that legitimate government drew its mandate from neither Kings nor Gods, but from the people. What other acceptable justification of power or authority can there be?

Today democracy is being challenged by large corporations and financial institutions that can override or circumvent democratic accountability. It would be irresponsible to take the survival of democracy for granted. The struggle to renew and extend democracy is one of the most important of the twenty-first century.[40]

But while defending democracy, it must be re-iterated that it is, and should not be, everything. There are practical and moral limits to democratic decision-making. For practical reasons we cannot make more than a tiny fraction of important decisions by democratic vote. And democratic majority rule should not be able to overturn human rights.

WHY RIGHTS ARE IMPORTANT

Rights were central for Enlightenment thinkers and for the original *Left*. But many on the socialist Left treat them with suspicion. They are regarded as expressions of Western individualism, or of the class interests of the bourgeoisie.

Rights have an individualistic character because they exist to protect the individual from the unwarranted actions of authority, even if those actions are willed by the majority. As Jeremy Waldron put it, our rights are 'those of our individual interests which would be wrong or unreasonable to sacrifice for the greater good of others'. But on the other hand, rights are not entirely egotistic or self-regarding because they must be universal. To protect rights for ourselves, we have an interest in preserving the rights of others. These are 'interests that require moral protection in the case of all human individuals'.[41]

The most fundamental right is over our lives and bodies, to be unmolested by torture or violence. Secondary rights include the right to own property. A great empirical lesson from the twentieth century is that democracy does not endure without the right to private property. Many on today's Left have yet to learn that lesson. But it was well understood by the original *Left*.

There is no rock-solid justification for any set of rights. Alasdair MacIntyre made much of this omission in his book *After Virtue*. But it is vital to continue the conversation concerning the philosophical grounding of rights.[42]

The failure to justify rights does not mean that we should follow MacIntyre and other anti-Enlightenment thinkers. It is an elementary philosophical stricture that a lack of proof of existence does not itself imply non-existence. Concerning rights, if we cannot prove their existence then this does not necessarily mean they do not exist. The open-endedness of the discourse on rights can be taken as a source of encouragement, especially if we regard the process of enquiry as incremental and evolutionary. The fact that we do not reach a final proof does not mean that the effort is worthless.

Edmund Burke argued in 1790 that claims concerning democracy and rights could not be established by reason alone. In large part it was a matter of experience. The constitution and laws of a state had to be tested historically. The development of suitable governing principles and institutions was an 'experimental science'. Since Burke we have seen many experiments in institutional design. From these experiences we are able to draw some conclusions.

One experimental result is solid, and buttressed by the overwhelming evidence raised earlier in this chapter. Governments that remove, or fail to protect, human rights and democracy are much more likely to lead to repression, famine, war and human misery. Furthermore, while the maintenance of private property rights has not guaranteed other liberties, the removal of private property rights has universally led to totalitarianism and has compromised other rights as well.

On the basic question of rights, what more evidence do we need? The twentieth century has shown what happens when rights in general are limited, and when rights to property in particular are removed. This ample experimental evidence suggests that the rhetoric of rights is not illusory. It is not merely bourgeois apologetics. It is not simply a smokescreen for Western imperialism. Rights and democracy matter for human survival and fulfilment.

The West has committed many atrocities. The deliberate strategic bombing of thousands of civilians in Germany and Japan in the Second World War is one of many examples. More recently, the West has been involved in torture in Guantanamo, Iraq, Afghanistan and elsewhere. No excuses justify these outrages.

But, without condoning these crimes, inhabitants of the developed West enjoy more freedom and security than people in countries that lack democracy or adequately protected rights. Western democracy and rights, while far from perfect, have major, positive effects. They are intrinsically worthwhile; they are not fake.

Having considered this compelling evidence, what arguments do philosophers give for human rights? There are several prominent approaches. Considerations of rights in ethical theory often start from the basic requirements for human beings to lead an acceptable life and to avoid harm. These include basic rights to health care and education, as well as freedom from torture or arbitrary imprisonment.

A distinction is made between claim rights and liberty rights. A claim right is a right one holds against others who owe a corresponding duty to the right holder. Examples could include the rights to health care, housing or education. Liberty rights are rights to choose any action that is not itself prohibited under the adopted system of rights. Examples include freedom of movement, worship, assembly or expression.[43]

As noted in preceding chapters, many Enlightenment justifications of rights were based on their 'natural and inalienable' character, including the claim that they were bestowed by God. In modern approaches, the role of the state in the provision of welfare and other rights is often underlined. There is concern about communities as well as individuals. Rights are considered in the international as well as the national arena. Also proclaimed are the rights of future generations to a planet that is habitable in terms of climate and ecology.

There are two dominant modern approaches toward the justification of rights. They are the interest theory and the will theory. Advocates of the interest theory (a needs-based approach) argue that the principal function of human rights is to protect and promote certain essential human interests, particularly concerning well-being, personal development and protection from harm. Human rights are among the necessary conditions for human well-being. The universality of human rights is grounded on these basic, indispensable requirements, which we all share because of the enduring commonalities in our biological, psychological and social nature.[44]

In slight contrast, the will (or agency-based) theory starts from the claim that human agency and autonomy bestow the possibility of freedom, and this ought to constitute the core of any account of rights. Hence the rights to such things as an adequate diet, private property and political participation all derive ultimately from a right to liberty.[45] But both approaches end up discussing universal human interests and needs.

The fundamental right over our lives and bodies, unmolested by torture or violence, stems from our basic need for survival. The rights to liberty and to private property derive from the universal right to a degree of autonomy and to the means of self-development. Notwithstanding our general dependence on others, we have the right to as much self-determination as possible that is consistent with the common good.

While upholding the basic liberal values of the Enlightenment, we should not presume that they are absolute and beyond modification. We have learned these moral values from long experience, and we should not rule out the possibility that we may learn more, including from non-Western cultures.

Philip Kitcher has argued that moral values and principles should be seen not as fixed truths, but as a 'social technology' with provisional solutions to the problems that arise in the process of living together as humans. Ethical commands are not divine revelations, but ethical practices that have evolved over tens of thousands of years, as members of our species have worked out how to live together and prosper.[46]

This evolutionary and pragmatic approach avoids the pitfalls of both absolutism and relativism. Unlike relativism, it does not accept that one moral claim is as good as any other. Moral values are right and good to the extent that they allow people to live acceptable lives together. But these values may have to be adapted as new circumstances arise and we learn from experience.

An example of a new circumstance requiring new rights was the transition from smaller-scale, hunter-gatherer communities to larger economic units requiring a much more complex division of labour. Hunter-gatherer societies rely on norms of sharing and cooperation, which depend on face-to-face interaction. Larger-scale societies cannot rely on face-to-face interactions, except in smaller subunits, such as families. In these circumstances, the right to private property becomes relevant in order to enable a degree of autonomy and self-development.

In modern, knowledge-intensive capitalism, rights to information become relatively more important, as outlined in the final chapter of this book.

CONCLUSION: FINDING THE WAY

Among other different meanings, the term 'Right' has come to mean a preference for market solutions, while the Left has for much longer been associated with state intervention and ownership. Ironically, this is the reverse of the original meanings of these terms. In 1789 the *Right* advocated state monopolies and some state intervention, while the original *Left* advocated free markets. These huge shifts of meaning have caused enormous confusion.

This chapter concludes with two depictive figures which might help to unravel the mess. The first figure (7.1) places a number of thinkers and ideologies within a box, where the left to right dimension concurs with the original meaning of *Left* and *Right*.

The term *social democracy* appears in the figures. It has had different meanings in the past. It is used here according to the dominant interpretation today. Social democracy refers to a form of market economy, with democracy, a welfare state and some redistributive taxation of income and wealth.[47]

Communism refers here to Soviet-style systems, which lack democracy and allow a limited role for markets or private enterprise. Libertarianism is

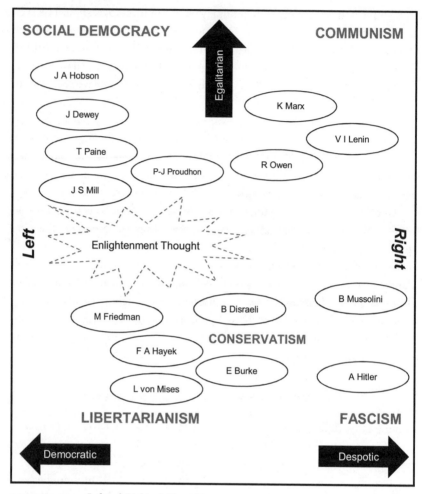

FIGURE 7.1. *Left* and *Right*—A Truer Picture

This figure is speculative and approximate, but concurs with the original meanings of *Left* and *Right*. 'Communism' and 'social democracy' correspond to their usage today, rather than earlier meanings. The positioning of all items on the vertical and horizontal scales is approximate and illustrative, rather than exact.

used in its now-dominant sense to refer to a market economy with individual commercial freedom and a limited state.[48] Fascism refers to an economy with markets and private enterprise, overshadowed by an authoritarian, undemocratic, interventionist state with limited human rights.

The vertical scale in figure 7.1 refers to the degree of concern for greater equality of opportunity and for economic equality, as well as political and legal equality. The horizontal scale concerns the form of government, with democracy toward the left and despotism toward the right.

Precise positioning on the vertical and horizontal scales is difficult and would depend on what aspects are given more weight. For example, while some Communist countries may have achieved less inequality in terms of income or wealth, they suffered greater inequalities of power and effective rights. It all depends on the relative weightings given to economic and political equality.

By 'democracy' on the horizontal scale, it is not meant majority decision-making over anything and everything. All major democratic theorists accept that there are some rights that should not be overturned by votes. The *Left* in the figure refers to the supremacy of some form of representative democracy, within a constitutional and legal framework, with equality under the law and other basic human rights. It may be seen as a composite index, involving aspects of democracy and basic rights.

By these criteria, Marxism is not on the *Left* but on the *Right*. Marxism rejects the universality of rights. Marxist regimes have falsely claimed to be democratic. But in practice, both the denial of universal rights and the concentration of economic power in the hands of the state mean that genuine democracy is unviable in Marxist regimes.

In addition, as shown later in chapter 10, some prominent libertarians—such as Ludwig von Mises and Friedrich Hayek—sometimes prioritized the defence of private property over democracy and other human rights. So they took a radical position over private property but they were not nearly as *Left* on questions such as democracy.

Figure 7.1 simplifies a much more complex picture, and it excludes attitudes to private property and common ownership. These could form an important third dimension. Not all points within this imaginary three-dimensional box would be viable. For instance, it has been argued above that democracy is incompatible with widespread common ownership. Hence rights to private property underpin democracy and some other human rights.

A possible fourth dimension (again omitted from the figures) is highlighted by a recent empirical survey of political attitudes in the UK. In addition to divisions of opinion over matters such as economic policy and state intervention, this study found a significant 'communitarian-cosmopolitan dimension', where 'communitarian' refers to more nationalist, localist and conservative attitudes, including opposition to immigration, gay marriage and the European Union.[49]

The second figure (7.2) rotates the preceding one anti-clockwise by ninety degrees. It conforms much more with typical usages of the terms 'Left' and

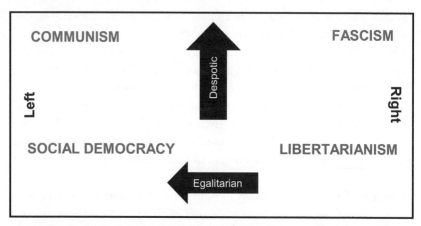

F I G U R E 7.2. Left and Right—The Misleading Modern Metamorphosis
This figure rotates the preceding one anti-clockwise by ninety degrees. It conforms to typical usages of the terms 'Left' and 'Right' today. By transposing the Left-Right terminology onto the question of egalitarianism, the democratic-despotic dimension now lacks an accepted positional terminology. Hence this dimension, concerning democracy and basic rights, may be neglected. Yet each upward incremental movement of a millimetre in this box—thereby decreasing the levels of democracy and rights—may be measured in millions of twentieth-century deaths. The dimension concerning democracy and rights needs to be highlighted once more, alongside the question of equality. That is why Figure 7.1 is to be preferred.

'Right' today. But by transposing the Left-Right terminology onto the question of egalitarianism, the democratic-despotic dimension here lacks an accepted positional terminology. Hence democracy and rights may be neglected.

Consider this: each upward incremental movement of a millimetre in the box in figure 7.2—thereby decreasing the levels of democracy and rights—may be measured in millions of twentieth-century deaths. The vertical dimension is literally vital—a matter of life and death. This movement is from *Left* to *Right*. This strengthens the case for reversing the ninety-degree turn back to the original in figure 7.1. *Left* and *Right* should be left and right.

The Left should return to its almost-forgotten roots on the *Left*, and make the struggle for liberty and democracy central to its message, alongside the pursuit of greater economic and political equality. In this struggle it will find allies among those free-market libertarians who are more enthusiastic in their support for democracy. But a revived social democratic *Left* will also propose judicious regulation of markets, especially of global financial markets, with measures to reduce economic inequality. Together these would be its distinctive and defining aims.

CHAPTER 8

After Vietnam:
The Left Descends into
Cultural Relativism

What we see in such cases is an odd phenomenon indeed. Highly intelligent people, people deeply committed to the good of women and men in developing countries, people who think themselves as progressive and feminist and antiracist, are taking up positions that converge . . . with the positions of reaction, oppression, and sexism. Under the banner of their radical and politically correct 'antiessentialism' march ancient religious taboos, . . . ill health, ignorance, and death.

Martha Nussbaum, 'Human Functioning and Social Justice' (1992)

From the late 1960s to the early 1970s, the movement against the Vietnam War radicalized millions of young people on a global scale. It was an immense upsurge of protest, not only against the war but also against the hypocrisy and conservative values of preceding generations.

The lure of the Soviet Union had been undermined by the Hungarian Uprising of 1956 and it was reduced further by the Soviet invasion of Czechoslovakia in August 1968. Maoism was an attraction for some from the Left, but they were then mostly unaware of its dreadful legacy of famine, killing and torture. Others turned to Trotskyist sects, to leftist social democracy, to radical liberalism, to anarchism or to alternative lifestyles.

But the anti-war movement was united in its condemnation of American aggression in Vietnam. Pictures of napalmed children and massacres of unarmed civilians were broadcast on the media. South Vietnam was a brutal dictatorship propped up by American military power. The Communist regime in North Vietnam seemed no worse. It was easy to become cynical about claims that the United States was a bulwark of democracy and human rights.

No defence of US foreign policy is offered here. In the twentieth century, both Britain and the United States have shown that democracies can kill innocent civilians on a massive scale. Also, during the Cold War, the West in opposition to Communism propped up several repressive dictatorships in South America, Africa and Asia.

But murderous or repressive behaviour by a democratic power abroad does not mean that the limited rights and flawed democratic institutions at home can be disregarded, or treated as fake.

As noted in the preceding chapter, Noam Chomsky claimed that Western democracy and rights are a sham. He was not alone. With similar effect, the left-ist cultural theorist Kwame Anthony Appiah wrote of 'Eurocentric hegemony posing as universalism'. The political theorist Nicholas Rengger considered whether universal human rights were a new form of imperialism or 'a mask for Western interests'. The Marxist economist Samir Amin diagnosed *The Liberal Virus*. This is seen as a sickness afflicting the world, where the US rhetoric of human rights and democracy is little more than a cynical, hypocritical device to gain power over global resources and maximize profits for business.[1]

But there was another prominent response. It focused crucially on cultural differences. Western discourses on democracy and human rights were seen as inappropriate for other cultures. Western thought emphasizes the rights of the individual, and hence the human rights agenda is an expression of Western individualism. This response can be described as *normative moral relativism*; more frequently it is described as *cultural relativism*.

Such relativist views incubated within anthropology in the early twentieth century. They evolved and spread massively in the climate of protest against Western aggression in the Vietnam War. Among their bizarre manifestations were feminists refusing to condemn horrendous acts against women. This chapter criticizes cultural relativism and ends with further arguments in favour of universal human rights.

ANTHROPOLOGY AND CULTURAL RELATIVISM

Influential American anthropologists such as Franz Boas (1858–1942) insisted that cultures differ in their moral values. Boas warned that we should not jump to the conclusion that the moral values of our culture are right and those from other cultures are wrong. So far, so good. But many of his students made additional and less tenable claims.

For example, in the 1930s, the influential anthropologist Ruth Benedict declared indifference between 'equally valid patterns of life'. Less cautiously than her teacher Boas, she suggested that we should refrain from criticizing the morality of any foreign culture. Yet her ethical tolerance in the anthropological field is inconsistent with her noted intolerance of racism and sexism in

Western society. If we cannot criticize other cultures, then we lack universal standards to criticize our own. Her global opposition to discrimination and injustice would be devalued if it were simply regarded—in her own morally relativist terms—as a product of her own culture. Her position had internal contradictions.[2]

By the 1940s, Benedict and other students of Boas were dominant in the American Anthropological Association. The term *cultural relativism* began to be widely used. In 1947, in response to the drafting of the Universal Declaration of Human Rights, the Executive Board of the American Anthropological Association submitted a 'Statement on Human Rights' to the United Nations. The statement is believed to be drafted by Melville Herskovits—another student of Boas. It asked: 'How can the proposed Declaration be applicable to all human beings, and not be a statement of rights conceived only in terms of the values prevalent in the countries of Western Europe and America?'[3]

This was an extraordinary response for the time. The Allies had just defeated Nazism and fascism in Europe and Asia. It was odd to call for 'tolerance' and 'respect' for all cultures, including those that had committed genocide. Especially in those circumstances, it was important to underline basic human rights and values.

The 1947 statement by the American Anthropological Association included some embarrassing arguments. For instance it claimed: 'Respect for differences between cultures is validated by the scientific fact that no technique of qualitatively evaluating cultures has been discovered'. In response, the legal philosopher James Nickel pointed out: 'This bizarre argument attempts to justify a norm of tolerance by asserting that there is no way of justifying moral and legal norms'. Nickel then noted the internal contradiction: if norms are impossible to justify, then we cannot promote norms of diversity and tolerance. Furthermore, the question of what cultural practices should be *respected* is quite independent of whether techniques of cultural *evaluation* are available.[4]

Another argument in the 1947 statement was: 'The individual realizes his personality through his culture, hence respect for individual differences entails a respect for cultural differences'.[5] The meaning of 'respect' in these quotes is unclear. Does it mean 'try to understand the way in which cultures engender particular behaviours'? Or does it mean 'tolerate and refrain from moral criticism'? Or does it mean 'give our moral approval'?

Consider an imaginary culture where unwanted or delinquent children are tortured, chopped up by a specialist butcher and their meat is sold to be eaten as a delicacy. The individual butcher would be realizing 'his personality through his culture'. But it does not follow that we should tolerate or refrain from criticizing the infant-butcher or his cannibal consumers. The last-quoted sentence is both imprecise and a *non sequitur*.

The statement by the American Anthropological Association ignored an important fact. While different cultures deal with their problems in a huge variety of ways, many of these problems are equivalent for all cultures, including the basic needs to provide for food, shelter, warmth, individual development, human interaction and social cohesion. Some moral evaluation of different cultures may be possible on the basis of the degree and manner that these different needs are satisfied.

MORAL AND CULTURAL RELATIVISMS TODAY

It is a commonplace observation that what may be a moral or binding rule in one culture may not be so in another. This valid and uncontroversial observation, that different cultures have different ethical codes and systems of rules, can be more precisely described as *descriptive cultural relativism* or as *descriptive moral relativism*. But counting as a moral rule in a community is not the same thing as being a *valid* moral rule. The cultural specificity of many moral judgments does not justify a *normative moral relativism*, where one person's morality is deemed as good as any other.

Henceforth we shall follow prevailing practice and refer to this normative version as *cultural relativism* for short. The descriptive relativism of Boas and others is not contested. By contrast, the normative relativism of his students was a serious problem. Cultural relativism in this sense goes beyond matters of mere understanding to assert normative neutrality between different cultural practices.

Anthropologists have rightly and amply pointed out that practices that we find obnoxious or barbaric in other cultures often perform socially useful functions in the particular contexts in which they operate. Within those societies these practices may facilitate social cooperation, prevent violence, help to resolve conflicts and so on. For example, the Mayan practice of human sacrifice in Central America helped to sustain Mayan social cohesion and social order. But that does not mean that it was acceptable, or that we must refrain from passing a moral judgment about it.

Some of these arguments, concerning the way in which specific ritual practices can allegedly facilitate social cooperation and cohesion, are redolent of classical functionalist arguments in anthropology and sociology, where the existence of a practice was purportedly explained by its social function. Functionalism was rightly criticized for its incapacity to accommodate intra-social conflicts, including internal disputes over such practices. It is a static and conservative approach that fails to explain social change.[6]

We know that there can be multiple alternative ways of facilitating social cooperation and cohesion. There can be different cultural practices or institutional arrangements, which form different equilibria in different societies. But not all of them are morally acceptable. We have to be very careful not to jump to the conclusion that Western moral values are superior. But that does not mean that we should reach no judgmental conclusion at all.

Consider changes of norms within cultures. As recently as the 1970s, in several developed countries, it was deemed acceptable to pay women a wage lower than that paid to the men who were doing the same work. It was claimed that employing women was riskier for the firm, as women could get pregnant and then leave the job for a while. The lower wages for women were said to reflect this risk.

This gender discrimination gave women a lower incentive to seek paid employment than men. At the same time there was a widespread cultural norm that women should do most of the cleaning, cooking and childcare at home. The willing acceptance of this role by many women also deterred them from seeking paid employment outside. This was a cultural equilibrium. People of both genders believed in stereotypical gender roles and voluntarily accepted them. It provided some social stability and created a clear, functional, gender-based division of labour.

Were feminists wrong to oppose these assumed roles and cultural norms? The logic of cultural relativism suggests that they were: people should refrain from criticizing prevalent cultural values.

The fact that this gender discrimination was a cultural equilibrium does not mean that it was moral or just. The feminist movement attacked the problem on both sides, by campaigning for equal pay and for shared participation of men in household chores. Eventually, laws were brought in to enforce equal pay. Many men accepted that they should take on work in the household that was traditionally done by women. A new equilibrium was reached where more women participated in paid employment.[7]

By ruling out any moral condemnation of any set of prevailing cultural norms, cultural relativists are unable to support such changes. Cultural relativism is an extraordinarily conservative doctrine.

Similarly, some ultra-individualists suggest that as long as all participants are voluntary, and no one is forced to act against his or her will, then we should refrain from criticizing a particular cultural practice. This position also turns out to be conservative, but this time in libertarian clothing.

Would such libertarians accept many social practices, including sex with children, female genital mutilation or even Mayan human sacrifice, as long as the victims consented to their ordeal? A problem with the criterion of voluntariness is that people can be duped or pressured into an agreement. Only a reckless version of libertarianism would ignore the problem of unwarranted consent and overlook the need to protect children, the brainwashed or the less competent from being victims of their own misguided approval. It is far better to stick to Enlightenment principles here and uphold inalienable rights and basic needs that cannot be traded away, even when there is consent.[8]

Cultural relativists deny that other cultures should adopt Western views concerning democracy or human rights. They claim that different moral rules prevailing in other cultures are 'equally valid'. The notion of universal human rights is thus abandoned, along with any guiding notion of morality.

Of course, individuals vary in their moral beliefs. Some people argue that because different cultures disagree on moral rules there cannot be universally valid moral rules. But we should not then abandon all moral judgments, or jump to the conclusion that one moral claim is as valid as any other. Disagreement about the truth does not mean that there is no truth. If I wake up and think it is Saturday, when my partner says it is Friday, this does not mean that it is neither. Similarly, we cannot draw the conclusion from the fact that different cultures have different moral codes that there cannot be a universal morality.

Relativists claim that 'morality is subjective', so there cannot be universal moral rules. But the whole point about a moral claim is that it transcends individual preference and is purportedly universal. 'My personal preference is that you should not kill people' does not have the same moral status as 'thou shalt not kill'. Morality is more than mere preference.

How do we know whether a moral rule is universally valid? Good question. But the fact that we may be unsure how to justify a rule does not make that rule invalid. It also does not imply that there are no valid moral rules. Ignorance of what is valid does not imply that every possible claim is invalid. Of course, this does not itself imply that there *are* valid moral rules, but absence of evidence is not evidence of absence.

Cultural relativism is internally contradictory. It denies that our normative values are valid or suitable for other cultures. But this too is a normative claim. Why should this normative claim (that we should not impose our normative values on other cultures) be adopted by others in different cultures? By the logic of cultural relativism, thinkers in other cultures are not obliged to be cultural relativists. The whole argument is self-defeating.[9]

Cultural relativists remove themselves from any discussion of normative morality. They reject a key premise of all post-Enlightenment discussions in ethics and elsewhere: they deny that there are right and wrong answers that might eventually be discovered through reason and experience. Consequently, cultural relativists either withdraw from the discussion or uphold indefensibly that contradictory moral claims can all be correct. Cultural relativism fails as an ethical or meta-ethical stance because it cannot arbitrate over moral disagreements.

Cultural relativism implies that if an act is morally permitted in a culture, then it must be tolerated by outsiders, even if it is regarded as wrong elsewhere. To accept such a version of moral relativism is to undermine an essential feature of morality itself—that it is absolute and inescapable. Because this vital feature is denied, such a relativist cannot believe in *any* moral judgment.

Cultural relativism often ends up reducing morality to a matter of preference, and claiming that any such preferences are culturally conditioned. But the whole point about morality, as many philosophers have insisted, is that morality transcends matters of convenience or preference. Cultural relativism abandons morality and descends into nihilism or amoralism.[10]

Many cultural relativists join forces with Marxists and other utilitarians. They all claim that morality is superficial. Morality is the fake and diversionary language of rich elites or cultural imperialists. Instead they propose that there are different cultural norms, or different class interests, or different individual preferences. The multiple rhetorics of cultural relativism, class struggle or utilitarian individualism all converge toward amoralism.

By the 1970s, suspecting Western hypocrisy, many on the Left ceased to appeal to universal moral values or rights. That territory was left open for the Right, who quickly claimed the high ground on rights and morality. It was left to the Right to defend the moral achievement of the Enlightenment. The outcome was disastrous for the Left, when it abandoned much of its moral appeal. The Left became dominated by Enlightenment sceptics and 'anything goes' relativists. This appalling wrong turning led to a catastrophic decline in intellectual respect for the Left, from which it has yet to recover.

But even worse, as shown in the following section, the Regressive Left did not simply abandon the high ground of democracy and rights. Cultural relativism led some prominent leftist feminists to abandon genuine feminism as well.

HOW SOME FEMINISTS DOWNPLAY WOMEN'S RIGHTS

Feminists rightly point out that for millennia, discourses on politics and ethics have been almost completely dominated by men. Furthermore, with examples such as 'the rights of man' the language exhibits a gender bias that down-grades the status and concerns of women. Women are thus rightly suspicious of attempts by men to argue for particular rights. Just as we should scrutinize claims by the West to represent universal moral values, we should also be cautious about claims by men that their moral principles apply to all human-ity. Some prominent feminists have gone further to endorse the view that we cannot impose our values or moral principles on other cultures.

Germaine Greer became a leftist leader of the global feminist movement. Her iconic book *The Female Eunuch* became an international bestseller in 1970. Her thesis was that consumerism and the nuclear family repress women, both personally and sexually. She has claimed to be an anarchist or a Marxist, as well as a feminist. Her Marxism was re-affirmed in a television interview as late as 2008. She also said she was committed to 'permanent revolution'. Yet despite her claimed Marxism, with its culturally universal aim of socialism, she gravitated toward cultural relativism.

She also abandoned key values of the Enlightenment. When controversy erupted over the alleged blasphemy against Islam in Salman Rushdie's 1988 novel *The Satanic Verses*, Greer refused to sign a petition in favour of freedom of expression.[11]

In her 1999 book *The Whole Woman*, Greer argued that attempts to outlaw the practice of female genital mutilation amounted to 'an attack on cultural identity'. She compared the practice to the commercialized cult of female beautification in the West. Strictly, by careful wording, she supported neither, but she tolerated mutilation and she attacked universal values and rights. She accused the West of holding double standards. To assert the right of women not to be mutilated was to 'reinforce our notions of cultural superiority'.[12]

Greer had academic allies on this issue. In her 1995 essay on 'Rethinking Female Circumcision', the anthropologist Melissa Parker accused those con-cerned about the practice of female genital mutilation as 'lending credence to fierce moral judgements and campaigns aimed at remaking other cultures in their own image'. The 'intense emotions aroused by the subject [of female circumcision] among Western researchers are, to a large extent, influenced by Euro-American discourses and debates which have little or nothing to do with the study populations [in Africa]'.[13]

'Who are we to say?' they cry. If you feel repugnance, or see a violation of moral principles or women's rights, then you are a victim of 'Euro-American discourses and debates' that supposedly do not apply to other cultures. Other feminists have argued (more convincingly) that our feelings and emotions are important, alongside conversation and reason. But now Greer and Parker instruct us to disregard our feelings because they are conditioned by 'Euro-American discourses and debates'.

The cultural relativists went even further. In parts of India it is an ancient custom—called *sati*—for widows to be burned alive (voluntarily or involuntarily) on their husbands' funeral pyres. This was often seen as duty and a heroic sign of respect for the deceased husband and his family. In 1829 the practice was outlawed by the British East India Company, who had estimated more than five hundred instances of *sati* per year in their Indian territories. Subsequent colonial and postcolonial authorities in India upheld the ban. But some cultural relativists see this as an unwarranted attempt to impose Western standards on a different culture.

There is also dowry murder, where after failed attempts to extract higher dowries, Indian wives are burned alive or killed in other ways by their husbands or in-laws. This is a growing problem. Current estimates for India suggest over two thousand cases of bride-burning and a further six thousand dowry murders per year. Dowry murders run into the thousands annually in Pakistan and they have also been recorded in Iran.

The journalist Nick Cohen rightly mocked the pretentious and tortured prose of Western leftish academic apologists, who questioned our moral repugnance against practices such as *sati* and dowry murder. These apologists accused Western critics of 'interfering' in cultures that are different from theirs. The critics were imperialist agents of cultural globalization, forcing Western views on others. Cohen translated the obscurantist and obnoxious discourse of the apologists into brief, understandable English, boiling it down to its ridiculous and reactionary core argument: 'It is racist to oppose sexists'. But if we cannot oppose sexism because of cultural differences, then we cannot oppose racism too.[14]

In a forceful counter-blast against the apologists, Elizabeth M. Zechenter pointed out that such cultural relativism, 'no matter how nuanced, inevitably provides the logical justification for such inhumane practices' as widow-burning. It is appalling that some leading members of the feminist movement have been reduced to such disgraceful apologetics for brutality.[15]

UNIVERSAL HUMAN RIGHTS: FROM ABANDONMENT TO RE-INSTATEMENT

If unchallenged, the logic of cultural relativism would destroy the foundation of progressive and emancipatory thinking from the Enlightenment. Cultural relativists and postmodernists tell us that there is there is no such thing as objective reality or truth. Hence Enlightenment science must be a myth. We are also told that Enlightenment values are simply a reflection of bourgeois or Western interests. Enlightenment values are ideological devices to subjugate all cultures in the grand hegemonic project for Western-style globalization.

Proponents of these arguments have reacted against Western atrocities and aggression. But their flawed arguments would open the door to other forms of subjugation, oppression and evil. Drawn to their logical conclusions, they would end up condoning anything from cannibalism through witch-burning to Nazism.

The Universal Declaration of Human Rights was adopted by the General Assembly of the United Nations in 1948. It is an imperfect document and it has been subject to much scholarly scrutiny. One criticism is that it places too much emphasis on the individual, whereas Eastern cultures place more emphasis on the community and the social whole. There is scope for reconsideration here. But we should not concede too much.

While extreme individualists sometimes forget that individual self-realization comes only through interaction and cooperation with others in a community, we should also acknowledge that communities and families can often be regressive and discriminatory. Consider the community pressures in some cultures for child marriage, widow-burning or female genital mutilation. Protection from community or family injustices, especially in circumstances where we are dependent on communities and families for our livelihood and development, is precisely why many rights have to be framed in individual terms.

The academic and politician Michael Ignatieff argued: 'Western defenders of human rights have traded too much away. In the desire to find common ground with Islamic and Asian positions and to purge their own discourse of the imperial legacies uncovered by the postmodernist critique, Western defenders of human rights norms risk compromising the very universality they ought to be defending'.[16]

There is little substance in fears that universal rights would undermine other cultures. Zechenter pointed out that the general principles involved do not necessarily erode cultural specificities: 'Contrary to the assertions and fears of relativists, human rights universalism does not take away decision-making powers from individual cultures, nor does it have demoralizing and homogenizing effects'. She went on to argue that the Western origin of universal rights does not make them any less global in their validity:

Nor is there any evidence to show that universalism is merely a form of uncritical ethnocentric Western conspiracy designed to undermine non-Western cultures. It may well be that universal human rights ideals were first recognized and developed in the West, but that does not mean such ideals are alien to non-Western cultures. Similarly, while the development of international human rights law during the last forty years was primarily spearheaded by Western nations, it does not mean that the resulting international human rights regime is ethnocentric and unjust.[17]

We should also remind ourselves of the context of the 1948 Universal Declaration of Human Rights. As Ignatieff pointed out: 'the declaration was not so much a proclamation of the superiority of European civilization as an attempt to salvage the remains of its Enlightenment heritage from the barbarism of a world war just concluded. . . . A consciousness of European savagery is built into the very language of the declaration's preamble'. With awareness of the atrocities of fascism in Europe and elsewhere, this preamble noted that 'disregard and contempt for human rights have resulted in barbarous acts which have outraged the conscience of mankind'. As Ignatieff continued:

> The declaration may still be a child of the Enlightenment, but it was written when faith in the Enlightenment faced its deepest crisis. In this sense, human rights norms are not so much a declaration of the superiority of European civilization as a warning by Europeans that the rest of the world should not reproduce their mistakes.

Ignatieff went on to argue that one of those mistakes was 'idolatry of the nation-state, causing individuals to forget the higher law commanding them to disobey unjust orders'. Consequently:

> Unless the disastrous heritage of European collectivism is kept in mind as the framing experience in the drafting of the declaration, its individualism will appear to be nothing more than the ratification of Western bourgeois capitalist prejudice. In fact, it was much more: a studied attempt to reinvent the European natural law tradition in order to safeguard individual agency against the totalitarian state.[18]

In summary, normative cultural relativism is intellectually bankrupt and politically dangerous. While we are obliged to respect many aspects of other cultures, there are common universal values that we should also acclaim. Protection of the individual is important in any culture, and it does not necessarily imply a narrow, self-oriented individualism.

Twentieth-century anthropologists have done great service by showing us the huge variety of cultural norms and practices around the world. They have rightly warned us that practices that we take for granted in the West are not necessarily the only, or right, way. But at the same time, many anthropologists have diverted our gaze away from important commonalities across cultures.

There is strong evidence of human cultural and normative universals. Donald E. Brown has described more than four hundred statistical regularities in every known culture. These include ideas of fairness and taking turns, admiration for generosity, condemnation of murder and rape, restrictions on violence, concepts of property and inheritance, and distinctions between actions that are willed and actions that are not under self-control. Similarly Shalom H. Schwartz identified a set of values that were nearly universal in forty-four countries. The idea that lying is wrong is found in virtually all religions. These human universals endure despite other major cultural variations.[19]

It is likely that their universality derives in part from their positive role in the survival of individuals and groups. We are divided into different cultures, but we are all human beings, descended from common ancestors who had to deploy and adapt their cultural knowledge to survive. While the anthropologists of the first half of the twentieth century pointed to cultural diversity, and showed that beliefs about goodness and morality varied around the world, we also have to take note of those shared practices and beliefs that have helped humans globally for their survival. These shared practices and beliefs are not necessarily morally justified, but they are important indicators of what kind of moral norms are important for human survival.[20]

As noted in the preceding chapter, many argue that the principal function of human rights is to protect and promote certain essential human interests, particularly concerning well-being, personal development and protection from harm. Human rights help us secure the necessary conditions for human well-being. Human rights are hence universal, reflecting the commonalities in our biological, psychological and social nature.[21]

CODA

The Vietnam War was a seminal event for the worldwide Left. While cultural relativism was strengthened, it had other very different effects on the thinking of major segments of the Left. Vietnam was one of several struggles against colonialism and its legacies. Hence the massive protest against the Vietnam War injected energy into other important movements, including the (ultimately successful) campaign against Apartheid in South Africa and the (still-unresolved) struggle for the rights of the Palestinian people.

Marxists had always faced the problem that their prophesied proletarian revolution in the developed countries had never arrived, and showed no sign of arriving. An outburst of militant anti-colonial movements gave the Marxist Left a new hope to bring socialism closer. Borrowing from Mao Zedong and others, the idea of Third World struggle against 'Western imperialism' became fashionable. The proletariat had let Marxism down: the new saviours were those downtrodden by imperialism in poor countries. Through their victories, the rich countries would be jolted into revolution.[22]

This shift within Marxism was not confined to Maoists. To gain advantage in the Cold War, particularly in the Third World arena, the Soviet Union endorsed several anti-colonial struggles and postcolonial regimes. Third World struggles were also supported by Trotskyists, some of whom gained funding from dictators like Muammar Gaddafi and Saddam Hussein.

The new Third World focus of the Left had major consequences. It led to the support of movements or regimes that were illiberal, authoritarian, fanatical or religious. Key principles of the Enlightenment were jettisoned.

The Left also changed its position on Israel. The Left had been sympathetic to the plight of the Jews after the Holocaust. Many had supported the Zionist idea of a Jewish state and the formation of Israel in 1948. But Israel was supported by the West and it was engaged in violent struggle against Palestinian forces and postcolonial states in the Middle East. So it was seen as an agent of Western imperialism. It became the enemy. As Dave Rich wrote: 'Since the 1960s, the idea has spread across the left that Zionism is a racist ideology and that Israel is a Western colonial implant in the Middle East'. For many, illegal occupations and brutalities committed by Israel made this argument seem more plausible. The Left's sympathy for Zionism was reduced. Many called for a single, integrated, secular state of Palestine.

Others went further to support anti-Semitic, terrorist organizations such as Hamas and Hezbollah, who wish to destroy Israel. Today, people claiming to be 'anti-Zionist' now dominate the UK Labour Party. Literally, this would mean a denial of Israel's right to exist and would suggest support for its extermination.

Israel's governments should be criticized for its disproportionate use of force and its routine rejection of UN resolutions. But without careful thought and firm political leadership, the language of blaming Israel can slip into the rhetoric of blaming Jews. Add the age-old perception that Jews are rich from their devious pickings in business and finance. Stir in the more recent mantras of anti-imperialism and of a class struggle against the rich. We end up with a dangerous brew of anti-Semitism that closely resembles Nazism. In this context, anti-Semitism has now re-appeared, not only on the fringes, but also within a major party on the Left.[23]

Hamas and Hezbollah fight for Palestine, but they are explicitly wedded to an anti-Semitic and extreme Islamist ideology. Many of their Left supporters seem comfortable with this. This complete about-turn, on the foundational question of religion by many on the Left, is the subject of the next chapter.

CHAPTER 9

Final Full Turn:
The Left Condones Reactionary
Religion

As religious beliefs are deeply held and religious culture produces much of value, many liberal-minded people are wary about having arguments with the religious. They have forgotten what the men and women of the Enlightenment knew. All faiths in their extreme form carry the possibility of tyranny because they place the revealed word of whatever god or gods they happen to worship above the democratic will of electorates.

Nick Cohen, *What's Left* (2007)

Intelligence Squared is an organization that arranges high-profile debates about important topics around the world. Several Intelligence Squared debates have been broadcast globally on BBC World to audiences of up to eighty million, and they are available on YouTube.

A dramatic Intelligence Squared debate was broadcast in October 2009. The motion for dispute was: 'The Catholic Church is a force for good in the world'. In favour of the motion were the Catholic Archbishop John Onaiyekan (from Nigeria) and Ann Widdecombe (a retired British Conservative politician). Opposing the motion were Christopher Hitchens (an Anglo-American author and journalist) and Stephen Fry (a famous British actor and television presenter).

The conservative British newspaper *The Telegraph* ran a report on the debate, which was headlined: 'Catholics humiliated by Christopher Hitchens and Stephen Fry'. The author of the report was the journalist Andrew Brown—himself a Catholic. According to him, the supporters of the motion were 'comprehensively trounced'. A vote taken among the auditorium audience before the debate was 678 in favour of the motion and 1,102 against. After the debate the vote shifted to only 268 in favour with a devastating 1,876 against.

According to the journalist, Hitchens and Fry were able to swing the debate by listing one after another the 'wicked things' that have been done in the name of the Catholic Church. They attacked the Catholic teaching on homosexuality. More than anything they focused on the 'institutionalisation of the rape and torture and maltreatment of children'.[1]

Let us consider another event. It is imaginary. It is unlikely to happen. It would be a large, TV-broadcast, YouTube-accessible debate on 'Islam is a force for good in the world'. It would have excellent and educated proponents and opponents. The imaginary opponents might focus on alleged 'wicked things' associated with Islam, citing the forms of justice prescribed in some prominent versions of Sharia law (such as mutilation and stoning to death); the condoned murder of blasphemers, apostates or homosexuals; and religious laws discriminating against women.

Below I will consider some of the rights or wrongs of this imaginary opposition's case. But the account in the preceding paragraph is an imagined event—these are words of fiction. Instead I wish first to consider the public reaction to the event if it actually happened. I am not going to consider the reaction of intolerant religious extremists who shun all dispute and debate. I wish to consider the possible reaction of part of the educated and enlightened Western Left.

First, it is possible that the statements made by the opposition in either the real or imaginary debate might be (or may become) illegal under British law. In 2005 the British Labour government under Tony Blair began to push the 'Racial and Religious Hatred Bill' through Parliament. Labour originally tried to criminalize 'deliberately insulting' a religion. Under this original draft, the *Charlie Hebdo* cartoons of Mohammed would have probably been deemed criminal. The original draft of the bill would have made 'abusive and insulting' words against a religion a criminal offence, even if they were not intended to stir up hatred against adherents of a religion.

This draft bill was widely and strongly criticized. It was eventually amended in the House of Lords, requiring the intention—and not just the possibility—of stirring up religious hatred to constitute a breach of the law. The amended draft returned to the House of Commons. There the Labour government attempted to reverse the change, but a revolt of some Labour MPs led to a close-run defeat. The amended act passed into law in 2006.

Second, the opposition in the imaginary debate would certainly be accused of *Islamophobia*. A problem here is that the much-contested word has more meanings than it has letters. Does it literally mean fear of Islam? Or criticism of Islam? Or hatred of Islam? Or persecution of Muslims? Its intended meaning can range from scholarly criticism of Islamic doctrines to racist acts against ethnic groups who are Muslim. These are obviously very different. Informed academics have criticized the term for its serious ambiguities. For example, Erik Bleich wrote in a prestigious academic journal that 'there is no widely accepted definition of Islamophobia that permits systematic comparative and causal analysis'.[2]

Sadly there is extensive prejudice and discrimination against Muslims. Muslim minorities in developed countries are frequently subjected to discrimination, abuse, threats and violence. There are anti-Muslim fanatics who would wish to deport them, or to do them severe harm. Some Muslims in Western countries live in fear. These problems are extremely serious and have to be addressed. No one should live in fear of violence or repression. Freedoms of belief and worship should be vigilantly protected.

There is strong evidence that Muslims face acute discrimination at work in Britain, France, the United States and elsewhere.[3] This is a very serious problem, contravening individual rights, and it needs energetic remedial action. But this should not involve restriction on the criticism of a religion: freedom of expression (short of incitement to violence) is also a human right.

In his election campaign, US President Donald Trump repeatedly called for Muslims to be banned from entering the United States. This amounts to discrimination on the grounds of religion and encourages other bigots to do the same.

Also in 2016, several French towns banned the burkini swimwear, leading to incidents of French police obliging women to uncover their heads. The *burqa* is different: it has been (rightly or wrongly) banned in France on the grounds that the full covering of the face is demeaning for women, and it could be used as a means of concealment of identity or weapons by terrorists.[4] By contrast, the burkini hugs the body and leaves the face uncovered. The attempt to ban the burkini showed shameful anti-Muslim prejudice by some local authorities.

But calling this prejudice *Islamophobia* is misleading. It is unjustified intolerance of a minority group. In all such cases, anti-Muslim 'prejudice' or 'discrimination' would be much better terms than *Islamophobia*, which has the effect of closing down criticism of religion.

While firmly condemning all such discrimination against minorities, the task at hand is to address the role of religion. Following Enlightenment thinkers, we should criticize the way that religion has been used as a means to legitimate legal and political authority. This is principally to do with the promotion of a system of law derived from a religion, rather than from a secular, democratically legitimated, legislative authority.

As noted below, other religious texts, including the Old Testament, urge believers to punish transgressors, subdue women, kill homosexuals and execute apostates. The problem is not just the sacred word: it is the degree to which a religious community has assimilated into modern post-Enlightenment societies, and accepted—at least in practice—that they cannot treat religious texts as supreme law.

Christians and Jews used to see religion as the grounding of all law. Some still do. But to a large extent they have modernized and accepted secular authority. The failure of Islam to modernize adequately has created problems for the Left, especially after its shift away from its Enlightenment roots. In the name of multi-culturalism or Third World struggle, many leftists have become apologists for religious authority. Misguided by cultural relativism or 'anti-imperialism', they have failed to make a stand in favour of the vital freedom to criticize religion. Some have gone even further to side with Islamic extremism in the 'anti-imperialist' struggle.

CRITICISM OF A RELIGION IS NOT RACISM

Many intelligent people wrongly regard criticism of Islam as racist or xenophobic. As noted previously, the American actor Ben Affleck described criticism of some Islamic beliefs as 'racist'. An academic article that couples 'Islamophobia' with 'racism' in its title has been published in a leading sociological journal. An article published in the thoughtful and progressive *Guardian* newspaper was titled: 'Islamophobia is racism, pure and simple'.[5]

All this again confuses criticism of a religious doctrine with hostility to an ethnic group. They are entirely different things, notwithstanding the fact that many Muslims are non-white and suffer racist abuse and discrimination. Emphatically, criticism of Islam as a doctrine does not imply hostility to Muslims as persons: it does not imply hostility to any ethnic group.

At least in Britain, Muslims are the most ethnically diverse followers of any single religion. Globally, there are numerous white Muslims, as well as many Muslims of multiple Asian and African ethnicities. This makes nonsense of the confused allegation of 'anti-Muslim racism'.[6]

Refraining from criticism of religion does not help the assimilation of Muslims or any other religious group. On the contrary, the Enlightenment values of tolerance, freedom of speech, freedom of worship and respectful debate can demonstrate a way forward, help to integrate those communities, and reduce the climate of fear and the threat of persecution. Mutual understanding is the basis of all tolerance. Yet all understanding requires the possibility of critical engagement.

Racism and anti-Muslim discrimination are serious problems and we should stand up against them. But this should not curtail criticism of religion.

These things have to be carefully separated, even when they are conflated by others. As the writer and broadcaster Kenan Malik wrote in his article entitled 'The Islamophobia Myth': 'The charge of "Islamophobia" is all too often used not to highlight racism but to stifle criticism'.[7]

Yet in the 2015 British general election campaign, the then Labour Party leader Ed Miliband—and putative future Prime Minister—spoke out strongly against 'Islamophobia'. Even after criticism by secularists, he did not define what it meant. He pledged to strengthen the law against it—whatever it means. In an interview with *The Muslim News* on 24 April 2015, Miliband mentioned Islamophobia and promised: 'We are going to make it an aggravated crime. We are going to make sure it is marked on people's records with the police to make sure they root out Islamophobia as a hate crime'.[8]

Ed Miliband has degrees from the University of Oxford and the London School of Economics. Hence he must be aware that the term *phobia* derives from the Greek *phobos*, meaning *fear* or *panic*. Did he want to make a particular fear or panic an 'aggravated crime'? Miliband surely intended a different meaning, but he was trying to make something 'an aggravated crime' without being clear what it was.

Note also Miliband's undefined use of the term *hate crime*. This was the same term used appropriately by the police in Charleston, South Carolina, in the United States, after the racist murder of nine African Americans in a church in January 2015. Yet criticism of religion is entirely different from racist murder. It is preposterous to place them in the same category. There is a severe danger that loose terms like 'Islamophobia' and 'hate crime' become the means of restricting free speech, including the vital right to criticize a religion.

On 11 January 2015, along with David Cameron, François Hollande, Angela Merkel and other world leaders, Miliband joined the 'Je Suis Charlie' march in Paris, in favour of freedom of expression and in protest against the murder of the *Charlie Hebdo* journalists by Islamist fanatics. With about one and a half million people on the streets, this was the largest demonstration in French history. But if Miliband had become Prime Minister in the May 2015 election, he might have made illegal the publication in Britain of the *Charlie Hebdo* cartoons for 'deliberately insulting' a religion.

Criticism of religion can offend people. This is why it is always important to stress the universal human rights to worship and to live without fear, molestation, discrimination and violence. We have to create a climate where criticism of religion is possible, and the right to worship is upheld and protected.

RELIGION AND THE SOURCES OF LAW

Protection of the right to worship does not mean that human rights can be overridden by a religion. Any rules of behaviour that derive from a religion should be subservient to both the morality of human rights and state laws that are consistent with those rights.

Most religions have a lot to answer for. Christianity has been responsible for atrocious wars, genocides, persecutions, tortures, slavery and much else. The Old Testament preaches genocide and depicts a vengeful God who murders many innocents and sometimes instructs his chosen people to commit genocide.[9]

Leviticus (20:13) describes all homosexual acts as 'detestable' and legally punishable by death. According the religious laws set out in to Deuteronomy 13:6-10, everyone who renounces the true God must be stoned to death.

The Bible is also spine-chilling in its discrimination against women. Deuteronomy (22:20-21) instructs that if a bride is found not to be a virgin, then she must be stoned to death at the door of her home.

None of these religious laws is overturned by the New Testament. Jesus himself is reported as saying: 'Think not that I am come to destroy the law, or the prophets: I am not come to destroy, but to fulfil. . . . Till heaven and earth pass, one jot or one tittle shall in no wise pass from the law, till all be fulfilled' (Matthew 5:17-18). St Paul in Colossians (3:18) and in Ephesians (5:22-24) instructed women to submit to the commands and desires of their husbands.

The Catholic Church has a bleak history of authoritarianism and repression. Apart from the abuse of children and the persecution of homosexuals, until 1966 it forbade Catholics from reading works by Montaigne, Voltaire, Copernicus, Galileo, Francis Bacon, Blaise Pascal, John Milton, John Locke, René Descartes, Denis Diderot, Victor Hugo, Jean-Jacques Rousseau, Baruch Spinoza, Immanuel Kant, David Hume, Thomas Browne, Jean-Paul Sartre and Simone de Beauvoir.

But for most (sadly not all) Christians and Jews today, the Old Testament is no longer regarded as supreme law. It does not trump state laws. Believers are not generally obliged by their religion to punish those that break its rules. Believers agree to accept the authority of democratic states, even if they contradict their religion.

Crucially, despite sharing its Abrahamic roots with Judaism and Christianity, Islam currently sustains a different relationship between law and society. The imprecise rhetoric of 'Islamophobia' obscures all this. Those that label criticism of Islam as racism inadvertently and misleadingly shift attention onto ethnic or racial characteristics, thus ignoring the social rules and norms that religions infuse into cultures. To consider the place of any religion in the Enlightenment project we need to consider how that religion works, at the level of the promulgation and practical enforcement of its social rules.

Christianity became the dominant religion in the West when, in the fourth century AD, the Roman Emperor Constantine favoured it, and suppressed other religions. Then established as the official religion of the Roman and Byzantine Empires, it came to dominate the elites of medieval Europe and spread via colonialism to other continents. Although some were willing converts, many other ordinary people were obliged to become Christian because their rulers hitched onto that faith. It was largely a top-down process, often imposed by higher authorities.

Even before the destruction of Jerusalem by the Romans in 70 AD, the Jews were dispersed throughout the Roman Empire. Catastrophic destruction in their homeland in Judea led to a further diaspora. The Jews were always in a minority in the places that they were tolerated. They retained their religion and customs, but otherwise adapted as much as possible to local laws and traditions. For example, laws that required them to kill apostates (Deuteronomy 13:6–10) were eventually abandoned in deference to the laws in their host country. Adaptation was the necessary (but sadly sometimes insufficient) price for their survival.

By contrast, Islam was rarely the creed of an adaptable minority. Even when it was imposed by conquest, it was sustained from below. It has remained to a large degree a devolved system, with rules enforced by religious conversion and the dedication of its adherents. It offers powerful incentives for conversion and strong disincentives against apostasy (i.e. abandonment or renunciation of the religion).

RELIGIONS AND SECULAR STATES

The Enlightenment affirmed religious tolerance and freedom of worship. It also promoted the separation of church from state, which has been fully achieved in at best a few countries.

In Britain, the Church of England is not yet completely separated from the state. For example, the monarch is obliged to be a member of the Church of England and its bishops have automatic seats in the House of Lords.

Zionism was set up as a movement to create a state for the Jewish people. The original Zionists wanted to set up a secular state. But in some spheres of state authority, Israel since its formation in 1948 has institutionalized a special place for Judaism. For example, all recognized marriages in Israel must be presided over by a rabbi. Such laws are a problem for Israeli citizens who do not adhere to Judaism.

Turning to Islam, a minority of the forty-nine countries with majority Muslim populations have purportedly separated religion from the state. In most of these minority cases, secularism has been imposed from outside by a colonial power or from inside by a dictatorship. In other minority cases the secularism is nominal rather than effective, because of weak or failed states.

The minority cases include nine countries where secularism has been imposed; these nine, from Albania to Uzbekistan, were formerly under Communist rule. Six sub-Saharan African countries have majority Muslim populations, with relatively weak and nominally secular states that generally do not override the local practice of Islamic law. North African countries were partly secularized by colonial rule and by subsequent dictatorships.

Since its declaration as a republic in 1923, Turkey is often cited as a secular country. It is at a higher level of economic development than most other Muslim nations. But the Turkish state discriminates in favour of Sunni Muslims and pays the wages of Sunni imams out of revenues from national taxes. It also funds education in the Sunni Islamic religion in state schools. There is a Department of Religious Affairs, directly under the Prime Minister's control, responsible for controlling the Sunni Muslim religion, including the vetting of sermons in mosques. Since Recep Tayyip Erdoğan became Prime Minister in 2003 and President in 2014, Turkey's secularism has been further undermined.

There is no clear case of a predominantly Muslim country that has become fully secular through a democratic process. The few Muslim-majority democracies include Tunisia, where secularization was imposed by the pre-2011 dictatorship, and Turkey, where secular reforms were implemented after the revolutionary establishment of the Republic of Turkey in 1923. Today, in both cases, democracy is limited and fragile. In other cases, secularism was imposed by colonial powers, through Communist rule or by authoritarian military regimes.

THE HISTORY AND NATURE OF ISLAM

Today Islam has about 1.6 billion followers—about 23 per cent of the global population. After Christianity, it is the second-largest religion by number of adherents.

The rise and spread of Islam is an astonishing story. Born in about 570 AD in Mecca in Arabia, Mohammed worked as a merchant. In about 610 he reported revelations that he believed to be from God. These were recorded by his companions in the Qur'an. Mohammed and his followers began to preach to the people, imploring them to follow the one true God. In 622 they established a political and religious authority in the city of Medina. Its constitution allowed religious freedoms for Jewish and Christian minorities and established taxes and legal institutions. In 629 Mohammed and his followers conquered Mecca; much of Arabia became united under Islamic rule.

After Mohammed's death in 632, Islam spread into Syria and Persia. By 750 it had surged westward across North Africa, conquering Iberia and reaching the south of France. Then it spread further eastward, into India. Groups of Muslim traders settled as far away as China and Indonesia.

The period from 750 to 1258 is known as the Islamic Golden Age. Firmly bonded by a shared religion, the legal and institutional framework that had been developed by Mohammed and his disciples proved to be highly effective for maintaining social order and for promoting economic, scientific and cultural development.

For example, the Islamic legal framework of the *waqf*—a form of private foundation devoted to charitable service—was used to establish many social facilities, including hospitals. Founded in 859, the University of Al Karaouine in Morocco was the first degree-awarding university in the world. Under Islam there were hugely impressive developments in science and mathematics. Islam's many Golden Age achievements in art, architecture and literature endure as outstanding accomplishments to this day.[10]

From the thirteenth century, Islam spread with Muslim trade networks and in some cases by conquest. It extended into sub-Saharan Africa, Central Asia and the Malay Archipelago. Under the Ottoman Empire, Islam spread to South-East Europe, Crimea and the Caucasus.

The extraordinary intercontinental and multi-ethnic spread of Islam cannot be explained simply in terms of a combination of military strength and religious zeal. The explanation lies in the manner in which Islam fuses together religion with law and the state. Language itself reflects this fusion: the Arabic word for religion is *din*, which can also be translated as 'submission to law and order'.

The Qur'an is a legal as well as a religious text. It contains many rules that Muslims must follow in their daily lives and their relations with others. It ordains a personal regimen of devotion and ritual, involving faith, prayer, charity, fasting and pilgrimage. It includes laws and rules governing all sorts of affairs, from within the family and business to dealing with non-believers.

The Qur'an is often supplemented by the Hadith, which was developed by Islamic scholars in the ninth century. The Hadith is allegedly based on the words and deeds of Mohammed, but there is no single, agreed version. Nevertheless, it often has served as a supplement to the Qur'an in matters of legal and religious doctrine. The Qur'an and Hadith make up the body of Sharia law, but Islamic sects disagree on some matters of inclusion and interpretation.

In many respects, the detailed rules in the Qur'an and Hadith are impressive. Although they often fail by modern liberal and egalitarian norms, they show concern for everyone in the community and they are designed to bind Muslim societies together to enhance their harmony and prosperity.

This highly sophisticated and relatively advanced system of social and economic rules helps to explain Islam's achievements in its Golden Age, when other societies in Europe and elsewhere were languishing in backwardness and enduring disorder.

The Qur'an requires that different Islamic tribes and clans cooperate together in their common subjugation to God. Formerly a merchant, Mohammed took great care to specify rules to ensure that contracts between Muslims would be enforced, that their property rights would be respected and that everyone's prosperity could be enhanced through cooperation and trade.

Hence Islam draws much of its power from its provision of socioeconomic rules that extend far beyond the activities of worship and ceremonial commemorations of birth, maturity, marriage and death. Islam provides a complex legal system governing the spheres of work and civil society, as well as of the family. The enforcement of these rules relies primarily on religious adherence and devotion, with less reliance on legal authority buttressed by the state.

In Islamic societies, the legitimation of legal authority is by religion, acting at the social base. All authority is legitimized by God, rather than by democracy or anything else. Laws in particular are seen as immutable commands by God, rather than the decrees of any human authority.

Islamic religious and legal rules developed in communities where states were often weak and societies were fragmented into tribes and clans. Although Islamic legal texts decree that rulers have the duty to enforce laws, many of these laws are derived from religious sources and believers also have an obligation to enforce them. Courts played an important role, but some important aspects of justice were devolved to individual Muslims. Islam assigns the right of enforcement of many laws directly to the believer.

Islam spread over a vast territory, encompassing many different languages and ethnicities. It did not rely on a strong, centralized, state apparatus. The shared, engrained, cultural dedication to religious rules made a smaller state possible.[11]

Believers have a duty to follow the Qur'an, including when it requires them to punish others. The Qur'an is seen as the word of God, which believers have a duty to obey. And there are several passages in the Qur'an that ask true Muslims to punish those who disobey God's rules. As long as they carefully follow his instructions, God gives permission to Muslims to take the law into their own hands.

Consequently, many legal rules in Islam are enforced bottom-up, by the authority of God as devolved to believers, rather than top-down by the authority of courts or governments. As the Islamic scholar Michael Cook put it:

> What we see here is the presence, within the mainstream of Islamic thought, of a strikingly . . . radical value: the principle that an executive power of the law of God is vested in each and every Muslim. Under this conception the individual believer as such has not only the right, but also the duty, to issue orders pursuant to God's law, and to do what he can to see that they are obeyed.[12]

The massive spread of Islam, from Iberia in the West, to the Malay Archipelago and parts of China in the East, created a huge intercontinental zone for trade with effective legal-religious mechanisms for the enforcement of contracts. It did not require a unified state apparatus to police this zone. Islamic societies enforced contracts through their fusion of religion and law: believers would honour their agreements, even if they were between strangers, because they were made in the sight of a just and merciful God.

The enforcement of Islamic legal-religious rules required the inculcation of the strictures in the Qur'an and Hadith into every Muslim. For this reason, Islamic societies have promoted mass religious education, particularly of males.

Originally, this powerful fusion of religion with law created the conditions for impressive economic growth, at least until the fourteenth century. The scientific and cultural achievements of Islam were built upon this prosperity.

SUCCESSES AND FAILURES OF MODERNIZATION

Europe developed later, and took a very different path. It eventually created national trading zones on the basis of the growing military and legal powers of its nation states. This process began in Western Europe around the late fifteenth century, with the development of stronger nation states in Spain, Portugal, France and England. This was much later than the wide-ranging commerce of the Islamic world, which by contrast was achieved without the development of strong states.

But the Islamic system had an unforeseen problem. It was designed in an era when economic growth and technological advance were slow. It presumed a virtually static society, without further structural or technological changes. But as technology, urbanization and the scale of productive activity advanced, new rules were needed to improve economic efficiency. But because the Qur'an was deemed to be the word of God, it could not be altered by any political or legal authority. There could be disputes over interpretation, but the word of God could not be changed. Consequently, in the absence of powerful rival authority, it was difficult to modify legal and other rules.

Christians and Jews also upheld religious texts as the word of God, and religious rules as legally and morally binding. But in these cases, evolving circumstance and history have allowed most adherents to accept state laws as well.

In Christian Europe most ordinary people were denied access to the Biblical texts until the Reformation. In England the Bible was not widely available in English until the seventeenth century, at a time when a large majority of the population was illiterate. The Bible was used selectively and deviously by those in power to maintain the authority of the state and of the nobility. They did not devolve matters of judgment or punishment to ordinary people.

The chronic disadvantage of the ruling-class monopoly of access to religious texts in Christian Europe was the suppression and ignorance of the population. But the top-down imposition of Christianity did allow for more flexibility. Official doctrine could shift as new circumstances and interests emerged. When mass education belatedly spread in Europe in the late nineteenth century, its peoples were already entering a more secular and enlightened age.

Judaism adapted for different reasons. Dispersed from their homeland, the Jews had to survive as minorities within other states. While keeping their religion, they otherwise adapted to local laws and customs.

In contrast, despite its enormous achievements from the eight to the thirteenth centuries, Islam was much less adaptable. It relied on educated local observance from the bottom up. Within a state it was typically the religion of the majority rather than a minority.

This limited adaptability helps to explain why Islamic countries were eventually overtaken economically by the rising powers in Western Europe. In his meticulous studies of this process, the economist Timur Kuran has identified a number of institutional brakes on Islamic economic development, from the fifteenth century to modern times. They include the rigid inheritance laws in the Qur'an. These were designed to ensure that wives and children all gained a portion of the wealth of the deceased, but they disallowed the passing on of agglomerated wealth that could be used in larger-scale enterprise.

In addition, while Europe from the thirteenth century was developing the legal form of the corporation, which eventually became the foundation of large-scale mercantile and industrial endeavour, non-human legal persons (such as corporations) were prohibited by the Qur'an.[13]

ISLAM'S DIFFICULTIES WITH MODERNIZATION

The relatively unadaptable nature of Islamic institutions meant that rules and laws that emerged in underdeveloped tribal society were preserved, with relatively little amendment, into the modern era. Let us consider some examples.

By the standards of Europe before 1750, many Islamic rules were relatively progressive, including the rules concerning women. Until recently, severe discrimination against women was the norm throughout the world, including in medieval Europe; women were often treated as chattels. In Britain, married women could not own property until 1882.

The Qur'an and Hadith were written by men, for men and they give instructions to men. Their rules make the husband the head of the household, who may take up to four wives as long as he can treat them all fairly. If a wife is disobedient, then her husband may beat her. A woman's inheritance is unequal to, and generally less than, a man's. A daughter's inheritance is usually half that of her brother's. In legal proceedings under Sharia law, a woman's testimony before a court is worth half that of a man's, so it takes at least two female witnesses to counter the testimony of one man.

The Qur'an forbids adultery between a man and the wife of another man. The specified punishment is flogging. But the Qur'an explicitly allows the rape of unbelievers when they are owned captives or slaves. Some passages in the Qur'an seem to forbid homosexuality. While this has been a matter of interpretative dispute, in most of the Islamic world today, homosexual acts are illegal and sometimes carry the death penalty.

Slavery has been widespread for thousands of years. The Qur'an and Hadith do not abolish slavery, but try to avoid some of its injustices. The enslavement of other Muslims is strictly forbidden. This was at a time when Christians could enslave fellow believers, as well as others. But as an unintended consequence, the prohibition on Muslim enslavement led to a massive importation of slaves from outside, particularly through Islamic military conquest. The Qur'an clearly sanctions violent and repressive actions against unbelievers.

The codification of laws for slaves led paradoxically to a substantial extension of the Islamic slave trade.

Although no specific penalty is specified in the Qur'an, Muslim jurists in the seventh century imposed a death penalty for apostasy. It is decreed in some versions of the Hadith; many modern Muslims still advocate this punishment.[14] Islam is a political as well as a religious system; hence exit from its belief system is akin to treason, as well as defiance of God. But punishment for apostasy is clearly against freedom of choice in religion, as codified in the United Nations Universal Declaration of Human Rights.

The rules in both the Qur'an and Hadith are dependent on context and interpretation. Although what is written is important, the problem is not simply the literal rules themselves. Salafism is the most conservative wing of Islam and its Wahhabi variant is prominent in Saudi Arabia. These sects interpret the rules more strictly, with the most severe punishments. In recent decades, Salafism has spread rapidly and globally. Conservative Islam is also a major force behind the adoption of the *burqa*.

In the twenty-first century, many Islamic rules appear as hugely anachronistic, discriminatory and demeaning. The problem is not simply that these discriminatory doctrines are in their scriptures: similar rules can be found in the Bible. But in the main, Christianity and Judaism have modernized. It is a matter of cultural practice and not simply Holy Scripture.

In appraising any religion, it is important not to overemphasize scriptural doctrine and overlook cultural practices and institutional structures within a faith. We do not routinely require Christians or Jews to renounce the discriminatory laws in Leviticus or Deuteronomy. That is because they do not bear upon the practices of most of their followers.

A key problem with Islam is that many of its adherents have not yet modernized and accepted the practical supremacy of secular law. Backward cultural practices, often transmitted from less developed countries with weak legal systems, have survived among Muslims, and are sustained by the religious customs of immigrant communities. Many Muslims do not accept the authority of secular law and democratic government above that of their religion. Many Muslims live in, or originate from, underdeveloped countries that have not experienced an equivalent of the Enlightenment.

The Islamic fusion of law with religion created a largely conservative system of belief. In addition, the devolution of rights of legal judgment and punishment to individual believers contrasts with legal norms in the modern West, where citizens are prohibited from taking the law into their own hands. This state monopolization of political and legal power is an important hallmark of modernization.

Partly as a result of Western colonialism, several Islamic countries began to modernize in the nineteenth century. The changes were most marked in the areas of commercial law, and less so in aspects of family and community life. In other spheres, modernization was more limited.

Notably, few if any Islamic countries are stable and secure democracies. One of the barriers to democracy is the retention of legal and political powers in the hands of clans and religious sects, and the consequent failure to develop strong national states that draw legitimacy and support from the people as a whole.[15]

For this reason, it was naïve of some leading Western politicians to expect that the overthrow of Saddam Hussein in Iraq in 2003 would lead to a flowering of democracy. Iraq was an artificial creation of Western colonialism and is deeply divided along religious-sectarian and ethnic lines. Such a riven society would be difficult to keep together, except by colonial or homegrown despotism.

For similar reasons, with the single, fragile exception of Tunisia, no country experiencing the Arab Spring uprisings of 2010–2012 has developed into a democracy. The outcomes have been either authoritarian government or sectarian civil war. The causes of these failures are multiple and complex, but one is the nature and social structure of Islam and its institutions.

THE NEED FOR ASSIMILATION AND REFORM

Many Muslims, like members of other faiths, are kind and peace-loving people. Many have moved to developed countries and embraced Enlightenment norms and values. Many live and work in harmony with others. But others have turned into terrorists and murdered innocent civilians in their home countries.

Hassan Butt was born in Luton in England in 1980. In 2000 he travelled to Pakistan and worked for the Taliban and other jihadists against the West. Subsequently he renounced his anti-Western views. His reports of the jihadist mentality are chilling: 'What drove me and many of my peers to plot acts of extreme terror within Britain, our own homeland and abroad, was a sense that we were fighting for the creation of a revolutionary state that would eventually bring Islamic justice to the world'. Butt went on to explain that 'Islamic theology, unlike Christian theology, does not allow for the separation of the state and religion . . . [they] are considered to be one and the same'. Consequently, since no righteous Islamic state is deemed to exist, the extremists have 'declared war on the whole world'.

But some on the so-called Left shunned Butt's remarks against jihad. They disowned him for betraying the struggle against 'Western imperialism'. He was also criticized by one member of the 'Stop the War' movement, who is a leading supporter of the Muslim Brotherhood, for his unjustified 'call to change the face of Islam'.[16]

There is a substantial, ongoing debate about the possibilities for reform within Islam. It involves Muslims as well as non-Muslims. Optimists argue that Islam, or a modernized version of it, is fully compatible with democracy and secular values. It is beyond the scope of this book to go into this debate, but some have found grounds for optimism. The main points that need to be established here are the following.

First, traditional Islam—like many other religions—is at odds in a number of respects with Enlightenment values of liberty and equality. Traditional Islam is not of the *Left*: it is a conservative creed that harks back to medieval times. Similar degrees of conservativism are found among other religions, including in some Christian sects. But the peculiar, devolved or bottom-up patterns of Islamic rule enforcement and punishment, and the enduring fusion of Islamic religion with law, are major drags on its modernization.

Second, many Muslims living in Western democracies have promoted unreformed and discriminatory versions of Islamic law. This represents a problem for any society that is based on Enlightenment principles, and which requires obedience to laws that are enacted by the state. It creates major difficulties for integration and assimilation. Such a society must, of course, protect the freedoms of Muslims and others to worship, to express themselves and to obtain a livelihood. Cultural and religious diversity can greatly enrich a modern nation, but only if the state legal system and overarching secular values remain healthy and intact. Such a diverse society requires a just legal system and strong secular values, not least to protect the human rights of members of minority religions or ethnicities.

Finally, the strident leftist rhetoric of 'Islamophobia'—advanced among others by politicians trying to capture the votes of Muslims in Western democracies—has blocked serious discussion of the merits and demerits of Islamic institutions and has disabled careful and scholarly attempts by Muslims and others to identify where these institutions are in need of reform. The rhetoric of 'Islamophobia' makes any criticism of the doctrines of Islam difficult, and it does no service to those Muslims who are trying to identify discriminatory and illiberal practices in their culture, and to develop a Muslim-led movement for modernization and assimilation.

THE 'ANTI-IMPERIALIST STRUGGLE': HOW THE
FAR LEFT EMBRACED MILITANT ISLAM

Much of the Left has failed to get to grips with these problems. It has even sided with Islam for reasons of political expediency. In 1920 Soviet Russia organized in Baku the Congress of the Peoples of the East. In their attempt to undermine the Western powers, the Communists made alliances with nationalist and jihadist movements. The historian E. H. Carr wrote about this event: 'Muslim beliefs and institutions were treated with veiled respect . . . The Muslim tradition of jihad, or holy war against the infidel, was harnessed to a modern crusade of oppressed peoples against the imperialist oppressors, with Britain as the main target'.[17] This was a fateful precedent. There are many recent examples of Left alliances with Islam, along with tolerance of theocratic rule, for 'anti-imperialist' motives.

Michel Foucault was once a darling theoretician of the Left. He was a member of the French Communist Party from 1950 to 1953. Eventually, he searched for other sources of inspiration. In 1978 he travelled to Iran and met opposition leaders who were to become involved in the dramatic revolution against the Shah in the following year. Returning to France, he visited the Ayatollah Khomeini, who was then in exile in Paris. Foucault expressed admiration for Khomeini's Islamist revolutionary movement. In a bizarre *hommage* redolent of his compatriot Jean-Jacques Rousseau, Foucault saw Khomeini as reflecting 'the perfectly unified collective will' of the Iranian people.

Foucault argued—presciently as it turned out—that Islamism was to become a major political force in the region. He proposed respect and support, rather than hostility. He depicted the 1979 Iranian Revolution as 'the first great insurrection against global systems'. But this 'great insurrection' led to a brutal Islamic regime in Iran, which repressed women, tortured and executed political dissenters, killed homosexuals, and persecuted non-Muslim minorities. Foucault was once asked in an interview why he had not protested against the persecution of intellectuals under Khomeini. His response was to support their repression, on the grounds that Iran 'did not have the same regime of truth as ours'. He thus descended into the reactionary apologetics of moral and cultural relativism.[18]

Since 1979, the official line of several Far Left groups is 'critical support' for the Iranian theocratic regime in its 'anti-imperialist struggle' against the West. Some have gone so far as to express similar support for the murderous, so-called Islamic State in Iraq and Syria. Others argue that Western 'imperialism' is more of an enemy to human emancipation than the Islamic State. Some Far Left groups took sides in the Iran–Iraq War of the 1980s to side with Iran.[19]

Nick Cohen has related how a huge and honourably motivated protest in Britain against the 2003 invasion of Iraq was led astray by the Trotskyist leaders of 'Stop the War'. These leaders advocated support for all resistance against the American and British invaders. That meant supporting al-Qaeda and other homicidal sects. Critics attempting to distance themselves from the suicide bombers and murderers of innocents were accused of 'anti-Islamic racism'. It is once again necessary to point out again that Islam is a religion and not a race.

The leaders of 'Stop the War' had recruited to their cause a British branch of the Muslim Brotherhood, known as the Muslim Association of Britain. Its leader, Yusuf al-Qaradawi, advocated suicide bombings against civilians, killing Muslim apostates, executing fornicators and gays, female genital mutilation, and the 'light' beating of disobedient or rebellious wives. In such a manner, a group of far leftists embraced a reactionary version of Islam.[20]

Also, disturbingly, the Left's failure to criticize the extreme rhetoric of some of their Muslim allies created a space for anti-Semitism to fester. This problem has now seeped into the Labour Party. As Trevor Phillips, former Chair of the Commission for Racial Equality, put it: 'Labour's determination to win support from Muslim communities has meant too often a blind eye has been turned to inconvenient attitudes, such as the unfair treatment of women or hostility to Jews'. Curtailment of criticism of Islam has led to a tolerance of extreme positions, some of which are anti-Semitic. Attempts from the Left as well as the Right to blame 'the Jews' for the world's ills are now sadly commonplace.[21]

In 2016 the British Labour MP Naz Shah was obliged to apologize for a series of posts on Facebook in 2014 where she endorsed a suggestion that Israel should be removed from its current location and set up instead in the United States. A number of other Labour Party members have been suspended or expelled for alleged anti-Semitism, including the former Mayor of London Ken Livingstone.[22]

The Labour leader Jeremy Corbyn has praised and taken tea on the parliamentary terrace with the Islamist leader Sheikh Raed Salah, despite the fact (as confirmed in a British court) that Salah is a notorious anti-Semite. Corbyn once described it as his 'honour and pleasure' to host 'our friends' from Hamas in Parliament. Hamas's charter states: 'The time will not come until Muslims will fight the Jews (and kill them); until the Jews hide behind rocks and trees, which will cry . . . there is a Jew hiding behind me, come on and kill him!'

Assuming that Corbyn is not anti-Semitic, it is difficult to excuse him taking 'honour and pleasure' from meeting and having such 'friends'.[23]

These cases show how Far Left toleration of Islamist extremism, and their choice of unsavoury Islamist allies in 'the struggle against Western imperialism', have opened the door for anti-Semitism to enter mainstream politics.

WHERE THE MODERATE LEFT HAS FAILED

While the Far Left sided with Islam, the more moderate Left in some countries ducked the problems of assimilation and reform. Since 1950, developed countries in Europe and elsewhere have experienced large-scale immigration, particularly from former colonies. Many of these immigrants had limited experience of any Western-style democracy and had an inadequate appreciation of universal human rights. Many of the immigrants came from rural areas in undeveloped countries, where the state was weak and social and business interactions were governed by custom and religion, based on ties of loyalty to family and clan.

Faced with this issue, many progressive politicians adopted a stance of ultra-tolerance and inaction. Consider the question of language. Should immigrants be obliged to learn the language of their new country, so that they can understand its culture and its laws? Some countries take this on board: a requirement that immigrants into Sweden learn Swedish has long been in place. Other countries have active assimilation programmes.

But such an assimilationist policy in Britain was highly controversial as late as 2001. In that year, Labour MP Ann Cryer bravely argued that many UK Muslims were held back economically and educationally by language difficulties. The problem was especially severe among Muslim women. But she was faced with criticism and scorn from the Left. Shahid Malik, a senior member of the Commission for Racial Equality and a member of the Labour Party National Executive Committee, and subsequently a Labour MP and government minister, responded to Cryer: 'Her arguments are sinister and they have no basis in fact . . . she is doing the work of the extreme right wing'.[24]

2001 was of course the year of the al-Qaeda attacks on New York and Washington, which led to the deaths of 2,977 innocent people from 90 countries. The relationship between Islam and the West was thrust to the forefront of public debate. The nineteen airplane hijackers came from Saudi Arabia and three other Muslim-majority countries.

But subsequently it became clear that young people, born and bred in democratic countries, could murder innocent civilians in the name of Islam. On

7 July 2005, a group of young, British-born Islamist suicide bombers killed fifty-two and injured about seven hundred people in London. Similar home-grown terrorist outrages have followed in other countries. The problem of Muslim integration has been pushed into the limelight.

MORE FAILURE: FAITH SCHOOLS AND DIVIDED COMMUNITIES

Schooling must be central to any viable integration programme. Young people need to learn about the struggles for democracy, independence, rights and human emancipation throughout the world. They should be aware not only of different cultures and religions, but also of the claims of Enlightenment thinkers to establish universal values and sustain inalienable rights. They should be free to discuss and evaluate all these things, from criticism of the Enlightenment to criticism of any religion.

Such a broad education is less likely in a school that is linked to one particular religion. Instead it would be more viable in secular schools with pupils from multiple religions, classes and cultures. Broad-based secular education is even more essential in multi-cultural and multi-faith societies.

To a large degree, the United States enforces a separation of church and state, and prohibits the public funding of religious schools. But faith schools are being promoted and funded by taxpayers' money in several countries, particularly in the UK. Even in secular France, some independent religious schools receive state funding, including many Catholic and a few Muslim schools.

In the UK there is a long tradition of religious state schools. The deep political and cultural division of Northern Ireland has been long underpinned by the segregation of Protestant from Catholic schools. In 2011 about one-third of state-funded schools in England were faith schools. Of these, 68 per cent were Church of England schools and 30 per cent were Roman Catholic. There were also smaller numbers of Jewish, Muslim, Sikh and Hindu state-funded faith schools. But a majority of public opinion seems to be against state-funded faith schools. Yet few UK politicians dare to question existing policy. Both the Conservative and Labour Parties support the idea of state-funded faith schools.[25]

One of the most energetic advocates of publicly funded faith schools was the former Labour Prime Minister Tony Blair. After coming to power in 1997, he promoted a programme of expansion of faith schools, involving multiple religions. But a 2001 report commissioned by Bradford City Council concluded that its communities were becoming increasingly isolated along racial, cultural and religious lines, and that faith-segregated schools were fuelling the divisions. The report was prophetic. During that year there were riots in Bradford, which spread to other northern cities. Yet in the same year the Labour government proposed a large increase in the number of state schools run by religious organizations.

By 2002 there was a major public row, with accusations that some pupils were being taught creationism in science lessons and others were being instilled (including by Christian fundamentalists) that homosexual acts are against God's law. Campaigners for women's rights expressed concern that conservative religious teachers were instructing young girls that women should take a secondary role in society.[26]

David Bell—then Chief Inspector of Schools—warned in a January 2005 speech to the Hansard Society that a traditional Islamic education did not equip Muslim children for living in modern Britain. He said: 'I worry that many young people are being educated in faith-based schools, with little appreciation of their wider responsibilities and obligations to British society'. He continued:

> We must not allow our recognition of diversity to become apathy in the face of any challenge to our coherence as a nation . . . I would go further and say that an awareness of our common heritage as British citizens, equal under the law, should enable us to assert with confidence that we are intolerant of intolerance, illiberalism and attitudes and values that demean the place of certain sections of our community, be they women or people living in non-traditional relationships.[27]

His comments were condemned as 'irresponsible' and 'derogatory' by some senior Muslims, but supported by Trevor Phillips, then Chair of the Commission for Racial Equality. In another lecture Bell said: 'We can choose . . . whether we want to bring our diversity together in a single rainbow or whether we allow our differences to fester into separate cultures and separate communities'.[28]

Yet, even after the July 2005 London bombings, and until his resignation from office in 2007, Prime Minister Blair continued to promote faith schools. Phillips came to the conclusion that increasing self-segregation of British communities along ethnic and religious lines was a major threat to national integration and to Enlightenment values. Young people were being brought up with insufficient awareness of these values, in closed communities where extremism could fester.

Ken Livingstone, the leftist Mayor of London, attacked Phillips for 'pandering to the right'. During a televised discussion, the prominent Labour Minister David Miliband shook his head and described Phillips's remarks about community segregation as 'fatuous'.[29]

Ed Husain was born and educated in Britain, where he obtained a master's degree. He was drawn toward extreme versions of Islam and was persuaded that Western democracies were irredeemably corrupt and must be replaced by theocracies based on Islamic law. After several years he renounced his former extremism, but retained his Islamic faith. In an interview he pointed out:

> The result of 25 years of multiculturalism has not been multicultural communities. It has been mono-cultural communities. Islamic communities are segregated. Many Muslims want to live apart from mainstream British society; official government policy has helped them do so. I grew up without any white friends. My school was almost entirely Muslim. I had almost no direct experience of 'British life' or 'British institutions'.[30]

British policymakers have welcomed diversity. But they define needs and rights via the ethnic categories into which people were placed, using those divisions to shape public policy. The result has been a more fragmented society, which has nurtured extremism. The failure of British liberal society to spread its own values of inclusiveness and tolerance is alarming. In the name of multiculturalism, Britain has become a more divided society, where Enlightenment values are often sidelined or unknown. We know that opinion polls can be inaccurate, but consider the following:

In a 2004 poll of five hundred British Muslims, attacks on the United States by al-Qaeda or other similar groups were viewed as 'justified' by 13 per cent. Another 15 per cent said they did not know whether such attacks were wrong or right.[31]

A detailed report in 2007 by the Policy Exchange think tank revealed that 37 per cent of young British Muslims want Sharia law in Britain, 36 per cent of young British Muslims think apostates should be killed and 13 per cent of young British Muslims said they 'admired' al-Qaeda.[32]

The same Policy Exchange report revealed that 37 per cent of sixteen- to twenty-four-year-old British Muslims preferred to send their children to Islamic schools, compared to 25 per cent of forty-five- to fifty-four-year-old Muslims and 19 per cent of those older than fifty-five years.[33]

There are many other polls with similar results. Most alarmingly, extremist views are more common among younger than older British Muslims. Previous policies of integration have largely failed and the problem in some respects is getting worse, not better.

CONCLUSION: AN HONEST AND
PROGRESSIVE WAY FORWARD

It is very sad that we have to remind ourselves, over two centuries since Voltaire—but we need an atmosphere where the defects of any religious doctrine or practice can be criticized. Leftist condemnations of 'Islamophobia' and absurd confusions such as 'anti-Islamic racism' prevent the creation of such an atmosphere.

In 2004 the progressive Left (and vigilantly anti-racist) journalist Polly Toynbee was proclaimed by the Islamic Human Rights Commission as the winner of their 'Most Islamophobic Media Personality' award. In her words, she received this award because she 'had challenged the legitimacy of the idea of Islamophobia and warned of the danger to free speech of trying to make criticism of a religion a crime akin to racism'. She rightly noted that the 'occasional note of reason from moderate Islamic groups is so weak it hardly makes itself heard'. She highlighted the difficulties involved in starting a serious dialogue on this issue.[34]

The failure to distinguish racism from criticism of religion sadly remains widespread. Many on the Left have done excellent work since the 1970s in campaigning against racism, fascism and discrimination. But the frequent confusion of criticism of religion with racism has diverted their efforts.

It cannot be repeated often enough that fears about Islam as a belief system are not equivalent to bigotry toward Muslims. Racism and persecution of Muslims are serious problems and should be vigilantly opposed. But the option to criticize Islam, or any other belief system, is an important right, and it should be protected.

In 2015 *The Huffington Post* commissioned a poll that found 56 per cent of British people in their sample think that Islam is 'a major' or is 'some' threat to Western liberal democracy. These results were published in an article with the headline: 'More than half of Britons see Muslims as a threat'. This conflation of concerns about a doctrine with perceptions of individuals is inexcusable. It depicts critics of Islam as hostile to Muslims as individuals. To repeat: fears about Islam as a belief system are not equivalent to bigotry toward Muslims.[35]

It has already been noted that in March 2014 the anti-racist Hope not Hate campaign group circulated an appeal for funds to campaign against a political party because it had held a closed session discussing Sharia law. Also, in its attempts to counter anti-Islamic sentiment, Hope not Hate has called for limits to freedom of expression, to prohibit 'hate speech' against a religion.[36]

Clearly the danger here is that critical discussion of Sharia law might itself be regarded as 'hate speech'. Hope not Hate seems to put them both in the same box. If there is a case for the prohibition of 'hate speech' then it must be clearly and carefully confined to cases where people explicitly and unmistakably incite acts of violence. The right to criticize, even if it causes offence, should be protected. In the false name of hope, Hope not Hate is undermining Enlightenment liberties and values. This is the path back to medievalism.

In a more informed vein, the authors of the 2007 Policy Exchange report argued for a change of approach. The government and others 'should stop emphasising difference and engage with Muslims as citizens'. Policies of 'group rights or representation' for specific Islamic communities are likely to alienate other sections of the Muslim population further. These well-informed remarks went against much of the then-current local and national government policy.

The authors continued: 'The exaggeration of Islamophobia does not make Muslims feel protected but instead reinforces feelings of victimisation and alienation'. They also called for 'a broader intellectual debate in order to challenge the crude anti-Western, anti-British ideas that dominate cultural and intellectual life. This means allowing free speech and debate, even when it causes offence to some minority groups'.[37]

First we need to be honest. Extremist religions of all kinds can threaten liberal, democratic and Enlightenment values. Christianity in particular has been violently repressive and brutal. Some religious sects today are fanatical and intolerant. But traditional Islam has presented additional problems, including within Muslim communities in Western democracies, because of its fusion of law and religion, and its devolution of alleged rights of punishment to individuals.

We can criticize other religions with minimal chances of violent retaliation. But if we publish cartoons of Mohammed then we risk our lives. There are numerous exceptions, but many Muslims will regard it as their sacred duty to kill us, and will applaud others that do so.

This problem has nothing whatsoever to do with race or ethnicity. It stems from the religiously motivated, devolved mechanisms of reactionary rule enforcement and punishment within Islam, combined with the growth of more extreme Islamic doctrines. We should recognize this problem, as well as the hugely valuable past, present and potential contributions of Islamic culture to Western democracies.

The problems posed by Islam are understood by several serious and liberal-minded scholars. Consider the issue of human rights. On this point, the academic Michael Ignatieff wrote: 'The challenge from Islam has been there from the beginning'.

Ignatieff noted how the delegation from Saudi Arabia objected to parts of the Universal Declaration of Human Rights when it was being drafted in 1947. They raised particular objection to Article 16, relating to free marriage choice, and Article 18, relating to freedom of religion. The Saudi delegate to the committee examining the draft of the declaration argued that these articles meant the imposition of Western values on long-established Islamic institutions. On the basis of these objections, the Saudi delegation refused to ratify the declaration. Ignatieff pointed out that attempts to reconcile Islamic and Western traditions concerning rights have largely failed. And since the 1970s the stance of Islam toward Western formulations of human rights has grown more hostile. Ignatieff continued:

> When the Islamic Revolution in Iran rose up against the tyrannical modernization imposed by the shah, Islamic figures began to question the universal writ of Western human rights norms. They have pointed out that the Western separation of church and state, of secular and religious authority, is alien to the jurisprudence and political thought of the Islamic tradition. And they are correct. The freedoms articulated in the Universal Declaration of Human Rights make no sense within the theocratic bias of Islamic political thought. The right to marry and establish a family, to freely choose one's partner, is a direct challenge to the authorities in Islamic society that enforce the family choice of spouse, polygamy, and other restrictions on women's freedom.[38]

These issues need to be openly discussed in a civilized manner. They should not be swept under the carpet.

Successive British Prime Ministers have reacted to the threat of Islamist extremism by calling for 'British values'. After claims that some schools in Birmingham were promoting Islamist extremism, in 2014 the Conservative Prime Minister David Cameron outlined plans to put the promotion of 'British values' at the heart of the national curriculum for schools. This is now official policy: 'Schools should promote the fundamental British values of democracy, the rule of law, individual liberty, and mutual respect and tolerance of those with different faiths and beliefs'.[39]

But the official government document outlining this policy mentions respect and tolerance for other races but fails to mention discrimination against women or gays. It rightly mentions the freedom to 'choose and hold' any faith, but not the freedom to exit a religion without sanction. It mentions 'individual liberty' only once and fails to uphold freedom of non-violent expression, including when it may cause offence. Are these omissions an accident, or are they designed not to offend a particular religious minority? No prizes are offered for the answer.

Another major problem here is not the values as such, but their nationalistic description as 'British'. It would be a poor school that failed to inform its pupils of the multiple historical errors involved with the 'British values' label. The Magna Carta of 1215 promoted the rule of law, but it applied to England and not the whole of Britain. While it was an important symbolic agreement, it had limited effect on powerful medieval monarchs.[40] Democracy was not invented in Britain: ancient Athens and Viking Iceland are much earlier precursors. Dating from the late eighteenth century, the United States and France have much earlier claims to the values of liberty and religious tolerance. Britain legally discriminated against Protestant Nonconformists and Catholics until the nineteenth century, and it still bars any Catholic from becoming its sovereign.

Apart from being misleading and inaccurate, the label of 'British values' would hardly be effective in preventing a young Muslim from being radicalized. On the contrary, the label can help bolster the perception that Britain and the rest of the West are at war against Islam. The insular and nationalistic labelling readily allows the distortion that 'British values' are being promoted by the UK authorities in a global effort to counter Islam.

It would be more accurate and effective to label values such as democracy, the rule of law, individual liberty and freedom of worship as 'universal values' or 'Enlightenment values'. They are not simply values that British residents and citizens should adopt. Other countries should promote these values too.

There is an ironic divergence of reactions. On the one hand, some Islamic groups and paranoid 'Stop the War' activists see governmental promotion of 'British values' as 'anti-Muslim'. On the other hand, successive British governments have overlooked elements of Islamic doctrine or practice that are in need of reform. Yet attention to these points is necessary as part of a package of Enlightenment values that would help to facilitate the integration of Muslim communities in British society.[41]

But there are signs of hope. Many Muslims are engaged in open discussions about the possible reform of Islam, on the measures needed to integrate their communities into Western society and on the best means to deradicalize young Islamic extremists.

Consider how one courageous and principled Muslim reacted to Northern Ireland Pastor James McConnell, when he provocatively described Islam as 'satanic' and 'spawned in hell'. McConnell was prosecuted under the Communications Act 2003, which was passed when the Labour Party was in power in the UK. It broadly prohibits the electronic broadcast of 'offensive' material.

With immense principle and courage, the Muslim imam and scholar Dr Muhammad Al-Hussaini declared publicly that he was willing to go to prison to defend the free speech of McConnell. Al-Hussaini called the decision to press ahead with the prosecution 'extraordinary' and said it was 'quite contrary to our country's tradition of freedom of expression'. He said, 'It is of utmost concern that, in this country, we uphold the freedom to discuss, debate and critique religious ideas and beliefs—restricting only speech which incites physical violence'.

This is an example of a courageous Muslim accepting and fervently defending free speech, despite his strong disagreement with McConnell's views on Islam. Al-Hussaini, rather than those that pass such restrictive and ill-advised laws, should be given our support.[42]

The statements of many Muslim leaders who have strongly condemned Islamist terrorism should also be welcomed. But unfortunately, an insufficient number of Muslim leaders consider that some of the roots of Islamist terrorism lie in the doctrines and institutions of Islam itself. Islam is in need of reform and modernization to bring it into the post-Enlightenment era. This too has to be recognized, by Muslims and others.

To some extent there is progress on this front. In an immensely positive development, the 'Muslim Reform Movement' was launched in 2015. In their inaugural statement they defended freedom of speech, gender equality, a secular state and the UN Declaration of Universal Human Rights. They noted explicitly that freedom of speech included the right to criticize Islam: 'Ideas do not have rights. Human beings have rights'.[43]

By contrast, the blanket and ill-defined leftist rhetoric of 'Islamophobia' does not help those Muslims who are struggling to reform and modernize their religion. Instead, the more conservative leaders of Muslim communities protect their old-fashioned or reactionary views behind its smokescreen. Modernizing Muslims are thus impaired by an unwitting coalition of liberals, leftists and Muslim conservatives.[44]

Initiatives to preserve liberal values in a multi-faith and multi-ethnic world should be welcomed. In addition, the lost Left of the twenty-first century needs to re-establish its links with the Enlightenment and its project to separate church from state. Within any society, freedom of worship should be protected, as well as the freedom to criticize religion.

CHAPTER 10

Two Open Letters to Friends

I have seen the morals of my time, and I have published these letters.

Jean-Jacques Rousseau, *Julie, ou la Nouvelle Héloïse* (1761)

In the eighteenth century it was fashionable to lay out a political argument as a letter to a real or imagined recipient. This epistolary form was used by Edmund Burke, Thomas Paine and Mary Wollstonecraft. A fictional interrogator in the preface to Jean-Jacques Rousseau's *Julie* asked if the letters in the novel were fictional or real. You may ask the same question about the letters below. I can think of several people to whom it would be fitting to send them. I have chosen this form, with one letter to a libertarian and the other to a leftist, principally because it allows me to triangulate my own position over a range of topics.

DEAR SWEET LIBERTY

Since the 1970s, the pro-market, libertarian views with which you identify have enjoyed a massive revival. They used to be mocked. Now they are mainstream. But also they have been misunderstood.

Some wrongly suggest that any free-market opposition to socialism must be conservative or fascist. But I never regarded your pro-market libertarianism as conservative or fascist. Libertarian and classical liberal values are in strong opposition to fascism, and to conservative values that undermine individual rights or bestow special privileges.

But some of your leaders did blot their copybook by dallying with dictatorships. In a book originally published in 1927, Ludwig von Mises praised fascism as 'an emergency makeshift' that 'has, for the moment, saved European civilization'. This brief statement cannot be excused, despite the facts that it was in a book that was otherwise devoted to the promotion of classical liberal values and that von Mises was a Jew who eventually had to flee the Nazis. From 1932 to 1934 von Mises continued as an economic adviser in Austria, even to the 'Austro-fascist' or 'clerical fascist' government of Chancellor Engelbert Dollfuss, who assumed dictatorial powers, closed down Parliament, smashed the trade unions and banned several political parties. This does not mean that von Mises was a fascist, but other economists would have drawn the line at advising them.[1]

The idea that temporary dictatorships, even if murderous, might sometimes be necessary rubbed off onto von Mises's student, Friedrich Hayek. Hayek argued that democracy, while desirable, can be temporarily dispensable, particularly in defence of private property. He believed that democracy and liberty would follow, once private property rights were secure. But these consequences are not automatic: there are many undemocratic and oppressive regimes that retain private property.

Augusto Pinochet may have saved private property rights in Chile. But he imposed a vicious dictatorship that tortured an estimated thirty thousand civilians and murdered over three thousand. The right to life and freedom from torture are existentially more basic, and hence even more important, than the right to property. Hayek visited Pinochet's Chile and he failed to condemn these atrocious abuses of human rights. Hayek inspired and silently condoned Pinochet. Hayek's silence over abuses of basic human rights cannot be excused by his age: he was still publishing major books in the 1970s.[2]

I oppose classical socialism because it inadvertently crushes human rights and leads to dictatorship. Von Mises and Hayek (temporarily) tolerated some dictatorships and their removal of some basic human rights, including the rights of *habeas corpus* and to live without torture. While earlier liberals had emphasized human rights, private property rights and democracy, in their reaction against socialism, von Mises and Hayek seemed to elevate private property rights over everything else. But private property rights require the protection of all actual or potential owners from torture or extermination. Basic human rights and democracy are vital, as well as the right to private property.

Admittedly, for moral and practical reasons, the democratic principle of majority rule cannot have free reign over everything, especially when it comes to human rights. If rights are inalienable, then they cannot be removed by any vote. But this does not justify brutal dictatorship.

UK Prime Minister Margaret Thatcher claimed to be a one of your ideological sisters. In 1999 she thanked the former dictator Pinochet for 'bringing democracy to Chile'. Clearly, while addressing someone who in 1973 overthrew a democratically elected government, she invested the term *democracy* with an esoteric, Thatcherite meaning. In truth, Pinochet was a torturer and an assassin.[3]

Thatcher also supped with South African Apartheid. As late as 1987 she declared that the African National Congress, led by Nelson Mandela, was 'a typical terrorist organisation'. She continued: 'Anyone who thinks it is going to run the government in South Africa is living in cloud-cuckoo land'. She underestimated the brilliant, forgiving and humane leadership of Mandela.[4]

Similarly, in 1986 the US President Ronald Reagan vetoed a Congressional bill that would have imposed sanctions on the Apartheid regime in South Africa. After taking office in 1981, Reagan moved to overturn an arms embargo that the former President Jimmy Carter had imposed on Guatemala for its abysmal record on human rights. Reagan funded death squads in Nicaragua and propped up dictatorships in Argentina, Brazil, Chile and elsewhere.

Did you speak out then? I did not hear many voices from your stable. Most protest came from the Left. The silence of your co-thinkers was deadly. It helped to associate pro-market libertarianism with the Right.

Prominent libertarians have supported some dictatorships because they have defended private property. But defending property rights is no excuse for riding roughshod over other human rights. The death squads and torturers are not somehow absolved when they defend the private property of the rich.

Like you, I wish to distinguish pro-market libertarianism from support for dictatorships. The latter does not necessarily follow from the former. Like you, I oppose all dictatorships and I support democracy and human rights, including rights to property.

Despite their political deficiencies, the theoretical critique of collectivist socialist planning by von Mises and Hayek is one of the most important intellectual achievements of the twentieth century.[5] They showed decisively that by marginalizing private enterprise and markets, socialist economies would stifle innovation and technical progress, as well as threaten liberties. The experience of Soviet-style regimes in the twentieth century has born this out.

While the Left were quick to label all critics of socialism as 'Right', this positional labelling is misleading. Your thread of liberty goes back to the French revolutionaries, the American Founding Fathers and the English Levellers. If you are a democratic libertarian, then you are a genuine part of the original *Left*.[6]

But that is both your strength and your problem. I shall explain why below. I give greater stress than you to the problem of inequality within capitalism. I value liberty no less highly, but I believe that the state has a greater and necessary role than you envisage in protecting liberty and in bringing prosperity.

Just as you showed that completely collectivist socialist planning was un-workable, your free-market utopia, with everything being traded as property, is also unfeasible. Furthermore, it overlooks major developments in modern capitalist economies that I shall discuss below.

It is no accident that your core principles were promoted by the Levellers in the 1640s, the American revolutionaries of the 1770s and the French *Left* of the 1790s. Apart from large landowners, the French and English market economies were then dominated by small-scale producers, from peasants to petty manufacturers. The United States was initially a country of small farmers and tradesmen. Contemporary discourses on liberty, property, trade and anti-monopoly addressed the world of the small-scale producer.

They were prior to the rise of industrial capitalism, which enhanced the economic need for organized mass education, social security and healthcare, along with regulations and bureaucracies to ensure that markets worked ef-fectively and consumers were protected. All this required higher taxes and a bigger state.

We now have a capitalism overshadowed by huge corporations. It is coordi-nated by a global financial system that is dominated by large banks and other massive financial institutions. Debt is now a major commodity, and asset bub-bles based on debt are major potential destabilizers of the system. Today, much production is of services rather than physical goods. Much property consists of intellectual or other intangible property. Information played a vital role in all past economies, but in the highly complex economies of the twenty-first century, everything depends on continuous processing of vast and increasing amounts of diverse information, on a global scale. These colossal develop-ments challenge your eighteenth-century view of the economy and raise new questions concerning liberty, property and the role of the state.

I know that you and many of your fellow libertarians would protest against oligopolistic power, and you call for greater competition. But you have paid insufficient attention to the fact that unless there are countervailing measures, the big players in competitive markets will always try to create niches or oli-gopolies, and thereby concentrate their economic power. By such means, they will try to protect themselves against competition. Capitalism has persistently displayed inbuilt tendencies toward oligopoly.

The reaction of von Mises and Hayek to the growth of the large corporation was inadequate and unrealistic. Von Mises regarded the separation of owner-ship and control as inefficient, anti-competitive and the result of intrusion by government. Hayek similarly blamed the existence of large corporations on the state—as if the state is always responsible for what goes wrong. Sure enough, state legislatures have played the leading role in developing the legal form of the corporation. But legislatures are also involved in the legal constitution of property, markets and smaller firms, all of which you take for granted.[7]

Your mentors overlook other sources of oligopolistic power and yearned for a return to an individualistic economy of small-scale entrepreneurs and producers. The huge economies of scale of some large-scale economic units are underestimated. Your mentors never adequately came to grips with the modern corporation and the dynamic role it has often played in the development of capitalism and modern technology.

Von Mises and Hayek favoured a system dominated by private property and contractual exchange. But their depiction of these vital institutional features was inadequate. They failed to distinguish between property and possession. Property involves legal rights established by legislative and judicial institutions. Instead, adopting extremely wide and vague notions of market and exchange, von Mises saw ownership as *de facto* 'having' something, or control of the services that derive from a good, thus removing the issue of legal rights from the notion of property. Although property rights were central to their argument, their understanding of them was defective. They did not acknowledge the role of the state in the constitution and maintenance of private property rights. A private enterprise economy requires an effective state and a statutory legal system to sustain it.[8]

Von Mises's definition of exchange was also too broad and vague. He saw all action, even by an isolated individual, as 'exchange', thus ignoring the exchange of legal rights and obligations. Von Mises also adopted a near-universal definition of the market as 'the social system of the division of labour under private ownership of the means of production'. He described any economy with a division of labour, where production was vaguely under some 'private' control, as a 'market' economy, without mention of legal contracts or legal ownership.[9]

These loose criteria could apply to almost all social formations in human history. They make no conceptual distinction between commercial and non-commercial exchanges, such as for example between prostitution and consensual sex. Overall, the Austrian economists' positive case for private property and markets was weakened by a serious dilution in meaning of those terms. Their concepts of property, exchange and market were eviscerated. The near ubiquity of their definitions robbed them of much meaning. They lacked adequate concepts to understand the market economy that they favoured.

You have rightly promoted the rule of law, but the notion of law adopted by some of your mentors is inadequate. Hayek, for example, reduced law to custom. His evolutionary portrayal of law, as an experimental search for universal principles of justice, downplayed the need for strong countervailing power. Hayek relied too often on exhortations for individual freedom and the rule of law, with inadequate attention to the power relations that are necessary for their preservation. Countervailing power has to be legitimate even in the eyes of the state, and sufficiently independent and powerful to be enforced, even against the erring rich and mighty in politics or business.[10]

In the great twentieth-century debate on capitalism versus socialism, both sides gave insufficient attention to legal rules and structures: they failed to characterize the rival systems adequately. The proponents of socialism played with general equilibrium models that were supposed to fit all worlds; they ignored key, specific, institutional features of both capitalism and socialism. Von Mises and Hayek inadequately specified the nature of private property and exchange, rendering them as near-universal phenomena. Neither side considered the more specific institutions that helped bring about the dramatic economic take-off of capitalism around 1800.

One of the major positive contributions of your mentors has been to focus on the nature and central role of knowledge in the economy. They emphasized that knowledge is localized, is often tacit and dispersed, and cannot readily be communicated to a large collective body. They had a much more sophisticated appreciation of the nature of knowledge than their opponents, who tried to use unrealistic neoclassical models to defend socialism.[11]

But your mentors largely overlooked the extent to which the contractual transfer of information has some curious features that challenge standard understandings of contract and exchange.

First, once acquired by its buyer, codifiable information can often be easily reproduced in multiple copies, and possibly sold to others. This can place the seller at a disadvantage. Accordingly, there may be licences, patents or other restrictions to prevent the buyer from selling it on. Second, codifiable information has the peculiar property that, once it is sold, it also remains in the hands of the seller. Information is not a 'normal' commodity that changes hands from seller to buyer when it is purchased. Third, as the Nobel economist Kenneth Arrow wrote: 'there is a fundamental paradox in the determination of demand for information: its value for the purchaser is not known until he has the information, but then he has in effect acquired it without cost'. If we knew what we were going to buy then we would no longer need to buy it.[12]

Consequently, in an economy involving substantial exchanges of information, it is sometimes difficult or even counter-productive to follow Hayek's advice and establish clear 'rules which, above all, enable man to distinguish between mine and thine'. Information challenges the bounds of exclusive and individual property. What is possessed cannot always be clearly defined, because to define it fully is to give it away. It is not always possible or efficient to break up information into discrete pieces and give each one an ownership tag. It is often difficult to determine who discovered the information in the first place, or who can claim legal title to its ownership. An information-rich society challenges the meaning and boundaries of what is mine and what is thine.[13]

Information is a non-rival good that often can be easily shared. Its use by one person does not diminish its usability by another. But private ownership of intellectual assets involves exclusive concentrations of rights and a general denial of readily available user rights to others. But such exclusive property rights are necessary for informational assets to be used as collateral. Your pro-market logic requires knowledge to be privatized. But the resulting denial of the cheaply acquired benefits of the shared possession of non-rivalrous information assets can generate remarkable inefficiencies.

Both planning and market competition operate with least difficulty when there are large numbers of commodities of a similar type. But the days of producing widgets are gone. Modern developed economies are dominated by highly varied services, and many physical commodities are exceedingly intricate. There is much more processing of complex information. Every transaction in every economy has always been unique, but in capitalism today every individual transaction is more distinctive and idiosyncratic. The delivery of each service varies through time and context, sometimes to a large degree. Consider the detailed and responsive services of a household carer or a hospital nurse, or the diverse and varying contents of newspapers or books.

In a complex, non-widget economy, extensive detailed planning from the centre of such services is impossible. But also, while market competition may remain a spur for efficiency and innovation, it cannot readily minimize prices as standard textbooks suggest. These complexities have opened up a major additional role for the state, not in central planning but in setting trading standards and regulating markets.

Furthermore, the infinite extension and subdivision of ownership in a densely interconnected knowledge economy can create an 'anti-commons' where interconnected rights obstruct investment and trade. This problem applies particularly to patents and other intellectual property and has become more severe in increasingly knowledge-intensive economies. The ubiquitous imposition of legal rules 'to distinguish between mine and thine' can deprive many people of information that is vital for their work or well-being. Capitalism is challenged by increasing knowledge intensity: to survive, capitalism must limit its own use of private property and the market mechanism.[14]

As capitalism has become more complex, these informational needs have become much greater, implying a greater need for some public provision alongside a vibrant private sector. While much information and knowledge cannot be shared (because of tacitness, interpretative difficulty or inaccessibility), much else can, and this can be of huge productive value. Consequently, the benefits of private and contractual provision of some information may be much less than the overall opportunity costs of charging a price for its use. A healthy market system itself depends on the incompleteness of markets for information; some crucial data must be unowned and available freely.

Consider the phenomenal growth of the Internet. In the early 1990s, CERN (the European Organization for Nuclear Research) developed key elements of the Internet infrastructure. They were released to the public for free, to ensure that the information technology would become widespread. Similarly, many software programs and even operating systems are available free of charge. The Internet has vastly stimulated markets, but not all its components or enablers were marketed. Modern capitalism has reduced the marginal cost of many additional informational goods and services to near zero, making them nearly free and open to non-market modes of distribution.[15]

Especially in a technologically complex capitalism, in order to evaluate what is being bought, effective consumer choice often requires some scientific and technical knowledge. Consequently, informed choice in a market economy requires effective public education in science. This problem was addressed by liberal thinkers such as John Dewey, who saw education and democracy as facilitating public debate about science and its objectives.[16]

While state intervention in the economy is often confounded by problems of complexity and distributed knowledge, the state can sometimes intervene effectively as a coordinator, enabler, information processor and strategic leader. As Hayek put it: 'It is the character rather than the volume of government activity that is important'.[17]

Your mentors expound a theory of money and finance that is more suited to the seventeenth century than the twenty-first. It treats money primarily as a commodity-based medium of exchange and overlooks the crucial role of the state in the development of modern financial systems, involving the buying and selling of debt. Your theory is ill-equipped to deal with the congenital instability of capitalism and the growth of huge financial institutions.[18]

Your mentors developed a powerful critique of comprehensive central planning but offered little detailed practical advice for reform or development within capitalism, other than to privatize public enterprises, encourage competition, minimize outside regulation, and shrink the scale and powers of the state to the practical minimum. These are more like slogans than detailed, practical policies.

Your mentors failed to consolidate their victory in the socialist calculation debate and develop the foundations of practical policy. By refusing a 'mixed economy' or any other intermediate position, they shifted to an extreme, playing an ideological rather than a detailed practical role for policymakers or politicians. In pursuing market imperatives without restraint, they failed to explain why any non-market institution, such as the family, should be retained.

But Hayek and others understood that a free-market economy cannot work when individuals lack education and lack the basic necessities for survival as economic agents. For this reason Hayek advocated legislation to limit working hours, state assistance for social and health insurance, state-financed education and research, a guaranteed basic income, and other welfare measures. Hayek also proposed a Keynesian-style, counter-cyclic government strategy to deal with fluctuations in economic activity.[19]

But he overlooked the mechanisms that generate greater inequality in modern corporate capitalism. These include the returns from the ownership of collateralizable assets, including tangible and intangible property. Although he moved in the direction of social democracy in some respects, he entirely neglected the problem of growing inequalities in the distribution of wealth.[20]

Your libertarian friends may dismiss such concerns about inequality as envy. But even if we assume that all incomes reflect effort and skill, massive inequality of wealth remains. Much of the inequality of wealth found within capitalist societies results from inequalities of inheritance.[21]

Extreme inequalities in the distribution of wealth are unfair and dysfunctional. They undermine principles of sympathy and solidarity upon which every society depends. As the philosopher John Finnis argued: 'what is unjust about large disparities of wealth in a community is not the inequality as such but the fact that . . . the rich have failed to redistribute that portion of their wealth which could be better used by others for the realization of basic values in their own lives'.[22]

Some redistribution of wealth can be justified on the grounds of greater satisfaction of human needs, including the need for widespread education and personal development. For example, you favour entrepreneurship: moderate wealth redistribution can give more people the chance of being entrepreneurs.

Your blanket opposition to trade unions is also unjustified. You overlook the fact that labour and capital are fundamentally dissimilar, and can never meet together on a level playing field. The owner of capital can make money while on holiday in the Cayman Islands, while the owner of labour is obliged to be present when and where his or her labour is hired.

The owner of capital can use such assets as collateral to borrow money and invest further in profit-making schemes. Short of slavery, labour cannot be used as collateral, and the wage labourer cannot use his or her capacity to work as collateral to obtain a secured loan. Because of these asymmetries, trade unions can have an important role in redressing the balance. As John Kenneth Galbraith pointed out, trade unions are an important source of countervailing power in modern capitalism.[23]

Even in a system of small-scale producers there are limits to the use of markets. You generally favour markets over other allocation systems, but do you recognize these limits? Is a market a solution to every problem? If so, why not argue for the dissolution of marriage and its replacement by a market system of prostitutes, baby-selling and hired household services? Rightly, you do not. But why do you fail to specify the circumstances where markets are inappropriate or cannot work, and why do you fail to explain these limitations? A better defence of markets and private property would know better their limitations.

Markets cannot work everywhere, partly because we rely on zones of intimate, interpersonal interaction that build trust and transcend the monetary calculus of cost and reward. Market systems always rely on non-market institutions, such as the household and the state. You ignore the fact that capitalism cannot ever be a 100 per cent market system. There always will be missing markets.

For example, a system of wage labour cannot in principle tie every worker down in employment contracts for the rest of his or her life. This would be tantamount to slavery. Under capitalism there never can be complete futures markets for labour.

Consequently, as the great economist Alfred Marshall pointed out, employers may not invest adequately in the skills of workers in the fear that they might quit their jobs and the investment would be wasted. This is an argument for substantial state intervention in the training and skill development of workers.[24]

And then there is the question of climate change. You are in the very bad company of Tea Party activists and climate-change deniers who cannot accept that the market is not the solution to every problem, or deny climate change because it might legitimate some state intervention to deal with the threat to our climate.

For example, the prominent free-market libertarian Václav Klaus has persistently denied that human activity is leading to climate change. In June 2007, when he was President of the Czech Republic, Klaus wrote an article in the *Financial Times* entitled 'Freedom, not climate, is at risk'. Therein he described policies that try to deal with environmental problems as 'the biggest threat to freedom, democracy, market economy and prosperity. . . . This ideology wants to replace the free and spontaneous evolution of mankind by a sort of central (now global) planning'. Of course, dealing with climate change will require concerted action by states. But the remedial policies proposed by leading experts in the area are very far from the imagined bogeyman of global central planning. Klaus used the post-communist scare phrase of 'central planning' to reject any kind of state intervention to deal with the problem.[25]

Problems such as climate change require not only state intervention but also the moral commitment of many citizens to goals and policies that do not necessarily serve their own narrow self-interest. Many of your fellow libertarians share with Marxists a view that individuals are entirely greedy and self-interested, at least in their economic lives, with little concern for justice or morality. As Adam Smith argued long ago, this view of human nature is deeply flawed.[26]

The example of climate change shows that people are not always the best judges of their own welfare, simply because many adults do not understand climate science. They do not accept the scientific evidence of global warming, or the reasons why this is becoming a serious problem. Of course, it can be politically dangerous to presume that one person knows better than another. But it is sometimes true. And presuming otherwise, that anyone's opinion is as good as anyone else's, would lead to a toleration of ignorance and inconsistency.

Your rightful defence of universal rights and equality under the law should not lead to an equally positive ethical evaluation of all opinions. Some opinions are defective. Human development and flourishing requires some moral and pedagogic authority.

In summary, there are good arguments for moving away from your extreme *Left* (in the original sense) position, to admit some role for the state in a vibrant market economy. Important areas for state intervention include the provision of free or subsidized mass education, the universal provision of at least basic healthcare, the tackling of excessive inequalities in the distributions of income and wealth, and the regulation of the financial sector with Keynesian measures to reduced market volatility and instability.

The international financial system is also unstable, as demonstrated in the Great Crash of 2008. There is a case here for stronger national and international regulation of financial markets. Pre-Keynesian policies of austerity have also failed globally. As Keynes argued in the 1930s, economies cannot be revived by cutting aggregate effective demand.[27]

But in several other important ways, I am with you politically on the *Left* (in the original sense of that term) because I see liberty and rights as fundamental to a civilized society.[28]

DEAR FRATERNAL COMRADE

As I understand your position, you have dropped some of the orthodoxies of Marxism, but still hold onto much of that creed. You still wish to nationalize several major companies and you believe in the class struggle as the motif of history. You admire Tony Benn, and you may have supported the retro-Marxist Jeremy Corbyn as leader of the British Labour Party. Your co-thinkers are plentiful in leftist parties in Europe. The Great Crash of 2008 renewed your confidence, suggesting perhaps that the end of capitalism is nigh.

I know where you are coming from. I've been there myself. I still share some of your basic values and attitudes. We both are concerned about extreme inequalities of income and wealth; poverty and destitution; low wages; appalling working conditions; the lack of access to good education; inadequate healthcare provision; discrimination by race, gender, sexuality or beliefs; the ravaging of the planet by uncaring corporations or governments; the threat of climate change; and illegal or unjustified wars.

We both claim to be democrats and protectors of human rights and liberties. But thenceforth our differences begin. Your allies sometimes argue that rights such as freedom of speech are not the first priority, especially for someone starving and deprived of adequate shelter or healthcare. You are right to prioritize to the most fundamental of human needs. But other rights remain vital. They are of intrinsic worth: they are essential for human flourishing. They are also part of a constellation of freedoms and autonomous powers that are important for a dynamic and innovative economy.

You say that you are in favour of human rights. But I do not think that you give enough attention to the politico-economic conditions that are necessary to sustain human rights and democracy. On this point I criticized Sweet Liberty for relying on individual pressure alone as sufficient to counter powerful vested interests that might undermine democracy or freedom. Individuals are not enough: modern democracies require a balance of *orga-*

nized, countervailing powers. But your position on this point is even weaker than hers.

In your enthusiasm for collectivization, nationalization and strong state intervention in the economy, you underestimate the problem of concentration of power in the state machine. Personally, I am in favour of some public ownership. Partly it depends on the nature of the service and its strategic role in the economy. Good cases could be made for the public provision of railways, education, healthcare and some housing, to name a few examples. I also accept a strategic economic role for the state. There has to be state regulation of the financial system, to avoid overlending in booms and cumulative collapse in recessions. As I said to Sweet Liberty, history has shown the value of both public enterprise and judicious state intervention.[29]

But we must also realize the dangers in all this. We should avoid an excessive concentration of economic power in state bureaucracies, as well as in large corporations. Just as we should embrace a pluralist democracy we should embrace a pluralist economy. There needs to be an extensive plurality of separate, autonomous, economic powers.

Many of your co-thinkers do not sufficiently understand that a plurality of economic powers and institutions requires private property rights and the ability to trade resources on markets. Otherwise, power would reside in large state bureaucracies. Without privatization, some devolution of power to local units was attempted in Stalin's Soviet Union and Mao's China. Although some decision-making was successfully devolved, without separate legal status and property rights, such devolution was limited and precarious. It could be readily retracted and reconcentrated at the centre when the periphery was deemed to misbehave.

Effective and enduring decentralization requires the devolution of legal ownership and rights to make contracts. Leading socialists such as Beatrice Webb, Sidney Webb, G. D. H. Cole and Karl Polanyi failed to understand this.[30]

The abolition or marginalization of private property rights is unviable in any dynamic, large-scale economy. Furthermore, such attempted moves would lead to concentrations of economic power that pose a strong threat to democracy, rights and liberties. In no historical case of such concentrations of power have meaningful democracy or adequate liberty survived. Of course, there are examples of despotic capitalism too, so private property and markets are not guarantors of democracy and liberty. Private property and markets are *necessary* but *insufficient* conditions for freedom. Democracy and liberty need *more* than private property and markets, but they need them nevertheless.

Here you have a problem. Unlike the original *Left*, you dislike markets. Tony Benn was a classic example, counter-poising 'democracy' to 'market forces' without realizing that they are part-complements rather than feasible substitutes. This statement that he made in the House of Commons in 1990 is typical: 'I do not share the general view that market forces are the basis of personal liberty'. Note his use of the term *market forces* to demonize 'markets' as dangerous impersonal powers, which are somehow beyond human agency or responsibility. In fact, markets are unavoidable outcomes of a large-scale society based on private property, with rights to sell and buy that property. Benn argued for extensive common ownership instead of 'market forces'. He wanted liberty and democracy. But while private property has existed without liberty or democracy, they have never prospered under widespread common ownership.[31]

Numerous academic intellectuals continue to propose the abolition of private property or markets. For example, the Massachusetts Institute of Technology–educated economist and socialist Michael Albert wrote: 'I am a market abolitionist. I know markets are going to be with us for some time to come, but I also know—or hope—that in time we will replace them entirely'. The Harvard-educated economist and socialist Robin Hahnel similarly upheld a vision of a marketless economy: 'I do not believe that markets have any role to play in a truly desirable economy . . . our long run goal should be to replace markets entirely with some kind of democratic planning'.

The influential Marxist and 'critical realist' philosophers Roy Bhaskar and Andrew Collier supported 'a form of socialism which is neither a market economy nor a command economy nor a mix of the two, but a genuine extension of pluralistic democracy into economic life'. We are not told how this market-free system would work, particularly in terms of the organization of complex, large-scale production and incentives to work and innovate.

The socialist philosopher John O'Neill claimed to 'puncture the case for a market economy' and argued for the moneyless, non-market, international associationism, as sketched in outline by the socialist philosopher Otto Neurath. O'Neill outlined the ethical limitations of the market, but without detailing any plausible alternative. But even if markets were ethically flawed, without a viable and humane alternative we are obliged to tolerate them. We should have learned, from the experiences of the twentieth century, that non-market alternatives can be much worse ethically.[32]

The statements reported above are extreme in outlawing any form of market arrangement, even at the fringes of an otherwise planned economy. Their unqualified use of the term *market* signals a prohibition of all contractual exchanges of goods of services and the wholesale abolition of the right to sell property, if not the abolition of all private property rights. By ending a mixed economy and removing multiple economic sources of countervailing power, this would put liberty and democracy in danger.

Hence there are severe perils in your unchecked vision of a state-run economy. History tells us that there can be dangers in attempting to bring it about without vigilant protection of extensive rights to property. Consider the Chilean tragedy of 1973. The Marxist Pedro Vuskovic, who was Chilean Minister of Economic Affairs in the government of Salvador Allende from 1970 until 1972, declared in power that 'state control is designed to destroy the economic basis of imperialism and the ruling class by putting an end to the private ownership of the means of production'. He did not accept any role for a private sector. For idealistic socialists who see common ownership as human destiny, he was pushing along the preordained path of history. But for realists who wish to retain some significant private enterprise, such statements are illiberal and provocative.[33]

Although the 1970 election was lawful, the Allende government unconstitutionally expropriated private property without compensation. In August 1973 the Chilean Chamber of Deputies passed a resolution demanding that the government must end breaches of the constitution and abide by Chilean law. Pinochet's coup overturned the Allende government in September 1973. Thousands were killed and tortured. Nothing justifies Pinochet's murderous dictatorship. But misty-eyed, Marxist visionaries—with their quasi-religious belief in historical forces on their side—played a part in provoking brutal reactionaries.

You dislike commercialism. I do too. You dislike greed. I do too. You criticize markets as impersonal. They can be. You extol cooperation. I agree that it is vital for a healthy society. I agree that when a society attempts to bring everything down to a monetary value, there is a risk of humanity losing its moral compass and becoming spiritually bereft.

We have further agreements. Unlike von Mises and others, you and I adopt a historically specific view of contractual exchange. We can thus identify spheres of activity—such as the family—that are not run on the basis of businesslike contracts. Householders do not pay each other every time they do the cleaning or the washing up. These things can be done on the basis of cooperation and mutual understanding. You appreciate the difference between legal contracts and informal cooperation. You understand that fraternity and genuine altruism are possible.

But you omit one crucial problem: Soviet planners called it 'the curse of scale'.[34] Intimate, face-to-face reciprocity and cooperation are generally viable and sufficient for small communities only. The sphere of amity and cooperation relies on familiarity and personal contact: this limits the number of people involved. In small communities, interpersonal interaction can promote trust. Rule-breaking can be punished by shaming, shunning or loss of reputation. But these mechanisms rely on relatively small groups.

In large groups it is impossible to know everyone. Interpersonal mechanisms promoting trust and rule enforcement are less effective. They are driven to the fringes and recesses of the system. Large-scale societies must rely on markets, bureaucracy or both. Your valid complaint about the impersonality of markets can apply in triple strength to bureaucracy. The grave danger is that the impersonal market is replaced by even more impersonal bureaucracy.

Early communist and socialist plans for holding property in common were generally on a small scale. By contrast, Marx and Engels mistakenly assumed that cooperative mechanisms that can operate well in small-scale societies can easily be expanded ten-thousand-fold onto the national arena, from communities of hundreds to nations of millions. Logic and experience show that they cannot. The $1/n$ problem looms large.

As well as the political dangers of concentrated economic power in the hands of the state, you have not appreciated the insurmountable epistemic problems of bringing together all the knowledge and information required to plan a modern, complex economy. As noted in my letter to Sweet Liberty, like some advocates of competitive markets, you have failed to appreciate the consequences of a shift away from a widget-producing industrial system to a complex knowledge economy based on informational and other services. In such an economy, extensive detailed planning from the centre of such services is impossible. Instead the state has the major role in setting trading standards and regulating markets, which to a large degree remain indispensable.

You and your socialist predecessors have had over 150 years to describe in detail how a feasible socialism could work. You have all failed. On this topic, you have also failed to learn from experience, the results of which have been catastrophic.

Because of the absence of any practical outline of a feasible socialism, your comrade revolutionaries in Russia in 1917 and China in 1949 had to start almost from scratch. They failed. Large-scale comprehensive planning smothered innovation and led to a crushing bureaucracy and the curtailment of freedom. At great human cost, these cases confirmed what critics knew already, that classic socialism cannot work, at least while retaining democracy and liberty. Dozens of millions died as a result.

The twentieth century has run its course. Your time has run out: you have exhausted your options. To retain classic socialism in the face of these arguments and experiences is to add to the irresponsibility of your earlier comrades.

Once the problem of envisioning a democratic socialist future in large-scale societies is addressed, with serious attempts to answer practical questions of how information is gathered and transmitted, how resources are produced and distributed, and how everyone is enabled and incentivized to work well and to innovate, then it is realized that democratic socialism (at least in the classic sense of overwhelming public ownership) is unfeasible in any large-scale complex economy. For dynamism and efficiency there have to be competition, markets and a large private sector, as well as a state. Private ownership is also important for political reasons, to create zones of politico-economic power that can countervail state autocracy.

Once this is understood, then your game changes—irrevocably. Once it is realized that classical socialism cannot work (at least in a democratic and humane way) then you have to look for alternatives. Once it is acknowledged that private property and markets are indispensable in large-scale modern economies, then you have to accept them, warts and all. The best that can be done is to harness their benefits and minimize their deleterious effects.

The grand march of history toward socialism is exposed as a myth. Classical socialism and the victory of the proletariat disappear as icons. The proletariat is no longer the means of our deliverance. The myth of historic destiny falls. They are all revealed as dangerous dogmas.

History is no longer on your side. Like everyone else in the real world, you are faced with the messy task of making do and muddling through. The extent of public or private ownership is a matter not of ideology, but of what works best in particular circumstances. We salvage some viable cargo from the socialist wreckage, including the pursuit of social justice and the reduction of inequality. Otherwise the socialist vessel is sunk.

You may in part have realized this, to advocate a 'mixed economy' as Corbyn outlined for the British Labour Party.[35] So far, so good. But to tolerate a private sector is not the same thing as to defend it, or to recognize its virtues. My friend Sweet Liberty advocates private enterprise and markets. I asked her: what are their limits, and where are other structures superior? Now I ask you: you seem to prefer public over private enterprise, so are there any limits to this remedy? By contrast, are there any spheres of activity that you would in principle keep private? Do you recognize the advantages and vital importance of a substantial private sector? Unless you have solid answers to these questions, involving a defence of some substantial private enterprise, then your 'mixed economy' is just a halfway house on your intended route to old-fashioned socialism: it becomes a socialist slippery slope.

But after the costly experimental experience of socialism in the twentieth century, our only acceptable option for the foreseeable future is a modified form of capitalism. Existing varieties of capitalism indicate that different destinations are possible. We should also encourage worker cooperatives. We also need to address the major reform of the financial system, comparing different institutional solutions and selecting what works best. Perhaps, at some stage, the most developed economies may evolve beyond capitalism. But that is a long way off, and cannot be envisaged for the here and now. We need to experiment and to see what works.

In defending private property and retaining a major role for markets (at least in large-scale complex societies) my position is some way to the *Left* of yours. But you object to my labelling of *Left* and *Right*. You respond: 'Time has moved on since the 1790s. Words change their meanings and the modern use of Left is legitimate'.

But what is this modern usage? 'The modern Left stands for collectivism and equality' is your answer. I agree that equality is important. But you have flirted with totalitarian and one-party regimes that have sacrificed adequate legal systems that could have maintained equal legal rights. These regimes politicized the legal process and made legal equality nominal rather than real.

Some friends of the Chinese regime have defended the *hukou* system in China, which, by giving people a different status on the basis of their location, is a blatant violation of equality under the law. Furthermore, the degree of equality in the distribution of income that was achieved in Stalin's Soviet Union and Mao's China was not overwhelmingly impressive. Scandinavian capitalist countries are relatively egalitarian and have maintained democracy and liberty.[36]

Turning to collectivism, this has also been the creed of the Right. The word fascism derives from its symbolic use of the *fasces* of ancient Rome, with rods bound together to signify collective strength. Fascism subjected individualism to the collective whole. Similarly, nationalism extols the nation over the individual. If you insist that collectivism is Left, be warned that fascism and nationalism both incline in the same collectivist direction.

You and your comrades are fond of the term *democracy*. But why aren't you more vigilant in promoting democracy in China and other developing countries? The answer may be that you are suspicious of the Western neoliberal agenda and of the 'Washington Consensus'. Where so-called 'neoliberals' promote democracy, property rights and privatization, you react against them. Where they promote anti-corruption programmes in developing countries, you see this as a ploy to privatize their economies. I have heard some of your comrades *defending* corruption in developing economies such as China and India, on the grounds that 'it gets things done'. You point out that China has achieved rapid economic growth, with corruption and without democracy or clear property rights.

But, in response, China is still at a relatively low level of GDP per capita. Ample evidence suggests that intermediate and higher levels of development can benefit from democracy, clear property rights and a relatively independent legal system. Much evidence also suggests that corruption has negative effects on economic growth.[37]

I agree with you that the state plays an important strategic role in both developing and developed economies. But democracy, secure property rights and the minimization of corruption are also vital. They are virtues in themselves, as well as being needed to sustain economic dynamism. In your overreaction against pro-market liberalism, you downplay all this. Instead you promote a romanticized statism and sideline the importance of competition and markets. But your statism has never delivered the degree equality of wealth and power that you rightly desire. In your overreaction against pro-market liberalism, you have overlooked evidence that rebuts your case, and you have abandoned several key principles of the *Left*.

You protested against Western intervention in Afghanistan, Iraq, Libya and Syria. But your blanket opposition to military action by the West has led you to devalue Western ideals that derive from the Enlightenment. Your 'anti-imperialism' has biased you against its invaluable principles and ideals. Like Corbyn, you may be a sentimentalist for Cuban-style revolution, and you may side with Putin's Russia in its post-socialist posturing against the West.[38]

Your veneration of large state monopolies, your mistrust of private ownership and the failures of your colleagues concerning human liberty place you toward the *Right*, in the original sense of that term.

Instead you should move toward the genuine *Left*. Consider Thomas Paine—a man of the *Left* who wanted greater economic equality, but within the framework of a property-owning market economy. He offers the best route for you to move from the *Right* to a more genuine *Left*. Paine's ideas need to be updated and conjoined with those of other social liberals, including Thomas H. Green and John A. Hobson.

Do not simply cherry-pick the redistributive side of Paine and then downplay the rest. Paine was a champion of liberty—the kind of liberty that many on the Left have relegated in the past. This includes the right to own and trade private property. Paine did not simply want to take from the super-rich and give to the poor. He speaks today to the aspiring middle ranks of society, who want to get on with their small businesses or develop their professional skills.

They want protection from large corporations and from insensitive bureaucracies. They want a good secular education for their children, so that they too can achieve something in their lives and careers. They want decent healthcare to meet the misfortune of illness or accident. They accept an economic role for the state in providing infrastructure and a safety net for the poor, but they also see the protection of property and enterprise as vital.

Unlike your comrades, Paine never sneered at these people as 'petit-bourgeois' or 'middle class'. The many varied ranks of the aspiring middle are now your principal constituency. Ignore them at your political peril.

Your Left has played out. Globally it is in a deep political crisis. Social democratic or Labour politicians have tried to adjust. Some have abandoned their wholesale commitment to nationalization. A diminishing minority have stuck with a fading original socialism, to discover that it has very little political traction nowadays. They cling on, pointing to the crises and failures of capitalism while fortified by the ungrounded dogmas of the 'inevitability' of socialism and the proletariat as the 'universal class'.

More extreme versions of socialism have fared no better. In Britain the Left Unity Party hosted a minority that supported the so-called Islamic State in Iraq and Syria. Far Left groups perennially exhibit their nature as anti-democratic and unprotective of basic human rights. These outcomes are not accidental. They are the results of wrong turnings your Left has taken in the past.[39]

To find an alternative you have to ditch the old baggage that is holding you back. Classical socialism is dead. But, re-animated like a zombie, the word *socialism* retains currency. It is misleading for all and unattractive for many. It is time for it to be buried. We have to find a new language, with new icons. We have to learn from the past and look to the future.

CHAPTER 11

Capitalism and Beyond: Toward a New Old *Left*

God, grant me the serenity to accept the things I cannot change,
The courage to change the things I can,
And the wisdom to know the difference.

Reinhold Niebuhr, 'The Serenity Prayer' (1932)[1]

The twentieth century saw the death of socialism (at least as originally defined) and the rebirth of free-market libertarianism.[2] In the preceding chapter I suggested a return to neither, at least without major amendments, while adopting some of the major concerns of both. The broad libertarian case for rights and liberty is indispensable, but libertarianism has to address the huge inequalities of wealth and massive concentrations of corporate and financial power within capitalism. The original libertarianism was designed for a different era, with small-scale enterprises in an economy dominated by material rather than intangible property. The massive inequalities within capitalism have been the concern of the Left, but the Left has too often run roughshod over rights and liberties. It needs to learn the lessons of the disastrous failure of socialism in the twentieth century.

So where does that leave us? First we need to improve our understanding of the nature of global capitalism. We need to appreciate what can and cannot be changed. We need to understand the mechanisms that generate inequality within the system so that we can develop policies that can deal with it, while retaining suitable incentives for work and enterprise.

We start from capitalism as we find it. Capitalism is a type of market system, but by its nature it cannot encompass markets for everything. In particular, we are prohibited from signing employment contracts that bind us for the rest of our lives. This has important consequences, as outlined below.

The partial absence of markets means that other institutions must step in. Here there can be a major role for the state, as long as it can intervene effectively. Capitalist economies are inevitably mixed economies, retaining an important role for the state and other institutions, as well as for markets. Some of the traditional arguments of free-market libertarians, who wish to minimize the state, are undermined.

On the other hand, those socialists who wish to abolish private property and markets have not learned the lessons of the twentieth century. We need to strike out on a course that is different from both. At the same time the libertarian defence of rights and the socialist concern about inequality must be retained.

Additional sections in this chapter address the problem of inequality, its sources and policies for its alleviation. More broadly, an experimental process of policy development is outlined in a section below on *evotopia*, inspired by John Dewey among others. The final section draws the threads together and sets out policy priorities for the new old *Left*.

CAPITALISM ALWAYS HAS MISSING MARKETS

It must be understood that capitalism can never be a 100 per cent market economy, and labour will always have disadvantages when compared with owners of capital. Given that we have no practical or acceptable alternative but to modify and tinker with capitalist economies, these indelible features of the system have to be taken into account when reforming their institutions.

We take it for granted that, after serving our contractual period of notice, we can quit our jobs. And we are not bound by employment contracts for the rest of our lives. This is part of our freedom. We are no longer slaves. But a strange consequence of this liberty is that capitalism cannot in principle be a complete market economy.

Generally, under capitalism, there can be no complete set of futures markets for the labour of existing or future workers. Although capitalism has meant a huge extension of property and markets, it has also, by freeing labour from servitude, created *missing* markets for labour futures. For there to be full futures markets for labour, all workers must be able to enter into contracts for every future instant in their expected working life. Such a complete curtailment of future discretion would be tantamount to voluntary bondage, limiting the freedom of workers to quit their employment. Paradoxically, pushing markets to their limits would mean the return of slavery for the workforce.[3]

There is some future contracting for labour, particularly when a student receives financial support for studies from a company in return for a commitment to work for some years in the firm. Also, in modern capitalism there are sometimes 'non-compete' agreements with skilled employees that prevent them for a while from leaving a firm and working for a rival. But these restrictive agreements are still far short of lifetime contracts.

Also the future supply of labour power is not something that can be contracted at source because within developed capitalism babies cannot legally be farmed and sold as commodities. Human infants and their future labour power are not themselves produced under capitalist conditions. If they were, it would not be capitalism. Consequently under capitalism there are unavoidable missing markets for the production of human resources.

This creates a problem for the employer with the existing workforce. If the employer spends money on employee training and skill development, then this investment is lost when the worker leaves. As a result, without compensatory arrangements, employers might under-invest in human learning and education. This problem of incentivizing investment in training, and retaining workers in the firms in which they have been trained, is intrinsic to capitalism.[4]

There are limited markets for future skills, and capitalism cannot deal with this problem by extending markets. Under capitalism there is a systemic problem of training workers with appropriate skills. This system shortfall has a number of possible remedies. The likelihood of worker exit might be reduced by distributing shares in the company to employees. There may be an additional role for state-aided training. Governments have subsidized employee training (with some success) in some countries and in some US states.[5]

The inevitability of missing markets within the system has profound consequences. Generally it means that markets cannot be the solution to everything and attempts to increase the power and scope of markets can be suboptimal. In addition, the problem of incentivizing the training of workers who are free to quit their jobs is exposed. It points to the need for substantial state intervention to fund training and education to ensure an adequate supply of skilled workers.

CAPITALISM AND INEQUALITY

At least nominally, capitalism embodies and sustains an Enlightenment agenda of freedom and equality. Typically there is freedom to trade and equality under the law, meaning that most adults—rich or poor—are formally subject to the same legal rules. But with its inequalities of power and wealth, capitalism darkens this legal equivalence. As Anatole France noted ironically: 'The law, in its majestic equality, forbids the rich as well as the poor to sleep under bridges, to beg in the streets, and to steal bread'. But this does not mean that legal equality is unreal or unimportant. On the contrary, legal equality is a vital element in the establishment of liberty and prosperity.[6]

In path-breaking empirical research, Richard Wilkinson and Kate Pickett revealed multiple deleterious effects of inequalities of income and wealth. Using data from twenty-three developed countries and from the separate states of the United States, they observed negative correlations between inequality, on the one hand, and physical health, mental health, education, child well-being, social mobility, trust and community life, on the other hand. They also found positive correlations between inequality and drug abuse, imprisonment, obesity, violence and teenage pregnancies. They suggested that inequality creates adverse outcomes through psychosocial stresses generated through interactions in an unequal society.[7]

What are the mechanisms within capitalism that exacerbate inequalities of income or wealth? Some inequality results from individual differences in talent or skill. But this cannot explain the huge gaps between rich and poor in many capitalist countries. Much of the inequality of wealth found within capitalist societies results from inequalities of inheritance. The process is cumulative: inequalities of wealth often lead to differences in education, economic power and further inequalities in income.[8]

To what extent can inequalities of income or wealth be attributed to the fundamental institutions of capitalism, rather than a residual landed aristocracy or other surviving elites from the pre-capitalist past? This question is more focused: instead of enquiring into all sources of existing inequality, we ask what mechanisms that are peculiar to capitalism exacerbate inequality? A familiar mantra is that markets are the source of inequality under capitalism. Can markets be blamed for inequality?[9]

In his hard-hitting analysis of growing inequality in the United States, Joseph E. Stiglitz wrote: 'Markets, by themselves, even when they are stable, often lead to high levels of inequality'. But he then modified this claim: 'Market forces played a role, but it was not market forces alone'. But blaming 'market forces' is not the same thing as blaming markets. Such 'forces' could be inequalities of power and wealth that operate within markets. In this case, the main factors involved in the explanation resemble the inequality that we are trying to explain. Then, in his chapter on 'markets and inequality', Stiglitz blamed not markets as such, but how they are 'shaped', along with other possible causes of inequality, including technological changes, advances in productivity, international shifts in comparative advantage and other important factors that are not strictly markets as such. Despite the rhetoric, Stiglitz did not show that markets can be blamed for inequality.[10]

In reality, of course, no market is perfectly competitive. When a seller has sufficient salable assets to affect market prices, then strategic market behaviour is possible to drive out competitors. If markets *per se* are to be blamed for inequality, then it has to be shown that competitive markets also have this outcome. Unless we can demonstrate their culpability, blaming competitive markets for inequalities of success or failure might be like blaming the water for drowning a weak swimmer.

To demonstrate that competitive markets are a source of inequality we would have to start from an imagined world where there was initial equality in the distribution of income, wealth and power, and then show how markets led to inequality. I know of no such theoretical explanation.

Markets involve voluntary exchange, where both parties to an exchange expect benefits. One party to the exchange may benefit more than the other; but there is no reason to assume that individuals who benefit more (or less) in one exchange will generally do so. And if some traders become more powerful in the market than others, then its competitiveness is reduced.

So if markets *per se* are not the root cause of inequality under capitalism, then what is? A clear answer to this question is vital if effective policies to counter inequality are to be developed. Capitalism builds on historically inherited inequalities of class, ethnicity and gender. By affording more opportunities for the generation of profits, it may also exaggerate differences due to location or ability. Partly through the operation of markets, it can also enhance positive feedbacks that further magnify these differences. But its generic sources of inequality lie elsewhere.

Precisely because waged employees are not slaves, they cannot use their lifetime capacity for work as collateral to obtain money loans. The very contractual freedom of workers denies them the possibility to use their labour assets or skills as collateral. By contrast, capitalists may use their property to make profits, and as collateral to borrow money, invest and make still more money. Differences become cumulative, between those with and without collateralizable assets, and between different amounts of collateralizable wealth. Even when workers become homeowners with mortgages, wealthier people in business can still race ahead.

Unlike owned capital, free labour power cannot be used as collateral to obtain loans for investment. At least in this respect, capital and labour do not meet on a level playing field. This asymmetry is a major driver of inequality.

Another consequence of missing futures markets for labour is that employers have diminished incentives to invest in the skills of their workforce. Especially as capitalism becomes more knowledge intensive, this can create an unskilled and low-paid underclass and further exacerbate inequality, unless compensatory measures are put in place. A socially excluded underclass is observable in several developed capitalist countries.

The foremost generator of inequality under capitalism is not markets but capital. This may sound Marxist, but it is not. I define capital differently from Marx and from most other economists and sociologists. My definition of capital corresponds to its enduring and commonplace business meaning. Capital is money, or the realizable money value of collateralizable property. Unlike labour, capital can be used as collateral and the loan obtained can help generate further wealth.[11]

Another source of inequality results from the inseparability of the worker from the work itself. By contrast, the owners of other factors of production are free to trade and seek other opportunities while their property makes money or yields other rewards. This puts workers at a disadvantage. Through positive feedbacks, even slight disadvantages can have cumulative effects.[12]

None of these core drivers of inequality can be diminished by extending markets or increasing competition. These drivers are congenital to capitalism and its system of wage labour. If capitalism is to be retained, then the compensatory arrangements that are needed to counter inequality cannot simply be extensions of markets or private property rights.

These ineradicable asymmetries between labour and capital mean that ultra-individualist arguments against trade unions are misconceived. In a system that is biased against them, workers have a right to organize and defend their rights, even if it reduces competition in labour markets.

REDUCING INEQUALITY

Over two hundred years ago, Thomas Paine set out arguments and methods for reducing inequality. But much of the wealth of his time was in land. Land and buildings are immobile, and can be readily assessed and taxed. Land ownership is still highly concentrated in a few hands, along with much additional wealth. Money capital can be easily moved around the world or hidden in foreign accounts.

Today we face problems of inequality even greater than those addressed by Paine. In the United States, the richest 1 per cent own 34 per cent of the wealth and the richest 10 per cent own 74 per cent of the wealth. In the UK, the richest 1 per cent own 12 per cent of the wealth and the richest 10 per cent own 44 per cent of the wealth. In France the figures are 24 cent and 62 per cent respectively. The richest 1 per cent own 35 per cent of the wealth in

Switzerland, 24 per cent in Sweden and 15 per cent in Canada. Although there are important variations, other developed countries show similar patterns of inequality within this range. The problem is extreme in the United States. Lower levels of inequality elsewhere are far from satisfactory, but they indicate what might be politically feasible for the currently more unequal countries.[13]

In an important book on inequality, Samuel Bowles and Herbert Gintis advocated wealth redistribution. They addressed problems of asymmetrical information in enterprises, schools and elsewhere and proposed redistributions of property in order to align the incentives of owners more closely with the incentives of users. While they proposed no ban on capitalist enterprises, they favoured workplace democracy and government provision of credit to worker cooperatives.[14]

In another work on inequality, Bruce Ackerman and Anne Alstott took up Paine's agenda in their proposal for a 'stakeholder society'. They argued that 'property is so important to the free development of individual personality that everybody ought to have some'. They echoed Francis Bacon: 'Wealth is like muck. It is not good but if it be spread'.[15]

To this end, home ownership is of positive value, as a means of widely extending ownership of collateralizable property. But there also needs to be a substantial amount of social housing available for rent, to cater for those unable to afford to buy their own homes. Significantly, the Right has promoted home ownership, while it has often been rebutted by the Left. This resistance comes from the Left's old-fashioned, overextended collectivism. By contrast, it is important for the Left to champion home ownership within an egalitarian and redistributive political programme.

Ackerman and Alstott stressed progressive taxes on wealth rather than on income. Echoing Paine, they proposed a large cash grant to all citizens when they reach the age of majority, around the benchmark cost of taking a bachelor's degree at private university in the United States. This grant would be repaid into the national treasury at death. To further advance redistribution, they argued for the gradual implementation of an annual wealth tax of 2 per cent on a person's net worth above a threshold of $80,000. Like Paine, they argued that every citizen has the right to share in the wealth accumulated by preceding generations. A redistribution of wealth, they proposed, would bolster the sense of community and common citizenship.

Increased wealth or inheritance taxes are likely to be unpopular because they are perceived as an attack on the wealth that we have built up and wish to pass on to our children or others of our choice. But the brilliance of Paine's 1797 proposal for a cash grant at the age of majority is that it offers a *quid pro quo* for wealth or inheritance taxes at later life. People will be more ready to accept wealth taxation if they have earlier benefitted from a large cash grant in their youth. Wealth would by recycled to younger generations rather than syphoned away.

Another form of wealth taxation that could be made more acceptable than others is to tax land values, as Henry George argued long ago. Land is a scarce (or limited) commodity that is subject to financial speculation and acquires value for those reasons. A tax on that unearned appreciation could be made politically acceptable.[16]

The more fortunate or successful can be persuaded to give up some of their advantages if they see the benefits for society as a whole. There is an interesting sporting parallel here. Sports involving league competitions, such as soccer in the UK, allow teams freely to pick the best players. Obviously, the richer and more successful teams have more money to recruit the better players, making these teams even richer and even more successful. This process of cumulative positive feedback ends up with a few rich teams dominating the league, and only rarely is another team able to break into the leading pack. Consequently, most of the public attention and money focuses on the few top teams.

But to counteract this prominence of a few teams, in the United States there is a 'National Football League Draft' system where the lowest-ranked teams have the first choices of the new players coming out of the colleges. The worse teams can choose the best players. Competition and mobility throughout the American National Football League are increased. As a result, the matches become more exciting, and the league gains more money from higher attendances and higher TV and other rights. This system shows that the more fortunate teams can be persuaded to give up money and power if they perceive benefits to the whole.[17]

In the economy, there are several ways of spreading power and influence more broadly. Employee shareholding in their enterprises is a flexible strategy for extending ownership of revenue-producing assets in society. In the United States alone, over ten thousand enterprises, employing over ten million workers, are part of employee ownership, stock bonus, or profit-sharing schemes. Employee ownership can increase incentives, personal identification with the enterprise and job satisfaction for workers. The evidence suggests that when employee ownership schemes and some employee participation in decision-making are combined, greater increases in profitability and productivity can be obtained.[18]

As modern capitalist economies become more knowledge intensive, access to education to develop skills becomes all the more important. Those deprived of such education suffer a degree of social exclusion, and, unless it is addressed, this problem is likely to get worse. Widespread skill-development policies are needed, alongside integrated measures to deal with job displacement and unemployment.[19]

The need for ongoing education is one argument for a basic income guarantee. Such a basic income would be paid to everyone out of state funds, irrespective of other income or wealth, and whether the individual is working or not. It is justified on the grounds that individuals require a minimum income to function effectively as free and choosing agents. The basic means of survival are necessary to make use of our liberty, to have some autonomy, to be effective citizens, to develop ethically and to participate in civil society. These are conditions of adequate and educated inclusion in the market world of choice and trade.[20]

A basic income would also reward otherwise unpaid work in care for the sick or elderly, which is often performed within families. A basic income would also encourage new entrepreneurs and creative artists. There would also be a huge saving in administration costs of often complex social security and welfare schemes. The level of the basic income does not have to be high. It can be set as a basic minimum for survival, thus retaining strong incentives for most people to seek additional sources of income.

Some forms of unconditional basic income have been pledged or introduced in several countries, including Brazil and Finland. Several developed countries have legal minimum income entitlements. In 1968, James Tobin, Paul A. Samuelson, John Kenneth Galbraith and another 1,200 economists signed a document calling for the US Congress to introduce a system of income guarantees and supplements. Winners of the Nobel Prize in Economics who fully support a basic income include Milton Friedman, Friedrich Hayek, James Meade, Herbert Simon and Robert Solow. Significantly, this idea cuts across the political spectrum.[21]

A related proposal, also redolent of Paine, was launched by the British Labour government in 2005. It introduced a Child Trust Fund with the aim of ensuring every child has savings at the age of eighteen, giving every child a financial boost that they could use for the purposes of education or enterprise. Children received an initial £250 subscription from the government. Family and friends could top up these trust funds. The child would attain control of the fund at age eighteen. Withdrawals could then be made but be exempt from taxation. A weakness of this particular scheme was its timidity. A greater government subscription would have been more redistributive and egalitarian in its consequences. Child Trust Funds were abolished by the coalition government that came to power in 2010.

A key challenge for modern capitalist societies, alongside the needs to protect the natural environment and enhance the quality of life, is to retain the dynamic of innovation and investment while ensuring that the rewards of the global system are more widely distributed. As Paine put it long ago:

> All accumulation, therefore, of personal property, beyond what a man's own hands produce, is derived to him by living in society; and he owes on every principle of justice, of gratitude, and of civilization, a part of that accumulation from whence the whole came.[22]

But the benefits of 'living in society' are not simply through the advantages of cooperation or the division of labour. Modern societies have developed complex institutions that have empowered innovations and massive expansions of wealth. The ultimate and indivisible accumulation is not simply of things, but of knowledge.

As Paine and others insisted, the right to private property is one of our basic human rights. Preceding chapters have supported a general right to private property, which derives from the universal rights to degrees of autonomy and self-development. This implies that private property should be widely distributed, rather than concentrated in a few hands. Notwithstanding our general dependence on others, we have right to as much self-determination as possible that is consistent with the common good.

In modern economies, substantial public ownership can also be effective in some sectors, but viable options for private enterprise are also crucial. In a system of private property, trade opens up possibilities of improvement through voluntary engagement with others. It is a vital means of social interaction in any complex, large-scale society.

The general right to private property needs to be modified in modern circumstances. First, we are no longer in economies dominated by agrarian activity or small trades. Activities necessary for self-development are entwined in more complex webs of institutional and technological interdependencies. While this does not diminish the importance of private property, it points to the need for institutions where it can be pooled, cooperatively and voluntarily, for productive activity, such as partnerships, cooperatives and corporations.

Second, a growing proportion of property in modern capitalism consists of informational assets and intellectual property, rather than the ownership of things. As noted in the preceding chapter, excessive property rights in informational assets can create an 'anti-commons' where divided, interconnected or concentrated rights obstruct investment and trade. Also modern capitalism has reduced the marginal cost of many additional informational goods and services to near zero, making them nearly free, and open to non-market modes of distribution. For the vitality of modern capitalism, as well as for the general development of the individual, it is important and feasible that much crucial information is available for free, while retaining a modernized copyright and patent system to retain incentives for innovation.[23]

Consequently, the right to private property in things must be qualified and transformed to include access to information that is vital for individual self-development. Access to such information has always been essential, and a basic right. But in modern economies it assumes a greater relative and absolute importance. It is realizable because of innovations such as the Internet. Private ownership of informational and intellectual property remains important, but must be limited, for fuller individual and economic development.

Hence we need an informational commons, where much information is freely available without payment. As much information as possible should be available on this commons, as long as sufficient incentives for the creation or discovery of new information are retained. The informational commons should be maximized, subject to any constraint imposed by arrangements that are necessary for the provision of new and useful information.

EVOTOPIA

The nineteenth and twentieth centuries have shown us the limitations of grand utopian schemes. Both the abolition of private property and markets, on the one hand, and any major contraction of the state, on the other hand, are unfeasible within a modern complex economy.

That complexity means that we must experiment with different forms of enterprise and organization, to determine what works best. The need for experimentation rather than fixed blueprints has been emphasized by diverse thinkers including John Dewey, Friedrich Hayek and Karl Popper. Here we focus on Dewey.[24]

Dewey's experimental and democratic approach to policy development relies critically on a system of institutionalized science and an adequate level of generalist education. In the context of uncertainty and complexity, Dewey favoured an experimental, process-oriented and participative democracy. Institutional design had to be cautious and experimental. The primary role of experts is to lay out the feasible policy alternatives and their likely consequences, and feed this information into informed public debate.[25]

Dewey stressed the need for an open-ended, flexible and experimental approach to dealing with human needs and the enhancement of welfare. He embraced a 'method of experimental and cooperative intelligence' based on democracy and science. He looked forward to the time when 'the method of intelligence and experimental control is the rule in social relations and social direction'.[26]

Dewey proposed a thorough and ingoing extension of democratic values. Habits of enquiry, respectful dialogue and public spiritedness had to be nurtured from the earliest years, in both the family and the school.

Dewey supported experimental, ongoing processes for improving policies and value judgments. They must rely on collective evaluation and debate to draw conclusions from the empirical outcomes of each trial. Policy judgments are tested by putting them into practice and considering through dialogue whether they enhance human life and lead to human flourishing.

We have basic and intermediate needs such as food, shelter, healthcare, security, a safe environment, interactions, education and autonomy. These objective and transcultural needs are essential for all human survival and self-realization. Their fulfilment requires the ability to participate in the social setting in which the individual operates.[27]

I introduced the term *evotopia* to describe a dynamic system that contrasts with fixed utopias, such as the socialist system of collective property or individualistic, free-market libertarianism. An evotopian approach should foster learning, enhance human capacities, systematically incorporate growing knowledge and adapt to changing circumstances. Science would be the guide for serving human needs, but many other moral and policy questions are matters for open and adaptive dialogue. An evotopia would embrace the following principles:[28]

Complexity, uncertainty and incomplete knowledge make any complete, comprehensive planning impossible. All policies are fallible, and hence they must be provisional and practically adaptable.

Much policy should be formulated by experimentation, and with a variety of institutions. Only on the basis of such a variety can policies and institutions be given any comparative and pragmatic evaluation.

Inbuilt structural variety is important for helping the system deal with and adapt to unforeseen changes: variety is essential to learning and adaptability at both the systemic and the individual level.

The impossibility of omniscience, in institutions or individuals, means that neither can be relied upon as a final judge of what is required. A learning, adapting system enjoins a democratic and participatory dialogue, covering both scientific and normative issues, in which the prevailing policies are repeatedly scrutinized.

Structural variety is a key evotopian principle. It is necessary to ensure that some degree of variability is continuously maintained and replenished. Also necessary is the capability to find solutions to the new problems that emerge.

The market has a vital, central, but qualified role in an evotopian economy. Failure to appreciate its essential role in a complex and innovative economy is a major leftist error. Devolved ownership and control provide scope for diversity and experimentation. Private property implies the ability to trade goods and services. Markets are processors and signallers of imperfect but essential price information.

But in principle the market cannot be relied upon as the single, supreme, regulatory institution. It is impossible to turn every human interaction into a legal contract. The evidence of numerous policy experiments in recent decades suggests that neither markets nor privatization are universal panaceas.[29]

Accordingly, flexibility and adaptability are not necessarily gained by giving markets more rein. A complex economy has a diversity of idiosyncratic goals and functioning principles, requiring overarching, non-market frameworks of communication and regulation. Carefully constructed frameworks of regulation can increase the capacity of the economy to innovate and adapt, and even improve the functioning of markets themselves.

Dynamic growth and flexibility can be thwarted by placing all subsystems under the dictates of the market. This is especially true with matters such as education, health and environmental policy, where everyone is affected by the actions of others: economists call these effects *externalities*. Better specifications of property rights can deal with some of these problems, but irreducible transaction costs make some public intervention necessary. The state is also necessary to ensure that markets, where they exist, work effectively.[30]

CONCLUSION: A NEW OLD *LEFT*

Markets, commodity exchange and private ownership existed for thousands of years before capitalism, and they will continue to exist, even if capitalism is eclipsed by new ways of organizing the production and distribution of wealth. We have to accept markets and much private property. To do otherwise is to ignore the twentieth-century lessons of devastating socialist failure. But from an acceptance of markets and private property, radical avenues can still be found. Some of these may lead beyond capitalism.

A system of commodity exchange devolves crucial decision-making to individuals and requires them to enter into contracts with others. The individual has to carry out numerous transactions and act responsibly. But people cannot function effectively in a system of contracts and markets if they are deprived of food, shelter, basic education or fruitful social interaction. Through engagement in a social culture, people acquire the education and capabilities to deliberate effectively and serve their autonomous goals. These are conditions for social inclusion.[31]

Hence effective libertarian political principles imply a welfare state. James Sterba established the need for welfare provision to ensure that the poor can exercise their (libertarian) rights to life and property. Justifying taxation, Michael Davis argued that beneficiaries of state services (such as public health programs that reduce epidemics and police services that improve personal security) have the duty to pay for them.[32]

The limits to markets also have to be understood. Capitalism involves the business corporation, which is not itself a market and is organized on different principles. Detailed arguments concerning externalities and other problems suggest that healthcare, education and protection of the natural environment are not best served by giving markets unrestricted reign.[33]

The birth of capitalism was stimulated by Enlightenment ideas of individual liberty and equality under the law. But rightly we lack the liberties to enslave others, trade in slaves or enslave ourselves. We have equal legal rights to use property to produce more wealth. But the owner of labour power is placed at two indelible disadvantages compared with the owner of non-labour assets. Because of the ban on slavery, he or she cannot be used as collateral for obtaining loans, and he or she cannot separate himself or herself from the deployment of his or her labour in production. The congenital and unavoidable 'contradictions' of capitalism are neither mass immiseration in a world of wealth, impelled clashes of class against class, nor capital accumulation undermining the rate of profit. They are systemic limitations to the Enlightenment principles of liberty and equality that are embedded in its being.

Key policies arise from these arguments. They include universal education, a welfare state, a guaranteed basic income, the promotion of worker cooperatives, employee share-ownership schemes, corporate law reform, inheritance taxation and vigilant public regulation of the financial system. Some of these policies find supporters across the now mislabelled *Left* and *Right*. They help consolidate the Enlightenment principles of human flourishing, autonomy and liberty that emerged with capitalism at its inception.

What are the policy priorities for the new old *Left*? Above all is the need to promote human flourishing and fulfilment, on the basis of providing for ascertained human needs, and also providing the means and liberties for self-fulfilment.

Instead of the dogmas of pro- or anti-public ownership, we need a public sector that steps in pragmatically where the market fails. The state can and should play a strategic role, particularly in developing transport and communications infrastructure and enhancing skills. A good case can be made for publicly arranged provision of railways, education, healthcare and some housing, for example. But what matters is the strategic effectiveness and efficiency of the public sector, and not first and foremost its size.

A healthy financial sector is vital to any economy based on private enterprise. Modern financial systems depend on both private initiative and state support. The state is essential to help constitute money and regulate finance. Paine's principle of reciprocal obligations derived from 'living in society' is relevant here. The banks depend on the state and the economy as a whole depends on the banks. State regulation of the banks is part of a vital *quid pro quo*.[34]

A number of issues flow from a supreme commitment to human flourishing. First is the problem of global poverty. Food, shelter and health are the most basic of human needs, without which we cannot survive. Unless these basic needs are satisfied then rights such as free expression and the pursuit of other goals are overshadowed. This is the fundamental motivation for a guaranteed basic income or other means to ensure livelihood and facilitate social engagement.

Second, we have basic developmental needs for parental care and education. Through such means we develop our potential as persons and learn to interact fruitfully with others. As economies develop their demands for skilled labour, education and training are vital means for participation, social inclusion and potential prosperity.

Third, because we depend on others both materially and psychologically, human flourishing requires an acknowledgement of our debts to others, through reciprocal engagement and social solidarity. The pitfall of some versions of political individualism is the mistaken notion that individual liberty and fulfilment are possible without this reciprocity and solidarity. Fully flourishing humans do not walk on the other side. Social solidarity implies individual charity, the willingness to pay reasonable taxes and support for policies that can help alleviate poverty and inequality.

Fourth, we must express solidarity with future generations by tackling the degradation of our natural environment and the problem of climate change. This will probably involve some sacrifices by this generation to deal with the climatic problems that threaten the next. The Enlightenment principles of liberty and human flourishing do not apply to current generations alone. For future generations to flourish we must safeguard the environment and deal with the problem of global warming.

Another major role for the state, as well as international cooperation between states, is to develop policies to address climate change. As noted in the preceding chapter, it is naïve to expect that the market will tackle this problem of its own accord. The state can create a regulatory framework that encourages innovation and entrepreneurship in fuel efficiency, renewable energy, recycling, public transport and so on.

Fifth, modern economies are ever-more complex due to incessant innovation in technology and institutions, and they are increasingly integrated on a global scale. Complexity and globalization create major political challenges, especially for the survival of meaningful democracy. Dani Rodrik argued that there is a 'fundamental political trilemma of the world economy: we cannot simultaneously pursue democracy, national determination, and economic globalization. If we want to push globalization further, we have to give up either the nation state or democratic politics'. His argument is that extended globalization requires the integration of nation states and the diminution of their independent powers, in favour of dominant superpowers or international institutions.

Rodrik rejected 'hyper-globalization' in favour of democracy and national determination. Hyper-globalization means pushing the integration of world markets even further, progressively reducing tariffs and eliminating protectionism. He argued that further gains along this dimension would be puny, and on the downside, that developing nations would be less able to establish and develop young industries in the face of fierce price competition from powerful global corporations.[35]

Globalization presents major political and economic challenges. Even if 'hyper-globalization' is avoided, we live in a world where each nation state interacts extensively with others. Each state depends on others for trade, security and collaboration to deal with global threats such as terrorism, disease and global warming. This limits the scope for full national autonomy.

In turn, the requirement of nations to collaborate to deal with such problems provides challenges for democracy. As international entanglements become greater, many supranational institutions—such as the World Bank, the European Union or the United Nations—emerge to facilitate cooperation and coordinate efforts. But putting these bodies under some kind of democratic control would be rife with problems. These international developments pose major questions on how democracy can be adapted for a more interdependent world, as well as strong challenges concerning its survival.

The interdependent world of today raises questions concerning the very nature of national citizenship. Just as Enlightenment thinkers protested against hereditary monarchies, because power was bestowed on individuals simply as a result of the accidental pedigree of their unchosen parents, we may protest today that the accident of being born in Bangladesh rather than Belgium should not bestow such vast differences in potential opportunity, expected wealth and longevity. National citizenship has become an anachronism. Immanuel Kant foresaw this problem and mooted the issue of world citizenship. But concomitant rights of free global movement, especially in a world of huge inequalities, would raise massive problems. This is a major international challenge for our century.

Notwithstanding all these challenges, the past two centuries have taught us the value of Enlightenment principles, particularly the importance of human rights, liberty and democracy. Those that would dilute or bypass such principles are deeply mistaken. This is especially the case when democracy itself is being threatened by globalization, large corporations, concentrated and reckless financial power, and proliferating supranational institutions that have limited democratic accountability.[36]

We may summarize these policy guidelines in the following way. The slogan of the French Revolution was *liberté*, *égalité*, *fraternité*. It should now be 'liberty, equality, democracy and solidarity':

Liberty. All people have basic human rights and liberties. Everyone has rights over his or her own body, and these preclude violence, torture and capital punishment. The exercise of liberty and choice requires the satisfaction of basic bodily, cognitive and relational needs, including food, shelter, education and social interaction. We have rights of free expression, of assembly and of worship, and rights to the ownership of property.

Equality. The law should not discriminate: everyone should be equal under the law. Access to the law must be universal, requiring provision of legal aid for the poor. The distributions of income and wealth should not be so extreme as to undermine social cohesion and solidarity. Extreme inequalities of income or wealth must be alleviated by careful and appropriate taxes and grants. They must be gauged to reduce inequality while encouraging wealth creation and property ownership.

Democracy. The ultimate legitimation of government is neither religion, tradition nor privilege, but the will of the people, expressed through a system of representative democracy. Some democracy is also important in other spheres of life, including local government and civil society. Democracy is also a crucial mechanism for social inclusion and civic education.

Solidarity. We have duties of solidarity to our family, to our community, to our nation, to all the people of the world and to future generations. No individual built up his or her wealth unaided and alone. He or she benefitted from others, at every level of society, and from the labours of past generations. Accordingly, we have reciprocal obligations to others, including the payment of taxes. These are recognition of the debts that we owe to our community and to our nation. We also have a duty to future generations, just as we benefitted from generations before: hence we must care for the natural environment and minimize the degradation of our planetary ecosystems and resources.

The Regressive Left has come to grief. Some have sunk into the mire of cultural relativism. Others have condoned reactionary religions and dictatorial regimes. The Left has to reverse and make a different turning, toward a modernized version of the Enlightenment politics of the original *Left*. The existing Left must return to what it once was—the foremost and most thoroughgoing champion of genuine and complete liberty, within a cohesive and caring society.

The first draft of this book was completed in late 2015, before the political earthquakes of 2016. During that fateful year, Donald Trump was elected President of the United States, Britons voted to leave the European Union, Turkey lurched toward dictatorship, Brazil ejected a democratically elected President, Russia extended its global influence and China tightened internal security while building military bases in the South China Sea.

It has become clear that, from America to Asia, authoritarian nationalism is on the march. The future of old international alliances is cast in doubt, raising a renewed spectre of global war. The global tectonic plates are now shifting. We may be moving toward an international crisis, as big as anything since 1945.

Within leading democracies, there are alarming developments. Torture is now endorsed by an elected US President. Journalists are threatened and in some countries imprisoned. Scientific findings on climate change are denied. Intellectuals and experts are ridiculed. Ignorance and dogma are celebrated. Truth is swamped by lies. Legislation protecting workers and the poor is undone. Minorities are attacked and made scapegoats. Racism is given licence. People suffer discrimination on the basis of their religious or other beliefs. Democratic systems are damaged. Judges and lawyers are treated as traitors. The rule of law is undermined.

In this dangerous new world, it matters less whether that railway is nationalized or whether electricity firms are in public ownership. Forms of ownership are always secondary to the actual provision and distribution of vital goods and services. What matters is what works.

But when our rights and liberties can no longer be taken for granted, secondary questions over forms of ownership move further down the ranking of priorities. Our human rights to life, liberty and opportunity matter above all.

The ubiquitous, trivializing idea that the Left is defined in terms of public provision, and Right as private provision, is historically recent. This book reveals the gross reversal of their original meanings. The contest between public and private ownership is also a polarization of lesser relevance in this world of rising authoritarian nationalism. Historically, rightist nationalism has often resorted to the nationalization of some companies when it suits the interests of the elite.

Our fundamental rights, our liberty and the rule of law are now increasingly threatened. Their defence becomes the great struggle of our time. This lesson is hardest for Americans and Britons, who were spared domestically from the jackboots of twentieth-century authoritarianism. Past struggles for British and American national liberty are beyond living memory. We have grown fat and lazy on the fruits of the liberal order. We have taken for granted its institutions and underestimated their fragility. We must repair our vigilance.

The struggle for liberty and equality has always been vital. When authoritarian nationalism emerged before, in the 1920s and 1930s, many radicals were then diverted by the delusions of classical socialism.

History is a good teacher, but only if we are prepared to listen. Unlike our grandparents in the crisis-ridden 1930s, we have seen the socialist experiments of the twentieth century and counted their cost in more than ninety million lives. History today provides stronger warnings against socialism. It is a wrong turning.

Social science today has more to teach us about the alternatives that we face. If we wish to learn, we can discover more about how markets work. Evidence and theory reveal the informational, organizational and other impediments to the kind of comprehensive national planning that was once proposed by most socialists. We can appreciate why countervailing politico-economic power, based on a strong private sector, is necessary to buttress democracy and to resist despotism. The twentieth century has taught us these lessons.

Attempts to build classical socialism and national collectivism are demonstrably unattractive options. Experiences in Russia, China, North Korea, Cuba, Venezuela and elsewhere have shown how severe limits on private ownership undermine countervailing power, crushing both democracy and freedom. We can explain why this occurs. There is a dwindling fantasy that classical socialism and meaningful democracy are compatible. But it is especially irresponsible in the light of history, and in the face of rising authoritarian nationalism.

The old Marxist mantra of bourgeoisie versus proletariat is also ungrounded in reality. Instead we have a highly fragmented working class, much of it aligned with authoritarianism and nationalism. Marxism relies on a quasi-religious and nonsensical belief that the working class—whatever it actually believes or strives for—carries our human destiny.

The large socialist and social democratic parties of Europe and elsewhere were founded on alliances of the organized working class and socialist intellectuals. Both parts of that coalition are in severe trouble, throughout Europe and elsewhere. The full-blooded classical socialism of Robert Owen and Karl Marx has been discredited: there has been no comparable Left philosophy to replace it. Buffeted by relentless globalization, the working class has also fragmented into countless specialisms, undermining the classic model of collective solidarity based on converging work-based interests.

Class struggle has mattered, but it has never been the main motor of history. What has mattered more have been struggles for power via the control of institutions, by individuals, dynasties, nations, religions or ideological movements.

Liberalism was one of those movements. It matured in the Enlightenment, based on the imperatives of equality and liberty. Liberalism rose up, in the English Civil War of the 1640s, in the American Revolution of the 1770s and in the French Revolution of 1789, in titanic struggles against despotism and oppression.

We must renovate the great traditions of liberalism that stem from the Enlightenment. The renewed rise of authoritarianism points to liberalism as the vital political movement of the modern age. But liberalism is a broad church. We may choose to reject the unfeasible, minimal statism of extreme pro-market libertarians. But if they are full defenders of human rights, then they are our allies against authoritarian nationalism.

We must avoid the past mistakes of Left and liberal thought. Faced with the challenges of changing, varied societies in the era of mass migration, sections of the liberal Left fell into the traps of ultra-tolerance and 'anything goes'. They forgot the vital institutions and values that are necessary to make any liberal society work, and they allowed conservative and discriminatory ideas to fester too long in some immigrant communities. These indulgences help the nationalist right in their racist crusades against immigrants and minorities.

Likewise, the Left does not serve its cause by campaigning against free speech, as some have done in their attempts to silence criticisms of Sharia law. Disapproval of some religious tenets can be warranted, even if these beliefs are upheld by a minority suffering discrimination. While it is necessary to prohibit incitement to violence, open criticism of conservative prejudices or practices is healthy. The dogmas of the oppressed—as well as of their oppressors—are not beyond reproach. The liberal Left should welcome careful criticism of religion and stop describing such disapproval as racist.

Neither is it racist to ask residents to learn the national language (or languages) so they can understand the prevailing laws and culture. Instead of defending medieval customs and values, the liberal Left should lead the struggle for assimilation, while celebrating the benefits of a diverse society. This would put the Left in a much stronger position, both to defeat racist nationalism and to defend the rights of minorities to live within the law and to worship as they please. A key strategic response to racism and to popular concerns about immigration is to focus on assimilation, rather than to condone backward practices and conservative religion. It is in the interests of everyone, including members of religious minorities, to stand up for liberal values.

The rise of authoritarian nationalism poses challenges for those who have defended private property and markets as if they were sufficient to guarantee liberty and human rights. We have noted how Ludwig von Mises aided pre-Nazi fascism in Austria and how Friedrich Hayek and Margaret Thatcher were silent over Augusto Pinochet's atrocities in Chile. How can Republicans defend pro-torture President Donald Trump? How can freedom-loving, pro-market members of the British Conservative Party support exit from the European Union, which is the biggest market on the planet and has facilitated a huge extension of human rights and democracy on that continent? Private property and markets are necessary but insufficient. The choice is now between authoritarian nationalism and liberal internationalism.

Liberalism is internally diverse. The use of the term *liberal* has differed between the English-speaking world, on the one hand, and Continental Europe on the other. Some strains of liberalism would reduce the economic role of the state. Yet there is another strain, going back to Thomas Paine, through John A. Hobson, William Beveridge and John Maynard Keynes, which emphasizes the importance of some state intervention and of a substantial welfare system. Without committing the mistake of socialism, this tradition addresses the problem of economic, as well as of political or legal, inequality. But all strains of liberalism are united on the importance of human rights and liberties.

We may be facing a generation of struggle to defend liberal democracy and human rights from authoritarian nationalism. There is a danger of a contraction of world trade and even of a major war. These threats make action more urgent. The Left is better equipped to win this struggle, as long as it understands and avoids the errors of its past.

NOTES

INTRODUCTION

1. See chapter 4 below. Throughout this book I use both the uncapitalized words 'communism' and 'socialism' to refer to any past, present or proposed society with common ownership (by the community, municipality or the national state) of most of the means of production. I use the capitalized word 'Communism' to refer to regimes with a self-described Communist Party in power. It was only with the Bolshevik Revolution that 'socialism' came to refer to a distinct stage between capitalism and communism. Lenin (1967, vol. 2, pp. 337–345) in his *State and Revolution* (1917) introduced this usage, partly to help defend the planned Bolshevik seizure of power against the criticism that Russia was insufficiently developed for socialist revolution. By contrast, Marx and Engels did not use the term *socialism* to refer to a future stage between capitalism and communism.

2. Stalin did not exterminate six million Jews, but many thousands of them were victims of his purges. And within the Soviet Union from 1939 to 1949 he ordered mass deportations and killings of Baltic, Caucasian, Polish, Slavic and Turkic peoples, with the aim of eliminating their cultures (Rummel 1990, Pohl 1999). Also in genocidal words, not in deeds, there is a little-known Marxist precedent. On 13 January 1849, in the *Neue Rheinische Zeitung* (a newspaper edited by Marx and Engels), Engels proclaimed that 'the disappearance from the face of the earth . . . of entire reactionary peoples' such as the Slavs would be a 'step forward' (Marx and Engels 1977, p. 238).

3. See Trotsky (1937).

4. See Lavoie (1985b).

5. See chapter 10 below.

6. See, for example, Wainwright (1994).

7. For the record, I opposed Western aggression in Vietnam. I was also against the 2003 invasion of Iraq. The fact that US President George W. Bush and UK Prime Minister Tony Blair attempted to justify the 2003 invasion in terms of the exportation of human rights and democracy does not mean that the invasion was justified. Promoting commendable institutions or values does not imply that they can or should be imposed by military force.

8. For example, Tariq Ali (2003), Seumas Milne (2004), John Pilger (Hinman and Pilger 2004) and the 'Stop the War' coalition (Bloodworth 2015c) urged indiscriminate support for all forms of anti-Western resistance in Iraq. These statements were made before that resistance revealed its full sectarian savagery, but they have not since been retracted, as far as I am aware. On Trotskyist support for the Iranian theocratic regime see Alexander (1985, p. 883). The extraordinary final quotation in this paragraph comes from a proposal by a minority group within the UK-based Left Unity Party (founded by the film director Ken Loach and others). This group supported ISIS as a 'stabilising force' with 'progressive potential' (Jones 2014, Sommers 2014). The fact that anyone could make such a proposal, particularly while describing himself as Left and socialist, is deeply shocking. In the following year, Alex Callinicos (2015) of the Socialist Workers Party (SWP) declared: 'Our job is to defeat Western imperialism, not ISIS'. Similarly, the SWP-led Stop the War coalition compared the 'internationalism and solidarity' of ISIS with that of the International Brigades who fought fascism in Spain in the 1930s (Independent 2015).

9. See Mayer (2014).

10. For an example of virulent opposition to anti-Sharia activists, see the rhetoric hurled at the 'One Law for All' campaign in Britain (Pitt 2014). The case of the English Defence League is different (see note immediately below) but both are crudely lumped together by some Left critics as 'Islamophobic'.

11. Thuggish nationalist groups such as the English Defence League (EDL) have (a) criticized aspects of Islamic doctrine such as Sharia law, (b) opposed violent Islamist extremism, (c) attracted racists and fascists, and (d) opposed the building of new mosques and tolerated calls for the violent destruction of existing ones (Wikipedia 2016a). But just as the EDL has conflated these four themes, so too have their strongest opponents. By opposing all EDL actions without reservation, many of its most forceful critics have entangled these issues. But (a) and (b) are very different from (c) and (d). The freedom to criticize (without threat of violence) a religion and to oppose religious extremism should be vigorously defended. But racism, fascism and attacks on the freedom of worship should all be strongly condemned.

12. The former UKIP leader Nigel Farage has a history of racist and even fascist views (Crick 2013).

13. In 2015 Hope not Hate published a long list of 'anti-Muslim' individuals and organizations (Mulhall and Lowes 2015). Alongside fascist and racist bigots, the list smears peaceful campaigners against Sharia law such as Melanie Phillips, Ayaan Hirsi Ali and the Lawyers' Secular Society.

14. See Rawlinson (2013).

CHAPTER ONE

1. Boehm (2012) provides a graphic account of the likely nature of human foraging societies circa forty-five thousand years ago.

2. See the discussions and estimates of tribal group size in Dunbar (1993, 2010, 2011), Richerson and Boyd (1999, 2001) and Boehm (2012). On the evolution of cooperation in communities through *group selection*, see Darwin (1871), Sober and Wilson (1998), Bowles and Gintis (2011), Boehm (2012) and Hodgson (2013).

3. See Bar-Yosef (1998).

4. See Fukuyama (2011, ch. 17) and Hodgson (2015, ch. 3).

5. Hampton's (1984) anthology of radical thinking is a valuable source, but it is mostly confined to England. In this chapter we venture a little further, but the great wisdom of some other countries and continents is sadly omitted.

6. Quotes from John Ball can be found in Hampton (1984, pp. 50-51).

7. See Hampton (1984, pp. 74-75).

8. Lilburne's words are quoted in Robertson (1951, p. 3). Brailsford (1961) is an invaluable and well-researched history of the Levellers, but it gives insufficient emphasis to their defence of private property. See Woodhouse (1951), Morton (1975) and Otteson (2003) for collections of Leveller tracts and speeches.

9. See Mises (1985, pp. 47, 51), Hayek (1960, 1973, 1979), Caldwell and Montes (2015) and chapter 10.

10. The *Agreement of the People* proclaimed that men aged twenty-one or over, but 'not being servants, or receiving alms', should have the vote (Morton 1975, p. 268). Accordingly, 'the Levellers consistently excluded from their franchise proposals two substantial categories of men, namely, servants or wage-earners, and those in receipt of alms or beggars' (Macpherson 1962, p. 107).

11. For the Leveller defence of private property see Robertson (1951, pp. 85-89), Woodhouse (1951, p. 75), Brailsford (1961, p. 315), Macpherson (1962, pp. 152-153) and Manning (1976, pp. 295-296).

12. On Leveller attitudes to the enclosure movement see Brailsford (1961, pp. 233, 431-433, 449-450, 526) and Hill (1975, p. 119). The quotation is from Hill (1961, p. 111).

13. See Morton (1975, p. 276).

14. Lilburne quoted in Robertson (1951, p. 87).

15. The term '$1/n$ problem' was suggested to me by Bob Rowthorn in 1992. It is not the only argument against large-scale socialism, but it is one of the simplest and profoundest. The problem of incentives in large-scale organizations is also a theme of Mancur Olson Jr's (1965) classic book.

16. See Morton (1975, p. 273).

17. See Brailsford (1961, p. 274) and Hampton (1984, p. 188).

18. Quotation is from Benn (2009). Benn (2009) mooted that by referring to the earth's 'common treasury' the Levellers justified 'common ownership and a classless society'. This is unfounded. The notion of a 'common treasury' of land and other natural wealth bestowed by God was commonplace in the seventeenth century, and it was only occasionally used as an argument for communism, as with the Diggers. By contrast, for the Levellers and others, ownership was justified by independent labour, not by any original gift from God. Benn and Brockway were long-standing Labour Party Members of Parliament. Brockway (1980) failed to define socialism clearly and he did not give any documented support to his assertion that the Agitators and Levellers were socialists.

19. Excerpts from Winstanley's writing are found in Hampton (1984, pp. 197-200, 212-214, 225-227, 229-238, 247-255). From 1649 to 1660 England was described as a Commonwealth rather than a Kingdom. Note that the term *commonwealth* did not imply common or collective ownership. It referred to 'public welfare' or 'general good or advantage'. The original phrases 'the common-wealth' and 'the common weal' come from the old meaning of 'wealth' as 'well-

being'. Under Cromwell, it expanded from its original sense of 'public welfare' to refer also to a republic, in which supreme power was supposedly vested in the adult male population, rather than in a monarch.

20. Kant (1929, p. 7).

21. Burke (1790; 1968, pp. 151–152).

22. Paine's response is in the first part of his *Rights of Man* (1791) (see Paine [1945, vol. 1]).

23. Quoted in Levin (2014, p. 113).

24. See Dewey (1916, 1935, 1938, 1939), Ryan (1995), Evans (2000) and Hodgson (2013, ch. 10).

25. Engels, *Socialism: Utopian and Scientific* (1892) in Marx and Engels (1962, vol. 2, p. 117).

26. Robinson (1998, p. 261).

27. See the magnificent studies by Ostrom (1990) of the management of 'common pool resources'. Concerning so-called 'primitive communism', it did not involve shared ownership in a developed legal sense. Veblen (1898, p. 358) pointed out that ownership and property were later institutional developments: 'no concept of ownership, either communal or individual, applies in the primitive community. The idea of communal ownership is of a relatively later growth'. Common access or usage does not imply common property rights, in their full legal meaning, with third-party adjudication and state legislatures. Before the emergence of modern states, property was no more than the customary powers of kinship groups, not legal title sanctioned by legal institutions (Fukuyama 2011, pp. 66–71).

28. See Manuel and Manuel (1979, p. 557).

CHAPTER TWO

1. Stewart (1951, p. 114).

2. Montesquieu (1748, bk. xi, ch. vi). The developmental importance of countervailing power is now widely stressed in modern institutional theory. See North, Wallis and Weingast (2009); Acemoglu and Robinson (2012); and Hodgson (2015).

3. During the Terror, more than 16,000 were executed with some semblance of legal process. An estimated 250,000 died during the savage repression of the revolt in the Vendée in the west. Maybe 14,000 more died elsewhere at the hands of mobs (Doyle 2002, pp. 257–259).

4. See Gauchet (1997, pp. 242–245).

5. See Soboul (1977, pp. 56–85).

6. See Doyle (2002, pp. 137, 142).

7. But in 1792 neither women, male servants, nor unemployed males had the vote (Doyle 2002, p. 193).

8. Caute received academic endorsement when Donald Mattheisen (1985, p. 26) wrote of the 'fundamental commitment to popular sovereignty' as 'the classic touchstone of the European left for the past 200 years'.

9. Quotations are from Caute (1966, pp. 26, 28, 34, 35).

10. On Brissot see Loft (2002).

11. See Caute (1966, 28).

12. See Caute (1966, p. 30).

13. Stewart (1951, pp. 165–166, 231); North, Wallis and Weingast (2009, pp. 206–207); Hodgson (2015, pp. 302–303). But this revolutionary experiment in free-market ultra-individualism

was short-lived. Crucially, there were no civil mechanisms to set standards or codes of conduct. Corporations were later re-instated. They were enshrined in Napoléon Bonaparte's legal code of 1807.

14. Tawney (1921, p. 56), Manuel and Manuel (1979, p. 565).

15. Caute (1966, pp. 34–35).

16. See Rose (1978), Manuel and Manuel (1979, pp. 568–577), Kolakowski (1978, pp. 184–187), Birchall (1996) and Mazauric (2009).

17. On the links between Babeuf, Blanqui and Marx, see Fishman (1970, pp. 26–83).

18. On Mignet, Thiers and others, see Comninel (1987, ch. 3) and Doyle (2002, p. 450). On Blanqui, see Fishman (1970, ch. 3). The quotations are found in Marx and Engels (1962, vol. 2, p. 452) and Marx (1973, pp. 67, 79).

19. See Cobban (1964), Taylor (1967) and Doyle (2002, pp. 451–453).

20. Comninel (1987, pp. 200, 202, 205).

21. Hodgson (2015, pp. 63–66).

22. In the preface above, I stated that when I explain the original meaning of the term *Left*, the reader should not automatically assume that I adopt that position. I reveal more of my own normative views in later chapters.

23. The French Declaration of the Rights of Man and of the Citizen of 1789 also saw the proclaimed rights as 'simple and incontestable' and recognized the 'auspices of the Supreme Being'. But it also regarded the 'source of all authority' as residing 'essentially in the nation' (Stewart 1951, pp. 113–114).

24. Babeuf (see Mazauric 2009, p. 258) criticized market competition because it (1) 'submerges conscientiously made products under a mass of deceptive goods contrived to dazzle the public' (2) 'achieves low prices only by obliging the worker to waste his skill in botched work, by starving him, by destroying his moral standards through lack of scruples' (3) 'gives the victory only to whoever has most money' and (4) 'ends up simply with a monopoly in the hands of the winner and the withdrawal of low prices'. Birchall (1996, p. 35) saw this as 'a devastating critique of the market economy which has lost none of its power two centuries later'. A more careful analysis of Babeuf's claims would note that criticisms (1) and (4) apply only to imperfectly competitive markets with imperfect information. They do not rebut a defence of markets that would find remedies in increasing competition and providing more transparent information concerning product quality. Criticism (2) may have some truth in particular labour markets at particular times, but is so far unproven as a general principle. Criticism (3) holds water, but the source of the problem is inequality, rather than markets as such. Babeuf failed to show how competitive markets generate inequality, or how the problems that he claimed for markets could be avoided in a large-scale, collectivized and planned economy.

CHAPTER THREE

1. See Beck (2009). Palin (2009, p. 146) quoted Paine's 1776 words: 'If there must be trouble, let it be in my day, that my children may have peace'. She used this quote to support cuts in government budgets. In fact, the text quoted from Paine was part of a rallying cry for liberty and US independence. Palin went rogue also in terms of scholarship and historical accuracy. Command of the facts was never her strongest suit.

2. See Paine (1945, vol. 1, pp. 434, 607) and Foner (1945). Claeys (1989, p. 198) criticizes Foner for this distortion.

3. Paine (1948, pp. 276, 331). Fast resigned from the US Communist Party in the late 1950s.

4. Quote from Benn (2000). According to Benn, Attlee's words were spoken shortly after the First World War. See Attlee (1937) for further statements in support of common ownership.

5. See Rentoul (1995).

6. See Benn (1979, 1981). The quote is from Benn (1982, p. 125). On mixed economies see, for example, Nelson (1981, 2003), Kenworthy (1995), Martinez (2009) and Mazzucato (2013).

7. But travellers along this road, inspired by Paine, included the English radical William Cobbett (1763–1835), the Uruguayan liberator José Gervasio Artigas (1764–1850) and the American abolitionist John Brown (1800–1859).

8. See Kramnick (1977, p. 527; 1981, pp. 127–138). Thompson (1968) provided a superb account of radicalism in England from the 1790s to the 1830s, but ultimately he regarded Paine and his followers as exponents of 'petit-bourgeois individualism' (p. 841) rather than of universal human rights.

9. See Levin (2014) for a lively discussion of Burke and Paine on rights.

10. See Paine (1948, p. 16).

11. See Keane (1995, pp. 116–117). Notably, Marxism proposes to bring much in civil society within the province of the state. For an excellent critique see Polan (1984).

12. See Paine (1948, p. 15).

13. Paine (1945, vol. 1, p. 357; 1948, pp. 191–192). Following Montesquieu, Condorcet and others, Paine proposed a version of the *doux-commerce* thesis. Hirschman (1982) elaborated on this in his magnificent discussion of different attitudes to the market.

14. See Paine (1945, vol. 1, pp. 357–358; 1948, p. 192).

15. See Keane (1995, pp. 190–191).

16. See Benn (1979, 1981). Polan (1984) is an excellent critique of Lenin's utopian democracy.

17. See Claeys (1989, p. 89) and Keane (1995, pp. 126, 260–261, 353–354).

18. See Paine (1945, vol. 2, pp. 373, 375).

19. See Lamb (2010, pp. 489–493) on this point. Both Locke and Paine used the term *property* in a broad and loose sense, embracing both customary possession and the modern legal concept of property. On the distinction between property and possession see Commons (1924), Heinsohn and Steiger (2013) and Hodgson (2015).

20. Paine (1797; 1945, vol. 1, p. 612), Lamb (2010, pp. 493–496).

21. Paine (1797; 1945, vol. 1, p. 612), Lamb (2010, pp. 502–506). Technically, in terms of property law, Paine proposed that private landowners should retain *usus* rights and rights of alienation, but were not entitled to all the *usus fructus* rights. Part of the *usus fructus* revenues should go to the state, in commemoration of the original gifts of nature. See Honoré (1961) on different rights relating to ownership.

22. Paine (1797; 1945, vol. 1, p. 612).

23. Paine (1797; 1945, vol. 1, p. 620).

24. Paine (1945, vol. 1, p. 357; 1948, p. 192). In Hodgson (2015), I show that maximal free-market capitalism would lack adequate incentives for the training of workers and this necessitates some intervention by the state.

25. See Paine (1797; 1945, vol. 1, p. 613). In terms of purchasing power in 2016, £15 converts to roughly £1,600 or $2,000. But, as a fraction of the UK's GDP in 1797, £15 converts to about £83,000 or $106,000 as an equivalent share of the UK's GDP in 2016.

26. See Lamb (2010) and also King and Marangos (2006).

27. On Spence see Ashraf (1983) and Bonnett (2007).

28. See Keane (1995, p. 427).

29. Recorded by O'Meara (1822, vol. 1, p. 249).

30. Paine (1797; 1945, vol. 1, pp. 612, 617).

31. See Claeys (1989, pp. 95, 99).

32. See United Nations (1948).

33. The modern literature on rights is extensive and complex. See, for example, Gewirth (1978), Finnis (1980), Nickel (1987), Waldron (1988), Jones (1994) and Ignatieff (2001).

34. Another exception is the appeal for female political rights in the *Appeal of One Half of the Human Race*, written by William Thompson and Anna Wheeler and published in 1825 (Taylor 1983, pp. 17, 22–24, 29, 34, 36–37, 52, 55). The first association in Britain agitating for women's suffrage appeared in Sheffield in 1851.

35. See, for example, Finnis (1980), Nickel (1987), Doyal and Gough (1991) and Gough (2000, 2004).

36. See Hegel (1942) and Waldron (1988).

37. For an insightful book-length comparison of the ideas of Burke and Paine see Levin (2014). But Levin overstresses Paine's individualism and underplays his commitment to social solidarity.

38. See Paine (1948, pp. 181, 233). North, Wallis and Weingast (2009, pp. 194–202) give a good account of 'fear of faction' around that time.

39. See, for example, Galbraith (1952, 1969); Moore (1966); North, Wallis and Weingast (2009); and Hodgson (2015).

40. See Levin (2014, pp. 135–140) for an excellent account of Burke's defence of political parties.

CHAPTER FOUR

1. As an exception, More's *Utopia* envisioned cities of between sixty thousand and one hundred thousand adults. By contrast, the utopian socialists proposed smaller communities, generally of fewer than two thousand inhabitants.

2. See Taylor (1975). See also Gide and Rist (1915, pp. 198–231), Manuel and Manuel (1979, pp. 590–640) and Kolakowski (1978, pp. 187–192).

3. The quotation is from Lavoie (1985b, p. 217).

4. The quotation is from Kolakowski (1978, p. 198).

5. See Gide and Rist (1915, pp. 245–255) and Manuel and Manuel (1979, pp. 641–675).

6. Harris (2010) argued that science is a sufficient basis for morality. For criticisms of claims that science can provide adequate ethical guidance see Joyce (2006) and Hodgson (2013, pp. 94–99).

7. This rejection is discussed in the next chapter. See Gide and Rist (1915, p. 258) and Reibel (1975).

8. See Lallement (2012).

9. On Owen see Gide and Rist (1915, pp. 235–244), Harrison (1969), Manuel and Manuel (1979, pp. 676–693), Kolakowski (1978, pp. 193–198) and Claeys (1991). I agree with much in Hain's (2015) book, but his brief attempt to cast Owen as a champion of 'industrial democracy' and of 'modern participatory democracy' is inaccurate (Hain 2015, p. 140).

10. The quoted words are from Owen (1991, pp. 277–278)—originally published in 1820. The pioneers of twentieth-century behaviourist psychology include John B. Watson, Ivan Pavlov and B. F. Skinner.

11. Harrison (1969, p. 78).

12. The quoted words are from Owen (1991, p. 298)—originally published in 1820.

13. See Darwin (1871), Sober and Wilson (1998), Bergstrom (2002), De Waal (2006), Bowles and Gintis (2011), Boehm (2012) and Hodgson (2013).

14. See Claeys (1991, p. xxviii) and Harrison (1969).

15. See Owen (1991, p. 362).

16. See Harrison (1969, pp. 214–215), Manuel and Manuel (1979, p. 687) and Claeys (1991, pp. xxi–xxix).

17. See Owen (1991, pp. 336–338).

18. See Claeys (1991, p. xvi) and Harrison (1969, p. 76).

19. See Harrison (1969, pp. 76, 164–169). There were later attempts to form Owenite communities in the United States, but with little success. Several American Fourierist communities lasted a bit longer, but they had all disappeared by about 1860.

20. See Harrison (1969, pp. 169–175).

21. See Harrison (1969, p. 186).

22. The quote is from Owen (1991, p. 362). Marx and Engels in the *Communist Manifesto* also sought the 'abolition of private property' (Marx 1973, p. 80). See Beer (1940), Bestor (1948) and Landauer (1959) on the history and meaning of the word 'socialism'. Proposals for 'market socialism' in the 1930s attempted to *simulate* markets within a planning system, rather than to establish true markets with private ownership (Lange 1936–1937, Dickenson 1939).

23. See Gregory (1983). The evidence suggests that Engels was not a socialist in 1842. For Engels's 1843 account of his contacts with the Manchester Owenites see Marx and Engels (1975a, pp. 385–389). The Owenite meetings in Manchester impelled Engels to write a study of Continental socialism, including discussions of Saint-Simon and Fourier, which he published in two parts in the Owenite journal of the Rational Society in November 1843 (Marx and Engels 1975a, pp. 392–408). Marx first advocated the abolition of private property in his essay 'On the Jewish Question' (Marx and Engels 1975a, pp. 146–174), which was written in the autumn of 1843.

24. The quotation on Watts is from Sutton (2014). Watts (1842) followed Thompson (1827) and others in seeing profit, rent and interest all as unjust expropriation from the labouring class.

25. See Podmore (1906, vol. 2, pp. 600 ff.).

26. See Kuhn (1962), Lakatos (1976), Laudan (1977, 1981), Kitcher (1993) and others.

27. See United Nations (1948).

28. The quotations are from Finnis (1980, pp. 146, 169). See also Hegel (1942) and Waldron (1988). But these claims are less persuasive when applied to corporate-owned property.

29. Jefferson (1822).

30. See Ostrom (1990). She also considered some larger-scale cases, but the enforcement mechanisms are different. Reputation is an enforcement mechanism that can apply to organizations as well as individuals, but other ways of developing trust typically depend on face-to-face contact. For example, in a short book, G. A. Cohen (2009) used the fable of cooperative behaviour on a camping trip to establish principles of socialism. He downplayed the problem of sustaining cooperation in larger-scale communities without the possibility of intensive, interpersonal dialogue and monitoring.

CHAPTER FIVE

1. Marx and Engels (1962, vol. 2, p. 121).

2. To Marx's *Capital* I would add milestone contributions by Thorstein Veblen, John R. Commons, Max Weber, John Maynard Keynes, Joseph Schumpeter and Friedrich Hayek.

3. See Marx and Engels (1991, p. 284) and Marx (1973, p. 80). Marx never clearly defined the term *economic*, but hinted at the sphere of material production.

4. See Hodgson (1974) and van Parijs (1980) for critiques of this theory.

5. Marx and Engels (1962, vol. 2, p. 117).

6. See Marx (1973, pp. 80–81).

7. See my discussions of Marxism elsewhere (Hodgson 1999, 2006, 2015). I build here on some of that material.

8. See Marx (1971, pp. 20–21). As well as 'base' and 'superstructure', Marx (1976a, p. 178) used other metaphors, such as depicting legal relations as a mirror reflection of the 'economic' reality. Marx also referred to legal relations as illusions (Kline 1987).

9. In the social sciences the term *economic* is used in several different ways. Meanings range from connotations of 'material production' to being concerned with 'economy' in a sense of cost-reduction or efficiency. 'Economics' is regarded by many economists as the study of choice under conditions of scarcity. But not all economists define their subject in this way. There is no unanimity over the meaning of terms such as 'economy', 'economic' or 'economic relations'.

10. See Marx (1973, p. 67 n.).

11. Marx (1981, p. 1025, emphasis added). For a fuller discussion of the views on property by Marx and others, see Hodgson (2015). Kline (1987) showed that Marx basically treated legal rights, concerning property and contract, for example, as illusory.

12. Quotations are from Marx (1974, p. 344). By contrast with Marx, the American institutional economist John R. Commons (1924) wrote *The Legal Foundations of Capitalism*. For Commons, law was not the superstructure: law served as a major part of the foundation of social classes and of the economic system.

13. See Marx and Engels (1975b, p. 37; 1976, p. 88).

14. See Marx and Engels (1962, vol. 2, pp. 134–135).

15. See Kolakowski (1978, p. 372).

16. See Marx and Engels (1976, p. 49). On later Marxist usages of the words 'communism' and 'socialism', see note 1 in the introduction above.

17. See Marx (1973, pp. 80–81, 86–87, 323).

18. See Marx (1978, p. 434; 1976b, p. 207) and Campbell (2011).

19. See Webb and Webb (1920, esp. pp. 342–343).

20. This enduring failure is also evident in later socialist writings, such as Benn (1979, 1981) and Ralph Miliband's (1994, pp. 71, 96) call 'for a radical extension of democracy' that 'absolutely depends on a growing socialisation of the economy'.

21. See Lavoie (1985b, pp. 20–21).

22. See the discussion of Michels's work in chapter 6 below.

23. See, for example, Cole (1920, p. 141). In a book arguing against neoliberalism and austerity, Hain (2015, pp. 140–145) attempted to construct a historical tradition of democratic 'libertarian socialism', using Owen and Cole as foremost exemplars. But as noted above, Owen did not favour democracy and he was much more a paternalist than a libertarian. Cole, on the other hand, advocated decentralization and democracy, but failed to show how they could function and endure in a nationalized economy without private property. Also, for Cole, the abolition of capitalism trumped both decentralization and democracy. Chapter 7 below cites quotations from Cole from 1941, where he expressed preferences for both Stalinism and Nazism over nationalism and capitalism.

24. See especially Cole (1920, pp. 141–147; 1948, p. 101). See also Cole (1917, 1932).

25. See Dale (2010, pp. 20–28) for an account of Polanyi's socialist proposals. Polanyi's attempt to simulate the market, without devolved ownership or profits, was a forerunner of the blackboard models of socialism by Lange (1936–1937) and Dickenson (1939), and it retains all their limitations (as noted in the following section). Polanyi's conceptual framework, including his concept of 'embeddedness', is critically examined in Hodgson (2017).

26. The quoted words are from Attlee (1937, pp. 15–16). See Thompson (1988) for a historical account of the enduring opposition to private property and markets within the socialist tradition.

27. See Benn (1979, 1981, 1982, 2000) and Hahnel (2005). Of the two, Hahnel is more specific in terms of details, and thereby more revealing in terms of impracticalities.

28. For the benefits of worker participation on productivity see, for example, Doucouliagos (1995). The exact quote from Wilde is: 'The problem with socialism is that it will take up too many evenings' (Wilde 2000, p. 238).

29. Hodgson (2010) discussed some rare instances where Schäffle's critique of socialism has been mentioned, and gave some possible reasons for the extreme neglect of his contribution.

30. The quote is from Schäffle (1908, p. 57). His other works on socialism include Schäffle (1870, 1874, 1885, 1892).

31. See Zhou (1996) and Coase and Wang (2012). Olson's (1965) theory is also relevant in this context.

32. Schäffle thus prefigured Olson's (1965, p. 71) argument concerning 'the need for coercion implicit in attempts to provide collective goods to large groups'.

33. See Schäffle (1892, pp. 37, 73).

34. See Schäffle (1892, pp. 416–419).

35. See Murrell (1991).

36. See Mises (1920), Lange (1936–1937) and Dickenson (1939).

37. For good accounts of the socialist calculation debate see Vaughn (1980), Murrell (1983), Lavoie (1985a), Steele (1992) and Boettke (2000, 2001).

38. See Dickenson (1939) and Hayek (1948, pp. 194, 199).

39. See Dickenson (1939, pp. 9, 191) and Lange (1987, p. 23).

40. See Hayek (1948, pp. 46, 33).

41. See Hayek (1948, pp. 78–79; 1989, p. 4).

42. See Nelson (1981, 2003), Kenworthy (1995), Chang (1997, 2002b), Evans and Rauch (1999), Reinert (2007), Martinez (2009) and Mazzucato (2013).

43. On the limits to contracts see, for example, Durkheim (1984), Fox (1974), Hodgson (1988), Satz (2010) and Sandel (2012). On the roles of trust, justice and morality in markets see Smith (1759, 1776), Zak (2008) and Hodgson (2013).

44. See Marx (1974, pp. 353–354), Gide and Rist (1915, p. 258) and Reibel (1975).

45. See Proudhon (1969). The notion of contract without a legal system and a state is unviable (Hodgson 2015). Hence anarchism can be seen as yet another wrong turning for the Left. Marxists doctrinally converge with anarchists in looking forward to the abolition of the state after communism is well established. But this too was wishful thinking.

46. See Marx (1974, p. 80).

47. On the insufficiency of incentives for skill training in capitalist firms see Marshall (1920, p. 565). On claims concerning the suboptimality of cooperatives see Ward (1958, 1967), Vanek (1970, 1972) and Hansmann (1996). Most of these arguments use equilibrium models and do not underline the dynamic skill-enhancing advantages of worker cooperatives. Learning is basically an out-of-equilibrium process and once we consider dynamic efficiency, then the prominent suboptimality proofs become irrelevant. The arguments and evidence in Pagano (1985); Bonin, Jones and Putterman (1993); Hodgson (1999); Dow (2003); Gagliardi (2009); and Zamagni and Zamagni (2010) suggest that cooperatives are even more viable economically than the Ward-Vanek models suggest.

48. See Chapple (1980). Alley was imprisoned during the Cultural Revolution, but he survived. The term *Gung Ho* derives from the Chinese phrase *Gong He*, which means 'work together in harmony'. United States Marine Corps Major Evans Carlson was a friend of Alley. Carlson picked up the term *Gung Ho* to help instil the idea of 'working together in harmony' in his troops. Then *Gung Ho* became the title of a 1943 American war film. It thus acquired the very different connotation of aggressive, reckless enthusiasm.

49. Furthermore, when Marx described wage labour as 'slavery' he thereby belittled the advantages of voluntary employment over forced labour. His repeated rhetorical claim, that wage labourers are also enslaved, diminished the massive historical importance of the abolition of slavery. Marx described wage labour as 'slavery' in the *Communist Manifesto* (written with Engels) (Marx 1973, p. 74), in *Wage Labour and Capital* (Marx and Engels 1962, pp. 80, 92, 98), in *Capital* (Marx 1976a, p. 875) and in the *Critique of the Gotha Programme* (Marx and Engels 1989, p. 91).

50. See, for example, Marx (1975, p. 347) and Draper and Lipow (1976). The quotation is from Luxemburg (1912).

CHAPTER SIX

1. See Marx and Engels (1962, vol. 2, p. 117) and Marx (1973, p. 80).

2. See Marx and Engels (1975a, pp. 146–174). For a useful discussion of writings by Marx on contract and property see Kline (1987).

3. The quotations are from Marx (1974, pp. 344, 347–348) and Marx and Engels (1991, p. 283). These quotations do not show that Marx failed to uphold any rights. But they indicate

that he believed that discussion of rights was a secondary and diversionary matter for the socialist movement.

4. There is clear evidence of moral motivations, even in the economic sphere (Minkler 2008, Hodgson 2013). For relevant discussions of the motivational roles of justice and morality see also Smith (1759), De Waal (2006) and Joyce (2006). Many mainstream economists also disregard moral motivation in the economy (Etzioni 1988; Hodgson 2013, 2015).

5. See Schumpeter (1942, p. 167). For superior evaluations of the socialist calculation debate see Vaughn (1980), Murrell (1983), Lavoie (1985a), Steele (1992) and Boettke (2000, 2001).

6. The quotation is from Marx (1973, p. 86). Lukes (1985) has forcefully criticized Marx's 'extreme consequentialism'—which amounts to a neglect of any moral evaluation of the means, as long as they serve the ends. Screpanti (2007, ch. 2) has documented the reluctance of Marx and Engels to take a moral stance. Doyal and Gough (1991) have criticized Marxists who tried to abandon a concept of objective need, arguing that a reliance on such a category is unavoidable for policy.

7. Quotations are from Marx and Engels (1975b, p. 37).

8. The notion of 'false consciousness' comes from Engels's 1893 letter to Franz Mehring (Marx and Engels 1962, vol. 2, p. 497).

9. See Weber (1968, pp. 971 ff.).

10. See Michels (1915). Eventually Michels came to the unfortunate conclusion that the solution to this problem of oligarchy was the installation of charismatic leaders such as Benito Mussolini. He lost faith in representative democracy and countervailing stakeholder power.

11. See Michels (1915, p. 400).

12. See Marx (1973, pp. 79–80).

13. See Lenin (1967, vol. 2, pp. 334–335). For a brilliant critique of Lenin's 'democratic' vision of the dictatorship of the proletariat see Polan (1984). Polan showed that the notion of the 'dictatorship of the proletariat' in the writings of Marx, Engels and (especially) Lenin ended up submerging civil society into the state.

14. See Polan (1984, p. 77).

15. If the reader would forgive a short autobiographical note, in 1977 I argued that 'all power to the soviets' would discriminate against women and the self-employed (Hodgson 1977, pp. 76–78). Several people told me that my 1977 book (which was translated into several languages) had convinced them that the idea of 'smashing' parliamentary democracy was mistaken. A few years later I abandoned Marxism. I became convinced that Marxism itself had helped pave the way for both Leninism and Stalinism.

16. See Luxemburg (1970, p. 394).

17. See Lenin (1967, vol. 3, p. 49).

18. See Russian Socialist Federated Soviet Republic (1918).

19. For the Chinese constitution see People's Republic of China (2004). On the *hukou* system see Chan and Zhang (1999) and Chan and Buckingham (2008).

20. See Synopwich (1990).

21. These counter-factuals are difficult to assess. Some argue that the economic achievements of Stalin and Mao are exaggerated. It is beyond our scope to go further into this complex question.

22. During the nineteenth century, 'Social Democratic' parties in Europe were typically dominated by Marxists. But from the 1950s the term *social democracy* became more associated

with policies to promote greater equality and social justice within mixed, capitalist economies. This is the sense of the term that is used in this book.

23. On the general indispensability of the state for capitalism see Hodgson (2015), where arguments are presented against the alternative view that these institutions can emerge spontaneously. See also Commons (1924). On the strategic state see for example Nelson (2003), Kenworthy (1995), Chang (1997, 2002b), Evans and Rauch (1999), Reinert (2007), Martinez (2009) and Mazzucato (2013).

24. See Blair (2006) and Kirkpatrick (2005, pp. 24, 39, 157).

25. See Blair (1994).

26. See Cole (1920, e.g. pp. 25, 206) and Tawney (1921, p. 19). See Foote (1997, pp. 72–80) for a brief account of Tawney's ideas and his political shifts.

27. Quote from Tawney (1921, p. 53).

28. See Lukes (1985) and Trotsky, Dewey and Novak (1979).

29. See Heath, Jowell and Curtice (2001, p. 106). Echoing Blair, Miliband (2016) endorsed the same untenable separation between means and ends.

30. See Dewey (1922; 1939, p. 45).

CHAPTER SEVEN

1. Quoted in Overy (2009, p. 284).

2. See Shaw (1934, p. 361), Minney (1969) and Hollander (1998).

3. See Webb and Webb (1935). On the Labour Party's flirtation with the Soviet Union see Jones (1977).

4. Cole (1941, p. 104). On the same page, Cole opined that a Nazi-dominated Europe was preferable to the preceding 'impracticable' system of sovereign states: 'it would be better to let Hitler conquer all Europe short of the Soviet Union, and thereafter exploit it ruthlessly in the Nazi interest, than to go back to the pre-war order of independent Nation States with frontiers drawn so as to cut right across the natural units of production and exchange'.

5. See Robinson (1969, pp. 35–36).

6. See Robinson (1969, p. 19). For a recent study of the Cultural Revolution see Dikötter (2016).

7. See Robinson (1973, pp. 4, 13, 37).

8. For Robinson on Korea see Turner (1989, p. 90). Since 2000 the North Korean dictatorship has introduced some private enterprise and the economy has begun to grow, albeit at a slow rate.

9. See Thompson (1973, p. 77, emphasis added), Kolakowski (1974, pp. 4–5) and Judt (2006).

10. See Barsky (1997) and Cohen (2007, pp. 157–168).

11. See Bloodworth (2015a, 2015b, 2015c), Corbyn (2011, 2014) and RT News (2014). Corbyn helped to revive a post-Soviet version of the 'Russia Complex' that was a characteristic of the British Labour Party until the 1950s (Jones 1977). Russia is supported now, not because of any socialism, but because it is a major opponent of NATO and the West. For analyses of the Corbyn Left see Hirsh (2015), Baggini (2016) and Hodgson (2016a, 2016b, 2016c).

12. On Cuba see, for example, Reuters (2015).

13. See Cunliffe (2016).

14. See Cohen (2007, pp. 65–69; 2015) and Kennedy (2015).

15. See Cohen (2007, pp. 291–293) and BBC News (2003). To repeat: the existence of a dictatorship does not necessarily justify the use of force to overthrow it. War itself is a totalitarian instrument: it should be used only as a last resort. That point had not been reached in 2003. Legality was also lacking. Cohen's (2007) defence of the 2003 invasion of Iraq has detracted from the other very important arguments and evidence in his book.

16. See Alexander (1985, p. 883), Socialist Worker (1987) and Azarmehr (2006).

17. See Rummel (1990) and Courtois et al. (1999). The technical term for premature deaths is *excess mortality*.

18. Journalist (and adviser to Jeremy Corbyn) Seumas Milne (1990) suggested that estimates of deaths under Stalin by Robert Conquest (1968, 1986) and others were too high. This was quickly contradicted when more evidence became available in 1991 showing that earlier estimates, particularly by Conquest, were in the right ballpark (Milne 1990, Shiraz Socialist 2015).

19. A YouTube video by Jason Unruhe estimates the premature death toll under capitalism to be 1.6 billion (Unruhe 2010). But some of Unruhe's figures are spurious. Among those 'killed by capitalism' he includes three hundred million deaths from smoking-related diseases. But capitalism does not force people to smoke—and people under Communist regimes smoke as well. Unruhe spoils his case with bad statistics. But wars and repressions under capitalism have led undoubtedly to hundreds of millions of deaths. On deaths in colonial America see Rationalwiki (2015) and in British India see Wikipedia (2016h).

20. See Sen (1981, 1990). Some critics stress that the remedies for famine are more complex. But there is still widespread agreement that democracy is a valuable antidote.

21. Estimates of the number of excess deaths in the Great Leap Forward range from an official government figure of fifteen million to much higher claims of about forty-five million. See Dikötter (2010) and Yang (2012).

22. But there are further complications to the story and it has been a matter of ongoing debate. See Maoz (1997); Rummel (1997); Mousseau, Hegre and Oneal (2003); and Gartze (2007).

23. See Pinker (2011).

24. See Human Security Research Group (2013).

25. See Wejnert (2014).

26. See Williamson (1990, ch. 2). In 2004, Williamson himself rejected the widespread assumption that his notion of 'the Washington Consensus' corresponded to 'neoliberalism' (Mirowski and Plehwe 2009, p. 8).

27. The quotation is from Chang (2002a). See also Chang (2002c). Using a free-market slogan, Chang wittily opined that developing countries should be 'free to choose' their policies for development, rather than necessarily following a path imposed by the West. But not everything works, and these countries should learn from international experience.

28. Of course, GDP and GDP per capita are flawed measures of human welfare. For instance, they neglect unpaid work and environmental damage (Costanza et al. 2014). They are used here as preliminary and indicative.

29. World bank PPP (purchasing power parity) data from Wikipedia (2016f).

30. See, for example, Lee (2013).

31. In 1990 the collapse of the Japanese asset bubble ended its period of rapid growth. For data see Maddison (2007, pp. 337, 383).

32. For non-2012 data see Maddison (2003, pp. 466, 562). 2014 GDP per capita figures are IMF PPP data from Wikipedia (2016f).

33. For data see Maddison (2001, pp. 185, 215)

34. See the World Bank and IMF PPP data from Wikipedia (2016f).

35. See Gerring et al. (2005).

36. See Rodrik and Wacziarg (2005).

37. See Acemoglu et al. (2014). But Pozuelo, Slipowitz and Vuletin (2016) argue that the apparent empirical correlation between democracy and economic growth does not mean that the former causes the latter. Instead, they argue that economic turmoil is responsible for causing or facilitating many democratic transitions.

38. See Knutsen (2015).

39. See Galbraith (1962, 1969); Moore (1966); North, Wallis and Weingast (2009); and Hodgson (2015). The comparatively low number of mainland-registered, large Chinese corporations may in part result from fear of sequestration by a one-party state with a historic hostility to private enterprise.

40. See Streeck (2014).

41. See Waldron (1988, pp. 103–4).

42. See MacIntyre (1981).

43. See Jones (1994).

44. See, for example, Finnis (1980), Nickel (1987), Doyal and Gough (1991) and Gough (2000, 2004).

45. See, for example, Gewirth (1978, 1982).

46. See Kitcher (2011).

47. See, for example, Martin (1982).

48. Note that there is a difference between rights-based and consequentialist libertarians. Rights-based libertarians such as the Levellers, John Locke, Robert Nozick and Murray Rothbard emphasized inalienable individual rights. By contrast, consequentialist libertarians such as Ludwig von Mises, Friedrich Hayek, Milton Friedman or James Buchanan sought justification in what was ultimately deemed best for individual liberty or individual satisfaction. Marxists typically embrace non-individualist versions of consequentialism (Lukes 1985).

49. See Wheatley (2015).

CHAPTER EIGHT

1. See Appiah (1992, p. 58), Rengger (2011, p. 1173) and Amin (2004).

2. See Benedict (1934, p. 278).

3. For an early critique of Herskovits and other cultural relativists see Schmidt (1955).

4. See Executive Board, American Anthropological Association (1947, pp. 539, 542) and Nickel (1987, p. 169). In 1999 the American Anthropological Association adopted a revised position on human rights that belatedly superseded the flawed 1947 statement (American Anthropological Association 1999).

5. See Executive Board, American Anthropological Association (1947, p. 541).

6. An influential proponent of functionalism in sociology was Talcott Parsons (1975).

7. Multiple studies show that this shift is incomplete. On average, men still participate less in household chores and the average wages for women are still significantly lower because in many professions men dominate the more senior and higher-paid jobs. But these facts do not support cultural relativism.

8. For an example of a libertarian argument that is redolent of cultural relativism see Leeson (2014).

9. This point has been made by Zechenter (1997), Kanarek (2013) and others.

10. On the generic nature of moral claims see, for example, Hare (1952), Mackie (1977), Joyce (2006) and Hodgson (2013).

11. See Wikipedia (2016c).

12. See Greer (1999, pp. 3, 95–105).

13. See Parker (1995, pp. 506, 520). Parker's current academic position is in the Department of Global Health and Development in the London School of Hygiene and Tropical Medicine. At least Greer confined herself to a university department of English.

14. See Cohen (2007, pp. 101–104). His main targets were Narayan (1997) and a rave review that it received in an academic journal.

15. See Zechenter (1997, p. 30).

16. See Ignatieff (2001, pp. 63–64).

17. See Zechenter (1997, p. 341).

18. See Ignatieff (2001, pp. 65–66).

19. See Roberts (1979), Bok (1978, 1995), Finnis (1980, pp. 83–84, 97), Brown (1991), Schwartz (1994), Walzer (1994), Haidt and Joseph (2004), Nichols (2004) and Hodgson (2013).

20. On cultural group selection and morality see Darwin (1871), Boyd and Richerson (1985), Sober and Wilson (1998), De Waal (2006), Bowles and Gintis (2011), Boehm (2012) and Hodgson (2013).

21. See, for example, Finnis (1980), Nickel (1987), Doyal and Gough (1991) and Gough (2000, 2004).

22. See Fanon (1963).

23. Quotation from Rich (2016, p. 240), which provides a good historical analysis of the re-emergence of anti-Semitism on the Left. Leftists are divided on the question of a two-state solution in Israel and Palestine. While Jeremy Corbyn has recently affirmed support for a two-state solution, he has allied himself with Hamas and Hezbollah, who take a different position (Bloodworth 2015b). Sadly, even in Britain, anti-Semitism is not new on the Left. In 1881 the Marxist Henry Hyndman founded the Social Democratic Federation, which was Britain's first socialist party. Hyndman used anti-Semitic language and warned that Jewish business interests were planning 'an Anglo-Hebraic empire' across Africa (Rich 2016, p. 202).

CHAPTER NINE

1. See Brown (2009).

2. See Bleich (2011).

3. See Dobson (2014) and Sides (2015).

4. The *burqa* is not of Islamic origin and there is no clear support for it in the Qur'an. The covering of women's faces is a custom that originated in ancient Persia and Byzantium, more than a thousand years before the birth of Islam.

5. See Mayer (2014), Poynting and Mason (2007), Commission on the Future of Multi-Ethnic Britain (2000, p. 60) and Musharbash (2014).

6. See Sedghi (2013) and Wikipedia (2016e).

7. See Malik (2005).

8. See Chapman (2015) and National Secular Society (2015a).

9. For example, Genesis 18–19, Exodus 11–12, Numbers 21:2–3, Deuteronomy 20:16–17, Joshua 6:17, 21.

10. There is some evidence that Islamic legal institutions had a major effect on the law in medieval Europe, including the establishment of trial by jury in England and the development of charities and corporations (Hodgson 2015, pp. 94, 96, 225, 304, 322).

11. Fukuyama (2011, chs 13–15) explains how Islamic societies used large numbers of trained slaves in their armies and administrative bureaucracies, helping to create a state system that could partially transcend tribal and clan divisions by depending upon an alienated slave caste, which was torn from all family and other local ties and loyalties.

12. See Cook (2000, p. 9).

13. See Kuran (2004, 2010).

14. See Kuran (2010, p. 291) and Mirza, Senthilkumaran and Ja'far (2007, p. 5).

15. Controlling for levels of economic development and other factors, Fish (2002) showed empirically that Muslim-majority countries tend to be less democratic. One of his explanations is the relatively lower status of women. This is supported by data indicating lower female literacy rates and gender empowerment.

16. See Butt (2007), Cohen (2007, pp. 371–372) and Wikipedia (2016d). The National Chair of the Stop the War Coalition was Jeremy Corbyn, until he was elected as leader of the Labour Party in 2015.

17. See Carr (1966, p. 261).

18. See Cohen (2007, pp. 107–108) and Yang (2005).

19. See Jones (2014), Sommers (2014) and Callinicos (2015). On Trotskyist support for the theocratic Iranian regime see Alexander (1985, p. 883), Socialist Worker (1987) and Azarmehr (2006).

20. See Cohen (2007, ch. 10, esp. pp. 301–302, 305–306) and Wikipedia (2016j).

21. See Phillips (2016).

22. A parliamentary report published in October 2016 severely criticized Jeremy Corbyn for failing to deal adequately with the problem of anti-Semitism within the Labour Party (House of Commons Home Affairs Committee 2016).

23. See Bloodworth (2015b), Freedland (2016) and Stewart (2016). Rich (2016) gives an account of how anti-Semitism developed from the 1960s in the British Far Left and later spread into the Labour Party, coinciding with the rise of Corbyn's 'anti-imperialist' politics.

24. See BBC News (2001).

25. See Wikipedia (2016b).

26. See Gillard (2007).

27. See Bell (2005).

28. See Gillard (2007).

29. See Wikipedia (2016i) and White (2015).

30. Quoted in Palmer (2007) and Cohen (2007, p. 378). See also Husain (2007).

31. See Kamm (2004).

32. See Mirza, Senthilkumaran and Ja'far (2007, p. 5).

33. See Mirza, Senthilkumaran and Ja'far (2007, p. 5).

34. See Toynbee (2004).

35. See Sommers (2015).

36. See Rawlinson (2013).

37. See Mirza, Senthilkumaran and Ja'far (2007, pp. 7, 18).

38. See Ignatieff (2001, pp. 58–59).

39. See Department of Education (2014, p. 5).

40. See Turner (2003).

41. See Hussain (2015) for the 'Stop the War' position on 'British values'.

42. See National Secular Society (2015b) and Jones (2015). Pastor McConnell was eventually found 'not guilty' in January 2016.

43. See National Secular Society (2015c) on the Muslim Reform Movement.

44. The Hope not Hate campaign group published a long list of 'anti-Muslims' that includes Muslim reformers of Islam alongside violent, anti-Muslim bigots (Mulhall and Lowes 2015). See Nawaz (2015) for criticism of this list of 'anti-Muslim' persons and organizations. Persons listed include Melanie Phillips (the journalist), Ayaan Hirsi Ali (a prominent author, ex-Muslim and critic of Islam) and Tawfik Hamid (a Muslim who preaches a peaceful version of Islam that is compatible with universal human rights and who fled his Egyptian homeland because his life was threatened by Islamic militants). Originally on the list but removed after protest was Raquel Saraswati (a devout American Muslim woman who campaigns against violence that is carried out in the name of 'family honour'). The Hope not Hate list of 'anti-Muslim' organizations in the UK includes both violent fascist groups like the British National Party and peaceful campaigners such as the Lawyers' Secular Society (which opposes Sharia law). This flawed and incongruous document makes the dreadful mistake of putting critics of Islamic doctrines in the same box as violent bigots who wish to harm individual Muslims.

CHAPTER TEN

1. See Mises (1985, pp. 47, 51). Dollfuss was murdered by Nazi agents in 1934.

2. See Hayek (1960, 1973, 1979). Caldwell and Montes (2015) give a detailed account of Hayek's relationship with the Pinochet regime. Milton Friedman also visited Pinochet's Chile. But, in contrast to Hayek and Margaret Thatcher, Friedman (1991) declared: 'I have nothing good to say about the political regime that Pinochet imposed. It was a terrible political regime'. Friedman (1976) upheld that he was merely giving 'technical advice' and expressed 'profound disagreement with the authoritarian political system of Chile'. Later he claimed that he believed that the promotion of free markets in Chile would eventually undermine Pinochet's dictatorship. But Letelier (1976) alleged that CIA-funded Chicago economists conferred with the generals before the coup and gave them some semblance of academic legitimacy, as well as World

Bank loans when they gained power. Klein (2007) and Schliesser (2010) have documented and analysed the involvement of Friedman and his Chicago colleagues in advising Pinochet.

3. See BBC News (1999).

4. See Bevins and Streeter (1996). Pinochet ordered the 1976 assassination of Orlando Letelier, a minister of the former, democratically elected, Chilean regime, who had fled to the United States. Two people died in the resulting car bomb in Washington, DC (Franklin 2015). In an attempt to cover up his own culpability, Pinochet ordered that the agent in charge of the assassination should also be murdered.

5. Although Hayek may be seen as a libertarian, there were strong elements of Burkean conservatism in his thought. Hayek stressed the importance of careful experiment in institutional design and argued—like Burke—that institutions are repositories of much complex or tacit knowledge that cannot be understood by one individual alone.

6. Readers perplexed by this claim need to return to chapter 2 and its discussion of the origins of the terms *Left* and *Right*. See also figure 7.1.

7. See, for example, Mises (1949, p. 307) and Hayek (1948, p. 116). See also Hodgson (2015) for a critical discussion.

8. See Mises (1981, p. 27). The role of the state in constituting and protecting property is discussed in Hodgson (2015).

9. See Mises (1949, pp. 97, 257).

10. On law see Hayek (1973) and the critique in Hodgson (2015). Fukuyama (2011, ch. 17) provides a good account of the origins and nature of the rule of law. On countervailing power see Galbraith (1962, 1969); Moore (1966); North, Wallis and Weingast (2009); and Hodgson (2015).

11. By 'neoclassical' here I refer to the broad approach to economic theory that was dominant for most of the twentieth century, which involves equilibrium analysis and utility-maximizing agents. It is still prominent in standard textbooks. Samuelson (1947) popularized this label and he was a major exponent of this approach. Neoclassical economics has general equilibrium (Walrasian) and partial equilibrium (Marshallian) variants.

12. See Nelson (1959) and Arrow (1962, p. 616).

13. See Hayek (1948, p. 18).

14. See Heller (2008) and Pagano (2014). Polanyi (1944) argued that emerging capitalism limited the role of the market to prevent the dissolution of the social fabric. The argument here is different: the nature of information places limits on the market mechanism.

15. See Rifkin (2014).

16. See Dewey (1916, 1935, 1938, 1939), Ryan (1995), Evans (2000) and Hodgson (2013, ch. 10).

17. See Hayek (1960, p. 222). On the economic role of the state see Nelson (1981, 2003), Kenworthy (1995), Chang (1997, 2002b), Evans and Rauch (1999), Reinert (2007), Martinez (2009) and Mazzucato (2013).

18. See for example Keynes (1930, 1936), Minsky (1982, 1986), Ingham (2004, 2008) and Wray (2012).

19. See Hoppe (1994), Block (1996), Rodrigues (2012) and Hodgson (2015, ch. 12) on Hayek's alleged 'social democratic' views.

20. On processes that create inequality within capitalism see Piketty (2014) and Hodgson (2015, ch. 15).

21. See Bowles and Gintis (2002) and Credit Suisse Research Institute (2012).

22. See Finnis (1980, p. 174).

23. See Galbraith (1952, 1969).

24. See Marshall (1920, p. 565).

25. See Klaus (2007).

26. See Smith (1759) and Hodgson (2013).

27. See Keynes (1936) and Stiglitz (2010).

28. See chapter 2 above.

29. See Nelson (1981, 2003), Kenworthy (1995), Chang (1997, 2002b), Evans and Rauch (1999), Reinert (2007), Martinez (2009) and Mazzucato (2013).

30. See Cole (1917, 1932), Webb and Webb (1920) and Dale (2010).

31. The quote is from Hansard (1990).

32. See Benn (1979, 1981, 1982, 2000), Albert (2004), Hahnel (2007, p. 1157), Bhaskar and Collier (1998, p. 392) and O'Neill (1998, pp. 176–177).

33. Quotation from Moss (1973, p. 59). Similarly murderous reactions were provoked by the ill-advised and reckless Spartacus Uprising in Germany in 1919 (Watt 1969, Hodgson 1977) and by other Marxist adventures.

34. See Nove (1983, pp. 75 ff.).

35. See BBC News (2016).

36. See for example Pryor (1973) and Wiles (1974).

37. On democracy and economic growth see chapter 7 above. For studies showing the negative effects of corruption see Shleifer and Vishny (1993), Mauro (1995), Jain (2001), Mo (2001), Aidt (2003) and Pellegrini and Gerlagh (2004). It is vital to deal with private as well as public corruption (Hodgson 2013, ch. 7).

38. See Corbyn (2011, 2014).

39. On Left Unity see Jones (2014) and Sommers (2014). Consider also the implosion of the UK Socialist Workers Party (SWP) in 2014 as a result of its abysmal internal handling of accusations of rape made by women against a senior male SWP official. The SWP is a very poor exemplar of basic human rights and standards of justice. These attributes are not accidental: they are congenital to Marxism (see chapters 5 and 6).

CHAPTER ELEVEN

1. In Hodgson (1999)—before the possibility of adequate Internet searches—I was mistakenly informed of the source of the prayer. Others have wrongly attributed it to St Francis of Assisi. See Shapiro (2014).

2. This chapter draws on material from Hodgson (2013, ch. 10; 2015, chs 9, 15–16).

3. Some libertarians—such as Nozick (1974)—have argued that voluntary slavery should be permitted. Typically this goes with the assumption that the individual is always the best judge of his or her interests, and that these judgments where possible should be honoured. See Hodgson (2013) for a critique of this assumption.

4. See Marshall (1920, p. 565).

5. See Robinson and Zhang (2005), Holzer et al. (1993), Van Horn and Fichtner (2003).

6. The quotation comes from France (1894).

7. See Wilkinson and Pickett (2009).

8. See Bowles and Gintis (2002) and Credit Suisse Research Institute (2012).

9. Note that Marx (1976a) did not regard markets as the source of inequality. Instead, he located it historically in the 'primitive accumulation' that separated the workers from the means of production, and in the ongoing expropriation of surplus value in the sphere of production.

10. See Stiglitz (2012, pp. xiii, 28).

11. See Hodgson (2015, ch. 7) for a defence of this definition and criticism of the misuse of the term *capital*. My definition of capital is close to that of Joseph Schumpeter, Max Weber and John Hobson, among others. Piketty (2014) used a similar definition of capital and provided evidence in support of differential capital ownership as a driver of inequality.

12. See Marshall (1920, p. 565).

13. Data are from 2010 and Credit Suisse Research Institute (2012). See also Piketty (2014) for extensive data on inequality.

14. See Bowles and Gintis (1999). Another inspiring book with policies to counter inequality is Atkinson (2015).

15. See Ackerman and Alstott (1999, p. 191). The Bacon quote can be found in Tawney (1921, p. 62) and many other places.

16. See George (1879).

17. See Wikipedia (2016g). I thank Colin Talbot for pointing this out to me.

18. See Kelso and Adler (1958); Bonin, Jones and Putterman (1993); Poole and Whitfield (1994); Doucouliagos (1995); Hubbick (2001); Robinson and Zhang (2005); and National Center for Employee Ownership (2012).

19. See Ashton and Green (1996); Crouch, Finegold and Sako (1999); Acemoglu and Autor (2011, 2012); and Cowen (2013).

20. See Van Parijs (1992, 1995) and Corning (2011).

21. A plan to introduce a basic income was also drafted by US President Richard Nixon, but then abandoned. Apparently he was persuaded by Karl Polanyi's (1944) notorious historical chapter on the Speenhamland Law that such measures would have an excessive downside risk (Bregman 2016). See Block and Somers (2003) for a critique of Polanyi's chapter on Speenhamland and the discussion in Hodgson (2016d).

22. Paine (1797; 1945, vol. 1, p. 620).

23. See Heller (2008), Pagano (2014) and Rifkin (2014).

24. See Dewey (1916, 1935, 1938, 1939), Popper (1945), Lindblom (1959, 1984), Nelson and Winter (1982, part VI), Hayek (1988) and Martinez Alier, Munda and O'Neill (1998).

25. For discussions see Gouinlock (1972, 1978), Ryan (1995), Evans (2000) and Hodgson (2013, ch. 10).

26. Quotations are from Dewey (1935, p. 92).

27. See Finnis (1980), Doyal and Gough (1991) and Gough (2000, 2004).

28. See Hodgson (1999).

29. See Nelson (1981, 2003), Kenworthy (1995), Chang (1997, 2002b), Martinez (2009) and Mazzucato (2013).

30. See Coase (1960), Traxler and Unger (1994), Chang and Rowthorn (1995), Vogel (1996) and Hodgson (2013).

31. See Gray (1993, pp. 306–314) and O'Neill (1998, chs 5–7).

32. See Sterba (1985) and Davis (1987).

33. See Reisman (1993), Davis (2001), Vatn (2005), Winston (2006) and Hodgson (2013).

34. On the nature of modern financial systems see Keynes (1930, 1936), Minsky (1982, 1986), Ingham (2004, 2008), Wray (2012) and Hodgson (2015).

35. See Rodrik (2011).

36. See Streeck (2014).

REFERENCES

Acemoglu, Daron, and Autor, David H. (2011) 'Skill, Tasks and Technologies: Implications for Employment Earnings', in Ashenfelter, Orley, and Card, David E. (eds) (2011) *The Handbook of Labor Economics*, vol. 4b (Amsterdam: Elsevier), pp. 1043–1072.

Acemoglu, Daron, and Autor, David H. (2012) 'What Does Human Capital Do? A Review of Goldin and Katz's *The Race between Education and Technology*', *Journal of Economic Literature*, 50(2), June, pp. 426–463.

Acemoglu, Daron, Naidu, Suresh, Restrepo, Pascual, and Robinson, James A. (2014) 'Democracy Does Cause Growth', National Bureau of Economic Research, Working Paper 2004, Cambridge, MA.

Acemoglu, Daron, and Robinson, James A. (2012) *Why Nations Fail: The Origins of Power, Prosperity, and Poverty* (New York: Random House; London: Profile).

Ackerman, Bruce, and Alstott, Anne (1999) *The Stakeholder Society* (New Haven, CT: Yale University Press).

Aidt, Toke S. (2003) 'Economic Analysis of Corruption: A Survey', *Economic Journal*, 113(8), November, pp. F632–F652.

Albert, Michael (2004) 'Market Madness', Znet. http://zcomm.org/znetarticle/market-madness -by-michael-albert-1/. (Retrieved 1 October 2014.)

Alexander, Robert J. (1985) *International Trotskyism, 1929–1985: A Documented Analysis of the Movement* (Durham, NC: Duke University Press).

Ali, Tariq (2003) *Bush in Babylon: The Re-colonisation of Iraq* (London: Verso).

American Anthropological Association (1999) 'Declaration on Anthropology and Human Rights'. http://www.aaanet.org/about/Policies/statements/Declaration-on-Anthropology -and-Human-Rights.cfm. (Retrieved 18 July 2015.)

Amin, Samir (2004) *The Liberal Virus: Permanent War and the Americanization of the World* (New York: Monthly Review Press).

Appiah, Kwame Anthony (1992) *In My Father's House: Africa in the Philosophy of Culture* (Oxford and New York: Oxford University Press).

Arrow, Kenneth J. (1962) 'Economic Welfare and the Allocation of Resources to Invention', in Nelson, Richard R. (ed.) (1962) *The Rate and Direction of Inventive Activity: Economic and Social Factors* (Princeton, NJ: Princeton University Press), pp. 609–625.

Ashraf, P. M. (1983) *The Life and Times of Thomas Spence* (Newcastle: Frank Graham).

Ashton, David, and Green, Francis (1996) *Education, Training and the Global Economy* (Cheltenham: Edward Elgar).

Atkinson, Anthony B. (2015) *Inequality: What Can Be Done?* (Cambridge, MA: Harvard University Press).

Attlee, Clement R. (1937) *The Labour Party in Perspective* (London: Gollancz).

Azarmehr, Potkin (2006) 'Iranian Fury in the SWP Meeting', 1 March. http://www.azarmehr .info/2006/03/iranian-fury-in-swp-meeting.html. (Retrieved 19 January 2016.)

Baggini, Julian (2016) 'Jeremy Corbyn Is a Great Populist. But That's No Good for Our Democracy', *The Guardian*, 25 July. https://www.theguardian.com/commentisfree/2016/jul/ 25/jeremy-corbyn-populist-democracy-mps. (Retrieved 10 September 2016.)

Barsky, Robert F. (1997) *Noam Chomsky: A Life of Dissent* (Cambridge, MA: MIT Press).

Bar-Yosef, Ofer (1998) 'The Natufian Culture in the Levant, Threshold to the Origins of Agriculture', *Evolutionary Anthropology*, 6(5), pp. 159–177.

BBC News (1999) 'Thatcher Stands by Pinochet', 26 March. http://news.bbc.co.uk/2/hi/ 304516.stm. (Retrieved 27 September 2015.)

BBC News (2001) 'MP Calls for English Tests for Immigrants', 17 July. http://news.bbc.co.uk/ 1/hi/uk/1436867.stm. (Retrieved 21 May 2015.)

BBC News (2003) 'Profile of George Galloway', 22 April. http://news.bbc.co.uk/1/hi/uk _politics/2966199.stm. (Retrieved 8 May 2015.)

BBC News (2016) 'Jeremy Corbyn Outlines Labour's Vision of a "New Economics"', 21 May. http://www.bbc.com/news/uk-politics-36351149. (Retrieved 21 October 2016.)

Beck, Glenn (2009). *Glenn Beck's Common Sense: The Case against an Out-of-Control Government, Inspired by Thomas Paine* (New York: Simon and Schuster).

Beer, Max (1940) *A History of British Socialism*, 2 vols (London: Allen and Unwin).

Bell (2005) 'Full Text of David Bell's Speech', *The Guardian*, 17 January. http://www .theguardian.com/education/2005/jan/17/faithschools.schools. (Retrieved 21 May 2015.)

Benedict, Ruth (1934) *Patterns of Culture* (New York: New American Library).

Benn, Tony (1979) *Arguments for Socialism* (London: Jonathan Cape).

Benn, Tony (1981) *Arguments for Democracy* (Harmondsworth: Penguin).

Benn, Tony (1982) *Parliament, People and Power: Agenda for a Free Society* (London: Verso).

Benn, Tony (2000) 'Commanding Heights'. http://www.pbs.org/wgbh/commandingheights/ shared/minitext/int_tonybenn.html. (Retrieved 21 May 2016.)

Benn, Tony (2009) 'Benn 10—What Would The Levellers Do Today?' 15 February. https:// seagreensociety.wordpress.com/tag/levellers-day/. (Retrieved 2 July 2015.)

Bergstrom, Theodore C. (2002) 'Evolution of Social Behavior: Individual and Group Selection', *Journal of Economic Perspectives*, 16(2), Spring, pp. 67–88.

Bestor, Arthur E., Jr (1948) 'The Evolution of the Socialist Vocabulary', *Journal of the History of Ideas*, 9(3), June, pp. 259–302.

Bevins, Anthony, and Streeter, Michael (1996) 'Nelson Mandela: From "Terrorist" to Tea with the Queen', *The Independent*, 8 July. http://www.independent.co.uk/news/world/ from-terrorist-to-tea-with-the-queen-1327902.html. (Retrieved 27 September 2015.)

Bhaskar, Roy, and Collier, Andrew (1998) 'Introduction: Explanatory Critiques', in Archer, Margaret S., Bhaskar, Roy, Collier, Andrew, Lawson, Tony, and Norrie, Alan (eds) (1998) *Critical Realism: Essential Readings* (London and New York: Routledge), pp. 385–394.

Birchall, Ian (1996) 'The Babeuf Bicentenary: Conspiracy or Revolutionary Party?' *International Socialism*, 72, September, pp. 29–47.

Blair, Tony (1994) *Socialism*, Fabian Pamphlet 565 (London: Fabian Society).

Blair, Tony (2006) 'The Full Text of Tony Blair's Letter to Michael Foot Written in July 1982'. http://www.telegraph.co.uk/news/uknews/1521418/The-full-text-of-Tony-Blairs-letter-to -Michael-Foot-written-in-July-1982.html. (Retrieved 22 January 2016.)

Bleich, Erik (2011) 'What Is Islamophobia and How Much Is There? Theorizing and Measuring an Emerging Comparative Concept', *American Behavioral Scientist* 55(12), pp. 1581–1600.

Block, Fred, and Somers, Margaret (2003) 'In the Shadow of Speenhamland: Social Policy and the Old Poor Law', *Politics and Society*, 31(2), June, pp. 283–323.

Block, Walter (1996) 'Hayek's Road to Serfdom', *Journal of Libertarian Studies*, 12(2), Fall, pp. 339–365.

Bloodworth, James (2015a) 'A Left-Wing Case against Comrade Jeremy Corbyn', *International Business Times*, 4 August. http://www.ibtimes.co.uk/james-bloodworth-left-wing -case-against-comrade-jeremy-corbyn-1513969. (Retrieved 9 July 2016.)

Bloodworth, James (2015b) 'Why Is No One Asking about Jeremy Corbyn's Worrying Connections?' *The Guardian*, 13 August. https://www.theguardian.com/commentisfree/2015/aug/ 13/jeremy-corbyn-labour-leadership-foreign-policy-antisemitism. (Retrieved 9 July 2016.)

Bloodworth, James (2015c) 'The Bizarre World of Jeremy Corbyn and Stop the War', *Politico*, 12 December. http://www.politico.eu/article/bizarre-world-of-jeremy-corbyn-and-stop-the -war-coalition-galloway-rees-iraq-far-left/. (Retrieved 25 April 2017.)

Boehm, Christopher (2012) *Moral Origins: The Evolution of Virtue, Altruism and Shame* (New York: Basic Books).

Boettke, Peter J. (ed.) (2000) *Socialism and the Market: The Calculation Debate Revisited* (London and New York: Routledge).

Boettke, Peter J. (2001) *Calculation and Coordination: Essays on Socialism and Transitional Political Economy* (London and New York: Routledge).

Bok, Sissela (1978) *Lying: Moral Choice in Public and Private Life* (New York: Pantheon).

Bok, Sissela (1995) *Common Values* (Columbia: University of Missouri Press).

Bonin, John P., Jones, Derek C., and Putterman, Louis (1993) 'Theoretical and Empirical Studies of Producer Cooperatives: Will Ever the Twain Meet?' *Journal of Economic Literature*, 31(3), September, pp. 1290–1320.

Bonnett, Alastair (2007) 'The Other Rights of Man: The Revolutionary Plan of Thomas Spence', *History Today*, 57(9), pp. 42–48.

Bowles, Samuel, and Gintis, Herbert (1999) *Recasting Egalitarianism: New Rules for Markets, States, and Communities* (London: Verso).

Bowles, Samuel, and Gintis, Herbert (2002) 'The Inheritance of Inequality', *Journal of Economic Perspectives*, 16(3), Summer, pp. 3–30.

Bowles, Samuel, and Gintis, Herbert (2011) *A Cooperative Species: Human Reciprocity and Its Evolution* (Princeton, NJ: Princeton University Press).

Boyd, Robert, and Richerson, Peter J. (1985) *Culture and the Evolutionary Process* (Chicago: University of Chicago Press).

Brailsford, H. N. (1961) *The Levellers and the English Revolution* (London: Cresset Press).

Bregman, Rutger (2016) 'Nixon's Basic Income Plan', *Jacobin*, 5 May. https://www.jacobinmag .com/2016/05/richard-nixon-ubi-basic-income-welfare. (Retrieved 15 May 2016.)

Brockway, Fenner (1980) *Britain's First Socialists: The Levellers, Agitators and Diggers of the English Revolution* (London: Quartet).

Brown, Andrew (2009) 'Intelligence Squared Debate: Catholics Humiliated by Christopher Hitchens and Stephen Fry', *The Telegraph*, 19 October. http://blogs.telegraph.co.uk/ news/andrewmcfbrown/100014133/intelligence-squared-debate-catholics-humiliated-by -christopher-hitchens-and-stephen-fry/. (Retrieved 17 May 2015.)

Brown, Donald E. (1991) *Human Universals* (New York: McGraw-Hill).

Burke, Edmund (1790) *Reflections on the Revolution in France and on the Proceedings in Certain Societies in London* (London: Dodsley).

Burke, Edmund (1968) *Reflections on the Revolution in France* (Harmondsworth: Penguin).

Butt, Hassan (2007) 'My Plea to Fellow Muslims: You Must Renounce Terror', *The Observer*, 1 July. http://www.theguardian.com/commentisfree/2007/jul/01/comment.religion1. (Retrieved 12 May 2015.)

Caldwell, Bruce J., and Montes, Leonidas (2015) 'Friedrich Hayek and His Visits to Chile', *Review of Austrian Economics*, 28(3), pp. 261–309.

Callinicos, Alex (2015) 'Our Job Is to Defeat Imperialism, Not ISIS', *Socialist Worker*, 17 November. https://socialistworker.co.uk/art/41713/Our+job+is+to+defeat+imperialism, +not+Isis. (Retrieved 1 December 2015.)

Campbell, Al (2011) 'Marx and Engels' Vision of a Better Society', *Forum for Social Economics*, 39(3), October, pp. 269–278.

Carr, E. H. (1966) *The Bolshevik Revolution*, vol. 3 (Harmondsworth: Pelican).

Caute, David (1966) *The Left in Europe since 1789* (London: Weidenfeld and Nicolson).

Chan, Kam Wing, and Buckingham, Will (2008) 'Is China Abolishing the *Hukou* System?' *China Quarterly*, 195, pp. 582–606.

Chan, Kam Wing, and Zhang, Li (1999) 'The *Hukou* System and Rural-Urban Migration in China: Processes and Changes', *China Quarterly*, 160, pp. 818–855.

Chang, Ha-Joon (1997) 'The Economics and Politics of Regulation: A Critical Survey', *Cambridge Journal of Economics*, 21(6), November, pp. 703–728.

Chang, Ha-Joon (2002a) 'The Real Lesson for Developing Countries from the History of the Developed World: "Freedom to Choose"', *History and Policy*, 1 August. http://www .historyandpolicy.org/policy-papers/papers/the-real-lesson-for-developing-countries-from -the-history-of-the-developed. (Retrieved 17 October 2015.)

Chang, Ha-Joon (2002b) 'Breaking the Mould: An Institutionalist Political Economy Alternative to the Neo-Liberal Theory of the Market and the State', *Cambridge Journal of Economics*, 26(5), September, pp. 539–559.

Chang, Ha-Joon (2002c) *Kicking Away the Ladder: Development Strategy in Historical Perspective* (Anthem Press: London).

Chang, Ha-Joon, and Rowthorn, Robert E. (eds) (1995) *The Role of the State in Economic Change* (Oxford: Clarendon Press).

Chapman, Hamed (2015) 'Labour Would Outlaw Islamophobia, Says Miliband in an Exclusive Interview', *The Muslim News*, 24 April. http://www.muslimnews.co.uk/newspaper/top-stories/labour-to-outlaw-islamophobia-says-miliband-in-an-exclusive-interview/. (Retrieved 17 May 2015.)

Chapple, Geoff (1980) *Rewi Alley of China* (Auckland: Hodder and Stoughton).

Claeys, Gregory (1989) *Thomas Paine: Social and Political Thought* (London and New York: Routledge).

Claeys, Gregory (1991) 'Introduction', in Owen, Robert (1991) *A New View of Society and Other Writings* (Harmondsworth: Penguin), pp. vii–xxxiv.

Coase, Ronald H. (1960) 'The Problem of Social Cost', *Journal of Law and Economics*, 3(1), October, pp. 1–44.

Coase, Ronald H., and Wang, Ning (2012) *How China Became Capitalist* (London and New York: Palgrave Macmillan).

Cobban, Alfred (1964) *The Social Interpretation of the French Revolution* (Cambridge: Cambridge University Press).

Cohen, G. A. (2009) *Why Not Socialism?* (Princeton, NJ, and London: Princeton University Press).

Cohen, Nick (2007) *What's Left? How the Left Lost Its Way* (London and New York: Harper).

Cohen, Nick (2015) 'Far Leftists Do Not Laugh about Mao to Mock Communism. They Laugh to Forget Communism', *The Spectator*, 26 November. http://blogs.new.spectator.co.uk/2015/11/far-leftists-not-laugh-mao-mock-communism-laugh-forget-communism/. (Retrieved 26 November 2015.)

Cole, George D. H. (1917) *Self-Government in Industry* (London: G. Bell).

Cole, George D. H. (1920) *Guild Socialism Re-Stated* (London: Parsons).

Cole, George D. H. (1932) *The Intelligent Man's Guide through World Chaos* (London: Gollancz).

Cole, George D. H. (1941) *Europe, Russia and the Future* (London: Gollancz).

Cole, George D. H. (1948) *The Meaning of Marxism* (London: George Allen and Unwin).

Commission on the Future of Multi-Ethnic Britain (2000) *The Future of Multi-Ethnic Britain: The Parekh Report* (London: Profile Books).

Commons, John R. (1924) *Legal Foundations of Capitalism* (New York: Macmillan).

Comninel, George C. (1987) *Rethinking the French Revolution: Marxism and the Revisionist Challenge* (London: Verso).

Conquest, Robert (1968) *The Great Terror* (London: Macmillan).

Conquest, Robert (1986) *The Harvest of Sorrow: Soviet Collectivization and the Terror-Famine* (Oxford: Oxford University Press).

Cook, Michael (2000) *Commanding Right and Forbidding Wrong in Islamic Thought* (Cambridge and New York: Cambridge University Press).

Corbyn, Jeremy (2011) 'Foreword', in Hobson, John A. (1902) *Imperialism: A Study*, facsimile reprint (Nottingham: Spokesman).

Corbyn, Jeremy (2014) 'Nato Belligerence Endangers Us All', *Morning Star*, 17 April. http://www.morningstaronline.co.uk/a-972b-Nato-belligerence-endangers-us-all. (Retrieved 20 September 2015.)

Corning, Peter A. (2011) *The Fair Society: The Science of Human Nature and the Pursuit of Social Justice* (Chicago: University of Chicago Press).

Costanza, Robert, Kubiszewski, Ida, Giovannini, Enrico, Lovins, Hunter, McGlade, Jacqueline, Pickett, Kate E., Ragnarsdóttir, Kristín Vala, Roberts, Debra, De Vogli, Roberto, and Wilkinson, Richard (2014) 'Time to Leave GDP Behind', *Nature*, 505, 16 January, pp. 283–285.

Courtois, Stéphane, Werth, Nicolas, Panné, Jean-Louis, Packowski, Andrzej, Bartošek, Karel, and Margolin, Jean-Louis (1999) *The Black Book of Communism: Crimes, Terror, Repression* (Cambridge, MA: Harvard University Press).

Cowen, Tyler (2013) *Average Is Over: Powering America beyond the Age of the Great Stagnation* (New York: Dutton).

Credit Suisse Research Institute (2012) *Credit Suisse Global Wealth Databook 2012* (Zurich: Credit Suisse Research Institute).

Crick, Michael (2013) 'Nigel Farage Schooldays Letter Reveals Concerns over Fascism', *Channel Four News*, 19 September. http://www.channel4.com/news/nigel-farage-ukip-letter-school-concerns-racism-fascism. (Retrieved 30 September 2016.)

Crosland, C. Anthony R. (1956) *The Future of Socialism* (London: Jonathan Cape).

Crouch, Colin, Finegold, David, and Sako, Mari (1999) *Are Skills the Answer? The Political Economy of Skill Creation in Advanced Industrial Countries* (Oxford: Oxford University Press).

Cunliffe, Rachel (2016) 'Corbyn Looks the Other Way as Venezuela Self-Destructs', 28 December. https://capx.co/corbyn-looks-the-other-way-as-venezuela-self-destructs-2016/. (Retrieved 18 January 2017.)

Dale, Gareth (2010) *Karl Polanyi: The Limits to the Market* (Cambridge: Polity Press).

Darwin, Charles R. (1871) *The Descent of Man, and Selection in Relation to Sex*, 2 vols (London: Murray; New York: Hill).

Davis, John B. (ed.) (2001) *The Social Economics of Health Care* (London and New York: Routledge).

Davis, Michael (1987) 'Nozick's Argument *for* the Legitimacy of the Welfare State', *Ethics*, 97, April, pp. 576–594.

Department of Education (2014) *Promoting Fundamental British Values as Part of SMSC in Schools* (London: Department of Education). https://www.gov.uk/government/uploads/system/uploads/attachment_data/file/380595/SMSC_Guidance_Maintained_Schools.pdf. (Retrieved 29 June 2015.)

De Waal, Frans B. M. (2006) *Primates and Philosophers: How Morality Evolved* (Princeton, NJ: Princeton University Press).

Dewey, John (1916) *Democracy and Education* (New York: Macmillan).

Dewey, John (1922) *Human Nature and Conduct: An Introduction to Social Psychology*, 1st ed. (New York: Holt).

Dewey, John (1935) *Liberalism and Social Action* (New York: G. P. Putnam's Sons).

Dewey, John (1938) *Logic: The Theory of Enquiry* (New York: Holt).

Dewey, John (1939) *Theory of Valuation* (Chicago: University of Chicago Press).

Dickenson, Henry D. (1939) *Economics of Socialism* (Oxford: Oxford University Press).

Dikötter, Frank (2010) *Mao's Great Famine: The History of China's Most Devastating Catastrophe, 1958–62* (London: Bloomsbury).

Dikötter, Frank (2016) *The Cultural Revolution: A People's History 1962–1976* (London: Bloomsbury).

Dobson, Roger (2014) 'British Muslims Face Worst Job Discrimination of Any Minority Group, According to Research', *The Independent*, 30 November. http://www.independent .co.uk/news/uk/home-news/british-muslims-face-worst-job-discrimination-of-any -minority-group-9893211.html. (Retrieved 30 September 2016.)

Doucouliagos, Chris (1995) 'Worker Participation and Productivity in Labor-Managed and Participatory Capitalist Firms: A Meta-Analysis', *Industrial and Labor Relations Review*, 49(1), October, pp. 58–77.

Dow, Gregory K. (2003) *Governing the Firm: Workers' Control in Theory and Practice* (Cambridge and New York: Cambridge University Press).

Doyal, Leonard, and Gough, Ian (1991) *A Theory of Human Need* (London: Macmillan).

Doyle, William (2002) *The Oxford History of the French Revolution*, 2nd ed. (Oxford and New York: Oxford University Press).

Draper, Hal, and Lipow, Anne G. (1976) 'Marxist Women *versus* Bourgeois Feminism', *Socialist Register*, pp. 179–226. https://www.marxists.org/archive/draper/1976/women/women .html. (Retrieved 23 July 2015.)

Dunbar, Robin I. M. (1993) 'Coevolution of Neocortical Size, Group Size, and Language', *Behavioral and Brain Sciences*, 16(4), December, pp. 681–694.

Dunbar, Robin I. M. (2010) *How Many Friends Does One Person Need? Dunbar's Number and Other Evolutionary Quirks* (London: Faber and Faber).

Dunbar, Robin I. M. (2011) 'Constraints on the Evolution of Social Institutions and Their Implications for Information Flow', *Journal of Institutional Economics*, 7(3), September, pp. 345–371.

Durkheim, Émile (1984) *The Division of Labour in Society*, trans. from the French 1893 edition (London: Macmillan).

Etzioni, Amitai (1988) *The Moral Dimension: Toward a New Economics* (New York: Free Press).

Evans, Karen G. (2000) 'Reclaiming John Dewey: Democracy, Inquiry, Pragmatism, and Public Management', *Administration and Society*, 32(3), July, pp. 308–328.

Evans, Peter, and Rauch, James E. (1999) 'Bureaucracy and Growth: A Cross-National Analysis of the Effects of "Weberian" State Structures on Economic Growth', *American Sociological Review*, 64, October, pp. 748–765.

Executive Board, American Anthropological Association (1947) 'Statement on Human Rights', *American Anthropologist*, New Series, 49(4), Part 1, October–December, pp. 539–543.

Fanon, Franz (1963) *The Wretched of the Earth* (New York: Grove Press).

Finnis, John (1980) *Natural Law and Natural Rights* (Oxford: Clarendon Press).

Fish, M. Steven (2002), 'Islam and Authoritarianism', *World Politics*, 55(1), October, pp. 4–37.

Fishman, William J. (1970) *The Insurrectionists* (London: Methuen).

Foner, Philip S. (1945) *The Life and Major Writings of Thomas Paine*, 2 vols (New York: Citadel Press).

Foote, Geoffrey (1997). *The Labour Party's Political Thought: A History*, 3rd ed. (London: Palgrave).

Fox, Alan (1974) *Beyond Contract: Work, Power and Trust Relations* (London: Faber and Faber).

France, Anatole (1894) *Le Lys Rouge* (Paris: Calmann Lévy).

Franklin, Jonathan (2015) 'Pinochet Directly Ordered Killing on US Soil of Chilean Diplomat, Papers Reveal', *The Guardian*, 8 October. http://www.theguardian.com/world/2015/oct/08/pinochet-directly-ordered-washington-killing-diplomat-documents-orlando-letelier-declassified. (Retrieved 8 October 2015.)

Freedland, Jonathan (2016) 'Labour and the Left Have an Antisemitism Problem', *The Guardian*, 18 March. https://www.theguardian.com/commentisfree/2016/mar/18/labour-antisemitism-jews-jeremy-corbyn. (Retrieved 8 October 2016.)

Friedman, Milton (1976) 'Reply to Citizen's Committee on Human Rights and Foreign Policy, "Advising Chile"', Letter to the Editor, *Newsweek*, 14 June.

Friedman, Milton (1991) 'Economic Freedom, Human Freedom, Political Freedom'. Lecture delivered 1 November 1991. http://calculemus.org/lect/07pol-gosp/frlect.html. (Retrieved 9 October 2015.)

Fukuyama, Francis (2011) *The Origins of Political Order: From Prehuman Times to the French Revolution* (London and New York: Profile Books and Farrar, Straus and Giroux).

Gagliardi, Francesca (2009) 'Financial Development and the Growth of Cooperative Firms', *Small Business Economics*, 32(4), April, pp. 439–464.

Galbraith, John Kenneth (1952) *American Capitalism: The Concept of Countervailing Power* (Boston: Houghton Mifflin).

Galbraith, John Kenneth (1962) *American Capitalism: The Concept of Countervailing Power*, 3rd ed. (Boston: Houghton Mifflin).

Galbraith, John Kenneth (1969) *The New Industrial State* (Harmondsworth: Penguin).

Gartzke, Erik (2007) 'The Capitalist Peace', *American Journal of Political Science*, 51(1), pp. 166–191.

Gauchet, Marcel (1997) 'Right and Left', in Nora, Pierre, and Kritzman, Lawrence D. (eds) (1997) *Realms of Memory: Conflicts and Divisions* (New York: Columbia University Press), pp. 242–245.

George, Henry (1879) *Progress and Poverty: An Inquiry into the Cause of Industrial Depression and Increase of Want with Increase of Wealth* (London: Kegan Paul).

Gerring, John, Bond, Philip J., Barndt, William T., and Moreno, Carola (2005) 'Democracy and Growth: A Historical Perspective', *World Politics*, 57(3), April, pp. 323–364.

Gewirth, Alan (1978) *Reason and Morality* (Chicago: Chicago University Press).

Gewirth, Alan (1982) *Human Rights: Essays on Justification and Applications* (Chicago: University of Chicago Press).

Gide, Charles, and Rist, Charles (1915) *A History of Economic Doctrines from the Time of the Physiocrats to the Present Day* (London: George Harrap).

Gillard, Derek (2007) 'Never Mind the Evidence: Blair's Obsession with Faith Schools', Education in England. http://www.educationengland.org.uk/articles/26blairfaith.html. (Retrieved 21 May 2015.)

Gough, Ian (2000) *Global Capital, Human Needs and Social Policies* (Basingstoke and New York: Palgrave Macmillan).

Gough, Ian (2004) 'Human Well-Being and Social Structures: Relating the Universal and the Local', *Global Social Policy*, 4, pp. 289–311.

Gouinlock, James (1972) *John Dewey's Philosophy of Value* (New York: Humanities Press).

Gouinlock, James (1978) 'Dewey's Theory of Moral Deliberation', *Ethics*, 88(3), April, pp. 218–228.

Gray, John (1993) *Post-Liberalism* (London and New York: Routledge).

Greer, Germaine (1970) *The Female Eunuch* (London and New York: Harper).

Greer, Germaine (1999) *The Whole Woman* (New York: Doubleday).

Gregory, David (1983) 'Karl Marx's and Friedrich Engels' Knowledge of French Socialism in 1842–43', *Historical Reflections*, 10(1), Spring, pp. 143–193.

Hahnel, Robin (2005) *Economic Justice and Democracy: From Competition to Cooperation* (London and New York: Routledge).

Hahnel, Robin (2007) 'The Case against Markets', *Journal of Economic Issues*, 41(3), December, pp. 1139–1159.

Haidt, Jonathan, and Joseph, Craig (2004) 'Intuitive Ethics: How Innately Prepared Intuitions Generate Culturally Variable Virtues', *Daedalus*, 133(4), Fall, pp. 55–66.

Hain, Peter (2015) *Back to the Future of Socialism* (Bristol: Policy Press).

Hampton, Christopher (ed.) (1984) *A Radical Reader: The Struggle for Change in England, 1381–1914* (Harmondsworth: Penguin).

Hansard (1990) 'Parliamentary Debates, 22 November 1990, Column 485'. https://www.publications.parliament.uk/pa/cm199091/cmhansrd/1990-11-22/Debate-6.html. (Retrieved 27 April 2015.)

Hansmann, Henry (1996) *The Ownership of Enterprise* (Cambridge: Cambridge University Press).

Hare, Richard M. (1952) *The Language of Morals* (Oxford: Oxford University Press).

Harris, Sam (2010) *The Moral Landscape: How Science Can Determine Human Values* (New York and London: Free Press).

Harrison, J. F. C. (1969) *Robert Owen and the Owenites in Britain and America* (London: Routledge and Kegan Paul).

Hayek, Friedrich A. (1948) *Individualism and Economic Order* (London and Chicago: George Routledge and University of Chicago Press).

Hayek, Friedrich A. (1960) *The Constitution of Liberty* (London and Chicago: Routledge and Kegan Paul, and University of Chicago Press).

Hayek, Friedrich A. (1973) *Law, Legislation and Liberty, Volume 1: Rules and Order* (London: Routledge and Kegan Paul).

Hayek, Friedrich A. (1979) *Law, Legislation and Liberty, Volume 3: The Political Order of a Free People* (London: Routledge and Kegan Paul).

Hayek, Friedrich A. (1988) *The Fatal Conceit: The Errors of Socialism; The Collected Works of Friedrich August Hayek, Vol. I*, ed. William W. Bartley III (London: Routledge).

Hayek, Friedrich A. (1989) 'The Pretence of Knowledge', *American Economic Review*, 79(6), December, pp. 1–7.

Heath, Anthony F., Jowell, Roger M., and Curtice, John K. (2001) *The Rise of New Labour: Party Politics and Voter Choices* (Oxford: Oxford University Press).

Hegel, Georg Wilhelm Friedrich (1942) *Philosophy of Right*, trans. from the German 1821 edition (Oxford: Oxford University Press).

Heinsohn, Gunnar, and Steiger, Otto (2013) *Ownership Economics: On the Foundations of Interest, Money, Markets, Business Cycles and Economic Development*, trans. and ed. Frank Decker (London and New York: Routledge).

Heller, Michael A. (2008) *The Gridlock Economy: How Too Much Ownership Wrecks Markets, Stops Innovation, and Costs Lives* (New York: Basic Books).

Hill, Christopher (1961) *The Century of Revolution 1603–1714* (London: Van Nostrand Reinhold).

Hill, Christopher (1975) *The World Turned Upside Down: Radical Ideas during the English Revolution* (Harmondsworth: Penguin).

Hinman, Pip, and Pilger, John (2004) 'Pilger Interview: Truth and Lies in the "War on Terror"', *Green Left* (Australia), 28 January.

Hirschman, Albert O. (1982) 'Rival Interpretations of Market Society: Civilizing, Destructive, or Feeble?' *Journal of Economic Literature*, 20(4), December, pp. 1463–1484. Reprinted in Hirschman, Albert O. (1986) *Rival Views of Market Society and Other Essays* (New York: Viking).

Hirsh, David (2015) 'The Corbyn Left: The Politics of Position and the Politics of Reason', *Fathom*, Autumn. http://fathomjournal.org/the-corbyn-left-the-politics-of-position-and -the-politics-of-reason/. (Retrieved 19 August 2016.)

Hodgson, Geoffrey M. (1974) 'The Theory of the Falling Rate of Profit', *New Left Review*, 84, March/April, pp. 55–82. Reprinted in Hodgson, Geoffrey M. (1991) *After Marx and Sraffa: Essays in Political Economy* (London: Macmillan).

Hodgson, Geoffrey M. (1977) *Socialism and Parliamentary Democracy* (Nottingham: Spokesman).

Hodgson, Geoffrey M. (1988) *Economics and Institutions: A Manifesto for a Modern Institutional Economics* (Cambridge and Philadelphia: Polity Press and University of Pennsylvania Press).

Hodgson, Geoffrey M. (1999) *Economics and Utopia: Why the Learning Economy Is Not the End of History* (London and New York: Routledge).

Hodgson, Geoffrey M. (2006) *Economics in the Shadows of Darwin and Marx: Essays on Institutional and Evolutionary Themes* (Cheltenham: Edward Elgar).

Hodgson, Geoffrey M. (2007) '*The Impossibility of Social Democracy* by Albert E. F. Schäffle', *Journal of Institutional Economics*, 3(1), April, pp. 113–125.

Hodgson, Geoffrey M. (2010) 'Albert Schäffle's Critique of Socialism', in Vint, John, Metcalfe, J. Stanley, Kurz, Heinz D., Salvadori, Neri, and Samuelson, Paul A. (eds) (2010) *Economic Theory and Economic Thought: Essays in Honour of Ian Steedman* (London and New York: Routledge), pp. 296–315.

Hodgson, Geoffrey M. (2013) *From Pleasure Machines to Moral Communities: An Evolutionary Economics without* Homo Economicus (Chicago: University of Chicago Press).

Hodgson, Geoffrey M. (2015) *Conceptualizing Capitalism: Institutions, Evolution, Future* (Chicago: University of Chicago Press).

Hodgson, Geoffrey M. (2016a) 'Corbyn, Brexit and the Impossibility of Democratic Absolutism', *New Politics*, 30 June. http://newpolitics.apps-1and1.net/corbyn-brexit-and-the -impossibility-of-democratic-absolutism. (Retrieved 1 October 2016.)

Hodgson, Geoffrey M. (2016b) 'On Jeremy Corbyn's "Obvious" Socialism', *New Politics*, 10 August. http://newpolitics.apps-1and1.net/on-jeremy-corbyns-obvious-socialism. (Retrieved 1 October 2016.)

Hodgson, Geoffrey M. (2016c) 'The Perils of Corbynista Populism', *New Politics*, 16 September. http://newpolitics.apps-1and1.net/the-perils-of-corbynista-populism. (Retrieved 1 October 2016.)

Hodgson, Geoffrey M. (2016d) 'The Muddled Mystique of Karl Polanyi', *New Politics*, 15 October. http://newpolitics.apps-1and1.net/the-muddled-mystique-of-karl-polanyi. (Retrieved 15 October 2016.)

Hodgson, Geoffrey M. (2017) 'Karl Polanyi on Economy and Society: A Critical Analysis of Core Concepts', *Review of Social Economy*, 75(1), March, pp. 1–25.

Hollander, Paul (1998) *Bernard Shaw: A Brief Biography* (Philadelphia: University of Pennsylvania Press).

Holzer, Harry J., Block, Richard N., Cheatham, Markus, and Knott, Jack H. (1993) 'Are Training Subsidies for Firms Effective? The Michigan Experience', *Industrial and Labor Relations Review*, 46(4), July, pp. 625–636.

Honoré, Antony M. (1961) 'Ownership', in Guest, Anthony G. (ed.) (1961) *Oxford Essays in Jurisprudence* (Oxford: Oxford University Press), pp. 107–147. Reprinted in the *Journal of Institutional Economics*, 9(2), June 2013, pp. 227–255.

Hoppe, Hans-Hermann (1994) 'F. A. Hayek on Government and Social Evolution: A Critique', *Review of Austrian Economics*, 7(1), pp. 67–93.

House of Commons Home Affairs Committee (2016) *Antisemitism in the UK* (London: House of Commons). http://www.publications.parliament.uk/pa/cm201617/cmselect/cmhaff/136/136.pdf. (Retrieved 16 October 2016.)

Hubbick, Elizabeth (2001) *Employee Share Ownership* (London: Chartered Institute of Personnel and Development).

Human Security Research Group (2013) *Human Security Report 2013: The Decline in Global Violence; Evidence, Explanation, and Contestation* (Vancouver: Simon Fraser University). http://www.hsrgroup.org/docs/Publications/HSR2013/HSRP_Report_2013_140226_Web.pdf. (Retrieved 25 April 2015.)

Husain, Ed (2007) *The Islamist: Why I Joined Radical Islam in Britain, What I Saw Inside, and Why I Left* (London: Allan Lane).

Hussain, Dilly (2015) 'How "British Values" Are Used as a Smoke Screen for Anti-Muslim Government Policies', Stop the War Coalition, 11 June. http://www.stopwar.org.uk/news/how-british-values-are-used-as-a-smokescreen-for-anti-muslim-government-policies. (Retrieved 11 June 2015.)

Ignatieff, Michael (2001) *Human Rights as Politics and Idolatry* (Princeton, NJ: Princeton University Press).

Independent (2015) 'Stop the War Has Been Accused of "Complimenting" ISIS', *The Independent*, 5 December 2015. http://i100.independent.co.uk/article/stop-the-war-has-been-accused-of-complimenting-isis—Wyg4nnxLql. (Retrieved 8 December 2015.)

Ingham, Geoffrey (2004) *The Nature of Money* (Cambridge: Polity Press).

Ingham, Geoffrey (2008) *Capitalism* (Cambridge: Polity Press).

Jain, Arvind K. (2001) 'Corruption: A Review', *Journal of Economic Surveys*, 15(1), February, pp. 71–120.

Jefferson, Thomas (1822) 'Thomas Jefferson to Cornelius Camden Blatchly, 1822'. http://famguardian.org/Subjects/Politics/thomasjefferson/jeff1550.htm. (Retrieved 12 September 2015.)

Jones, Benjamin (2014) 'Mission Creep on the Anti-War Left', *National Secular Society*, 19 November. http://www.secularism.org.uk/blog/2014/11/mission-creep-in-the-anti-war -left. (Retrieved 21 November 2014.)

Jones, Benjamin (2015) 'Preacher James McConnell Faces Prosecution for Calling Islam "Satanic"—The State Again Tramples over Free Expression', *National Secular Society*, 18 June. http://www.secularism.org.uk/blog/2015/06/preacher-james-mcconnell-faces -prosecution-for-calling-islam-satanic—the-state-again-tramples-over-free-expression. (Retrieved 26 June 2015.)

Jones, Bill (1977) *The Russia Complex: The British Labour Party and the Soviet Union* (Manchester: University of Manchester Press).

Jones, Peter (1994) *Rights* (Basingstoke: Macmillan).

Joyce, Richard (2006) *The Evolution of Morality* (Cambridge, MA: MIT Press).

Judt, Tony (2006) 'Goodbye to All That?' *New York Review of Books*, 21 September 2006.

Kamm, Oliver (2004) 'Impertinence and Impropriety', 16 March 2004. http://oliverkamm .typepad.com/blog/2004/03/impertinence_an.html. (Retrieved 21 May 2015.)

Kanarek, Jaret (2013) 'Critiquing Cultural Relativism', *The Intellectual Standard*, 2(2), Article 1. http://digitalcommons.iwu.edu/tis/vol2/iss2/1. (Retrieved 16 May 2015.)

Kant, Immanuel (1929) *Critique of Pure Reason*, trans. from the 2nd German edition (1787), with an introduction by Norman Kemp Smith (London: Macmillan).

Keane, John (1995) *Tom Paine: A Political Life* (London: Bloomsbury).

Kelso, Louis O., and Adler, Mortimer J. (1958) *The Capitalist Manifesto* (New York: Random House).

Kennedy, Dominic (2015) 'Shadow Chancellor Was Championed by Thug Chief of Revolutionary Party', *The Times*, 16 September. http://www.thetimes.co.uk/tto/news/politics/ article4558112.ece. (Retrieved 27 November 2015.)

Kenworthy, Lane (1995) *In Search of National Economic Success: Balancing Competition and Cooperation* (Thousand Oaks, CA, and London: Sage).

Keynes, John Maynard (1930) *A Treatise on Money, Vol. 1: The Pure Theory of Money* (London: Macmillan).

Keynes, John Maynard (1936) *The General Theory of Employment, Interest and Money* (London: Macmillan).

King, John E., and Marangos, John (2006) 'Two Arguments for Basic Income: Thomas Paine (1737–1809) and Thomas Spence (1750–1814)', *History of Economic Ideas*, 14(1), pp. 55–71.

Kirkpatrick, Frank (2005) *John Macmurray: Community beyond Political Philosophy* (Lanham, MD: Rowman and Littlefield).

Kitcher, Philip (1993) *The Advancement of Science: Science without Legend, Objectivity without Illusions* (Oxford and New York: Oxford University Press).

Kitcher, Philip (2011) *The Ethical Project* (Cambridge, MA: Harvard University Press).

Klaus, Václav (2007) 'Freedom, Not Climate, Is at Risk', *Financial Times*, 13 June. https://www .ft.com/content/9deb730a-19ca-11dc-99c5-000b5df10621. (Retrieved 13 June 2015.)

Klein, Naomi (2007) *The Shock Doctrine: The Rise of Disaster Capitalism* (New York: Henry Holt).

Kline, Donna C. (1987) *Dominion and Wealth: A Critical Analysis of Karl Marx's Theory of Commercial Law* (Dordrecht: Reidel).

Knutsen, Carl Henrik (2015) 'Why Democracies Outgrow Autocracies in the Long Run: Civil Liberties, Information Flows and Technological Change', *Kyklos*, 68(3), August, pp. 357–384.

Kolakowski, Leszek (1974) 'My Correct Views on Everything: A Rejoinder to Edward Thompson's "Open Letter to Leszek Kolakowski"', *Socialist Register*, 11. http:// socialistregister.com/index.php/srv/article/view/5323/2224#.VXBUKrFwYy8. (Retrieved 4 June 2015).

Kolakowski, Leszek (1977) 'Marxist Roots of Stalinism', in Tucker, Robert C. (ed.) (1977) *Stalinism: Essays in Historical Interpretation* (New York: Norton), pp. 283–298.

Kolakowski, Leszek (1978) *Main Currents of Marxism: The Founders* (Oxford and New York: Oxford University Press).

Kramnick, Isaac (1977) 'Religion and Radicalism: English Political Theory in the Age of the Revolution', *Political Theory*, 5(4), November, pp. 505–534.

Kramnick, Isaac (1981) 'Tom Paine: Radical Democrat', *Democracy*, 1(1), January, pp. 127–138.

Kuhn, Thomas S. (1962) *The Structure of Scientific Revolutions* (Chicago: University of Chicago Press).

Kuran, Timur (2004) 'Why the Middle East is Economically Underdeveloped: Historical Mechanisms of Institutional Stagnation', *Journal of Economic Perspectives*, 18(3), Summer, pp. 71–90.

Kuran, Timur (2010) *The Long Divergence: How Islamic Law Held Back the Middle East* (Princeton, NJ: Princeton University Press).

Lakatos, Imre (1976) *Proofs and Refutations* (Cambridge: Cambridge University Press).

Lallement, Michel (2012) 'An Experiment Inspired by Fourier: J. B. Godin's Familistere in Guise', *Journal of Historical Sociology*, 25(1), March, pp. 31–49.

Lamb, Robert (2010) 'Liberty, Equality, and the Boundaries of Ownership: Thomas Paine's Theory of Property Rights', *Review of Politics*, 72(3), Summer, pp. 483–511.

Landauer, Carl A. (1959) *European Socialism: A History of Ideas and Movements from the Industrial Revolution to Hitler's Seizure of Power*, 2 vols (Berkeley: University of California Press).

Lange, Oskar R. (1936–1937) 'On the Economic Theory of Socialism: Parts One and Two', *Review of Economic Studies*, 4(1), pp. 53–71, and 4(2), pp. 123–142.

Lange, Oskar R. (1987) 'The Economic Operation of a Socialist Society', two lectures delivered in 1942, *Contributions to Political Economy*, 6, pp. 3–24.

Laudan, Larry (1977) *Progress and Its Problems: Towards a Theory of Scientific Growth* (London: Routledge and Kegan Paul).

Laudan, Larry (1981) *Science and Hypothesis: Historical Essays on Scientific Methodology* (Dordrecht: Reidel).

Lavoie, Donald (1985a) *Rivalry and Central Planning: The Socialist Calculation Debate Reconsidered* (Cambridge: Cambridge University Press).

Lavoie, Donald (1985b) *National Economic Planning: What is Left?* (Cambridge, MA: Ballinger).

Lee, Keun (2013) *Schumpeterian Analysis of Economic Catch-up: Knowledge, Path-Creation, and the Middle-Income Trap* (Cambridge and New York: Cambridge University Press).

Leeson. Peter T. (2014) 'Human Sacrifice', *Review of Behavioral Economics*, 1, pp. 137–165.

Lenin, Vladimir Ilyich (1967) *Selected Works in Three Volumes* (London: Lawrence and Wishart).

Letelier, Orlando (1976) 'The Chicago Boys in Chile: Economic Freedom's Awful Toll', *The Nation*, 28 August. http://www.ditext.com/letelier/chicago.html. (Retrieved 21 December 2015).

Levin, Yuval (2014) *The Great Debate: Edmund Burke, Thomas Paine, and the Birth of Right and Left* (New York: Basic Books).

Lindblom, Charles E. (1959) 'The Science of "Muddling Through"', *Public Administration Review*, 19(1), pp. 79–88.

Lindblom, Charles E. (1984) *The Policy-Making Process* (Englewood Cliffs, NJ: Prentice-Hall).

Loft, Leonore (2002) *Passion, Politics, and Philosophie: Rediscovering J.-P. Brissot* (Westport, CT: Greenwood Press).

Lukes, Steven (1985) *Marxism and Morality* (Oxford: Oxford University Press).

Luxemburg, Rosa (1912) 'Women's Suffrage and Class Struggle'. https://www.marxists.org/archive/draper/1976/women/4-luxemburg.html. (Retrieved 23 July 2015.)

Luxemburg, Rosa (1970) *Rosa Luxemburg Speaks*, ed. and with an introduction by Mary-Alice Waters (New York: Pathfinder Press).

MacIntyre, Alasdair (1981) *After Virtue: A Study in Moral Theory* (London: Duckworth).

Mackie, John Leslie (1977) *Ethics: Inventing Right and Wrong* (Harmondsworth: Penguin).

Macpherson, Crawford B. (1962) *The Political Theory of Possessive Individualism: Hobbes to Locke* (Oxford: Oxford University Press).

Maddison, Angus (2001) *The World Economy: A Millennial Perspective* (Paris: OECD).

Maddison, Angus (2003) *The World Economy: Historical Statistics* (Paris: OECD).

Maddison, Angus (2007) *Contours of the World Economy, 1–2030 AD*, Essays in Macro-Economic History (Oxford and New York: Oxford University Press).

Malik, Kenan (2005) 'The Islamophobia Myth', *Prospect*, February. http://www.kenanmalik.com/essays/prospect_islamophobia.html. (Retrieved 14 June 2015.)

Manning, Brian (1976) *The English People and the English Revolution, 1640–1649* (London: Heinemann).

Manuel, Frank E., and Manuel, Fritzie P. (1979) *Utopian Thought in the Western World* (Oxford: Basil Blackwell).

Maoz, Zeev (1997) 'The Controversy over the Democratic Peace: Rearguard Action or Cracks in the Wall?' *International Security*, 22(1), Summer, pp. 162–198.

Marshall, Alfred (1920) *Principles of Economics: An Introductory Volume*, 8th ed. (London: Macmillan).

Martin, John (1982) 'The Meaning of Social Democracy', in Martin, John (ed.) (1982) *The Meaning of Social Democracy and Other Essays* (London: John Martin), pp. 3–19.

Martinez, Mark A. (2009) *The Myth of the Free Market: The Role of the State in a Capitalist Economy* (Sterling, VA: Kumarian Press).

Martinez Alier, Joan, Munda, Giuseppi, and O'Neill, John (1998) 'Weak Comparability of Values as a Foundation for Ecological Economics', *Ecological Economics*, 26(3), pp. 277–286.

Marx, Karl (1971) *A Contribution to the Critique of Political Economy* (London: Lawrence and Wishart).

Marx, Karl (1973) *The Revolutions of 1848: Political Writings—Volume 1* (Harmondsworth: Penguin).

Marx, Karl (1974) *The First International and After: Political Writings—Volume 3* (Harmondsworth: Penguin).

Marx, Karl (1975) *Early Writings* (Harmondsworth: Penguin).

Marx, Karl (1976a) *Capital*, vol. 1 (Harmondsworth: Pelican).

Marx, Karl (1976b) 'Marginal Notes on Wagner', in Dragstedt, Albert (ed.) (1976) *Value: Studies by Marx* (London: New Park), pp. 195–229.

Marx, Karl (1978) *Capital*, vol. 2, trans. David Fernbach from the German 1893 edition (Harmondsworth: Pelican).

Marx, Karl (1981) *Capital*, vol. 3 (Harmondsworth: Pelican).

Marx, Karl, and Engels, Frederick (1962) *Selected Works in Two Volumes* (London: Lawrence and Wishart).

Marx, Karl, and Engels, Frederick (1975a) *Karl Marx and Frederick Engels, Collected Works, Vol. 3, Marx and Engels: 1843-1844* (London: Lawrence and Wishart).

Marx, Karl, and Engels, Frederick (1975b) *Karl Marx and Frederick Engels, Collected Works, Vol. 4, Marx and Engels: 1844-1845* (London: Lawrence and Wishart).

Marx, Karl, and Engels, Frederick (1976) *Karl Marx and Frederick Engels, Collected Works, Vol. 5, Marx and Engels: 1845-1847* (London: Lawrence and Wishart).

Marx, Karl, and Engels, Frederick (1977) *Karl Marx and Frederick Engels, Collected Works, Vol. 8, Marx and Engels: 1848-1849* (London: Lawrence and Wishart).

Marx, Karl, and Engels, Frederick (1989) *Karl Marx and Frederick Engels, Collected Works, Vol. 24, Marx and Engels: 1874-1883* (London: Lawrence and Wishart).

Marx, Karl, and Engels, Frederick (1991) *Karl Marx and Frederick Engels, Collected Works, Vol. 45, Letters: 1874-1879* (London: Lawrence and Wishart).

Mattheisen, Donald J. (1985) 'Understanding Political Alignments in the Frankfurt Parliament: The Case for the Guttman Scale', *Historical Social Research*, 10(3), pp. 19–30.

Mauro, Paolo (1995) 'Corruption and Growth', *Quarterly Journal of Economics*, 110(3), August, pp. 681–712.

Mayer, Bill (2014) 'Real Time with Bill Maher: Ben Affleck, Sam Harris and Bill Maher Debate Radical Islam', 6 October. https://www.youtube.com/watch?v=vln9D81eO60. (Retrieved 7 June 2015.)

Mazauric, Claude (ed.) (2009) *Babeuf. Écrits. Textes choisis de Gracchus Babeuf* (Pantin: Le Temps des cerises).

Mazzucato, Mariana (2013) *The Entrepreneurial State: Debunking Public vs. Private Sector Myths* (London and New York: Anthem).

Michels, Robert (1915) *Political Parties: A Sociological Study of Oligarchical Tendencies of Modern Democracy* (New York: Hearst).

Miliband, David (2016) 'New Times: David Miliband on Why the Left Needs to Move Forward, Not Back', *New Statesman*, 21 September. http://www.newstatesman.com/

politics/uk/2016/09/new-times-david-miliband-why-left-needs-move-forward-not-back. (Retrieved 22 September 2016.)

Miliband, Ralph (1994) *Socialism for a Sceptical Age* (Cambridge: Polity Press).

Milne, Seumas (1990) 'Stalin's Missing Millions', *The Guardian*, 10 March. https:// shirazsocialist.wordpress.com/2012/09/29/seamas-milne-on-stalins-missing-millions/. (Retrieved 25 October 2015.)

Milne, Seumas (2004) 'The Resistance Campaign Is Iraq's Real War of Liberation', *The Guardian*, 30 June. https://www.theguardian.com/world/2004/jul/01/iraq.comment. (Retrieved 26 September 2016.)

Minkler, Lanse P. (2008) *Integrity and Agreement: Economics When Principles Also Matter* (Ann Arbor: University of Michigan Press).

Minney, Rubeigh J. (1969) *The Bogus Image of Bernard Shaw* (London: Frewin).

Minsky, Hyman P. (1982) *Can "It" Happen Again? Essays in Instability and Finance* (Armonk, NY: M. E. Sharpe).

Minsky, Hyman P. (1986) *Stabilizing an Unstable Economy* (New Haven, CT: Yale University Press).

Mirowski, Philip, and Plehwe, Dieter (eds) (2009) *The Road from Mont Pèlerin: The Making of the Neoliberal Thought Collective* (Cambridge, MA: Harvard University Press).

Mirza, Munira, Senthilkumaran, Abi, and Ja'far, Zein (2007) *Living Apart Together: British Muslims and the Paradox of Multiculturalism* (London: Policy Exchange). https://www .policyexchange.org.uk/wp-content/uploads/2016/09/living-apart-together-jan-07.pdf. (Retrieved 21 May 2015.)

Mises, Ludwig von (1920) 'Die Wirtschaftsrechnung im sozialistischen Gemeinwesen', *Archiv für Sozialwissenschaften und Sozialpolitik*, 47(1), April, pp. 86–121.

Mises, Ludwig von (1949) *Human Action: A Treatise on Economics* (London and New Haven, CT: William Hodge and Yale University Press).

Mises, Ludwig von (1981) *Socialism: An Economic and Sociological Analysis*, trans. from the 2nd (1932) German edition (Indianapolis: Liberty Classics).

Mises, Ludwig von (1985) *Liberalism in the Classic Tradition*, trans. Ralph Raico from the German 1927 edition (Irvington, NY: Foundation for Economic Education).

Mo, Pak Hung (2001) 'Corruption and Economic Growth', *Journal of Comparative Economics*, 29(1), March, pp. 66–79.

Monbiot, George (2003) 'Rattling the Bars', *The Guardian*, 18 November. http://www.monbiot .com/2003/11/18/rattling-the-bars/. (Retrieved 9 May 2015.)

Montesquieu, Charles-Louis (1748) *De l'esprit des lois* (Geneva).

Moore, Barrington, Jr (1966) *Social Origins of Dictatorship and Democracy: Lord and Peasant in the Making of the Modern World* (London: Allen Lane).

Morton, A. L. (1975) *Freedom in Arms: A Selection of Leveller Writings* (London: Lawrence and Wishart).

Moss, Robert (1973) *Chile's Marxist Experiment* (New York: John Wiley).

Mousseau, Michael, Hegre, Håvard, and O'Neal, John R. (2003) 'How the Wealth of Nations Conditions the Liberal Peace', *European Journal of International Relations*, 9(4), pp. 277–314.

Mulhall, Joe, and Lowes, Nick (2015) *The Counter-Jihad Movement: Anti-Muslim Hatred from the Margins to the Mainstream.* http://edition.pagesuite-professional.co.uk// launch.aspx?eid=9332fd52-02b8-4f71-a12e-030d311dda57. (Retrieved 15 December 2015.)

Murrell, Peter (1983) 'Did the Theory of Market Socialism Answer the Challenge of Ludwig von Mises? A Reinterpretation of the Socialist Controversy?' *History of Political Economy*, 15(1), Spring, pp. 92–105.

Murrell, Peter (1991) 'Can Neoclassical Economics Underpin the Reform of Centrally Planned Economies?' *Journal of Economic Perspectives*, 5(4), Fall, pp. 59–76.

Musharbash, Yassin (2014) 'Islamophobia Is Racism, Pure and Simple', *The Guardian*, 10 December. http://www.theguardian.com/commentisfree/2014/dec/10/islamophobia -racism-dresden-protests-germany-islamisation. (Retrieved 14 July 2015.)

Narayan, Uma (1997) *Dislocating Cultures: Identities, Traditions, and Third World Feminism* (London and New York: Routledge).

National Center for Employee Ownership (2012) 'A Statistical Profile of Employee Ownership'. http://www.nceo.org/articles/statistical-profile-employee-ownership. (Retrieved 18 September 2013.)

National Secular Society (2015a) 'Free Speech Campaigners Concerned by Ed Miliband's Vow to Ban "Islamophobia"—Without Defining What It Means', *National Secular Society*, 29 April. http://www.secularism.org.uk/news/2015/04/free-speech-campaigners -concerned-by-ed-milibands-vow-to-ban-islamophobia--without-defining-what-he-means. (Retrieved 17 May 2015.)

National Secular Society (2015b) 'Imam Joins Secularists and Christians in Defending Pastor James McConnell's Free Speech', *National Secular Society*, 24 June. http://www .secularism.org.uk/news/2015/06/imam-joins-secularists-and-christians-in-defending -pastor-james-mcconnells-free-speech. (Retrieved 26 June 2015.)

National Secular Society (2015c) 'Muslim Reform Movement Embraces Secularism and Universal Human Rights', *National Secular Society*, 8 December. http://www.secularism.org .uk/news/2015/12/muslim-reform-movement-embraces-secularism-and-universal-human -rights. (Retrieved 11 December 2015.)

Nawaz, Maajid (2015) 'The Left's Witch Hunt against Muslims', *The Daily Beast*, 14 December. http://www.thedailybeast.com/articles/2015/12/14/the-left-s-witch-hunt-against -muslims.html. (Retrieved 14 December 2015.)

Nelson, Richard R. (1959) 'The Simple Economics of Basic Scientific Research', *Journal of Political Economy*, 67(3), June, pp. 297–306.

Nelson, Richard R. (1981) 'Assessing Private Enterprise: An Exegesis of Tangled Doctrine', *Bell Journal of Economics*, 12(1), pp. 93–111.

Nelson, Richard R. (2003) 'On the Complexities and Limits of Market Organization', *Review of International Political Economy*, 10(4), November, pp. 697–710.

Nelson, Richard R., and Winter, Sidney G. (1982) *An Evolutionary Theory of Economic Change* (Cambridge, MA: Harvard University Press).

Nichols, Shaun (2004) *Sentimental Rules: On the Natural Foundations of Moral Judgment* (Oxford and New York: Oxford University Press).

Nickel, James (1987) *Making Sense of Human Rights: Philosophical Reflections on the Universal Declaration of Human Rights* (Berkeley: University of California Press).

North, Douglass C., Wallis, John J., and Weingast, Barry R. (2009) *Violence and Social Orders: A Conceptual Framework for Interpreting Recorded Human History* (Cambridge: Cambridge University Press).

Nove, Alexander (1983) *The Economics of Feasible Socialism* (London: George Allen and Unwin).

Nozick, Robert (1974) *Anarchy, State, and Utopia* (New York: Basic Books).

Nussbaum, Martha C. (1992) 'Human Functioning and Social Justice: In Defense of Aristotelian Essentialism', *Political Theory*, 20(2), May, pp. 202–246.

Olson, Mancur, Jr (1965) *The Logic of Collective Action* (Cambridge, MA: Harvard University Press).

O'Meara, Barry E. (1822) *Napoléon in Exile; or, A Voice from St. Helena*, 2 vols (London: Simpkin and Marshall).

O'Neill, John (1998) *The Market: Ethics, Knowledge and Politics* (London and New York: Routledge).

Ostrom, Elinor (1990) *Governing the Commons: The Evolution of Institutions for Collective Action* (Cambridge: Cambridge University Press).

Otteson, James R. (ed.) (2003) *The Levellers: Overton, Walwyn and Lilburne—Works by These and by Other British Levellers* (Bristol: Thoemme Press).

Overy, Richard (2009) *The Morbid Age: Britain and the Crisis of Civilisation, 1919–1939* (London: Allen Lane).

Owen, Robert (1991) *A New View of Society and Other Writings*, ed. and with an introduction by Gregory Claeys (Harmondsworth: Penguin).

Pagano, Ugo (1985) *Work and Welfare in Economic Theory* (Oxford: Basil Blackwell).

Pagano, Ugo (2014) 'The Crisis of Intellectual Monopoly Capitalism', *Cambridge Journal of Economics*, 38(6), November, pp. 1409–1429.

Paine, Thomas (1797) *Agrarian Justice: Opposed to Agrarian Law and to Agrarian Monopoly* (Philadelphia: Folwell).

Paine, Thomas (1945) *The Complete Writings of Thomas Paine*, ed. and with an introduction by Philip S. Foner (New York: Citadel Press).

Paine, Thomas (1948) *The Selected Work of Tom Paine*, ed. and with an introduction by Howard Fast (London: Bodley Head).

Palin, Sarah (2009) *Going Rogue: An American Life* (New York: Harper Collins).

Palmer, Alasdair (2007) 'Not in Their Name?' *The Telegraph*, 8 July. http://www.telegraph.co.uk/news/uknews/1556799/Not-in-their-name.html. (Retrieved 12 May 2015.)

Parker, Melissa (1995) 'Rethinking Female Circumcision', *Africa: Journal of the International African Institute*, 65(4), pp. 506–523.

Parsons, Talcott (1975) *Social Systems and the Evolution of Action Theory* (New York: Free Press).

Pellegrini, Lorenzo, and Gerlagh, Reyer (2004) 'Corruption's Effect on Growth and Its Transmission Channels', *Kyklos*, 57(3), pp. 429–456.

People's Republic of China (2004) 'Constitution of the People's Republic of China'. http://english.peopledaily.com.cn/constitution/constitution.html. (Retrieved 7 May 2015.)

Phillips, Trevor (2016) 'Why I Fear My Poisoned Party Has Lost Its Purpose', *Daily Mail*, 16 October. http://www.dailymail.co.uk/news/article-3842370/Trevor-Phillips-appalled-bigotry-heart-Labour.html. (Retrieved 18 October 2016.)

Piketty, Thomas (2014) *Capital in the Twenty-First Century* (Cambridge, MA: Belknap Press).

Pinker, Steven (2011) *The Better Angels of Our Nature: Why Violence Has Declined* (New York: Viking).

Pitt, Bob (2014) 'Secularists Assist Right-Wing Anti-Sharia Hysteria', *Islamophobia Watch*. 30 April. http://www.islamophobiawatch.co.uk/secularists-assist-right-wing-anti-sharia-hysteria/. (Retrieved 7 June 2015.)

Podmore, Frank (1906) *Robert Owen: A Biography*, 2 vols (London: Hutchinson).

Pohl, J. Otto (1999) *Ethnic Cleansing in the USSR, 1937-1949* (Westport, CT: Greenwood Press).

Polan, Anthony J. (1984) *Lenin and the End of Politics* (London: Methuen).

Polanyi, Karl (1944) *The Great Transformation: The Political and Economic Origins of Our Time* (New York: Rinehart).

Poole, Michael, and Whitfield, Keith (1994) 'Theories and Evidence on the Growth and Distribution of Profit Sharing and Employee Shareholding Schemes', *Human Systems Management*, 13(3), pp. 209-220.

Popper, Karl R. (1945b) *The Open Society and Its Enemies*, 2 vols (London: Routledge and Kegan Paul).

Poynting, Scott, and Mason, Victoria (2007) 'The Resistible Rise of Islamophobia: Anti-Muslim Racism in the UK and Australia before 11 September 2001', *Journal of Sociology*, 43(1), pp. 61-86.

Pozuelo, Julia Ruiz, Slipowitz, Amy, and Vuletin, Guillermo (2016) 'Democracy Does Not Cause Growth: The Importance of Endogeneity Arguments', Inter-American Development Bank, IDB Working Paper Series No IDB-WP-694.

Proudhon, Pierre Joseph (1969) *Selected Works* (New York: Doubleday).

Pryor, Frederick L. (1973) *Property and Industrial Organization in Communist and Capitalist Nations* (Bloomington: Indiana University Press).

Rationalwiki (2015) 'American Indian Holocaust', *Rationalwiki*. http://rationalwiki.org/wiki/American_Indian_Holocaust. (Retrieved 21 April 2015.)

Rawlinson, Kevin (2013) 'Anti-Ground Zero Mosque Campaigners Pamela Geller and Robert Spencer Barred from Entering Britain to Speak at an EDL Rally', *The Independent*, 26 June. http://www.independent.co.uk/news/uk/crime/antiground-zero-mosque-campaigners-pamela-geller-and-robert-spencer-barred-from-entering-britain-to-speak-at-an-edl-rally-8675251.html. (Retrieved 7 May 2015.)

Reibel, R. (1975) 'The Workingman's Production Association, or the Republic in the Workshop', in Vanek, Jaroslav (ed.) (1975) *Self-Management: The Economic Liberation of Man* (Harmondsworth: Penguin), pp. 39-46.

Reinert, Erik S. (2007) *How Rich Countries Got Rich . . . And Why Poor Countries Stay Poor* (London: Constable).

Reisman, David (1993) *The Political Economy of Health Care* (London: Macmillan).

Rengger, Nicholas (2011) 'The World Turned Upside Down? Human Rights and International Relations after 25 Years', *International Affairs*, 87(5), pp. 1159-1178.

Rentoul, John (1995) '"Defining Moment" as Blair Wins Backing for Clause IV', *The Independent*, 14 March. http://www.independent.co.uk/news/defining-moment-as-blair-wins-backing-for-clause-iv-1611135.html. (Retrieved 27 April 2015.)

Reuters (2015) '"There Is No Money": Cash-Strapped Cuba Is Forced to Cut Vital Imports', 16 October, *The Guardian*. http://www.theguardian.com/world/2015/oct/16/cuba-cash-shortage-imports-oil-commodities. (Retrieved 16 October 2015.)

Rich, Dave (2016) *The Left's Jewish Problem: Jeremy Corbyn, Israel and Anti-Semitism* (London: Biteback).

Richerson, Peter J., and Boyd, Robert (1999) 'Complex Societies: The Evolutionary Origins of a Crude Superorganism', *Human Nature*, 10, pp. 253–289.

Richerson, Peter J., and Boyd, Robert (2001) 'Institutional Evolution in the Holocene: The Rise of Complex Societies', in Runciman, Walter Garry (ed.) (2001) *The Origin of Human Social Institutions* (Oxford and New York: Oxford University Press), pp. 197–234.

Rifkin, Jeremy (2014) *The Zero Marginal Cost Society: The Internet of Things, the Collaborative Commons, and the Eclipse of Capitalism* (New York and London: Palgrave Macmillan).

Roberts, Simon (1979) *Order and Discipline: An Introduction to Legal Anthropology* (New York: St Martin's Press).

Robertson, D. B. (1951) *The Religious Foundations of Leveller Democracy* (New York: Kings Crown Press, Columbia University).

Robinson, Andrew M., and Zhang, Hao (2005) 'Employee Share Ownership: Safeguarding Investments in Human Capital', *British Journal of Industrial Relations*, 43(3), September, pp. 469–488.

Robinson, Guy (1998) *Philosophy and Mystification: A Reflection on Nonsense and Clarity* (London and New York: Routledge).

Robinson, Joan (1969) *The Cultural Revolution in China* (Harmondsworth: Penguin).

Robinson, Joan (1973) *Economic Management in China 1972* (London: Anglo-Chinese Educational Institute).

Rodrigues, João (2012) 'Where to Draw the Line between the State and the Market?' *Journal of Economic Issues*, 46(4), December, pp. 1007–1033.

Rodrik, Dani (2011) *The Globalization Paradox: Why Global Markets, States, and Democracy Can't Coexist* (Oxford and New York: Oxford University Press).

Rodrik, Dani, and Wacziarg, Romain (2005) 'Do Democratic Transitions Produce Bad Economic Outcomes?' *American Economic Review*, 95(2), pp. 50–55.

Rose, R. B. (1978) *Gracchus Babeuf: The First Revolutionary Communist* (Stanford: Stanford University Press).

RT News (2014) 'EU Adopts New Sanctions against Russia to Come into Force in "Next Few Days"', *RT News*, 8 September. https://www.rt.com/news/186148-eu-adopt-sanctions-russia/. (Retrieved 17 August 2016.)

Rummel, Rudolph J. (1990) *Lethal Politics: Soviet Genocide and Mass Murder since 1917* (New Brunswick, NJ: Transaction).

Rummel, Rudolph J. (1997) *Power Kills: Democracy as a Method of Nonviolence* (New Brunswick, NJ: Transaction).

Russian Socialist Federated Soviet Republic (1918) 'Article Two: General Provisions of the Constitution of the Russian Socialist Federated Soviet Republic', ch. 5. https://www

.marxists.org/history/ussr/government/constitution/1918/article2.htm. (Retrieved 19 April 2015.)

Ryan, Alan (1995) *John Dewey and the High Tide of American Liberalism* (New York: Norton).

Samuelson, Paul A. (1947) *Foundations of Economic Analysis* (Cambridge, MA: Harvard University Press).

Sandel, Michael (2012) *What Money Can't Buy: The Moral Limits of Markets* (London: Allen Lane).

Satz, Debra (2010) *Why Some Things Should Not Be for Sale: The Moral Limits of Markets* (Oxford and New York: Oxford University Press).

Schäffle, Albert E. F. (1870) *Kapitalismus und Sozialismus: Mit besonderer Rücksicht auf Geschäfts und Vermögensformen* (Tübingen: Laupp).

Schäffle, Albert E. F. (1874) *Quintessenz des Sozialismus* (Gotha: Perthes).

Schäffle, Albert E. F. (1885) *Die Aussichtslosigkeit der Socialdemokratie. Drei Briefe an einen Staatsmann zur Ergänzung der 'Quintessenz des Sozialismus'* (Tübingen: Laupp).

Schäffle, Albert E. F. (1892) *The Impossibility of Social Democracy: Being a Supplement to 'The Quintessence of Socialism'*, trans. A. C. Morant from the 4th German ed. (1885) with a preface by Bernard Bosanquet (London: Swan Sonnenschein; New York: Charles Scribner's Sons). Excerpted in Hodgson (2007, pp. 118–125).

Schäffle, Albert E. F. (1908) *The Quintessence of Socialism*, trans. under the supervision of Bernard Bosanquet from the 8th German edition of Schäffle (1874) (London: Swan Sonnenschein; New York: Charles Scribner's Sons).

Schliesser, Eric (2010) 'Friedman, Positive Economics, and the Chicago Boys', in Emmett, Ross B. (ed.) (2010) *The Elgar Companion to the Chicago School of Economics* (Cheltenham and Northampton, MA: Edward Elgar), ch. 14, pp. 175–195.

Schmidt, Paul F. (1955) 'Some Criticisms of Cultural Relativism', *Journal of Philosophy*, 52(25), 8 December, pp. 780–791.

Schumpeter, Joseph A. (1942) *Capitalism, Socialism and Democracy* (London: George Allen and Unwin).

Schwartz, Shalom H. (1994) 'Are There Universal Aspects in the Structure and Contents of Human Values?' *Journal of Social Issues*, 50(4), pp. 19–45.

Screpanti, Ernesto (2007) *Libertarian Communism: Marx, Engels and the Political Economy of Freedom* (London and New York: Palgrave Macmillan).

Sedghi, Ami (2013) 'UK Census: Religion by Age, Ethnicity and Country of Birth', *The Guardian*, 16 May. http://www.theguardian.com/news/datablog/2013/may/16/uk-census-religion-age-ethnicity-country-of-birth. (Retrieved 12 June 2015.)

Sen, Amartya K. (1981) *Poverty and Famines: An Essay on Entitlement and Deprivation* (Oxford: Clarendon Press).

Sen, Amartya K. (1990) 'Individual Freedom as a Social Commitment', *New York Review of Books*, 14 June.

Shapiro, Fred R. (2014) 'Who Wrote the Serenity Prayer?' *The Chronicle Review*, 28 April.

Shaw, George Bernard (1934) *Prefaces by Bernard Shaw* (London: Odhams Press).

Shiraz Socialist (2015) 'Stalinist Seumas's (Failed) Attempt to Take on Conquest', 5 August. https://shirazsocialist.wordpress.com/2015/08/05/stalinist-seumass-failed-attempt-to-take-on-conquest/. (Retrieved 25 October 2015.)

Shleifer, Andrei, and Vishny, Robert W. (1993) 'Corruption', *Quarterly Journal of Economics*, 108(3), August, pp. 599–617.

Sides, John (2015) 'New Research Shows That French Muslims Experience Extraordinary Discrimination in the Job Market', *The Washington Post*, 23 November. https://www .washingtonpost.com/news/monkey-cage/wp/2015/11/23/new-research-shows-that -french-muslims-experience-extraordinary-discrimination-in-the-job-market/. (Retrieved 30 September 2016.)

Smith, Adam (1759) *The Theory of Moral Sentiments; or, An Essay Towards an Analysis of the Principles by Which Men Naturally Judge Concerning the Conduct and Character, First of Their Neighbours, and Afterwards of Themselves* (London and Edinburgh: Millar, and Kincaid and Bell).

Smith, Adam (1776) *An Inquiry into the Nature and Causes of the Wealth of Nations*, 2 vols, (London: Strahan and Cadell).

Sober, Elliott, and Wilson, David Sloan (1998) *Unto Others: The Evolution and Psychology of Unselfish Behavior* (Cambridge, MA: Harvard University Press).

Soboul, Albert (1977) *A Short History of the French Revolution, 1789–1799* (Berkeley: University of California Press).

Socialist Worker (1987) *Socialist Worker*, 28 November. Quoted in https://libcom.org/library/ the-socialist-workers-party-iran-iraq-war-1987. (Retrieved 19 January 2016.)

Sommers, Jack (2014) 'Islamic State's "Progessive Potential" as "Stabilising Force" Debated by New Left Unity Party', *The Huffington Post*, 17 November. http://www.huffingtonpost .co.uk/2014/11/17/islamic-state-left-unity_n_6171252.html. (Retrieved 30 June 2015.)

Sommers, Jack (2015) '7/7 Bombings Anniversary Poll Shows More than Half of Britons See Muslims as a Threat', *The Huffington Post*, 3 July. http://www.huffingtonpost.co.uk/ 2015/07/03/77-bombings-muslims-islam-britain-poll_n_7694452.html. (Retrieved 25 April 2017.)

Steele, David Ramsay (1992) *From Marx to Mises: Post-Capitalist Society and the Challenge of Economic Calculation* (La Salle, IL: Open Court).

Sterba, James P. (1985) 'A Libertarian Justification for the Welfare State', *Social Theory and Practice*, 11(3), Fall, pp. 285–306.

Stewart, Heather (2016) 'Naz Shah Suspended by Labour Party amid Antisemitism Row', *The Guardian*, 27 April. https://www.theguardian.com/politics/2016/apr/27/naz-shah -suspended-labour-party-antisemitism-row. (Retrieved 10 October 2016.)

Stewart, John Hall (1951) *A Documentary Survey of the French Revolution* (New York: Macmillan).

Stiglitz, Joseph E. (2010) *Freefall: America, Free Markets, and the Sinking of the World Economy* (New York: Norton).

Stiglitz, Joseph E. (2012) *The Price of Inequality: How Today's Divided Society Endangers Our Future* (New York and London: Norton).

Streeck, Wolfgang (2014) *Buying Time: The Delayed Crisis of Democratic Capitalism* (London and New York: Verso).

Sutton, Charles William (2014) 'Watts, John (1818–1887)', *Dictionary of National Biography*, vol. 60. http://en.wikisource.org/wiki/Watts,_John_(1818-1887)_(DNB00). (Retrieved 12 April 2015.)

Synopwich, Christine (1990) *The Concept of Socialist Law* (Oxford: Clarendon Press).

Tawney, Richard H. (1921) *The Acquisitive Society* (London: Bell).

Taylor, Barbara (1983) *Eve and the New Jerusalem: Socialism and Feminism in the Nineteenth Century* (London: Virago).

Taylor, George V. (1967) 'Noncapitalist Wealth and the Origins of the French Revolution', *American Historical Review*, 72(2), January, pp. 469–496.

Taylor, Keith (ed.) (1975) *Henri de Saint Simon, 1760–1825: Selected Writings on Science, Industry and Social Organization* (New York: Holmes and Meier).

Thompson, Edward P. (1968) *The Making of the English Working Class*, 2nd ed. (Harmondsworth: Penguin).

Thompson, Edward P. (1973) 'An Open Letter to Leszek Kolakowski', *Socialist Register 10*. http://socialistregister.com/index.php/srv/article/view/5351#.VXBrZLFwYy8. (Retrieved 4 June 2015.)

Thompson, Noel (1988) *The Market and Its Critics: Socialist Political Economy in Nineteenth Century Britain* (London: Routledge).

Thompson, William (1827) *Labour Rewarded. The Claims of Labour and Capital Conciliated: or, How to Secure to Labour the Whole Products of Its Exertions* (London: Hunt and Clarke).

Toynbee, Polly (2004) 'We Must Be Free to Criticise without Being Called Racist', *The Guardian*, 17 August. http://www.theguardian.com/world/2004/aug/18/religion.politics. (Retrieved 14 July 2015.)

Traxler, Franz, and Unger, Brigitte (1994) 'Governance, Economic Restructuring, and International Competitiveness', *Journal of Economic Issues*, 28(1), March, pp. 1–23.

Trotsky, Leon D. (1937) *The Revolution Betrayed: What Is the Soviet Union and Where Is It Going?* (London: Faber and Faber).

Trotsky, Leon D., Dewey, John, and Novak, George (1979) *Their Morals and Ours: Marxist versus Liberal Views on Morality* (New York: Pathfinder Press).

Turner, Marjorie S. (1989) *Joan Robinson and the Americans* (Armonk, NY: M. E. Sharpe).

Turner, Ralph (2003) *Magna Carta: Through the Ages* (London and New York: Routledge).

United Nations (1948) *Universal Declaration of Human Rights*. http://www.ohchr.org/EN/UDHR/Documents/UDHR_Translations/eng.pdf. (Retrieved 11 January 2016.)

Unruhe, Jason (2010) '1.6 Billion Killed by Capitalism'. https://www.youtube.com/watch?v=qmYSNDr84M4. (Retrieved 17 May 2015.)

Vanek, Jaroslav (1970) *The General Theory of Labor-Managed Market Economies* (Ithaca, NY: Cornell University Press).

Vanek, Jaroslav (1972) *The Economics of Workers' Management* (London: Allen and Unwin).

Van Horn, Carl E., and Fichtner, Aaron R. (2003) 'An Evaluation of State-Subsidized, Firm-Based Training: The Workforce Development Partnership Program', *International Journal of Manpower*, 24(1), pp. 97–111.

Van Parijs, Philippe (1980) 'The Falling-Rate-of-Profit Theory of Crisis: A Rational Reconstruction by Way of Obituary', *Review of Radical Political Economics*, 12(1), Spring, pp. 1–16.

Van Parijs, Philippe (ed.) (1992) *Arguing for Basic Income: Ethical Foundations for a Radical Reform* (London and New York: Verso).

Van Parijs, Philippe (1995) *Real Freedom for All: What (If Anything) Can Justify Capitalism?* (Oxford: Clarendon Press).

Vatn, Arild (2005) *Institutions and the Environment* (Cheltenham and Northampton, MA: Edward Elgar).

Vaughn, Karen I. (1980) 'Economic Calculation under Socialism: The Austrian Contribution', *Economic Inquiry*, 18, pp. 535–554.

Veblen, Thorstein B. (1898) 'The Beginnings of Ownership', *American Journal of Sociology*, 4(3), November, pp. 352–365.

Vogel, Steven K. (1996) *Freer Markets, More Rules: Regulatory Reform in Advanced Industrial Countries* (Ithaca, NY: Cornell University Press).

Wainwright, Hilary (1994) *Arguments for a New Left: Answering the Free-Market Right* (Oxford: Basil Blackwell).

Waldron, Jeremy (1988) *The Right to Private Property* (Oxford and New York: Oxford University Press).

Walzer, Michael (1994) *Thick and Thin: Moral Argument at Home and Abroad* (Notre Dame, IN: University of Notre Dame Press).

Ward, Benjamin (1958) 'The Firm in Illyria: Market Syndicalism', *American Economic Review*, 48, pp. 566–589.

Ward, Benjamin (1967) *The Socialist Economy: A Study of Organizational Alternatives* (New York: Random House).

Watt, Richard M. (1969) *The Kings Depart: The Tragedy of Germany: Versailles and the German Revolution* (London: Weidenfeld and Nicholson).

Watts, John (1842) *Facts and Fictions of Political Economists* (Manchester: Heywood).

Webb, Sidney J., and Webb, Beatrice (1920) *A Constitution for the Socialist Commonwealth of Great Britain* (London: Longmans Green).

Webb, Sidney J., and Webb, Beatrice (1935) *Soviet Communism: A New Civilisation?* (London: Longmans Green).

Weber, Max (1968) *Economy and Society: An Outline of Interpretative Sociology*, 2 vols, trans. from the 1921–1922 German edition (Berkeley: University of California Press).

Wejnert, Barbara (2014) *Diffusion of Democracy: The Past and Future of Global Democracy* (Cambridge and New York: Cambridge University Press).

Wheatley, Jonathan (2015) 'Restructuring the Policy Space in England: The End of the Left-Right Paradigm?' *British Politics*, 10, pp. 268–285.

White, Michael (2015) 'Trevor Phillips Says the Unsayable about Race and Multiculturalism', *The Guardian*, 16 March. http://www.theguardian.com/uk-news/2015/mar/16/trevor -phillips-race-multiculturalism-blog. (Retrieved 21 May 2015.)

Wikipedia (2016a) 'English Defence League', *Wikipedia*. http://en.wikipedia.org/wiki/English _Defence_League. (Retrieved 20 January 2016.)

Wikipedia (2016b) 'Faith School', *Wikipedia*. http://en.wikipedia.org/wiki/Faith_school. (Retrieved 20 January 2016.)

Wikipedia (2016c) 'Germaine Greer', *Wikipedia*. http://en.wikipedia.org/wiki/Germaine _Greer. (Retrieved 20 January 2016.)

Wikipedia (2016d) 'Hassan Butt', *Wikipedia*. http://en.wikipedia.org/wiki/Hassan_Butt. (Retrieved 20 January 2016.)

Wikipedia (2016e) 'Islamophobia', *Wikipedia*. http://en.wikipedia.org/wiki/Islamophobia. (Retrieved 20 January 2016.)

Wikipedia (2015f) 'List of Countries by GDP (PPP) per Capita', *Wikipedia*. http://en .wikipedia.org/wiki/List_of_countries_by_GDP_(PPP)_per_capita. (Retrieved 20 January 2016.)

Wikipedia (2016g) 'National Football League Draft', *Wikipedia*. https://en.wikipedia.org/ wiki/National_Football_League_draft. (Retrieved 20 January 2016.)

Wikipedia (2016h) 'Timeline of Major Famines in India during British Rule', *Wikipedia*. http://en.wikipedia.org/wiki/Timeline_of_major_famines_in_India_during_British_rule. (Retrieved 20 January 2016.)

Wikipedia (2016i) 'Trevor Phillips', *Wikipedia*. http://en.wikipedia.org/wiki/Trevor_Phillips. (Retrieved 20 January 2016.)

Wikipedia (2016j) 'Yusuf al-Qaradawi', *Wikipedia*. http://en.wikipedia.org/wiki/Yusuf_al -Qaradawi. (Retrieved 20 January 2016.)

Wilde, Oscar (2000) *Oscar Wilde: A Life in Quotes*, ed. Barry Day (London: Metro).

Wiles, P. J. D. (1974) *Distribution of Income: East and West* (Amsterdam: North-Holland).

Wilkinson, Richard, and Pickett, Kate (2009) *The Spirit Level: Why More Equal Societies Almost Always Do Better* (London: Allen Lane).

Williamson, John (1990) 'What Washington Means by Policy Reform', in Williamson, John (ed.) (1990) *Latin American Adjustment: How Much Has Happened?* (Washington, DC: Institute for International Economics).

Winston, Clifford (2006) *Government Failure versus Market Failure: Microeconomics Policy Research and Government Performance* (Washington, DC: Brookings Institute).

Woodhouse, A. S. P. (ed.) (1951) *Puritanism and Liberty: Being the Army Debates (1647–9 from the Clarke Manuscripts with Supplementary Documents)* (Chicago: University of Chicago Press).

Wray, L. Randall (2012) *Modern Money Theory: A Primer on Macroeconomics for Sovereign Monetary Systems* (London and New York: Palgrave Macmillan).

Yang, Jisheng (2012) *The Great Chinese Famine, 1958–1962*, trans. Stacy Mosher and Guo Jian (New York: Farrar, Straus and Giroux).

Yang, Wesley (2005) 'The Philosopher and the Ayatollah', *The Boston Globe*, 12 June. http:// www.boston.com/news/globe/ideas/articles/2005/06/12/the_philosopher_and_the _ayatollah/ and http://www.kevin-anderson.com/wp-content/uploads/docs/anderson -book-review-foucault-yang.pdf. (Retrieved 8 May 2015.)

Zak, Paul J. (ed.) (2008) *Moral Markets: The Critical Role of Values in the Economy* (Princeton, NJ: Princeton University Press).

Zamagni, Stefano, and Zamagni, Vera (2010) *Cooperative Enterprise: Facing the Challenge of Globalisation* (Cheltenham and Northampton, MA: Edward Elgar).

Zechenter, Elizabeth M. (1997) 'In the Name of Culture: Cultural Relativism and the Abuse of the Individual', *Journal of Anthropological Research*, 53(3), Autumn, pp. 319–347.

Zhou, Kate Xiao (1996) *How the Farmers Changed China* (Boulder, CO: Westview Press).

INDEX